T0191738

Conquering Big Data with High Performance Computing

Ritu Arora
Editor

Conquering Big Data with High Performance Computing

 Springer

Editor
Ritu Arora
Texas Advanced Computing Center
Austin, TX, USA

ISBN 978-3-319-81589-3   ISBN 978-3-319-33742-5   (eBook)
DOI 10.1007/978-3-319-33742-5

Printed on acid-free paper

This Springer imprint is published by Springer Nature
The registered company is Springer International Publishing AG Switzerland

Preface

Scalable solutions for computing and storage are a necessity for the timely processing and management of big data. In the last several decades, High-Performance Computing (HPC) has already impacted the process of developing innovative solutions across various scientific and nonscientific domains. There are plenty of examples of data-intensive applications that take advantage of HPC resources and techniques for reducing the time-to-results.

This peer-reviewed book is an effort to highlight some of the ways in which HPC resources and techniques can be used to process and manage big data with speed and accuracy. Through the chapters included in the book, HPC has been demystified for the readers. HPC is presented both as an alternative to commodity clusters on which the Hadoop ecosystem typically runs in mainstream computing and as a platform on which alternatives to the Hadoop ecosystem can be efficiently run.

The book includes a basic overview of HPC, High-Throughput Computing (HTC), and big data (in Chap. 1). It introduces the readers to the various types of HPC and high-end storage resources that can be used for efficiently managing the entire big data lifecycle (in Chap. 2). Data movement across various systems (from storage to computing to archival) can be constrained by the available bandwidth and latency. An overview of the various aspects of moving data across a system is included in the book (in Chap. 3) to inform the readers about the associated overheads. A detailed introduction to a tool that can be used to run serial applications on HPC platforms in HTC mode is also included (in Chap. 4).

In addition to the gentle introduction to HPC resources and techniques, the book includes chapters on latest research and development efforts that are facilitating the convergence of HPC and big data (see Chaps. 5, 6, 7, and 8).

The R language is used extensively for data mining and statistical computing. A description of efficiently using R in parallel mode on HPC resources is included in the book (in Chap. 9). A chapter in the book (Chap. 10) describes efficient sampling methods to construct a large data set, which can then be used to address theoretical questions as well as econometric ones.

Through the multiple test cases from diverse domains like high-frequency financial trading, archaeology, and eDiscovery, the book demonstrates the process of conquering big data with HPC (in Chaps. 11, 13, and 14).
The need and advantage of involving humans in the process of data exploration (as discussed in Chaps. 12 and 14) indicate that the hybrid combination of man and the machine (HPC resources) can help in achieving astonishing results. The book also includes a short discussion on using databases on HPC resources (in Chap. 15). The Wrangler supercomputer at the Texas Advanced Computing Center (TACC) is a top-notch data-intensive computing platform. Some examples of the projects that are taking advantage of Wrangler are also included in the book (in Chap. 16).

I hope that the readers of this book will feel encouraged to use HPC resources for their big data processing and management needs. The researchers in academia and at government institutions in the United States are encouraged to explore the possibilities of incorporating HPC in their work through TACC and the Extreme Science and Engineering Discovery Environment (XSEDE) resources.

I am grateful to all the authors who have contributed toward making this book a reality. I am grateful to all the reviewers for their timely and valuable feedback in improving the content of the book. I am grateful to my colleagues at TACC and my family for their selfless support at all times.

Austin, TX, USA   Ritu Arora

Contents

Chapter 1
An Introduction to Big Data, High Performance Computing, High-Throughput Computing, and Hadoop

Ritu Arora

Abstract Recent advancements in the field of instrumentation, adoption of some of the latest Internet technologies and applications, and the declining cost of storing large volumes of data, have enabled researchers and organizations to gather increasingly large datasets. Such vast datasets are precious due to the potential of discovering new knowledge and developing insights from them, and they are also referred to as "Big Data". While in a large number of domains, Big Data is a newly found treasure that brings in new challenges, there are various other domains that have been handling such treasures for many years now using state-of-the-art resources, techniques and technologies. The goal of this chapter is to provide an introduction to such resources, techniques, and technologies, namely, High Performance Computing (HPC), High-Throughput Computing (HTC), and Hadoop. First, each of these topics is defined and discussed individually. These topics are then discussed further in the light of enabling short time to discoveries and, hence, with respect to their importance in conquering Big Data.

1.1 Big Data

Recent advancements in the field of instrumentation, adoption of some of the latest Internet technologies and applications, and the declining cost of storing large volumes of data, have enabled researchers and organizations to gather increasingly large and heterogeneous datasets. Due to their enormous size, heterogeneity, and high speed of collection, such large datasets are often referred to as "Big Data". Even though the term "Big Data" and the mass awareness about it has gained momentum only recently, there are several domains, right from life sciences to geosciences to archaeology, that have been generating and accumulating large and heterogeneous datasets for many years now. As an example, a geoscientist could be having more than 30 years of global Landsat data [1], NASA Earth Observation System data

R. Arora (✉)
Texas Advanced Computing Center, Austin, TX, USA
e-mail: rauta@tacc.utexas.edu

© Springer International Publishing Switzerland 2016
R. Arora (ed.), *Conquering Big Data with High Performance Computing*,
DOI 10.1007/978-3-319-33742-5_1

1

[2] collected over a decade, detailed terrain datasets derived from RADAR [3] and LIDAR [4] systems, and voluminous hyperspectral imagery.

When a dataset becomes so large that its storage and processing become challenging due to the limitations of existing tools and resources, the dataset is referred to as Big Data. While a one PetaByte dataset can be considered as a trivial amount by some organizations, some other organizations can rightfully classify their five TeraBytes of data as Big Data. Hence, Big Data is best defined in relative terms and there is no well-defined threshold with respect to the volume of data for it to be considered as Big Data.

Along with its volume, which may or may not be continuously increasing, there are a couple of other characteristics that are used for classifying large datasets as Big Data. The heterogeneity (in terms of data types and formats), and the speed of accumulation of data can pose challenges during its processing and analyses. These added layers of difficulty in the timely analyses of Big Data are often referred to as its variety and velocity characteristics. By themselves, neither the variety in datasets nor the velocity at which they are collected might pose challenges that are insurmountable by conventional data storage and processing techniques. It is the coupling of the volume characteristic with the variety and velocity characteristics, along with the need for rapid analyses, that makes Big Data processing challenging.

Rapid, Interactive, and Iterative Analyses (RIIA) of Big Data holds untapped potential for numerous discoveries. The process of RIIA can involve data mining, machine learning, statistical analyses, and visualization tools. Such analyses can be both computationally intensive and memory-intensive. Even before Big Data can become ready for analyses, there could be several steps required for data ingestion, pre-processing, processing, and post-processing. Just like RIIA, these steps can also be so computationally intensive and memory-intensive that it can be very challenging, if not impossible, to implement the entire RIIA workflow on desktop class computers or single-node servers. Moreover, different stakeholders might be interested in simultaneously drawing different inferences from the same dataset. To mitigate such challenges and achieve accelerated time-to-results, high-end computing and storage resources, performance-oriented middleware, and scalable software solutions are needed.

To a large extent, the need for scalable high-end storage and computational resources can be fulfilled at a supercomputing facility or by using a cluster of commodity-computers. The supercomputers or clusters could be supporting one or more of the following computational paradigms: High Performance Computing (HPC), High-Throughput Computing (HTC), and Hadoop along with the technologies related to it. The choice of a computational paradigm and hence, the underlying hardware platform, is influenced by the scalability and portability of the software required for processing and managing Big Data. In addition to these, the nature of the application—whether it is data-intensive, or memory-intensive, or compute-intensive—can also impact the choice of the hardware resources.

The total execution time of an application is the sum total of the time it takes to do computation, the time it takes to do I/O, and in the case of parallel applications, the time it takes to do inter-process communication. The applications that spend a majority of their execution time in doing computations (e.g., add and multiply operations) can be classified as compute-intensive applications. The applications that require or produce large volumes of data and spend most of their execution time towards I/O and data manipulation and be classified as data-intensive applications. Both compute-intensive and data-intensive applications can be memory-intensive as well, which means, they could need a large amount of main memory during runtime.

In the rest of this chapter, we present a short overview of HPC, HTC, Hadoop, and other technologies related to Hadoop. We discuss the convergence of Big Data with these computing paradigms and technologies. We also briefly discuss the usage of the HPC/HTC/Hadoop platforms that are available through cloud computing resource providers and open-science datacenters.

1.2 High Performance Computing (HPC)

HPC is the use of aggregated high-end computing resources (or supercomputers) along with parallel or concurrent processing techniques (or algorithms) for solving both compute- and data-intensive problems. These problems may or may not be memory-intensive. The terms HPC and supercomputing are often used interchangeably.

1.2.1 HPC Platform

A typical HPC platform comprises of clustered compute and storage servers interconnected using very fast and efficient network, like InfiniBand™ [5]. These servers are also called nodes. Each compute server in a cluster can comprise of a variety of processing elements for handling different types of computational workloads. Due to their hardware configuration, some compute nodes in a platform could be better equipped for handling compute-intensive workloads, while others might be better equipped for handling visualization and memory-intensive workloads. The commonly used processing elements in a compute node of a cluster are:

- *Central Processing Units* (CPUs): these are primary processors or processing units that can have one or more hardware cores. Today, a multi-core CPU can consist of up to 18 compute cores [6].
- *Accelerators and Coprocessors:* these are many-core processors that are used in tandem with CPUs to accelerate certain parts of the applications. The accelerators and coprocessors can consist of many more small cores as compared to a CPU. For example, an Intel® Xeon Phi™ coprocessor consists of 61 cores. An accelerator or *General Purpose Graphics Processing Unit* (GPGPU) can consist of thousands of cores. For example, NVIDIA's Tesla® K80 GPGPU consists of 4992 cores [7].

These multi-core and many-core processing elements present opportunities for executing application tasks in parallel, thereby, reducing the overall run-time of an application. The processing elements in an HPC platform are often connected to multiple levels of memory hierarchies and parallel filesystems for high performance. A typical memory hierarchy consists of: registers, on-chip cache, off-chip cache, main memory, and virtual memory. The cost and performance of these different levels of memory hierarchies decreases, and size increases, as one goes from registers to virtual memory. Additional levels in the memory hierarchy can exist as a processor can access memory on other processors in a node of a cluster.

An HPC platform can have multiple parallel filesystems that are either dedicated to it or shared with other HPC platforms as well. A parallel filesystem distributes the data in a file across multiple storage servers (and eventually hard disks or flash storage devices), thus enabling concurrent access to the data by multiple application tasks or processes. Two examples of parallel file systems are Lustre [8] and General Parallel File System (GPFS) [9].

In addition to compute nodes and storage nodes, clusters have additional nodes that are called login nodes or head nodes. These nodes enable a user to interact with the compute nodes for running applications. The login nodes are also used for software compilation and installation. Some of the nodes in an HPC platform are also meant for system administration purposes and parallel filesystems.

All the nodes in a cluster are placed as close as possible to minimize network latency. The low-latency interconnect, and the parallel filesystems that can enable parallel data movement, to and from the processing elements, are critical to achieving high performance.

The HPC platforms are provisioned with resource managers and job schedulers. These are software components that manage the access to compute nodes for a predetermined period of time for executing applications. An application or a series of applications that can be run on a platform is called a job. A user can schedule a job to run either in batch mode or interactive mode by submitting it to a queue of jobs. The resource manager and job scheduler are pre-configured to assign different levels of priorities to jobs in the queue such that the platform is used optimally at all times, and all users get a fair-share of the platform. When a job's turn comes in the queue, it is assigned compute node/s on which it can run.

It should be mentioned here that the majority of the HPC platforms are Linux-based and can be accessed remotely using a system that supports the SSH protocol (or connection) [10]. A pictorial depiction of the different components of an HPC platform that have been discussed so far is presented in Fig. 1.1.

1.2.2   Serial and Parallel Processing on HPC Platform

An HPC platform can be used to run a wide variety of applications with different characteristics as long as the applications can be compiled on the platform. A serial application that needs large amounts of memory to run and hence cannot be run on

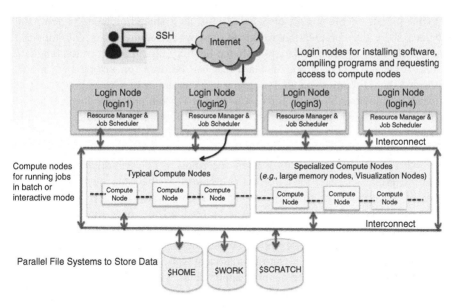

Fig. 1.1 Connecting to and working on an HPC platform

regular desktops, can be run on an HPC platform without making any changes to the source code. In this case, a single copy of an application can be run on a core of a compute node that has large amounts of memory.

For efficiently utilizing the underlying processing elements in an HPC platform and accelerating the performance of an application, parallel computing (or processing) techniques can be used. *Parallel computing* is a type of programming paradigm in which certain regions of an application's code can be executed simultaneously on different processors, such that, the overall time-to-results is reduced. The main principle behind parallel computing is that of divide-and-conquer, in which large problems are divided into smaller ones, and these smaller problems are then solved simultaneously on multiple processing elements. There are mainly two ways in which a problem can be broken down into smaller pieces—either by using data parallelism, or task parallelism.

Data parallelism involves distributing a large set of input data into smaller pieces such that each processing element works with a separate piece of data while performing same type of calculations. Task parallelism involves distributing computational tasks (or different instructions) across multiple processing elements to be calculated simultaneously. A parallel application (data parallel or task parallel) can be developed using the shared-memory paradigm or the distributed-memory paradigm.

A parallel application written using the shared-memory paradigm exploits the parallelism within a node by utilizing multiple cores and access to a shared-memory region. Such an application is written using a language or library that supports spawning of multiple threads. Each thread runs on a separate core, has its private memory, and also has access to a shared-memory region. The threads share the computation workload, and when required, can communicate with each other by writing data to a shared memory region and then reading data from it. OpenMP [11] is one standard that can be used for writing such multi-threaded shared-memory parallel programs that can run on CPUs and coprocessors. OpenMP support is available for C, C++, and Fortran programming languages. This multi-threaded approach is easy to use but is limited in scalability to a single node.

A parallel application written using the distributed-memory paradigm can scale beyond a node. An application written according to this paradigm is run using multiple processes, and each process is assumed to have its own independent address space and own share of workload. The processes can be spread across different nodes, and do not communicate by reading from or writing to a shared-memory. When the need arises to communicate with each other for data sharing or synchronization, the processes do so via message passing. Message Passing Interface (MPI) [12] is the de-facto standard that is used for developing distributed-memory or distributed-shared memory applications. MPI bindings are available for C and Fortran programming languages. MPI programs can scale up to thousands of nodes but can be harder to write as compared to OpenMP programs due to the need for explicit data distribution, and orchestration of exchange of messages by the programmer.

A hybrid-programming paradigm can be used to develop applications that use multi-threading within a node and multi-processing across the nodes. An application written using the hybrid-programming paradigm can use both OpenMP and MPI. If parts of an application are meant to run in multi-threaded mode on a GPGPU, and others on the CPU, then such applications can be developed using Compute Unified Device Architecture (CUDA) [13]. If an application is meant to scale across multiple GPUs attached to multiple nodes, then they can be developed using both CUDA and MPI.

1.3   High-Throughput Computing (HTC)

A serial application can be run in more than one ways on an HPC platform to exploit the parallelism in the underlying platform, without making any changes to its source code. For doing this, multiple copies of the application are run concurrently on multiple cores and nodes of a platform such that each copy of the application uses different input data or parameters to work with. Running multiple copies of serial applications in parallel with different input parameters or data such that the overall runtime is reduced is called HTC. This mechanism is typically used for running parameter sweep applications or those written for ensemble modeling. HTC applications can be run on an HPC platform (more details in Chaps. 4, 13, and 14) or even on a cluster of commodity-computers.

Like parallel computing, HTC also works on the divide-and-conquer principle. While HTC is mostly applied to data-parallel applications, parallel computing can be applied to both data-parallel and task-parallel applications. Often, HTC applications, and some of the distributed-memory parallel applications that are trivial to parallelize and do not involve communication between the processes, are called embarrassingly parallel applications. The applications that would involve inter-process communication at run-time cannot be solved using HTC. For developing such applications, a parallel programming paradigm like MPI is needed.

1.4   Hadoop

Hadoop is an open-source software framework written in Java that is commonly used for Big Data processing in mainstream computing domains [14]. It runs on a shared-nothing architecture, that is, the storage and processing resources are all distributed, and it functions in HTC mode. Basically, the shared-nothing architecture on which Hadoop runs is commonly built as a cluster of commodity hardware resources (nodes), and hence, is in contrast to HPC platforms that are built using high-end hardware elements.

There are three main modules or software components in the Hadoop framework and these are a distributed filesystem, a processing module, and a job management module. The Hadoop Distributed File System (HDFS) manages the storage on a Hadoop platform (hardware resource on which Hadoop runs) and the processing is done using the MapReduce paradigm. The Hadoop framework also includes Yarn which is a module meant for resource-management and scheduling. In addition to these three modules, Hadoop also consists of utilities that support these modules.

Hadoop's processing module, MapReduce, is based upon Google's MapReduce [15] programming paradigm. This paradigm has a map phase which entails grouping and sorting of the input data into subgroups such that multiple map functions can be run in parallel on each subgroup of the input data. The user provides the input in the form of key-value pairs. A user-defined function is then invoked by the map functions running in parallel. Hence, the user-defined function is independently applied to all subgroups of input data. The reduce phase entails invoking a user-defined function for producing output—an output file is produced per reduce task. The MapReduce module handles the orchestration of the different steps in parallel processing, managing data movement, and fault-tolerance.

The applications that need to take advantage of Hadoop should conform to the MapReduce interfaces, mainly the Mapper and Reducer interfaces. The Mapper corresponds to the map phase of the MapReduce paradigm. The Reducer corresponds to the reduce phase. Programming effort is required for implementing the Mapper and Reducer interfaces, and for writing code for the map and reduce methods. In addition to these there are other interfaces that might need to be implemented as well (e.g., Partitioner, Reporter, and OutputCollector) depending upon the application needs. It should also be noted that each job consists of only one map and one reduce function. The order of executing the steps in the MapReduce paradigm is fixed. In case multiple map and reduce steps are required in an application, they cannot be implemented in a single MapReduce job. Moreover, there are a large number of applications that have computational and data access patterns that cannot be expressed in terms of the MapReduce model [16].

1.4.1 Hadoop-Related Technologies

In addition to the modules for HDFS filesystem, job scheduling and management, and data processing, today Hadoop covers a wide ecosystem of modules that can be used with it to extend its functionality. For example, the Spark [17] software package can be used for overcoming the limitation of the almost linear workflow imposed by MapReduce. Spark enables interactive and iterative analyses of Big Data. A package called Hadoop Streaming [18] can be used for running MapReduce jobs using non-Java programs as Mapper and Reducer, however, these non-Java applications should read their input from standard input (or stdin) and write their data to standard output (or stdout). Hence this package can be used only for those applications that have textual input and output and cannot be directly used for applications that have binary input and output. Hive is another software package that can be used for data warehouse infrastructure and provides the capability of data querying and management [19]. A list of additional Hadoop packages or projects is available at [12].

1.4.2 Some Limitations of Hadoop and Hadoop-Related Technologies

Hadoop has limitations not only in terms of scalability and performance from the architectural standpoint, but also in terms of the application classes that can take advantage of it. Hadoop and some of the other technologies related to it pose a restrictive data format of key-value pairs. It can be hard to express all forms of input or output in terms of key-value pairs.

In cases of applications that involve querying a very large database (e.g., BLAST searches on large databases [20]), a shared-nothing framework like Hadoop could necessitate replication of a large database on multiple nodes, which might not be feasible to do. Reengineering and extra programming effort is required for adapting legacy applications to take advantage of the Hadoop framework. In contrast to Hadoop, as long as an existing application can be compiled on an HPC platform, it can be run on the platform not only in the serial mode but also in concurrent mode using HTC.

1.5 Convergence of Big Data, HPC, HTC, and Hadoop

HPC has traditionally been used for solving various scientific and societal problems through the usage of not only cutting-edge processing and storage resources but also efficient algorithms that can take advantage of concurrency at various levels. Some HPC applications (e.g., from astrophysics and next generation sequencing domains) can periodically produce and consume large volumes of data at a high processing rate or velocity. There are various disciplines (e.g., geosciences) that have had workflows involving production and consumption of a wide variety of datasets on HPC resources. Today, in domains like archaeology, and paleontology, HPC is becoming indispensable for curating and managing large data collections. A common thread across all such traditional and non-traditional HPC application domains has been the need for short time-to-results while handling large and heterogeneous datasets that are ingested or produced on a platform at varying speeds.

The innovations in HPC technologies at various levels—like, networking, storage, and computer architecture—have been incorporated in modern HPC platforms and middleware to enable high-performance and short time-to-results. The parallel programming paradigms have also been evolving to keep up with the evolution at the hardware-level. These paradigms enable the development of performance-oriented applications that can leverage the underlying hardware architecture efficiently.

Some HPC applications, like the FLASH astrophysics code [21] and mpiBLAST [16], are noteworthy in terms of the efficient data management strategies at the application-level and optimal utilization of the underlying hardware resources for reducing the time-to-results. FLASH makes use of portable data models and file-formats like HDF5 [22] for storing and managing application data along with the metadata during run-time. FLASH also has routines for parallel I/O so that reading and writing of data can be done efficiently when using multiple processors. As another example, consider the mpiBLAST application, which is a parallel implementation of an alignment algorithm for comparing a set of query sequences against a database of biological (protein and nucleotide) sequences. After doing the comparison, the application reports the matches between the sequences being queried and the sequences in the database [16]. This application exemplifies the usage of techniques like parallel I/O, database fragmentation, and database query segmentation for developing a scalable and performance-oriented solution for querying large databases on HPC platforms. *The lessons drawn from the design and implementation of HPC applications like FLASH and mpiBLAST are generalizable and applicable towards developing efficient Big Data applications that can run on HPC platforms.*

However, the hardware resources and the middleware (viz., Hadoop, Spark and Yarn [23]) that are generally used for the management and analyses of Big Data in mainstream computing have not yet taken full advantage of such HPC technologies. Instead of optimizing the usage of hardware resources to both scale-up and scale-out, it is observed that, currently, the mainstream Big Data community mostly prefers to scale-out. A couple of reasons for this are cost minimization, and the web-based nature of the problems for which Hadoop was originally designed.

Originally, Hadoop used TCP/IP, REST and RPC for inter-process communication whereas, for several years now, the HPC platforms have been using fast RDMA-based communication for getting high performance. The HDFS filesystem that Hadoop uses is slow and cumbersome to use as compared to the parallel filesystems that are available on the HPC systems. In fact, myHadoop [24] is an implementation of Hadoop over the Lustre filesystem and hence, helps in running Hadoop over traditional HPC platforms having Lustre filesystem. In addition to the myHadoop project, there are other research groups that have also made impressive advancements towards addressing the performance issues with Hadoop [25] (more details in Chap. 5).

It should also be noted here that, Hadoop has some in-built advantages like fault-tolerance and enjoys massive popularity. There is a large community of developers who are augmenting the Hadoop ecosystem, and hence, this makes Hadoop a sustainable software framework.

Even though HPC is gradually becoming indispensable for accelerating the rate of discoveries, there are programming challenges associated with developing highly optimized and performance-oriented parallel applications. Fortunately, having a highly tuned performance-oriented parallel application is not a necessity to use HPC platforms. Even serial applications for data processing can be compiled on an HPC platform and can be run in HTC mode without requiring any major code changes in them.

Some of the latest supercomputers [26, 27] allow running a variety of workloads—highly efficient parallel HPC applications, legacy serial applications with or without using HTC, and Hadoop applications as well (more details in Chaps. 2 and 16). With such hardware platforms and latest middleware technologies, the HPC and mainstream Big Data communities could soon be seen on converging paths.

1.6 HPC and Big Data Processing in Cloud and at Open-Science Data Centers

The costs for purchasing and operating HPC platforms or commodity-clusters for large-scale data processing and management can be beyond the budget of a many mainstream business and research organizations. In order to accelerate their time-to-results, such organizations can either port their HPC and big data workflows to cloud computing platforms that are owned and managed by other organizations, or explore the possibility of using resources at the open-science data centers. Hence, without a large financial investment in resources upfront, organizations can take advantage of HPC platforms and commodity-clusters on-demand.

Cloud computing refers to on-demand access to hardware and software resources through web applications. Both bare-metal and virtualized servers can be made available to the users through cloud computing. Google provides the service for creating HPC clusters on the Google Cloud platform by utilizing virtual machines and cloud storage [28]. It is a paid-service that can be used to run HPC and Big Data workloads in Google Cloud. Amazon Web Service (AWS) [29] is another paid cloud computing service, and can be used for running HTC or HPC applications needing CPUs or GPGPUs in the cloud.

The national open-science data centers, like the Texas Advanced Computing Center (TACC) [30], host and maintain several HPC and data-intensive computing platforms (see Chap. 2). The platforms are funded through multiple funding agencies that support open-science research, and hence the academic users do not have to bear any direct cost for using these platforms. TACC also provides cloud computing resources for the research community. The Chameleon system [31] that is hosted by TACC and its partners provides bare-metal deployment features on which users can have administrative access to run cloud-computing experiments with a high degree of customization and repeatability. Such experiments can include running high performance big data analytics jobs as well, for which, parallel filesystems, a variety of databases, and a number of processing elements could be required.

1.7   Conclusion

"Big Data" is a term that has been introduced in recent years. The management and analyses of Big Data through various stages of its lifecycle presents challenges, many of which have already been surmounted by the High Performance Computing (HPC) community over the last several years. The technologies and middleware that are currently almost synonymous with Big Data (e.g., Hadoop and Spark) have interesting features but pose some limitations in terms of the performance, scalability, and generalizability of the underlying programming model. Some of these limitations can be addressed using HPC and HTC on HPC platforms.

References

1. Global Landcover Facility website (2016), http://glcf.umd.edu/data/landsat/. Accessed 29 Feb 2016
2. NASA's Earth Observation System website (2016), http://eospso.nasa.gov/. Accessed 29 Feb 2016
3. National Oceanic and Atmospheric Administration (2016), http://oceanservice.noaa.gov/facts/currentmon.html. Accessed 29 Feb 2016
4. National Oceanic and Atmospheric Administration (2016), http://oceanservice.noaa.gov/facts/lidar.html. Accessed 29 Feb 2016

5. Introduction to InfiniBand (2016), http://www.mellanox.com/pdf/whitepapers/IB_Intro_WP_190.pdf. Accessed 29 Feb 2016
6. Intel® Xeon® Processor E5-2698 v3 (2016), http://ark.intel.com/products/81060/Intel-Xeon-Processor-E5-2698-v3-40M-Cache-2_30-GHz. Accessed 29 Feb 2016
7. Tesla GPU Accelerators for Servers (2016), http://www.nvidia.com/object/tesla-servers.html#axzz41i6Ikeo4. Accessed 29 Feb 2016
8. Lustre filesystem (2016), http://lustre.org/. Accessed 29 Feb 2016
9. General Parallel File System (GPFS), https://www.ibm.com/support/knowledgecenter/SSFKCN/gpfs_welcome.html?lang=en. Accessed 29 Feb 2016
10. The Secure Shell Transfer Layer Protocol (2016), https://tools.ietf.org/html/rfc4253. Accessed 29 Feb 2016
11. OpenMP (2016), http://openmp.org/wp/. Accessed 29 Feb 2016
12. Message Passing Interface Forum (2016), http://www.mpi-forum.org/. Accessed 29 Feb 2016
13. CUDA (2016), http://www.nvidia.com/object/cuda_home_new.html#axzz41i6Ikeo4. Accessed 29 Feb 2016
14. Apache Hadoop (2016), http://hadoop.apache.org/. Accessed 29 Feb 2016
15. J. Dean, S. Ghemawat, MapReduce: simplified data processing on large clusters. Commun. ACM **51**(1), 107–113 (2008). doi:10.1145/1327452.1327492
16. H. Lin, X. Ma, W. Feng, N. Samatova, Coordinating computation and I/O in massively parallel sequence search. IEEE Trans. Parallel Distrib. Syst. 529–543 (2010). doi:10.1109/TPDS.2010.101
17. Apache Spark (2016), http://spark.apache.org/. Accessed 29 Feb 2016
18. Hadoop Streaming (2016), https://hadoop.apache.org/docs/r1.2.1/streaming.html. Accessed 29 Feb 2016
19. Hive (2016), http://hive.apache.org/. Accessed 29 Feb 2016
20. S.F. Altschul, W. Gish, W. Miller, E.W. Myers, D.J. Lipman, Basic local alignment search tool. J. Mol. Biol. **215**(3), 403–410 (1990)
21. The FLASH code (2016), http://flash.uchicago.edu/site/flashcode/. Accessed 15 Feb 2016
22. HDF5 website (2016), https://www.hdfgroup.org/HDF5/. Accessed 15 Feb 2016
23. Apache Yarn Framework website (2016), http://hortonworks.com/hadoop/yarn/. Accessed 15 Feb 2016
24. S. Krishnan, M. Tatineni, C. Baru, Myhadoop—hadoop-on-demand on traditional HPC resources, chapter in Contemporary HPC Architectures (2004), http://www.sdsc.edu/~allans/MyHadoop.pdf
25. High Performance Big Data (HiDB) (2016), http://hibd.cse.ohio-state.edu/. Accessed 15 Feb 2016
26. Gordon Supercomputer website (2016), http://www.sdsc.edu/services/hpc/hpc_systems.html#gordon. Accessed 15 Feb 2016
27. Wrangler Supercomputer website (2016), https://www.tacc.utexas.edu/systems/wrangler. Accessed 15 Feb 2016
28. Google Cloud Platform (2016), https://cloud.google.com/solutions/architecture/highperformancecomputing. Accessed 15 Feb 2016
29. Amazon Web Services (2016), https://aws.amazon.com/hpc/. Accessed 15 Feb 2016
30. Texas Advanced Computing Center Website (2016), https://www.tacc.utexas.edu/. Accessed 15 Feb 2016
31. Chameleon Cloud Computing Testbed website (2016), https://www.tacc.utexas.edu/systems/chameleon. Accessed 15 Feb 2016

Chapter 2
Using High Performance Computing
for Conquering Big Data

Antonio Gómez-Iglesias and Ritu Arora

Abstract The journey of Big Data begins at its collection stage, continues to analyses, culminates in valuable insights, and could finally end in dark archives. The management and analyses of Big Data through these various stages of its life cycle presents challenges that can be addressed using High Performance Computing (HPC) resources and techniques. In this chapter, we present an overview of the various HPC resources available at the open-science data centers that can be used for developing end-to-end solutions for the management and analysis of Big Data. We also present techniques from the HPC domain that can be used to solve Big Data problems in a scalable and performance-oriented manner. Using a case-study, we demonstrate the impact of using HPC systems on the management and analyses of Big Data throughout its life cycle.

2.1 Introduction

Big Data refers to very large datasets that can be complex, and could have been collected through a variety of channels including streaming of data through various sensors and applications. Due to its volume, complexity, and speed of accumulation, it is hard to manage and analyze Big Data manually or by using traditional data processing and management techniques. Therefore, a large amount of computational power could be required for efficiently managing and analyzing Big Data to discover knowledge and develop new insights in a timely manner.

Several traditional data management and processing tools, platforms, and strategies suffer from the lack of scalability. To overcome the scalability constraints of existing approaches, technologies like Hadoop[1], and Hive[2] can be used for addressing certain forms of data processing problems. However, even if their data processing needs can be addressed by Hadoop, many organizations do not have the means to afford the programming effort required for leveraging Hadoop and related technologies for managing the various steps in their data life cycle. Moreover, there

---

A. Gómez-Iglesias (✉) • R. Arora
Texas Advanced Computing Center, The University of Texas at Austin, Austin, TX, USA
e-mail: agomez@tacc.utexas.edu; rauta@tacc.utexas.edu
http://www.tacc.utexas.edu

© Springer International Publishing Switzerland 2016
R. Arora (ed.), *Conquering Big Data with High Performance Computing*,
DOI 10.1007/978-3-319-33742-5_2

13

are also scalability and performance limitations associated with Hadoop and its related technologies. In addition to this, Hadoop does not provide the capability of interactive analysis.

It has been demonstrated that the power of HPC platforms and parallel processing techniques can be applied to manage and process Big Data in a scalable and timely manner. Some techniques from the areas of data mining, and artificial intelligence (viz., data classification, and machine learning) can be combined with techniques like data filtering, data culling, and information visualization to develop solutions for selective data processing and analyses. Such solutions, when used in addition to parallel processing, can help in attaining short time-to-results where the results could be in the form of derived knowledge or achievement of data management goals.

As latest data-intensive computing platforms become available at open-science data centers, new use cases from traditional and non-traditional HPC communities have started to emerge. Such use cases indicate that the HPC and Big Data disciplines have started to converge at least in the academia. It is important that the mainstream Big Data and non-traditional HPC communities are informed about the latest HPC platforms and technologies through such use cases. Doing so will help these communities in identifying the right platform and technologies for addressing the challenges that they are facing with respect to the efficient management and analyses of Big Data in a timely and cost-effective manner.

In this chapter, we first take a closer look at the Big Data life cycle. Then we present the typical platforms, tools and techniques used for managing the Big Data life cycle. Further, we present a general overview of managing and processing the entire Big Data life cycle using HPC resources and techniques, and the associated benefits and challenges. Finally, we present a case-study from the nuclear fusion domain to demonstrate the impact of using HPC systems on the management and analyses of Big Data throughout its life cycle.

2.2   The Big Data Life Cycle

The life cycle of data, including that of Big Data, comprises of various stages such as collection, ingestion, preprocessing, processing, post-processing, storage, sharing, recording provenance, and preservation. Each of these stages can comprise of one or more activities or steps. The typical activities during these various stages in the data life cycle are listed in Table 2.1. As an example, data storage can include steps and policies for short-term, mid-term, and long-term storage of data, in addition to the steps for data archival. The processing stage could involve iterative assessment of the data using both manual and computational effort. The post-processing stage can include steps such as exporting data into various formats, developing information visualization, and doing data reorganization. Data management throughout its life cycle is, therefore, a broad area and multiple tools are used for it (e.g., database management systems, file profiling tools, and visualization tools).

Table 2.1 Various stages in data life cycle

Data life cycle stages	Activities
Data collection	Recording provenance, data acquisition
Data preprocessing	Data movement (ingestion), cleaning, quality control, filtering, culling, metadata extraction, recording provenance
Data processing	Data movement (moving across different levels of storage hierarchy), computation, analysis, data mining, visualization (for selective processing and refinement), recording provenance
Data post-processing	Data movement (newly generated data from processing stage), formatting and report generation, visualization (viewing of results), recording provenance
Data sharing	Data movement (dissemination to end-users), publishing on portals, data access including cloud-based sharing, recording provenance
Data storage and archival	Data movement (across primary, secondary, and tertiary storage media), database management, aggregation for archival, recording provenance
Data preservation	Checking integrity, performing migration from one storage media to other as the hardware or software technologies become obsolete, recording provenance
Data destruction	Shredding or permanent wiping of data

A lot of the traditional data management tools and platforms are not scalable enough for Big Data management and hence new scalable platforms, tools, and strategies are needed to supplement the existing ones. As an example, file-profiling is often done during various steps of data management for extracting metadata (viz., file checksums, file-format, file-size and time-stamp), and then the extracted metadata is used for analyzing a data collection. The metadata helps the curators to take decisions regarding redundant data, data preservation and data migration. The Digital Record Object Identification (DROID) [8] tool is commonly used for file-profiling in batch mode. The tool is written in Java and works well on single-node servers. However, for managing a large data collection (≥ 4 TB), a DROID instance running on a single node server, takes days to produce file-profiling reports for data management purposes. In a large and evolving data collection, where new data is being added continuously, by the time DROID finishes file-profiling and produces the report, the collection might have undergone several changes, and hence the profile information might not be an accurate representation of the current state of the collection.

As can be noticed from Table 2.1, during data life cycle management, data movement is often involved at various stages. The overheads of data movement can be high when the data collection has grown beyond a few TeraBytes (TBs). Minimizing data movement across platforms over the internet is critical when dealing with large datasets, as even today, the data movement over the internet can pose significant challenges related to latency and bandwidth. As an example, for transferring approximately 4.3 TBs of data from the Stampede supercomputer

[18] in Austin (Texas) to the Gordon supercomputer [11] in San Diego (California), it took approximately 210 h. The transfer was restarted 14 times in 15 days due to interruptions. There were multiple reasons for interruptions, such as filesystem issues, hardware issues at both ends of the data transfer, and the loss of internet connection. Had there been no interruptions in data transfer, at the observed rate of data transfer, it would have taken 9 days to transfer the data from Stampede to Gordon. Even when the source and destination of the data are located in the same geographical area, and the network is 10 GigE, it is observed that it can take, on an average, 24 h to transfer 1 TB of data. Therefore, it is important to make a careful selection of platforms for storage and processing of data, such that they are in close proximity. In addition to this, appropriate tools for data movement should be selected.

2.3 Technologies and Hardware Platforms for Managing the Big Data Life Cycle

Depending upon the volume and complexity of the Big Data collection that needs to be managed and/or processed, a combination of existing and new platforms, tools, and strategies might be needed. Currently, there are two popular types of platforms and associated technologies for conquering the needs of Big Data processing: (1) Hadoop, along with the related technologies like Spark [3] and Yarn [4] provisioned on commodity hardware, and, (2) HPC platforms with or without Hadoop provisioned on them.

Hadoop is a software framework that can be used for processes that are based on the MapReduce [24] paradigm, and is open-source. Hadoop typically runs on a shared-nothing platform in which every node is used for both data storage and data processing [32]. With Hadoop, scaling is often achieved by adding more nodes (processing units) to the existing hardware to increase the processing and storage capacity. On the other hand, HPC can be defined as the use of aggregated high-end computing resources (or Supercomputers) along with parallel or concurrent processing techniques (or algorithms) for solving both compute and data-intensive problems in an efficient manner. Concurrency is exploited at both hardware and software-level in the case of HPC applications. Provisioning Hadoop on HPC resources has been made possible by the myHadoop project [32]. HPC platforms can also be used for doing High-Throughput Computing (HTC), during which multiple copies of existing software (e.g., DROID) can be run independently on different compute nodes of an HPC platform so that the overall time-to-results is reduced [22].

The choice of the underlying platform and associated technologies throughout the Big Data life cycle is guided by several factors. Some of the factors are: the characteristics of the problem to be solved, the desired outcomes, the support for the required tools on the available resources, the availability of human-power for programming new functionality or porting the available tools and applications to the aforementioned platforms, and the usage policies associated with the platforms. The characteristics of the data collection—like size, structure, and its current location—along with budget constraints also impact the choice of the underlying computational resources. The available mechanisms for transferring the data collection from the platform where it was created (or first stored), to where it needs to be managed and analyzed, is also a consideration while choosing between the available underlying platforms. The need for interactive and iterative analyses of the data collection can further impact the choice of the resource.

Since the focus of this chapter is on HPC platforms for Big Data management, we do not discuss the Hadoop-based platforms any further. In the following section, we discuss HPC platforms for managing and processing Big Data, which also have wider applicability and generalizability as compared to Hadoop. We further limit our discussion to the HPC resources available at the open-science data centers due to their accessibility to the general audience.

2.4 Managing Big Data Life Cycle on HPC Platforms at Open-Science Data Centers

With the advancement in hardware and middleware technologies, and the growing demand from their user-communities, the open-science data centers today offer a number of platforms that are specialized not only on handling compute-intensive workloads but also on addressing the need of data-intensive computing, cloud-computing, and PetaScale storage (e.g., Stampede, Wrangler [21], Chameleon [5], and Corral [6]). Together, such resources can be used for developing end-to-end cyberinfrastructure solutions that address the computing, analyses, visualization, storage, sharing, and archival needs of researchers. Hence, the complete Big Data life cycle can be managed at a single data center, thereby minimizing the data movement across platforms located at different organizations. As a case-in-point, the management and analysis of Big Data using the HPC resources available at the Texas Advanced Computing Center (TACC) is described in this section and is illustrated in Fig. 2.1.

2.4.1 TACC Resources and Usage Policies

The Stampede supercomputer can be used for running compute-intensive and data-intensive HPC or HTC applications. It is comprised of more than 6400 Dell PowerEdge server nodes, with each node having two Intel® Xeon E5 processors and an Intel® Xeon Phi™ Coprocessor. Stampede also includes a set of login nodes, large-memory nodes, and graphic nodes equipped with Graphics Processing Units

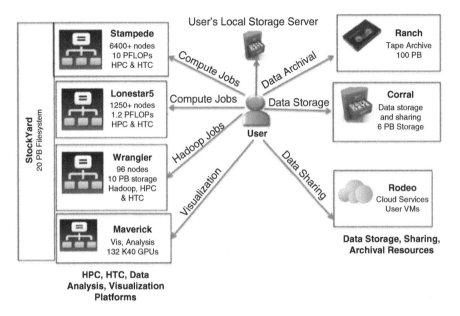

User's Local Storage Server

Stampede
6400+ nodes
10 PFLOPs
HPC & HTC

Lonestar5
1250+ nodes
1.2 PFLOPs
HPC & HTC

Wrangler
96 nodes
10 PB storage
Hadoop, HPC
& HTC

Maverick
Vis, Analysis
132 K40 GPUs

StockYard
20 PB Filesystem

Compute Jobs

Data Archival

Compute Jobs

Data Storage

Hadoop Jobs

User

Visualization

Data Sharing

Ranch
Tape Archive
100 PB

Corral
Data storage
and sharing
6 PB Storage

Rodeo
Cloud Services
User VMs

Data Storage, Sharing,
Archival Resources

HPC, HTC, Data
Analysis, Visualization
Platforms

Fig. 2.1 TACC resources used for developing end-to-end solutions

(GPUs) for data analysis and visualization. It has additional nodes for providing filesystem services and management. Depending upon the Big Data workflow of the end-user, Stampede can be used for data preprocessing, processing, post-processing, and analyses.

The Wrangler supercomputer is especially designed for data-intensive computing. It has 10 PetaBytes (PBs) of replicated, high-performance data storage. With its large-scale flash storage tier for analytics, and bandwidth of 1 TB per second, it supports 250 million I/O operations per second. It has 96 Intel ® Haswell server nodes. Wrangler provides support for some of the data management functions using iRods [12], such as calculating checksums for tracking the file fixity over time, annotating the data and data sharing. It supports the execution of Hadoop jobs in addition to regular HPC jobs for data preprocessing, processing, post-processing, and analyses. It is very well-suited for implementing data curation workflows.

Like Stampede, the Lonestar5 [14] supercomputer can also be used for running both HPC and HTC workloads. It also supports remote visualization. Maverick [15] is a computational resource for interactive analysis and remote visualization.

Corral is a secondary storage and a data management resource. It supports the deployment of persistent databases, and provides web access for data sharing. Ranch [17] is a tape-based system which can be used for tertiary storage and data archival. Rodeo [18] is a cloud-computing resource on which Virtual Machines (VMs) are provisioned for users. It can be used for data sharing and storage purposes.

A user can access TACC resources via an SSH connection or via a web interface provided by TACC (TACC Visualization Portal [20]). All TACC resources have low-latency interconnect like Infiniband and support network protocols like rsync and Globus online [9] for reliable and efficient data movement. Due to the proximity of the various resources at TACC to each other and the low-latency connection between them, the bottlenecks in data movement can be significantly mitigated. The various computing and visualization resources at TACC are connected to a global parallel filesystem called Stockyard. This filesystem can be used for storing large datasets that can, for example, be processed on Stampede, visualized on Maverick, and then can be moved to Corral or Ranch for permanent storage and archival. It has an aggregated bandwidth of greater than 100 gigabytes per second and has more than 20 PBs of storage capacity. It helps in the transparent usage between different TACC resources.

TACC resources are Linux-based, and are shared amongst multiple users, and hence, system policies are in place to ensure fair-usage of the resources by all users. The users have a fixed quota of the total number of files, and the total amount of storage space on a given resource. Both interactive and batch-processing modes are supported on TACC resources. In order to run their jobs on a resource, the users need to submit the job to a queue available on the system. The job scheduler assigns priority to the submitted job while taking into account several factors (viz., availability of the compute-nodes, the duration for which the compute nodes are requested, and the number of compute nodes requested). A job runs when its turn comes according to the priority assigned to it.

After the data processing is done on a given resource, the users might need to move their data to a secondary or a tertiary storage resource. It should also be noted that the resources at the open-science data centers have a life-span that depends upon the available budget for maintaining a system and the condition of the hardware used for building the resource. Therefore, at the end of the life of a resource, the users should be prepared to move their data and applications from a retiring resource to a new resource, as and when one becomes available. The resources undergo planned maintenance periodically and unplanned maintenance sporadically. During the maintenance period, the users might not be able to access the resource that is down for maintenance. Hence, for uninterrupted access to their data, the users might need to maintain multiple copies across different resources.

2.4.2   End-to-End Big Data Life Cycle on TACC Resources

Even before the data collection process begins, a data management plan should be developed. While developing the data management plan, the various policies related to data usage, data sharing, data retention, resource usage, and data movement should be carefully evaluated.

At the data collection stage, a user can first store the collected data on a local storage server and can then copy the data to a replicated storage resource like Corral. However, instead of making a temporary copy on a local server, users can directly send the data collected (for example, from remote sensors and instruments) for storage on Corral. While the data is ingested on Corral, the user has the choice to select iRods for facilitating data annotation and other data management functions, or to store their data in a persistent database management system, or store the data on the filesystem without using iRods. During the data ingestion stage on Corral, scripts can be run for extracting metadata from the data that is being ingested (with or without using iRods). The metadata can be used for various purposes— for example, for checking the validity of files, for recording provenance, and for grouping data according to some context. Any other preprocessing of data that is required, for example, cleaning or formatting the data for usage with certain data processing software, can also be done on Corral.

At times, the data collection is so large that doing any preprocessing on Corral might be prohibitive due to the very nature of Corral—it is a storage resource and not a computing resource. In such cases, the data can be staged from Corral to a computational or data-intensive computing resource like Stampede, or Lonestar5, or Wrangler. The preprocessing steps in addition to any required processing and post-processing can then be conducted on these resources.

As an example, a 4 TB archaeology dataset had to be copied to the filesystem on Stampede for conducting some of the steps in the data management workflow in parallel. These steps included extracting metadata for developing visual-snapshots of the state of the data collection for data organization purposes [22], and processing images in the entire data collection for finding duplicate and redundant content. For metadata extraction, several instances of the DROID tool were run concurrently and independently on several nodes of Stampede such that each DROID instance worked on a separate subset of the data collection. This concurrent approach brought down the metadata extraction time from days to hours but required a small amount of effort for writing scripts for managing multiple submissions of the computational jobs to the compute nodes. However, no change was made to the DROID code for making it run on an HPC platform. For finding the duplicate, similar and related images in a large image collection, a tool was developed to work in batch-mode. The tool works in both serial and parallel mode on Stampede and produces a report after assessing the content of the images in the entire data collection. The report can be used by data curators for quickly identifying redundant content and hence, for cleaning and reorganizing their data collection.

If the data life cycle entails developing visualization during various stages— preprocessing, processing, and post-processing, then resources like Maverick or Stampede can be used for the same. These resources have the appropriate hardware and software, like VisIt [23], Paraview [16], and FFmpeg [7], that can be used for developing visualizations.

After any compute and data-intensive functions in the data management work-flow have been completed, the updated data collection along with any additional data products can be moved to a secondary and tertiary storage resource (viz., Corral and Ranch). For data sharing purposes, the data collection can be made available in a VM instance running on Rodeo. In a VM running on Rodeo, additional software tools for data analysis and visualization, like Google Earth [10] and Tableau [19], can be made available along with the data collection. With the help of such tools and a refined data collection, collaborators can develop new knowledge from data.

2.5   Use Case: Optimization of Nuclear Fusion Devices

There are many scientific applications and problems that fit into the category of Big Data in different ways. At the same time, these applications can be also extremely demanding in terms of computational requirements, and need of HPC resources to run. An example of this type of problem is the optimization of stellarators.

Stellarators are a family of nuclear fusion devices with many possible configurations and characteristics. Fusion is a promising source of energy for the future, but still needs of a lot of efforts before becoming economically viable. ITER [13] is an example of those efforts. ITER will be a tokamak, one type of nuclear reactor. Tokamaks, together with stellarators, represent one of the most viable options for the future of nuclear fusion. However, it is still critical to find optimized designs that meet different criteria to be able to create a commercial reactor. Stellarators require complex coils that generate the magnetic fields necessary to confine the extremely hot fuels inside of the device. These high temperatures provide the energy required to eventually fuse the atoms, and also imply that the matter inside of the stellarator is in plasma state.

We introduce here a scientific use case that represents a challenge in terms of the computational requirements it presents, the amount of data that it creates and consumes and also a big challenge in the specific scientific area that it tackles. The problem that the use case tries to solve is the search of optimized designs for stellarators based on complex features. These features might involve the use of sophisticated workflows with several scientific applications involved. The result of the optimization is a set of optimal designs that can be used in the future. Based on the number of parameters that can be optimized, the size of the solution space which is composed of all the possible devices that could be designed, and the computational requirements of the different applications, it can be considered as a large-scale optimization problem [27].

The optimization system that we present was originally designed to run on grid computing environments [28]. The distributed nature of the grid platforms, with several decentralized computing and data centers, was a great choice for this type of problem because of some of the characteristics that we will later describe. However, it presented several difficulties in terms of synchronizing the communication of processes that run in geographically distributed sites as well as in terms of data movement. A barrier mechanism that used a file-based synchronization model was implemented. However, the amount of access to the metadata server did not normally allow to scale to more than a few thousand processes. The optimization algorithm has been since then generalized to solve any large-scale optimization problem [26] and ported to work in HPC environments [25].

A simplified overview of the workflow is depicted in Fig. 2.2. This workflow evaluates the quality of a given configuration of a possible stellarator. This configuration is defined in terms of a set of Fourier modes, among many other parameters, that describe the magnetic surfaces in the plasma confined in the stellarator. These magnetic fields are critical since they define the quality of the confinement of

Fig. 2.2 One of the possible
workflows for evaluating a
given configuration for a
possible stellarator. In this
case, any or all of the three
objectives codes can be
executed together with the
computation of the fitness
value

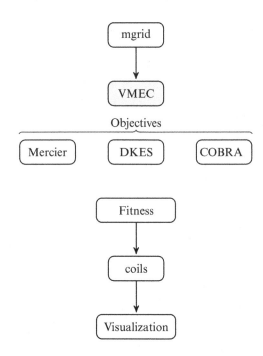

the particles inside of the device. A better confinement leads to lower number of particles leaving the plasma, better performance of the device, and less particles hitting the walls of the stellarator. Many different characteristics can be measured with this workflow. In our case, we use Eq. (2.1) to evaluate the quality of a given configuration. This expression is implemented in the `Fitness` step.

$$F_{fitnessfunction} = \sum_{i=1}^{N} \left\langle \left\| \frac{\vec{B} \times \vec{\nabla} |B|}{B^3} \right\| \right\rangle_i \tag{2.1}$$

In this equation, i represents the different magnetic surfaces in the plasma, whereas B represents the intensity of the magnetic field at each point of the surface. To calculate all of the values involved in this function, a workflow application must be executed, since no single application calculates all the data required in our optimization.

The magnetic surfaces can be represented as seen in Fig. 2.3, where each line represents a magnetic surface. The three figures correspond to the same possible stellarator at different angles, and it is possible to see the variations that can be found even between different angles. This needs very complex coils to generate the magnetic fields required to achieve this design.

The previous expression needs the value of the intensity of the magnetic field. We calculate that value using the VMEC application (Variational Moments Equilibrium Code [30]). This is a well-known code in the stellarator community

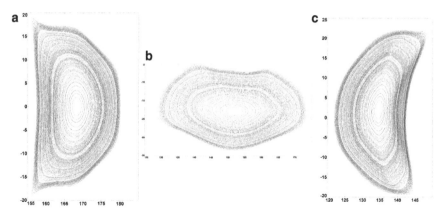

Fig. 2.3 Different cross-sections of the same stallarator design (0, 30 and 62 degrees angles)

with many users in the fusion centers around the world. It is a code implemented in Fortran. The execution time of this code depends on the complexity of the design that it is passed to it. Once it finishes, we calculate the Mercier stability [29] as well as the Ballooning [33] for that configuration. We can also run the DKES code (Drift Kinetic Equation Solver) [34]. These three applications are used together with the fitness function to measure the overall quality of a given configuration. Therefore, this can be considered a multi-objective optimization problem.

VMEC calculates the configuration of the magnetic surfaces in a stellarator by solving Eq. (2.2), where ρ is the effective normalized radius of a particular point on a magnetic surface, and θ and ϕ represent the cylindrical coordinates of the point.

$$B(\rho, \theta, \phi) = \sum_{mn} B_{mn}(\rho) \cos(m\theta - n\phi) \qquad (2.2)$$

With VMEC we are able to attain R_{mn} and Z_{mn} for a given point (ρ, θ, ϕ) and use these values in Eqs. (2.3), (2.4) and (2.2).

$$R(\rho, \theta, \phi) = \sum_{mn} R_{mn}(\rho) \cos(m\theta - n\phi) \qquad (2.3)$$

$$Z(\rho, \theta, \phi) = \sum_{mn} Z_{mn}(\rho) \sin(m\theta - n\phi) \qquad (2.4)$$

This is the most computationally demanding component of the workflow in terms of number of cycles required. It can also generate a relatively large amount of data that serves either as final result or as input for the other components of the workflow.

It can also be seen in the workflow how, as final steps, we can include the generation of the coils that will generate the magnetic field necessary to create the configuration previously found. Coils are a very complex and expensive component

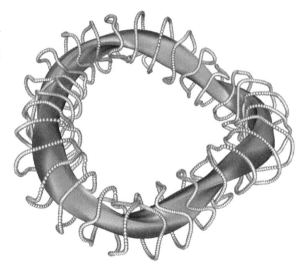

Fig. 2.4 Three modes
stellarator with required coils.
The *colors* describe the
intensity of the magnetic field
(Color figure online)

of the stellarators, so it is interesting to have this component as part of the
calculation. Finally, there is a visualization module that allows the researchers to
easily view the new configurations just created (as seen in Fig. 2.4).

Apart from the complexity of the type of problems that we tackle with this
framework and the amount of data that might be required and produced, another key
element is the disparity in terms of execution times for each possible solution to the
problem. Oftentimes, applications designed to work in HPC environments present
high-levels of synchronism or, at worst, some asynchronicity. The asynchronism
forces developers to overlap communication and computation. However, in the case
that we present here, the differences in the execution times of various solutions are
so large that specific algorithms need to be developed to achieve optimal levels of
resources' utilization. One of the approaches that we implemented consisted on a
producer–consumer model where a specific process generates possible solutions for
the problem (different Fourier modes) while the other tasks evaluate the quality of
those possible solutions (implement the workflow previously introduced).

2.5.1 Optimization

The workflow that we just described is used inside of an optimization algorithm to
find optimized solutions to the challenge of finding new stellarator's designs. In our
case, because of the complexity of the problem, with a large number of parameters
involved in the optimization and the difficulty to mathematically formulate the
problem, we decided to use metaheuristics to look for solutions to this problem.
Typically, algorithms used in this type of optimization are not designed to deal
with problems that are very challenging in terms of numbers of variables, execution

time, and overall computational requirements. It is difficult to find related work in the field that targets this type of problem. Because of this, we implemented our own algorithm, based on the Artificial Bee Colony (ABC) algorithm [31]. Our implementation is specially designed to work with very large problems where the evaluation of each possible solution can take a long time and, also, this time varies between solutions.

The algorithm consists of the exploration of the solution space by simulating bees foraging behavior. There are different types of bees, each one of them carrying out different actions. Some bees randomly explore the solution space to find configurations that satisfy the requirements specified by the problem. They evaluate those configurations and, based on the quality of the solution, will recruit more bees to find solutions close to that one. In terms of computing, this implies the creation of several new candidate solutions using a known one as base. Then, the processes evaluating configurations (executing the workflow previously described) will evaluate these new candidate solutions. Good known solutions are abandoned for further exploration if, after a set of new evaluations, the derived configurations do not improve the quality of known configurations.

Our algorithm introduces different levels of bees that perform different types of modifications on known solutions to explore the solution space. It takes advantage of the computational capabilities offered by HPC resources, with large number of cores available to perform calculations. Thus, each optimization process will consist of many different cores each one of them evaluating a different solution. As previously stated, a producer process implements the algorithm, creating new candidates based on the currently known solutions.

2.5.2   Computation on HPC

Because of the complexity of the problem, the number of processes required to carry out an execution of the algorithm is normally in the order of hundreds. For very large problems, it is normally necessary to use several thousand processes running for at least a week. Since HPC resources have a limit in the maximum wall-time for any given job, the algorithm incorporates a checkpointing mechanism to allow restarting the calculations from a previous stage.

While the programs involved in the optimization are written in C, C++ and Fortran, the optimization algorithm has been developed in Python. Since the algorithm is not demanding in terms of computational requirements, this does not present any overall problem in terms of performance. Moreover, we took special care using the most performant Python modules that we could use to perform the required calculations. Python also makes the algorithm highly portable: the optimization has been run on a number of HPC resources like Stampede, Euler[1] and Bragg.[2]

---
[1]http://rdgroups.ciemat.es/en_US/web/sci-track/euler.
[2]https://wiki.csiro.au/display/ASC/CSIRO+Accelerator+Cluster+-+Bragg.

Each evaluation of a possible stellarator might require a large number of files to be generated. The total number depends on the specific workflow that is being used for a given optimization. When considering the most simple case, the workflow generates up to 2.2 GB of data for each configuration as well as dozens of files, it is clear that this is a very large problem that it is also demanding from the data management point of view. This is, therefore, a data intensive problem. It is not a traditional data problem in terms of the amount of data that is required at a specific point in time, but it creates very large amounts of data, in a multitude of files and formats, and that data needs to be analyzed after being produced.

Taking into account that each optimization process requires the evaluation of thousands of configurations, it is also obvious that the total amount of data that is generated and managed by the application is large and complex.

One interesting aspect of this type of problem, where many different files are accessed during runtime, is that distributed filesystems like Lustre can run into problems with very high metadata load. In the case presented here, we take advantage of the fact that each node in Stampede has a local disk that can be used by the job that is running on that node. We can store intermediate files on that disk, specially those files that require many operations in a very short period of time. This way, we use the local disk for some very I/O intensive operations and the distributed parallel filesystem for the results and critical files.

As previously mentioned, this optimization system has been ported to different HPC resources. However, the capabilities provided by HPC centers that are considering a data centric approach simplifies the whole optimization process. The data being generated is challenging for some systems in terms of size and, as explained, in terms of the number of files. Also, the visualization that we will explain in the next section requires the data to be available on the systems used for this purpose. Sharing the filesystem between different HPC resources provides an optimal solution for not having to move data between systems. Finally, the data needs to be stored in secondary storage and archival systems so that it can be later retrieved for further optimizations or for querying some of the results already known.

2.5.3 Visualization Using GPUs

Being able to visualize the results that the optimization process generates is critical to understand different characteristics of those designs. As previously introduced, the workflow includes a module for visualizing the results that are found. The generation of the visualization file is very CPU demanding and constitutes a perfect candidate for being executed on GPUs. After running, it produces a SILO file that can be visualized using VisIt [23]. This was initially a C code running with OpenMP, but the time required for generating the visualization was so long that it made it difficult to use.

When running on many HPC centers, it is necessary to move files from the machine where the results is calculated to the machine used for visualization (if available). Although this is not a difficult task, it introduces an extra step that users many times avoid, only visualizing very specific results. The evaluation of the results as they are generated also becomes challenging.

Having a shared filesystem like Stockyard[3] at TACC, highly simplifies this process. Scientists only need to connect to the visualization resource (Maverick) and they already have access to the files that were generated or that are still being generated on a large HPC cluster. The possibility of visualizing the results immediately after they have been generated is very important since it allows researchers to provide guidance in real time to the optimization process.

2.5.4   Permanent Storage of Valuable Data

An important aspect of many scientific problems is the storage of the data that is generated by the scientific applications so that it can be later used for further analysis, comparison, or as input data for other applications. This is a relatively trivial problem when the amount of data that needs to be stored is not too large. In those cases, users can even make copies of the data on their own machines or on a more permanent storage solutions that they might have easily available. However, this approach does not scale well with the increase in the amount of datasets. Moving data over the networks between different locations is slow and does not represent a viable solution. Because of this, some HPC centers offer different options for the users to permanently store their data on those installations in a reliable manner.

In this use case, the optimization process can be configured to either simply keep the valid configurations that were found during the optimization process or to store all the results including all the files that are generated. The first case only creates up to several megabytes, normally below the gigabyte. However, the other mode, which is used to create a database of stellarator designs that can be easily accessed and used to find appropriate configurations that satisfy several different criteria will create large amounts of data and files.

HPC centers have different policies for data storage, including for example a quota and purge policies. Because of these policies, different strategies must be followed to ensure that the most valuable data is safely stored and can be easily retrieved when needed.

In the case of TACC, it has been previously described how Stockyard is useful for using the same data from different computational resources. However, Stockyard has a limit of 1 TB per user account. The amount of data produced by a single simulation might be larger than the overall quota allocated for a user. Stampede has a Scratch filesystem with up to 20 PB available. However, there is a purge policy that removes files after a given number of days.

---

[3]https://www.tacc.utexas.edu/systems/stockyard.

TACC provides other storage resources that are suitable for permanent storage of data. In our case, the configurations that have been created can be definitely stored in archival devices like Ranch or can be put into infrastructures devoted for data collections like Corral.

2.6 Conclusions

In this chapter, we presented some of the innovative HPC technologies that can be used for processing and managing the entire Big Data life cycle with high performance and scalability. The various computational and storage resources that are required during the different stages of the data life cycle are all provisioned by data centers like TACC. Hence, there is no need to frequently move the data between resources at different geographical locations as one progresses from one stage to another during the life cycle of data.

Through a high-level overview and a use-case from the nuclear fusion domain, we emphasized that by the usage of distributed and global filesystems, like Stockyard at TACC, the challenges related to the movement of massive volumes of datasets through the various stages of its life cycle can be further mitigated. Having all resources required for managing and processing the datasets at one location can also positively impact the productivity of end-users.

The complex big data workflows in which large numbers of small files can be generated, still present issues for parallel filesystems. It is sometimes possible to overcome such challenges (for example, by using the local disk on the nodes if such disks are present), but sometimes other specific resources might be needed. Wrangler is an example of such a resource.

References

1. Apache Hadoop Framework website. http://hadoop.apache.org/. Accessed 15 Feb 2016
2. Apache Hive Framework website. http://hive.apache.org/. Accessed 15 Feb 2016
3. Apache Spark Framework website. http://spark.apache.org/. Accessed 15 Feb 2016
4. Apache Yarn Framework website. http://hortonworks.com/hadoop/yarn/. Accessed 15 Feb 2016
5. Chameleon Cloud Computing Testbed website. https://www.tacc.utexas.edu/systems/chameleon. Accessed 15 Feb 2016
6. Corral High Performance and Data Storage System website. https://www.tacc.utexas.edu/systems/corral. Accessed 15 Feb 2016
7. FFmpeg website. https://www.ffmpeg.org. Accessed 15 Feb 2016
8. File Profiling Tool DROID. http://www.nationalarchives.gov.uk/information-management/manage-information/policy-process/digital-continuity/file-profiling-tool-droid/. Accessed 15 Feb 2016
9. Globus website. https://www.globus.org. Accessed 15 Feb 2016
10. Google Earth website. https://www.google.com/intl/ALL/earth/explore/products/desktop.html. Accessed 15 Feb 2016

11. Gordon Supercomputer website. http://www.sdsc.edu/services/hpc/hpc_systems.html#gordon. Accessed 15 Feb 2016
12. iRods website. http://irods.org/. Accessed 15 Feb 2016
13. ITER. https://www.iter.org/. Accessed 15 Feb 2016
14. Lonestar5 Supercomputer website. https://www.tacc.utexas.edu/systems/lonestar. Accessed 15 Feb 2016
15. Maverick Supercomputer website. https://www.tacc.utexas.edu/systems/maverick. Accessed 15 Feb 2016
16. Paraview website. https://www.paraview.org. Accessed 15 Feb 2016
17. Ranch Mass Archival Storage System website. https://www.tacc.utexas.edu/systems/ranch. Accessed 15 Feb 2016
18. Stampede Supercomputer website. https://www.tacc.utexas.edu/systems/stampede. Accessed 15 Feb 2016
19. Tableau website. http://www.tableau.com/. Accessed 15 Feb 2016
20. TACC Visualization Portal. https://vis.tacc.utexas.edu. Accessed 15 Feb 2016
21. Wrangler Supercomputer website. https://www.tacc.utexas.edu/systems/wrangler. Accessed 15 Feb 2016
22. R. Arora, M. Esteva, J. Trelogan, Leveraging high performance computing for managing large and evolving data collections. IJDC 9(2), 17–27 (2014). doi:10.2218/ijdc.v9i2.331. http://dx.doi.org/10.2218/ijdc.v9i2.331
23. H. Childs, E. Brugger, B. Whitlock, J. Meredith, S. Ahern, D. Pugmire, K. Biagas, M. Miller, C. Harrison, G.H. Weber, H. Krishnan, T. Fogal, A. Sanderson, C. Garth, E.W. Bethel, D. Camp, O. Rübel, M. Durant, J.M. Favre, P. Navrátil, VisIt: an end-user tool for visualizing and analyzing very large data, in *High Performance Visualization—Enabling Extreme-Scale Scientific Insight* (2012), pp. 357–372
24. J. Dean, S. Ghemawat, Mapreduce: simplified data processing on large clusters. Commun. ACM 51(1), 107–113 (2008). doi:10.1145/1327452.1327492. http://doi.acm.org/10.1145/1327452.1327492
25. A. Gómez-Iglesias, Solving large numerical optimization problems in HPC with python, in *Proceedings of the 5th Workshop on Python for High-Performance and Scientific Computing, PyHPC 2015*, Austin, TX, November 15, 2015 (ACM, 2015) pp. 7:1–7:8. doi:10.1145/2835857.2835864. http://doi.acm.org/10.1145/2835857.2835864
26. A. Gómez-Iglesias, F. Castejón, M.A. Vega-Rodríguez, Distributed bees foraging-based algorithm for large-scale problems, in *25th IEEE International Symposium on Parallel and Distributed Processing, IPDPS 2011 - Workshop Proceedings* Anchorage, AK, 16–20 May 2011 (IEEE, 2011), pp. 1950–1960. doi:10.1109/IPDPS.2011.355. http://dx.doi.org/10.1109/IPDPS.2011.355
27. A. Gómez-Iglesias, M.A. Vega-Rodríguez, F. Castejón, Distributed and asynchronous solver for large CPU intensive problems. Appl. Soft Comput. 13(5), 2547–2556 (2013). doi:10.1016/j.asoc.2012.11.031
28. A. Gómez-Iglesias, M.A. Vega-Rodríguez, F. Castejón, M.C. Montes, E. Morales-Ramos, Artificial bee colony inspired algorithm applied to fusion research in a grid computing environment, in *Proceedings of the 18th Euromicro Conference on Parallel, Distributed and Network-based Processing, PDP 2010*, Pisa, Feb 17–19, 2010 (IEEE Computer Society, 2010), pp. 508–512, ed. by M. Danelutto, J. Bourgeois, T. Gross. doi:10.1109/PDP.2010.50. http://dx.doi.org/10.1109/PDP.2010.50
29. C.C. Hegna, N. Nakajima, On the stability of mercier and ballooning modes in stellarator configurations. Phys. Plasmas 5(5), 1336–1344 (1998)
30. S.P. Hirshman, G.H. Neilson, External inductance of an axisymmetric plasma. Phys. Fluids 29(3), 790–793 (1986)
31. D. Karaboga, B. Basturk, A powerful and efficient algorithm for numerical function optimization: artificial bee colony (abc) algorithm. J. Glob. Optim. 39(3), 459–471 (2007)

32. S. Krishnan, M. Tatineni, C. Baru, myHadoop - hadoop-on-demand on traditional HPC resources. Tech. rep., Chapter in 'Contemporary HPC Architectures' [KV04] Vassiliki Koutsonikola and Athena Vakali. Ldap: framework, practices, and trends, in *IEEE Internet Computing* (2004)
33. R. Sanchez, S. Hirshman, J. Whitson, A. Ware, Cobra: an optimized code for fast analysis of ideal ballooning stability of three-dimensional magnetic equilibria. J. Comput. Phys. **161**(2), 576–588 (2000). doi:http://dx.doi.org/10.1006/jcph.2000.6514. http://www.sciencedirect.com/science/article/pii/S0021999100965148
34. W.I. van Rij, S.P. Hirshman, Variational bounds for transport coefficients in three-dimensional toroidal plasmas. Phys. Fluids B **1**(3), 563–569 (1989)

Chapter 3
Data Movement in Data-Intensive High Performance Computing

Pietro Cicotti, Sarp Oral, Gokcen Kestor, Roberto Gioiosa, Shawn Strande, Michela Taufer, James H. Rogers, Hasan Abbasi, Jason Hill, and Laura Carrington

Abstract The cost of executing a floating point operation has been decreasing for decades at a much higher rate than that of moving data. Bandwidth and latency, two key metrics that determine the cost of moving data, have degraded significantly relative to processor cycle time and execution rate. Despite the limitation of submicron processor technology and the end of Dennard scaling, this trend will continue in the short-term making data movement a performance-limiting factor and an energy/power efficiency concern. Even more so in the context of large-scale and data-intensive systems and workloads. This chapter gives an overview of the aspects of moving data across a system, from the storage system to the computing system down to the node and processor level, with case study and contributions from researchers at the San Diego Supercomputer Center, the Oak Ridge National Laboratory, the Pacific Northwest National Laboratory, and the University of Delaware.

P. Cicotti (✉) • L. Carrington
San Diego Supercomputer Center/University of California, San Diego
e-mail: pcicotti@sdsc.edu; lcarring@sdsc.edu

S. Oral • J.H. Rogers • H. Abbasi • J. Hill
Oak Ridge National Lab
e-mail: oralhs@ornl.gov; jrogers@ornl.gov; abbasi@ornl.gov; hilljj@ornl.gov

G. Kestor • R. Gioiosa
Pacific Northwest National Lab
e-mail: gokcen.kestor@pnnl.gov; roberto.gioiosa@pnnl.gov

S. Strande
San Diego Supercomputer Center
e-mail: strande@sdsc.edu

M. Taufer
University of Delaware
e-mail: taufer@udel.edu

© Springer International Publishing Switzerland 2016   31
R. Arora (ed.), *Conquering Big Data with High Performance Computing*,
DOI 10.1007/978-3-319-33742-5_3

3.1 Introduction

Today, a significant fraction of computing cycles and energy is consumed moving data; this is especially true in scientific, large-scale, and data-intensive computing. Over the years a data "red shift" has taken place: the data is moving farther away from the computing as the performance gap between latency in accessing data and computing throughput widens [46]. The Memory Wall is an example of this transition, from a performance perspective, from slow floating point (several cycles per operation) and fast load/store operations (one operation per cycle), to fast floating point (several operations completed per cycle) and slow load/store operations (hundreds of cycles per operation) [53].

To cope with the cost of moving data a significant amount of on-die resources are employed in increasingly complex memory hierarchies, a solution that is exacerbating the energy inefficiency and the complexity of the processor architecture at sub-micron technologies [10, 16]. In addition, the technology landscape changes dramatically due to the disruptive differences between technology nodes, and the introduction of new technology to overcome some of the challenges. Examples include the use of software-managed caches and scratchpads, pools of fast small on-die or on package memory, and deeper hierarchies topped by high-capacity non-volatile memory.

Emerging memory technologies are expected to dramatically alter the energy costs associated with the storage and movement of data. The traditional hierarchical organization of memory systems is evolving rapidly to encompass stacked memories [42], where competing 3D designs will impact the latency, bandwidth, capacity, and also the energy consumption. There is significant positive work on processors, using lower power circuits, voltage frequency scaling and other features that have held or reduced power consumption per socket as the potential (peak) floating point operations per clock continues to rise. Similarly, the energy cost associated with memory storage and movement will fall, from approximately 10 pJ/bit to near term forecasts that are single digit, eventually approaching 1 pJ/bit. Despite these advances, there may be substantial opportunity to further improve the efficiency of these memory systems by more accurately characterizing the bandwidth requirements of applications, and delivering proportional and balanced designs. There is a current dichotomy, even as these new memory technologies continue to increase memory bandwidth, there is significant evidence that memory access patterns are often latency-limited rather than bandwidth-limited, and that energy is being unnecessarily consumed by inappropriate designs. And while the cost of accessing near-processor memories is expected to improve, the overall cost of accessing data at the level of the hierarchy with the most capacity will keep increasing relative to the cost of computing. The capacity required for future many-core nodes will be provided by non-volatile memory technology; in the short term, even stacked non-volatile memory will be an order of magnitude slower than the volatile equivalent, and have higher energy costs, especially for write operations.

Given that the memory subsystem may continue to consume approximately 25 % of the total system energy, there should be significant pressure to find the appropriate balance of energy consumption versus delivered bandwidth.

Similar opportunities exist beyond the memory controller. Hybrid designs that use PCIe-based or custom interconnects must be designed to accommodate the application requirements, and balance those against the costs, including energy, for moving data to and from conventional and accelerator memories. This problem may be further extended, to the transfer of data from one node, whether single core multi-core, or hybrid, to another node, now across the node-interconnect. Bandwidth and latency decrease by an order of magnitude, but the energy costs increase substantially. Component, interconnect, processor, and accelerator designers must carefully consider the anticipated utilization of these memory structures versus the transistor, I/O pin, and energy budgets to ensure appropriate and proportional design balance.

The I/O requirements for future extreme scale systems combine fast bursty I/O (such as checkpoint/restart), smaller steady output (diagnostic logging) and larger data variable output (analysis and visualization output). Building a storage system that fulfills the requirements for each type of output is not feasible for Exascale systems.

This factor, combined with the increasing adoption of storage class memory (SCM), has led to shift from a homogeneous storage system to deeper, heterogeneous storage architecture. Each layer can serve as a cache for the layer below it, or be explicitly targeted for I/O by the application. Different I/O patterns can, therefore, be serviced without greatly constraining the design and capacity of the storage system.

The most common additional storage layer added to HPC systems is a burst buffer [41]. Burst buffers currently use NAND flash (or similar non-volatile memory technology) to provide an intermediate target for I/O operations, either available as a shared resource for a set of nodes (such as on the NERSC Cori system [23]) or as an on-node storage target (such as on the OLCF Summit system [33]). A more complex storage hierarchy can be envisioned that combines both techniques to optimize the system for a broader range of I/O patterns.

The aforementioned additions are storage layers contained within the high performance machine. An alternate is to enhance the storage system by augmenting it with fast SSD arrays. This is the technique used in the MilkyWay-2 (Tianhe-2) supercomputer at NUDT, China [54]. In MilkyWay-2 the SSD arrays are connected to a small number of I/O nodes, with transparent support provided by the file system in absorbing burst data.

A more comprehensive vision is described by Intel for Exascale I/O architecture. In Intel's version, not only are burst buffers added within the Exascale machine, but additional NVRAM targets are used in the back end storage system (connected through the site storage network) to host the metadata and "hot" data for the file system.

One additional aspect of these complex systems bears mentioning. Requiring applications to be re-written to adequately utilize a multi-tiered storage system is a fool's errand. Instead the file system must transparently handle this additional complexity, without being forced to move data unnecessarily.

Despite the differences in technology and scale, at every level of the system, from the processor to the storage, complexity and heterogeneity are increasing and so is the complexity of managing and optimizing data movement. The following Sections describe research efforts and experiences in dealing with data movement at the node-, system-, and center-level.

3.2 Node-Level Data Movement

Data movement within a shared memory node, loosely corresponds to locality of reference. In a single-core node, locality of reference only depends on the temporal and spatial locality of the single process running. In more recent multi-core Non Uniform Memory Access (NUMA) systems, the locality and data movement correlation becomes more complicated as data placement on different NUMA nodes and sharing resources, such as memory itself or caches, affects the performance and efficiency of each thread executing. On future systems there will be many cores per chip, in the order of a thousand or more, and certainly thousands on a single node. These cores will have to be organized hierarchically with different levels of coherent and non-coherent memories, and managing data movement and locality will be extremely challenging.

Modern architectures featuring accelerators and deep memory hierarchies, challenge programmers exposing an even greater imbalance in performance and efficiency between different memory types and configurations. In fact, managing the data transfer to and from device memory in accelerators, such as GPUs, is a significant hurdle in exploiting the potential of accelerators. Another example of the increasing complexity of managing data transfers comes from the internal memory of an accelerator, such as the Intel's Xeon Phi, in which memory is divided into pools of fast on-package memory and conventional DDR4 memory.

Finally, in emerging task-based programming models, like Concurrent Collections [15] and the Open Community Runtime (OCR) [1], locality cannot be managed only from within each single task. In these models, locality greatly depends on the data dependencies between tasks, the order of execution, and the placement of tasks. The scheduler must be able to manage locality, or to provide the capability to the user-level code to do so.

The case studies featured in this section present efforts in analyzing data movement and quantifying its energy cost.

3.2.1 Case Study: ADAMANT

In order to optimize locality and reduce data movement in applications, tools are needed to capture and analyze data-movement across all the levels of the hardware memory and storage system. The understanding gained by measuring and characterizing data-movement is required to truly co-design systems and algorithms that are high performance and energy efficient. Following the shift in costs from computing to data-movement, this approach changes the point of view of the system designer and parallel programmer from an instruction-centric view, to a data-centric view. The computational complexity of an application and its performance profile, based on a cost metric of instructions executed, is complemented with a metric of locality, characterizing a computation also by the amount of data moved and the distance traveled by data. As a characterization of a workload, this view supports models and methodologies for characterizing and predicting performance, and therefore impact optimization techniques for performance and energy efficiency.

The Advanced DAta Movement Analysis Toolkit (ADAMANT) project addresses these needs and aims at developing a methodology to characterize and analyze data movement. At the base of ADAMANT is a set of tools to create a unified view on data movement, not only to inform in algorithm design and performance tuning, but also to support a dynamic and adaptive computing environments in which applications, run-time systems, operating systems, and hardware cooperate to strive for maximal performance and energy efficiency. ADAMANT is a work in progress and here we provide an overview of its capability.

There are three phases in the analysis methodology proposed: capturing data life cycle, characterizing data movement, and analyzing the profile and devising optimizations. Figure 3.1 shows a high-level view of a deployment of ADAMANT. ADAMANT is loaded with a program, and collects information about the program from its binary and from the binary of the loaded libraries, then receives information from its extensions that plug into other frameworks, like the Precise Event Based Sampling [35] of the Intel Architecture, or instrumentation tools, like PEBIL [39] and pin [43].

By data life cycle we intend to identify data objects, from the time they are allocated in memory, statically, dynamically, or automatically, to the time they are deallocated (explicitly or the end of the application). Data objects are created in

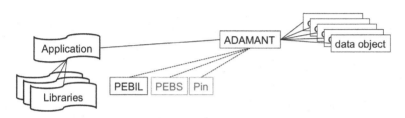

Fig. 3.1 Deployment view of ADAMANT

three main ways: statically (i.e., in the data section of a program and libraries), dynamically (i.e., on the heap), and automatically (i.e., on the stack). With the exception of statically allocated data, which can be identify at compile time, dynamically allocated and automatically allocated data come to existence at runtime, in a control-flow and input dependent manner. For example, the size of a dynamically allocated data object is in most cases determined during execution, and the allocation itself may be part of a conditional statement. When a program is loaded, ADAMANT scans the binary and the library loaded to resolve symbols and find size and start address of statically allocated data objects. Then, during the execution of the program, ADAMANT intercepts memory allocation and deallocation calls to update its data objects information accordingly.

Capturing data movement means detecting transfers between NUMA nodes and Last Level Caches (LLC), or between caches. Here we consider low level data transfer, as observed at the architectural level, rather than high level data movement, as defined in parallel algorithms (e.g. explicit communication via messages), with the latter being part of the final analysis phase. Data movement is observed at the architectural level when transfers occur between levels of the memory/storage hierarchy. Statistical summaries, such as hit/miss count and rate, summarize the behavior of the memory hierarchy and can be obtained from hardware performance counters [35] (or OS counters for transfer of memory pages) or via binary instrumentation; however, this information is generally representing hardware events but does not provide details specific about the data objects involved. To associate statistics to data objects is necessary to complement the general information obtained by counters with knowledge of the data objects accessed. ADAMANT maps this information to the directory of data objects discussed above. Figure 3.2 illustrates a view in which cache hit rates are reported for each variable. As an example, with this level of details it is possible to devise data placement policies that optimize data movement in heterogeneous memory hierarchies [18].

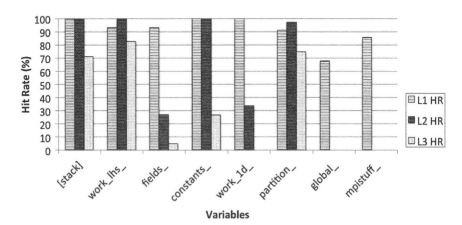

Fig. 3.2 Cache hit rates visualized per-variable in a block-tridiagonal solver

With the information about each object's access pattern and locality, it is possible to control the number of operations to slower memory (e.g. non-volatile memory) by carefully placing objects on the different memories available; in addition, if different hardware configurations are available, models based on this information can be used to select the optimal configuration.

In addition to the hardware counters mentioned, other metrics may be required to support analysis of locality and optimizations. There are different metrics that represent data movement and locality. Reuse distance is a platform-independent metric: assuming a given granularity (e.g. cache line size), a reference to a certain address has reuse distance d, where d is the number of unique addresses referenced since the last reference to that address [11]. Reuse distance can be used to characterize locality and approximate the behavior caches (hardware or software); for example, from the definition it follows that a reference must be satisfied by a fully-associative LRU cache with capacity greater than or equal to the reuse distance (a compulsory miss has infinite reuse distance) [11, 12]. Capturing reuse distance histograms is also a costly process [25]. ADAMANT seeks to combine binary instrumentation, heuristics, and on-line simulation to provide different levels of accuracy and performance: from tracing all load and store operations to sampling and modeling techniques combined with hardware counters.

The final phase involves interpreting the data provided by the tools and understand data movement, access patterns, and dependencies, as seen by the application. To build such a view, data objects and their information must be related to programming constructs, at the language level. The final view is based on a structure where data-objects have several reference points associated. The reference points will represent program constructs (instructions, loops, functions) that access the data objects. For each reference point, the association will include the fields that characterize the access pattern and related events, such as miss rates, etc. Objects can also be combined and nested, for example a collection of items can be allocated as a single array of structures (AoS), or as multiple arrays in a structure (SoA); recognizing this logical nesting of data types enables the analysis necessary to determine what organization is most efficient on a given architecture. Finally, it is informative to know where in the code a certain object is allocated, which variables persistently hold a reference to a data object, or even better name it in a meaningful way. This distinction is necessary because many objects are allocated in the same part of the program, which is the case anytime that a data object is not accessed via single reference and in fact, software engineering techniques and design patterns, such as the factory design pattern, promote this behavior. Containers of the C++ standard template library (STL) use a single default allocator, so simply tracking calls to the allocator would not be sufficient. ADAMANT provides the functionality to create this view such that programmers can understand data movement and improve locality in their applications.

3.2.2 Case Study: Energy Cost of Data Movement

The energy cost of powering and operating a large supercomputer is rapidly approaching its acquisition cost, and the U.S. Department of Energy (DOE) released clear indications that this trend is not sustainable. Data movement is anticipated to be a significant part of the energy cost, and significant work in reducing the energy cost of data movement is needed to reach the goal of creating next generation supercomputers that are two orders of magnitude more power- and energy-efficient than current Petascale systems [5].

Several circuits and micro-architecture techniques are under study or development to increase the power efficiency of future systems, including near-threshold voltage (NTV) operation levels, simplified core architectures, and massive thread levels. Projections show that the energy cost of register-to-register double precision floating point operations is expected to decrease by 10× by 2018 [5, 20], which would greatly improve the power efficiency of the entire system. However, the energy cost of moving data across the memory hierarchy is not expected to decrease at the same rate, hence the relative energy cost of data movement with respect to register-to-register floating point operations will increase. Additionally, deeper memory hierarchies, that also include non-volatile memory technologies (NVRAM) [9, 27, 34] and 3D-stacked on-chip DRAM [26, 42], will worsen the situation by adding an extra dimension to the data movement problem and increasing the distance of data from processor register. The combination of these two factors is often referred as the *energy wall*: in future Exascale systems, data movement will not only dominate performance, as in past generation supercomputers, but also the energy and power efficiency of the systems.

Despite its importance in the development of next generation large-scale systems, the energy cost of data movement has been evaluated only qualitatively [32] and mainly with architectural simulators at small scale [20]. Part of the problem with evaluating the energy cost of data movement for real applications and systems is the difficulty of accurately measuring power/energy consumption at the level of instructions, especially on systems with thousands of compute nodes. To provide for the lack of accurate power/energy instrumentation, power and energy models have been developed to accurately compute the energy cost of single instructions. However, in the case of data movement, these models need to be extended to account for the different latencies in moving data across the memory hierarchy. For example, on a AMD Opteron 6272 (Interlagos), the latencies of accessing the L1 data cache, the L2 cache, the L3, and main memory are 4, 12, 20 and 100 cycles, respectively. To make the problem more complicated, modern processors typically follow an out-of-order design and allow multiple instructions in flight. To take these considerations into account, power and energy models can be integrated with micro-benchmarks that enforce a specific processor behavior, such as always missing in the L1 cache and hitting the L2 cache. The energy cost of moving data across the memory hierarchy can then be accurately computed level by level, starting from the lowest level and then moving up to higher levels, and using a differential approach.

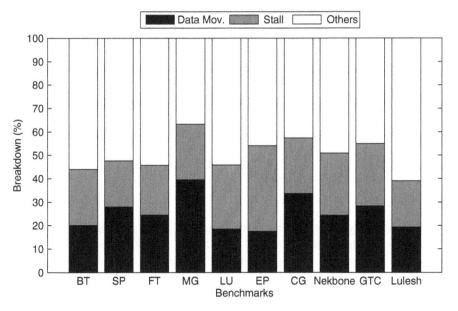

Fig. 3.3 Energy cost breakdown

For example, once the energy cost of moving data from the L1 cache to a register is known, the energy cost of moving data from the L2 to L1 can be computed starting from a micro-benchmark that always misses in the L1 and moves data from the L2 to register, and then subtracting the energy cost of moving data from the L1 cache to register. In this endeavor, particular attention must be paid to account for speculation, multiple in-flight operations, resource sharing, and data pre-fetching. Moreover, processors still consume energy even when stalled.

The methodology proposed in [36] accurately models the energy cost of moving data between any two levels of the memory hierarchy in a modern, out-of-order dual AMD Opteron 6272 processor. The methodology is then applied to several scientific applications from the U.S. DOE Exascale Co-Design Centers, the U.S. DOE Office of Science, and other well-know benchmarks [3]. Figure 3.3 reports the energy breakdown for each of these applications in three categories: Data Movement, Stall and Others. Data Movement includes the energy cost of moving data across the memory hierarchy; Stall represents the energy spent by the processor while waiting for data and control flow dependencies to be resolved; Other includes arithmetic, logic and control operations. The graph shows that 18–40 % of the energy of running an application is spent in moving data up and down the memory hierarchy and that 19–36 % of the total energy is wasted waiting for data and control flow dependencies to be solved (stalled cycles). The energy cost of moving data already account for a large part of the total energy consumption and, when combined with energy wasted while waiting, almost outweighs the energy spend in computation. On average, only about 50 % of the total energy cost is actually spent performing computation.

Table 3.1 Energy cost of moving data across the memory hierarchy in a AMD Interlagos 6227 system

Operation	Energy cost (nJ)	Δ energy (nJ)	Eq. ops
NOP	0.48	–	–
ADD	0.64	–	–
L1->REG	1.11	1.11	1.8 ADD
L2->L1	2.21	1.10	3.5 ADD
L3->L2	9.80	7.59	15.4 ADD
MEM->L3	63.64	53.84	99.7 ADD
stall	1.43	–	–
prefetching	65.08	–	–

The same study reports that the energy cost of moving data from the L1, L2, L3 and memory to register is equivalent to 1.8, 3.5, 15.4 and 99.7 times the energy cost of performing a register-to-register integer add operations as reported in Table 3.1. Assuming that the energy cost of computation decreases by a factor of 10× in the next few years, these rates will increase dramatically. Without intelligent memory management systems and task schedulers that increase data locality and reduce data movement, the data movement problem will exacerbate in the future and the energy cost of moving data will largely dominate the energy efficiency of the systems. From Table 3.1, it is also evident how the energy cost of moving data greatly increases for off-chip transfers. Moving data from memory (off-chip) to the L3 (on-chip) consumes 53.84 nJ, while moving data from the L3 to the L2 cache (both on-chip) only consumes 7.59 nJ. Finally, these results also point out that simpler processor design will increase energy efficiency by reducing the number of stalled cycles.

The study presented in this section provides a quantitative analysis of the energy cost of data movement on current systems using realistic, full-fledged applications. The findings can be used as the base for future analysis and projections, as well as a reference point in time for validation and evaluation of future prototype systems.

3.3 System-Level Data Movement

At the system level, data movement is required to satisfy data dependencies that occur between two computing elements. In general, this is the case for any parallel computation which is not embarrassingly parallel, and that is executing across a distributed memory systems, or parts of a work-flow executing concurrently in a pipelined fashion; in both cases, data movement is considered the communication part of the computation.

The common practice for reducing the cost of communication is to overlap computation with communication. With support from the network interface, communication requests are initiated and posted as soon as possible, and only later, when required by data dependencies or to claim resources, the transfers are checked for completion. This form of split-phase communication allows the computation to make progress in between the two phases, and essentially hide the latency of the communication [38].

There are two limitations to this approach. First, this approach can only improve performance by a limited amount that depends on the ratio and distribution of compute and communication phases and is ineffective when the communication costs dominates the computation cost, while even complicating the control flow of the program that needs to be restructured to expose opportunity for overlap [17]. Second, the energy cost has become a primary concern and this approach does nothing to reduce the energy cost of communication, and even increase the power draw of an application that now computes and communicates at the same time.

Alternative approaches have been sought for actually reducing the communication asymptotically and from an algorithmic point of view. Communication avoiding techniques, first proposed for linear algebra operations [22], reorder operations to reduce communication or trade communication for increased computation. This is the case, for example, in stencil computations: the ghost cells can be increased in depth to provide data for multiple iterations, at the cost of more operations to update also portions of the ghost cells. Other techniques include optimizations that change the work decomposition and the mapping of work and data, analyze data in situ, compress or reduce the dimensionality of data, or take advantage of features of the algorithm to heuristically avoid communication.

The case studies featured in this section present techniques to reduce data movement in the analysis of biology datasets and in graph searches.

3.3.1   Case Study: Graphs

In recent years, the exponential growth of data produced by simulations, scientific instruments, and sensors, resulted in many research initiatives for designing systems and methods to manage, analyze, and extract knowledge from large and often unstructured data sets. In the case of unstructured data, common system and algorithm design practices are challenged in that there is virtually no locality: the lack of structure in the data makes it almost impossible to decompose data in way that favors localized parallel analysis. That is often the case in emerging workloads from domains such as cybersecurity, biomedical informatics, and social networks.

To take advantage of locality, algorithm and system designers can look at other characteristics of the data. In graph search algorithms, a class of algorithms considered representative of many emerging analysis workloads, this can be the case when analyzing so called small-world graphs. This case study researched how to improve locality and avoiding communication, taking advantage of a characteristic of the dataset.

Graphs of small-world networks are a type of graph in which most nodes are not adjacent, but many have a common adjacent vertex. This means that there is a small subset of high-degree vertexes (the degree of the vertexes follows a power law distribution) and that the graph has a small diameter. This kind of graphs occurs in many domains, and numerous examples can be found in applications including social networks, computer networks, and gene networks. This case study discusses how this property of the graphs can be leveraged in the design of the algorithm and the computing system, thereby improving locality and avoiding communication. Specifically, by taking advantage of the distribution of edges in the graph, we show that the concept of caching can be applied to localize visit checks, significantly reduce communication, and consequently reduce the associated computation.

Despite the inherent randomness in the data access pattern, the search traverses many edges that are incident on a small number of high-degree vertexes; in the case of edges incident on remotely stored vertexes such traversal is an operation that requires communication but is essentially redundant after the vertex has been reached for the first time. The approach explored involves caching the remote vertexes that have been previously visited, and checking the cache before initiating any communication. This idea can be implemented modifying the algorithm and interfacing with a software cache; the cache can be a library or run as a service on dedicated resources.

Several implementations of the caching algorithm have been explored in Graph500 [6]. The Graph500 benchmarks were defined to define kernels that are a core part of analytics workloads, and include a breadth-first search (BFS) kernel. The BFS kernel consists in traversing a scale-free graph, randomly generated by a Kronecker generator [40], and constructing a BFS tree rooted in a randomly chosen vertex.

The reference parallel BFS in Graph500 implements a classic search algorithm based on a vertex queue. Starting from a root, a vertex is popped from the queue, and its adjacent vertexes that haven't been visited before are placed on the queue. The queue represents the frontier, and contains recently visited vertexes that may be connected to other vertexes that have not been visited yet. Checking that a vertex has not been visited and adding it to the queue, in parallel, requires communication if a remote process owns the vertex: if the vertex is local, bitmap has its *visited* status; otherwise a message is sent to the owner process.

The idea of improving locality by caching visited remote vertexes has been tested in several implementations: process-local caching, remote-shared caching, *memcached* caching, and accelerated memcached caching. Memcached is a distributed object caching system widely used to speedup database queries in web applications [31]. Memcached supports web applications that exhibit temporal locality, maintaining a key-value store accessible via TCP connections. The protocol is generic and supports keys and values of arbitrary size, and variants of basic get and set operations (plus other miscellaneous operations).

Local Caching (LC-BFS)   In this variant, each process maintains a vertex cache in memory. The cache is direct mapped and actually contains no value. A hit in the cache means that a vertex has been previously visited.

Remote Caching (RC-BFS)   In the remote caching variant, a different server process maintains the cache. Each MPI process connects via a TCP or MPI to the cache server, which can be shared, and queries the server to check whether a vertex is cached or not.

Memcached Caching (MC-BFS)   In this variant, like in RC-BFS, the cache is external but in this case it is implemented by a memcached server. A memcached server is used in a somewhat unusual way because no value needs to be effectively retrieved, and the cache is used only to check the presence of a key, which represents a visited vertex. Also in this case, the server can be shared. In addition, the server can be run on a dedicated appliance.

All the different variants have been tested on different systems to evaluate the methodology and compare different solutions. The systems used for the tests were a 4-node Nehalem cluster; two Sandy Bridge systems, Gordon and Stampede [2, 19]; and a dedicated Convey memcached appliance [8].

LC-BFS outperformed and scaled better than the reference implementation on up to 1024 cores, running on problems scales with a ratio of 2^{20} vertexes per core (edge factor of 16), a ratio that is comparable to the ratio found in several top results on the Graph 500 list. The speedup observed with respect to the reference implementation ranged from 1.6× to 2.4×, which is obtained by reducing the number of MPI messages by almost 50 % on 1024 cores.

One of drawbacks of LC-BFS is that each process has to allocate resources to the cache and that processes do not benefit from the caches of other processes. With a cache shared between sets of neighboring nodes, results with RC-BFS have shown a higher hit rate in the shared cache, and that potentially this approach can be more effective in reducing communication across the machine; however, at the scale tested, this benefit is not observed and RC-BFS did not improve over the reference. This design is only beneficial if the overhead of accessing a remote caching system is be compensated by the reduction of more expensive more expensive point-to-point communication.

Reducing the overhead of cache checks required testing and optimization in the communication, including using MPI instead of TCP/IP and coalescing messages. These optimizations were not all viable for MC-BFS, which turned out to be performing the worst. Despite modifications to MC-BFS to connect to a memcached server via UNIX socket, a change which improvement the observed performance by 10× with respect to the TCP variant, the memcached implementation was slower than the reference implementation, even on the Convey appliance. The protocol and communication required for memcached is simply not suited for this purpose (memcached is designed for very different workloads), and a general HPC system serving special needs at the rack level should use high performance communication primitives (e.g. MPI) and provide basic primitives that allow defining the needed services efficiently.

From a system design point of view, augmenting the design with a local programmable appliance, capable of providing shared high performance services to partitions of a system, can improve system level locality. However, existing caching systems designed for different environment may incur high overheads and not be

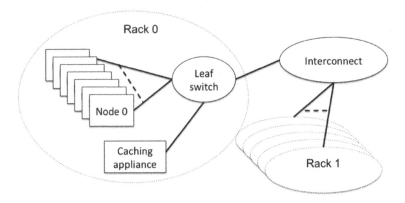

Fig. 3.4 Rack configuration with local cache server

suitable for high performance computing. Nevertheless, grouping nodes providing another locality tier, for example at the rack level, may be a viable solution in extreme large-scale systems where the latency difference between same-rack and across-system communication.

Figure 3.4 shows a system configuration in which several nodes connected to the same switch (e.g. all the nodes of a rack) share a cache server. This design has several benefits: the cost of maintaining the cache is shared, for example the memory to allocate the cache is reduced by avoiding replicating the cache in each process and competing with the memory required to store the graph; the caching system may be optimized for that single task; the cache is populated sooner which would likely result in higher hit rates; and finally, by physically localizing communication, low-latency messages are exchanged in place of long-latency messages going across multiple hops in the interconnect (similarly the energy cost of communication should be reduced).

3.3.2   Case Study: Map Reduce

State-of-the-art analysis methods based on clustering and classifications require comparing data in an iterative process. When big data are distributed across a large number of nodes, as will be the case for Exascale systems, even a small number of comparisons require unfeasible data movements and can ultimately have a negative impact on both performance and accuracy of the analysis. New methodologies that rely on optimized data movement are needed to analyze big data when distributed across the nodes of a computing system. A successful method for analyzing big scientific data from structural biology datasets in computational chemistry (i.e., molecular ensembles from docking simulations and trajectory snapshots from folding simulations) is proposed in [28, 55–57]. In general, structural biology datasets are high dimensional datasets including a high number of recorded data samples (n); for each sample one or multiple properties (or features) (p) are of interest (note that $n \gg p$) [49, 50]. The analysis of these high dimensional datasets (i.e., their clustering or classification) enables the scientists to pursue different objectives based on the type of data and features recorded such as identifying features that can be used to predict class memberships and finding recurrent patterns in datasets. To this end, the analysis method breaks the traditional constraint of centralized data analysis by modeling the data in a distributed manner on the local nodes and moving fewer selected metadata to rebuild a global view of key data properties. The analysis workload is tailored to suit the MapReduce paradigm workflow.

The effectiveness of the method for distributed datasets generated by protein-ligand docking simulations has been extensively proven in [28, 55–57]; these simulations deal with the docking of small molecules (also called ligands) into proteins involved in the disease process. When ligands dock well into a protein, they can potentially be used as a drug to stop or prevent diseases associated with the protein malfunction. Computationally, protein-ligand docking simulations are uncertain searches of a near-native ligand conformation in a large dataset of conformations that are docked in a protein; and a conformation is considered near-native if the Root-Mean Square Deviation (RMSD) of the heavy atom coordinates is smaller than or equal to two Angstroms from the experimentally observed conformation. Algorithmically, a docking simulation consists of a sequence of independent docking trials. An independent docking trial starts by generating a series of random initial ligand conformations; each conformation is given multiple random orientations. The resulting conformations are docked into the protein-binding site. Hundred of thousands attempts are performed in a distributed fashion. The resulting dataset consists of a very large number of docked ligand conformations that reside on multiple hard drives of the different nodes. Ligand conformations have to be compared to each other in terms of specific properties or features, including molecular geometries or location of a molecule in a pocket, presence of charges or a specific type of charges for an atom or sets of atoms, and presence of specific heavy atoms and their location.

Rather than migrating the resulting entire data to a centralized storage location for the clustering and classification, the specific property or the set of data properties of interest is encoded locally into a space of N-dimensional points by performing a space reduction. The space reduction enable the redefinition of the overall clustering and classification problem of molecular conformations into a density search problem within a domain of points that can be built, decomposed, and processed in a distributed manner. There is not a single way to capture and encode the properties; therefore multiple mapping techniques can assure the effectiveness in capturing diverse properties. When analyzing *large structural biology datasets* from protein-ligand docking simulations, the mapping transforms the space of millions of ligand conformations into a three-dimensional space by combining space projections and best-fit linear regressions. More specifically, each ligand with its three-dimensional

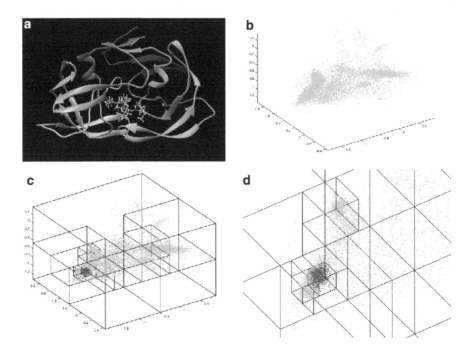

Fig. 3.5 Example of 3D data reduction and density space search for two million docked conformations of the protein-ligand complexes 1dif [57]. (**a**) 1hbv ligand in protein. (**b**) Metadata. (**c**) Octree. (**d**) Densest octant

(3D) atomic coordinates is encoded into a single 3D point (i.e., x, y, z) in the space by performing a geometry reduction. To this end, the 3D atoms of each conformation is projected on each of the three planes: (x, y), (y, z), and (z, x). Each projection results in a set of 2D points on the associated 2D plane. For each projection, the best-fit linear regression line of the 2D points is performed and the three lines' slope values as coordinates of the 3D point encoding the conformational geometry of its corresponding ligand. Figure 3.5a shows a ligand conformation docked in the HIV proteases for the *1dif* dataset generated with the Docking@Home simulations [49, 50]. Figure 3.5b shows the reduced space of 3D points generated by mapping each docked ligand conformation into a single point with the linear regression techniques.

To efficiently study the density of the redefined 3D space of points in a distributed manner, the whole multidimensional space is reshaped into local octrees that are built up dynamically on each node of the distributed system. Figure 3.5c shows an example of dynamically built octree. The octrees are explored through a binary search across the tree's levels moving up and down the tree levels to identify the octant that are the smallest in dimensions while at the same time are also the densest in number of points across the entire distributed systems. This subspace potentially contains the solution to the analysis problem [28]. Figure 3.5d shows a zoom-in of the selected octant; the points contained are associated to ligand conformations that were a posteriori validated as well docked into the protein-docking site.

The combination of mapping properties into metadata and searching for densest subspaces naturally fits into the MapReduce paradigm and can be implemented with different MapReduce frameworks e.g., Hadoop [21] and MapReduce-MPI [47]. Independently from the MapReduce framework considered, structural biology data with similar properties may be initially distributed across nodes randomly and result in multiple disjoint subsets. In this context, the analysis adopts an optimized movement of data that still allows the scientists to build a global knowledge of data properties while limiting data movement, avoiding communication congestion reducing energy consumptions. The node has a local vision of its ligand conformations and the associated 3D points (one per conformation) that populate its octree. Iteratively each node also builds a global vision of other nodes' octants by exchanging the counted densities for a given level of the octree's octants. Once ligands are mapped into 3D points, iterative chains of map and reduce jobs compute and sum up densities for the multiple, disjoint subspaces of the octree. In this optimized movement of data, nodes shuffle densities of subspaces that consists of a few floating point numbers rather than simulation data including hundreds of thousands molecules with their atomic coordinates. Results of the analysis of a dataset of ligand conformations sampled with Docking@Home for the 1dif ligand-HIV protease complex yield accuracy while enabling the analysis of larger datasets. The weak scalability presented in Fig. 3.6 and performed on Fusion, a 320-node computing cluster operated by the Laboratory Computing Resource Center at Argonne National Laboratory. The scalability results for a number of conformations that increases from 25 million ligands (64 GB) to 800 million ligands (2 TB), and for a number of nodes that increases from 8 nodes (64 cores) to 256 nodes (2048 cores), reveal that the analysis of the 1dif ligand-HIV protease complex dataset scales up to 500× in data size [57].

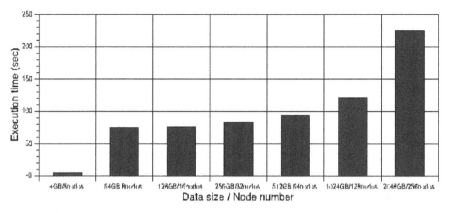

Fig. 3.6 Weak scalability of the 1dif ligand-HIV protease complex dataset on Fusion cluster

3.4 Center-Level Data Movement

At the center level, data moves and is shared between systems and instruments. In this context, data may be transferred to a center via networks, or created locally by instruments or computing systems, and when the life cycle of data does not begin and end on a single system, at large scale, managing the transfer is not trivial. Central to this scenario are the network of the center, and the file systems with the underlying storage systems.

In the data-centric file and storage system approach, data comes first. The data-centric model focuses on concurrently sharing data among multiple systems and eliminating unnecessary and expensive data movements. It strives to serve diverse I/O requirements and workloads generated on disparate computing resources. HPC centers are service providers, where multiple specialized computational resources provide different services. Some of these resources are designed to run simulations and generate data. Others provide post-processing or analysis of the generated data, while some are responsible for visualization of the raw or reduced data. The common denominator in all of these scenarios is data. Data must be shared among these systems in an efficient manner. Moreover, the users should not face unnecessary challenges in accessing their data from various systems.

Parallel file systems on large-scale computational systems are tightly coupled to a single simulation platform. This approach has resulted in the deployment of a dedicated file system for each computational platform. These dedicated file systems have created islands of data. As an example, users working on a visualization system cannot directly access data generated from a large-scale simulation on another system and must instead resort to manually transferring data between platforms. In addition to poor usability, dedicated file systems can make up a substantial percentage of total system deployment cost often exceeding 10 %. Data-centric file and storage system answer to all these technical challenges.

The two case studies that follow describe the design of storage and computing systems deployed at the Oak Ridge Leadership Computing Facility and the San Diego Supercomputer Center.

3.4.1 Case Study: Spider

In the past decade, the Oak Ridge Leadership Computing Facility (OLCF) at Oak Ridge National Laboratory (ORNL) has engaged in two large-scale storage system deployments (Spider 1 [48] and Spider 2 [45]), independent of the computing resource acquisitions for the Jaguar [13] and Titan [14] supercomputers. Spider 1 and 2 are data-centric, center-wide shared parallel file systems. Both systems were designed to meet the needs of a wide variety of OLCF user workloads, incorporating supercomputers, data analysis clusters, and remote data transfer systems. Spider 1 provided 240 GB/s peak I/O bandwidth and 10 PB of data storage; Spider II provides more than 1 TB/s of peak I/O bandwidth and 32 PB of storage. Both systems were built around the Lustre parallel file system [52], an open-source, community supported file system that is in use on more than 70 % of the Top500 systems [44]. The Spider 1 file system, deployed in 2008, was designed to provide a high-performance scratch space to scientific applications running on systems operated by the OLCF including the Jaguar supercomputer provided a transparent data sharing platform to all OLCF systems. Spider was a data-centric design and represented a significant departure from the traditional approach of tightly coupling a parallel file system to a single simulation platform and has also reduced operational costs and simplified the management of OLCF's storage environment.

At the time of the deployment of Spider, little was understood about the complexity of managing a single monolithic storage environment that provides center-wide access to simulation output. The OLCF team has spent years understanding the characteristics of the center-wide ecosystem. Significant effort was put into understanding network congestion as early attempts to validate the design of Spider 1 at scale yielded poor results. The concept of network locality was exploited to reduce contention/congestion and was dubbed Fine-Grained Routing (FGR) in LNET networks [24]. At the most basic level, FGR uses multiple Lustre LNET Network Interfaces (NIs) to expose physical or topological locality and each router has an InfiniBand-side NI that corresponds to the leaf switch it is plugged into. This work resulted in a 45 % increase in total delivered bandwidth to applications with no changes to the applications required. Since then, the FGR technique has been adopted by commercial products, such as the Cray's Sonexion. Lesson learned was that the network congestion will lead to sub-optimal I/O performance and identifying hot spots and eliminating them is key to realizing better performance. Careful placements of I/O processes and routers and better routing algorithms, such as FGR, are necessary for mitigating congestion.

The primary platform served by Spider was Jaguar, a 3.3 PFLOPS Cray XK6 machine, and one of the world's most powerful supercomputers. Since then, Jaguar has been upgraded into Titan. Titan is the largest GPU cluster in the world and it is a Cray XK7 system that couples the AMD 16-core Opteron 6274 processor, running at 2.4 GHz, with an NVIDIA "Kepler" K20 graphics processing unit (GPU) on each compute node. With 18,688 compute nodes, 710 TB of total system memory, and a peak performance of more than 20 PFLOPS, Titan is currently the number 2 machine on the Top500 list of supercomputers and the fastest supercomputer in the United States of America. The combination of CPUs and GPUs allows Titan, and future systems, to overcome the power and space limitations inherent in previous generations of HPC machines.

Titan is also one of the most energy-efficient systems in the world and came in at number three on the Green500 list in 2012, which ranks supercomputers based on their energy efficiency, in terms of calculations per watt of energy [30]. Titan's significant power savings are attributable to its hybrid CPU/GPU architecture. GPUs give Titan a tenfold boost in computing power, even though the system draws only modestly more power than a CPU-only system.

The compute power and scale of OLCF systems are key to achieving the U.S. Department of Energy's (DOE) mission for faster scientific discoveries and insights via computational simulations. Researchers from scientific domains including climate, combustion, fusion, astrophysics, and material science run massively parallel scientific simulations on Titan. Many scientific phenomena are better understood when the corresponding scientific simulation is run at a higher resolution (e.g. in time or space), or with more representative physics, at a higher computational complexity. Consequently, these simulations frequently run at very large scales, concurrently using tens or hundreds of thousands of cores. The scientific workflow then contains a series of data analysis and visualization jobs, run on smaller clusters, to glean insights from the vast amounts of data produced by the simulation.

In addition to Titan, the OLCF also hosts an array of other computational resources such as the visualization, end-to-end, and application development platforms. Each of these systems requires a reliable, high-performance and scalable file system for data storage. The next-generation Spider project (also known as Spider 2) was started in 2009, immediately after the commissioning of Spider 1. Spider 2 continued to adopt the decoupled approach in order to provide a center-wide storage system.

In order to provide a true integration between all systems hosted by the OLCF, a high-performance Scalable I/O Network (SION), has also been deployed. SION is a multi-stage InfiniBand network and enhances the current capabilities of the OLCF, providing connectivity between all OLCF systems and the Spider 2 file system.

Titan has 600 TB of main CPU memory. One key design principle was to checkpoint 75 % of Titan's memory in 6 min. Our earlier tests showed that a single SATA or near-line SAS hard disk drive can achieve 20–25 % of its peak performance under random I/O workloads (with 1 MB I/O block sizes). This drove the requirement for random I/O workloads of 240 GB/s at the file system level. Using system memory as the primary driver of file system bandwidth, it was calculated that Titan and other OLCF systems would require a 1 TB/s aggregate file system performance at the very least.

Spider 2 includes the 36 Data Direct Networks' SFA12KX block storage system units (SSUs), the Lustre file system, the scalable I/O network (SION), the Lustre router nodes, and the Lustre clients on the Titan compute nodes themselves. Other OLCF resources are connected to Spider 2 over the same SION. Each resource has its own set of Lustre routers for network traffic segregation. Spider 2's block storage subsystem comprises 20,160 2 TB near-line SAS disks that are organized into 2016 object storage targets (OSTs). 288 storage nodes are configured as Lustre object storage servers (OSS). 440 Lustre I/O router nodes are integrated into the Titan interconnect fabric. Titan provides 18,688 clients, all performing I/O. Each of these layers are tuned and optimized to derive optimal performance from the end-to-end I/O stack. The Spider storage system delivers a peak throughput of over 1 TB/s by optimizing each of these subsystems and how they interact with each other.

Large-scale distributed systems must take advantage of data locality to avoid the performance penalty of excessive data movement. Titan's network is based on the Cray Gemini interconnect that is configured as a 3D torus. I/O routers must be used to bridge Titan's Gemini interconnect to Spider's SION. OLCF's FGR implementation was updated to reflect Spider 2's decentralized SION and Titan's 3D torus architecture [29]. The SION deployment for Spider 1 utilized large director-class[1] Infiniband switches which were quite costly. The team chose to use smaller building blocks that were lower cost to increase other factors of the storage system, mainly capacity and performance and Spider 2 was designed with a decentralized InfiniBand fabric that consists of 36 leaf switches and multiple core switches. In this new design, clients choose to use a topologically close router that uses the NI of the desired destination Lustre OST. Clients have a Gemini-side NI that corresponds to a topological "zone" in the torus. The Lustre servers choose a router connected to the same InfiniBand leaf switch that is in the destination topological zone. This design decision has been good in terms of cost, but has made managing the SION slightly more difficult when new systems are added to the compute center, and also has the potential to be physical port bound at a point in the future. For the mixed I/O workloads, OLCF distributed the Titan I/O routers in a way that ensures fair sharing for all of the compute clients. The average distance between any client and its closest I/O router was optimized.

3.4.2 Case Study: Gordon and Oasis

In 2008, the National Science Foundation (NFS) released solicitation 08-573 requesting proposals to field data-intensive, high performance computing systems, defined as "systems with designs that are optimized to support research with very large data-sets or very large input-output requirements." The San Diego Supercomputer Center (SDSC) at the University of California, San Diego (UCSD) responded to this call with a proposal called Flash Gordon: A Data Intensive Computer. The system, which was designed in collaboration with Appro International Incorporated (now Cray) and other partners, sought to bridge the latency gap between main memory and rotating disk storage by using flash memory to provide a level of dense, affordable, low-latency storage to be configured as a very fast file system.

As a data-intensive system, Gordon achieved remarkable performance by combining technology that was highly innovative:

- 64 I/O nodes with an aggregate of 300 TB of high performance flash memory Each I/O node hosts 16 Intel 710 flash drives (enterprise grade MLC NAND-based SSDs).
- Dual-rail, 3D torus interconnect based on Quad Data Rate (QDR, 40 Gb/s) InfiniBand.
- Virtualized shared-memory nodes using ScaleMP's vSMP Foundation software.

---

[1]A director-class switch is loosely defined as a high port count switch connecting different fabrics.

- High-performance parallel file system that delivers sustained rates of 100 GB/s and a capacity of 4 PB, built on an Ethernet-based storage system that is globally available to SDSC's HPC systems via a high-performance 10 GbE network fabric.

At the time Gordon was proposed these technologies were not widely available, and deploying a system with this level of innovation was a significant undertaking; in particular, the integration of the I/O nodes, storage system, and the deployment of vSMP was challenging and precedent setting. The success of Gordon is therefore due also to substantial risk management through pre-production prototyping and testing, substantial and meaningful engagement with the NSF, and a concerted co-design effort between SDSC and Appro (Cray). SDSC carried out the majority of the testing and provided information to the vendor that helped shape the design. Gordon was made available to the academic research community via the NSF Extreme Science and Engineering Discovery Environment (XSEDE [51]) and will remain in production through August 2016.

In the end, Gordon was deployed as a 1024 node cluster, based on an 8-core, 2.6 GHz Intel Xeon E5 processor with Sandy Bridge architecture (E52670). Each of the dual-socket nodes has 64 GB of DDR3-1333 DRAM. There are 64 I/O nodes, each with sixteen 300 GB Intel 710 Series SSDs, for a total of 300 TB for the full system; in addition, the I/O nodes host LNet routers and serve as bridging gateways between the IB fabric and the Ethernet-based high performance Lustre parallel file system, called Data Oasis. The I/O nodes connect to Data Oasis via 10 GbE (two links per I/O node). Compute nodes and I/O nodes are connected via dual-rail QDR InfiniBand, based on Mellanox technology, forming a dual-rail 3D torus of switches. Compute nodes and I/O nodes are equipped with two QDR InfiniBand Host Channel Adapters (HCA), and are connected in groups of 16 compute nodes and one I/O node on a pair of switches (one for each rail of the 3D torus). The theoretical peak performance of Gordon is 341 TFLOPS.

Gordon is designed to form a hierarchical structure of storage levels. Each level has different capacity and performance characteristics. What follows is a description of each level, in decreasing order of bandwidth and increasing order of latency (capacities also increase when moving through the hierarchy).

The fastest storage option, available only on the vSMP nodes, is to create a volatile file system using the node's DRAM. Taking advantage of the aggregated memory of a vSMP node, a RAMFS file system is configured and mounted in the prologue script that starts a job. With a latency in the order of microseconds, this option has limited capacity (up to 1 TB of RAM), which depends on the number of nodes used and the memory requirements of the application, and the highest cost in terms of resources. In addition, the SSD's of the associated I/O node can been made available as a file system, providing an additional 4.8 TB of scratch storage, also made available via the users job submission script. The 16 compute nodes and I/O node provided as a single virtual image under vSMP is referred to as a Supernode. Outreach to new communities was a major element of the Gordon project, and several applications were identified that could take advantage of this configuration. vSMP nodes were deployed statically, with the number adjusted over time in response to user demand.

The next fastest, and more frequently used option is to employ the flash storage as temporary scratch space, in this case without the use of vSMP. For the duration of a job, each compute node mounts a single 300 GB flash drive to be used as scratch storage. Alternatively, projects can be granted allocation to use I/O nodes as dedicated resources and given access to run directly on an I/O node and its 4.8 TB of flash storage, which can be configured as a single RAIDed block device and file system. In the production configuration, the flash drives are remotely mounted using iSER (iSCSI Extensions for RDMA). Despite the loss of performance due to the software stack involved, the latency for accessing the remote flash drives is approximately 100 μs for random reads, and 400 μs for random writes.

Finally, the persistent and large-capacity level is the Data Oasis global parallel file system. Data Oasis was designed to meet Gordon's aggregate bandwidth requirement of 100 GB/s and is composed of 64 storage servers, each connected through dual-10 GbE links to the Gordon I/O nodes. While slower than either RAMFS or flash, it does have the advantage of being persistent across jobs and providing a higher degree of data integrity. All compute nodes have access to Data Oasis, which provide shared access to very large data sets. The bandwidth measured using the IOR benchmark, scaling from a compute node and I/O node pair to 48, ranged from 1.7 GB/s to approximately 75 GB/s. The results, as shown in Table 3.2, demonstrate good scaling to 48 I/O nodes, with a relative efficiency of more than 86 %. Scaling to 64 pairs effectively using all the I/O nodes was not possible since the Lustre file system was in production and shared with another HPC system at the time of testing, and such performance test would have required an interruption in service. However, based on the observed scaling, the projected performance at full scale would approximate 100 GB/s for both reads and writes.

Gordon I/O node design is a precursor of more recent burst buffer systems [41]. The I/O nodes provided both the SSDs *buffer*, as fast temporary scratch storage, and the connection to the large permanent global file system. Controlling the placement in the two levels is explicitly the applications/job responsibility. For example, many of the chemistry applications, such as Gaussian and GAMESS, need to store large integral files and then subsequently access them in a random manner. This usage pattern fits the intended usage of fast scratch storage, such as the remote flash, with input and final output of data to the Lustre file system. Since these applications can spend a significant fraction of the wall clock time in I/O, the greater locality of

Table 3.2 Lustre parallel file system performance

I/O nodes	Write GB/s	Read GB/s
1	1.7	1.8
2	3.4	3.4
4	6.0	6.7
8	11.3	13.0
16	24.7	23.7
32	50.7	50.8
48	75.4	74.5

the flash-based scratch storage and low latency of the flash drives (Intel 710 series specifications: 75 μs read, 85 μs write), substantial speedups can be obtained by using flash in this case. In addition, the use of flash relieves some of the pressure on the Data Oasis localizing the I/O traffic to the system interconnect, rather than the 10 GbE links and the remote storage system.

As a measure of capabilities to compare systems by their ability to store and rapidly access large amounts of data [37], the metric Data Motion Capability (DMC)[4] is defined as the sum of the capacities divided by the latencies at each level of the data hierarchy:

$$DMC = \sum_{i=0}^{levels} \frac{capacity_i}{latency_i}$$

where i is the number of data hierarchy levels in the data hierarchy of the machine. DMC combines aspects of capacity and speed for storing and accessing large data sets. These two attributes are paramount for data intensive computing, as data intensive computations read and write large amounts of data and accesses must be fast. Comparing Gordon to its contemporary XSEDE systems, Kraken and Ranger, shows greater DMC per FLOPS. Gordon has approximately the same data capability of Kraken but less than a third of its FLOPS computing capability (341 TFLOPS vs. 1200 TFLOPS), and 25 % more data capability than Ranger with less than two thirds of its FLOPS computing capability (341 TFLOPS vs. 580 TFLOPS). So while Gordon has a lower performance as measured by traditional HPC benchmarks, like LINKPACK, and is smaller in terms of core counts, it is better equipped to handle challenges associate with data intensive computing. If we restrict the comparison to I/O and FLOPS, then Gordon has a ratio of I/O performance to FLOPS of 0.29 GB/TFLOP. By contrast, Kraken, a system targeted at highly scalable applications, has a peak performance of 1.2 PFlops and a Lustre file system that performs at roughly 30 GB/s, resulting in an I/O to Flops ratio of 0.025 GB/TFlop [7]. At the time of its deployment, Gordon had the highest ratio of I/O to FLOPS of any system deployed in the NSF's XSEDE program.

3.5   About the Authors

Dr. Pietro Cicotti is a senior research scientist at the San Diego Supercomputer Center, where he is a member of the Performance Modeling and Characterization lab. He received his Ph.D. in Computer Science from the University of California, San Diego, in 2011. His research is focused on aspects of performance and efficiency in extreme-scale computing and on using modeling, simulation, and prototyping to co-design systems and applications. Recently, he has been investigating techniques to characterize, analyze, and optimize data movement in scientific applications.

Dr. Sarp Oral is a research scientist at the Oak Ridge Leadership Computing Facility (OLCF) of Oak Ridge National Laboratory, where he is a member of the Technology Integration Group and the task lead for the file and storage systems projects. His research interests are focused on computer benchmarking, parallel I/O and file systems, system and storage area networks and technologies. Dr. Oral holds a Ph.D. in Computer Engineering from the University of Florida.

Dr. Gokcen Kestor is a research scientist at the Pacific Northwest National Laboratory in the High-Performance Computing group. She received her Ph.D. from the Polytechnic University of Catalunya, Barcelona Spain, in 2013. Currently, her interests include programming models, fault tolerance and power/energy modeling.

Dr. Roberto Gioiosa is a senior research scientist at the Pacific Northwest National Laboratory (PNNL) in the High-Performance Computing Group. He received his Ph.D. in 2006 from the University of Rome "Tor Vergara", Rome Italy. In his career Prior to join PNNL in 2012, Dr. Gioiosa has worked at the Los Alamos National Laboratory (LANL), the Barcelona Supercomputing Center (BSC) and the IBM T.J. Watson Research Center, where he contributed to the development of the Compute Node Kernel for BG/Q systems. His research interests include operating systems, resilience, parallel runtime systems and performance/power modeling.

Shawn Strande is the Deputy Director at the San Diego Supercomputer Center. He has been involved with high performance computing since 1982 when he started his career at the NASA Ames Research Center performing wind tunnel tests and computational aerodynamics studies. Since then he has worked primarily in higher education and research computing at San Diego Supercomputer Center, the University of San Diego, and the National Center for Atmospheric Research. He holds an MS in Aeronautics and Astronautics from Stanford University, and a BS in Aeronautical Engineering from Cal Poly, Pomona.

Dr. Michela Taufer is the David L. and Beverly J.C. Mills Chair of Computer and Information Sciences and an associate professor in the same department at the University of Delaware. Taufer's research interests include scientific applications and their advanced programmability in heterogeneous computing (i.e., multi-core and many-core platforms, GPUs); performance analysis, modeling, and optimization of multi-scale applications on heterogeneous computing, cloud computing, and volunteer computing; numerical reproducibility and stability of large-scale simulations on multi-core platforms; big data analytics and MapReduce.

Jim Rogers is the Director, Computing and Facilities, for the National Center for Computational Sciences (NCCS) at Oak Ridge National Laboratory (ORNL). Jim has a BS in Computer Engineering, and has worked in high performance computing systems acquisition, facilities, integration, and operation for more than 25 years.

Hasan Abbasi is a research scientist at the Oak Ridge National Laboratory, Computer Science and Mathematics Division in the Scientific Data Group. His primary research interest is in techniques for Exascale computing such as performance understanding in end to end workflows, novel data management and storage methods, and OS and runtime support for task composition.

Jason Hill graduated from Iowa State University in 2004 with a Bachelors of Science in Computer Engineering. Since joining ORNL in 2007, he's been involved in designing, implementing, and maintaining large scale storage resources to support the OLCF's mission.

Dr. Laura Carrington is an Associate Research Scientist at University of California, San Diego and the director of the Performance Modeling and Characterization (PMaC) Lab at the San Diego Supercomputer Center. Her research interests are in HPC benchmarking, workload analysis, application performance modeling, analysis of accelerators (i.e., FPGAs, GPUs, and Xeon Phis) for scientific workloads, tools in performance analysis (i.e., processor and network simulators), and energy-efficient computing.

References

1. Open Community Runtime. https://xstackwiki.modelado.org/Open_Community_Runtime (2016)
2. Stampede - Dell PowerEdge C8220 Cluster with Intel Xeon Phi coprocessors. http://www.tacc.utexas.edu/resources/hpc (2016)
3. Advanced Scientific Computing Research (ASCR). Scientific discovery through advanced computing (SciDAC) Co-Design. http://science.energy.gov/ascr/research/scidac/co-design/ (2016)
4. S. Amarasinghe, D. Campbell, W. Carlson, A. Chien, W. Dally, E. Elnohazy, M. Hall, R. Harrison, W. Harrod, K. Hill, A. Snavely, ExaScale software study: software challenges in Extreme scale systems. Technical report, DARPA IPTO, Air Force Research Labs, 2009
5. S. Amarasinghe, M. Hall, R. Lethin, K. Pingali, D. Quinlan, V. Sarkar, J. Shalf, R. Lucas, K. Yelick, P. Balaji, P. C. Diniz, A. Koniges, M. Snir, S.R. Sachs, Report of the Workshop on Exascale Programming Challenges. Technical report, US Department of Energy, 2011
6. J.A. Ang, B.W. Barrett, K.B. Wheeler, R.C. Murphy, Introducing the graph 500, in *Proceedings of Cray User's Group Meeting (CUG)*, May 2010
7. T. Baer, V. Hazlewood, J. Heo, R. Mohr, J. Walsh, *Large Lustre File System Experiences at NICS*, Cray User Group, Atlanta, GA, May 2009
8. J.D. Bakos, High-performance heterogeneous computing with the convey hc-1. Comput. Sci. Eng. **12**(6), 80–87 (2010)
9. T. Barrett, M. Sumit, K. Taek-Jun, S. Ravinder, C. Sachit, J. Sondeen, J. Draper, A double-data rate (DDR) processing-in-memory (PIM) device with wideword floating-point capability, in *Proceedings of the IEEE International Symposium on Circuits and Systems*, 2006
10. K. Bergman, S. Borkar, D. Campbell, W. Carlson, W. Dally, M. Denneau, P. Franzon, W. Harrod, J. Hiller, S. Karp, S. Keckler, D. Klein, R. Lucas, M. Richards, A. Scarpelli, S. Scott, A. Snavely, T. Sterling, R.S. Williams, K. Yelick, K. Bergman, S. Borkar, D. Campbell, W. Carlson, W. Dally, M. Denneau, P. Franzon, W. Harrod, J. Hiller, S. Keckler, D. Klein, P. Kogge, R.S. Williams, K. Yelick, Exascale computing study: technology challenges in achieving exascale systems. Peter Kogge, editor and study lead (2008)
11. K. Beyls, E.H. D'Hollander, Reuse distance as a metric for cache behavior, in *Proceedings of the IASTED Conference on Parallel and Distributed Computing System*, 2001
12. K. Beyls, E.H. D'Hollander, Reuse distance-based cache hint selection, in *Proceedings of the 8th International Euro-Par Conference on Parallel Processing*, Euro-Par '02, London, 2002 (Springer-Verlag, UK, 2002, pp. 265–274)
13. A.S. Bland, R.A. Kendall, D.B. Kothe, J.H. Rogers, G.M. Shipman, Jaguar: the world's most powerful computer. Memory (TB) **300**(62), 362 (2009)

14. A.S. Bland, J.C. Wells, O.E. Messer, O.R. Hernandez, J.H. Rogers, Titan: early experience with the Cray XK6 at oak ridge national laboratory, in *Proceedings of Cray User Group Conference (CUG 2012)*, 2012
15. Z. Budimlić, M. Burke, V. Cavé, K. Knobe, G. Lowney, R. Newton, J. Palsberg, D. Peixotto, V. Sarkar, F. Schlimbach, S. Tacsirlar, Concurrent collections. Sci. Program. **18**(3–4), 203–217 (2010)
16. J.A. Butts, G.S. Sohi, A static power model for architects, in *Proceedings of the 33rd Annual ACM/IEEE International Symposium on Microarchitecture, MICRO 33* (ACM, New York, NY, 2000), pp. 191–201
17. P. Cicotti, Tarragon: a programming model for latency-hiding scientific computations. Ph.D. thesis, La Jolla, CA, USA, 2011. AAI3449479
18. P. Cicotti, L. Carrington, ADAMANT: tools to capture, analyze, and manage data movement, in *International Conference on Computational Science (ICCS)* San Diego, California, USA, 2016
19. P. Cicotti, M. Norman, R. Sinkovits, A. Snavely, S. Strande, *Gordon: A Novel Architecture for Data Intensive Computing* volume On the road to Exascale Computing: Contemporary Architectures in High Performance Computing, chapter 17. Chapman and Hall (2013)
20. B. Dally, Power, programmability, and granularity: the challenges of exascale computing, in *Proceedings of International Parallel and Distributed Processing Symposium* (2011), pp. 878–878
21. J. Dean, S. Ghemawat, MapReduce: simplified data processing on large clusters. Commun. ACM **51**(1), 107–113 (2008)
22. J. Demmel, Communication avoiding algorithms, in *Proceedings of the 2012 SC Companion: High Performance Computing, Networking Storage and Analysis*, SCC '12 (IEEE Computer Society, Washington, DC, 2012), pp. 1942–2000
23. J. Deslippe, B. Austin, C. Daley, W.-S. Yang, Lessons learned from optimizing science kernels for intel's knights landing. Comput. Sci. Eng. **17**(3), 30–42 (2015)
24. D. Dillow, G.M. Shipman, S. Oral, Z. Zhang, Y. Kim et al., Enhancing i/o throughput via efficient routing and placement for large-scale parallel file systems, in *Performance Computing and Communications Conference (IPCCC), 2011 IEEE 30th International* (IEEE, 2011), pp. 1–9
25. C. Ding, Y. Zhong, Predicting whole-program locality through reuse distance analysis, in *Proceedings of the ACM SIGPLAN 2003 Conference on Programming Language Design and Implementation, PLDI '03* (ACM, New York, NY, 2003), pp. 245–257
26. H. Dong, H. Nak, D. Lewis, H.-H. Lee, An optimized 3d-stacked memory architecture by exploiting excessive, high-density TSV bandwidth, in *IEEE 16th International Symposium on High Performance Computer Architecture (HPCA)* (2010), pp. 1–12
27. J. Draper, J. Chame, M. Hall, C. Steele, T. Barrett, J. LaCoss, J. Granacki, J. Shin, C. Chen, C. W. Kang, I. Kim, G. Daglikoca, The architecture of the diva processing-in-memory chip, in *Proceedings of the 16th International Conference on Supercomputing* (2002), pp. 14–25
28. T. Estrada, B. Zhang, P. Cicotti, R. Armen, M. Taufer, A scalable and accurate method for classifying protein–ligand binding geometries using a MapReduce approach. Comput. Biol. Med. **42**(7), 758–771 (2012)
29. M. Ezell, D. Dillow, S. Oral, F. Wang, D. Tiwari, D.E. Maxwell, D. Leverman, J. Hill, I/O router placement and fine-grained routing on titan to support spider II, in *Proceedings of Cray User Group Conference (CUG 2014)* (2014)
30. W.-C. Feng, K.W. Cameron, The green500 list: encouraging sustainable supercomputing. Computer **40**(12), 50–55 (2007)
31. B. Fitzpatrick, Distributed caching with memcached. Linux J. **2004**(124), 5 (2004)
32. R. Ge, X. Feng, S. Song, H.-C. Chang, D. Li, K.W. Cameron, PowerPack: energy profiling and analysis of high-performance systems and applications. IEEE Trans. Parallel Distrib. Syst. **21**(5), 658–671 (2010)
33. J.J. Hack, M.E. Papka, Big data: next-generation machines for big science. Comput. Sci. Eng. **17**(4), 63–65 (2015)

34. Y. Ho, G. Huang, P. Li, Nonvolatile memristor memory: device characteristics and design implications, in *IEEE/ACM International Conference on Computer-Aided Design* (2009), pp. 485–490
35. Intel Corporation. Intel® 64 and IA-32 Architectures Software Developer's Manual (2015)
36. G. Kestor, R. Gioiosa, D. Kerbyson, A. Hoisie, Quantifying the energy cost of data movement in scientific applications, in *The 16th IEEE International Symposium on Workload Characterization (IISWC)*, September 2013
37. P. Kogge, K. Bergman, S. Borkar, D. Campbell, W. Carlson, W. Dally, M. Denneau, P. Franzon, A. Snavely, W. Harrod, K. Hill, Exascale computing study: technology challenges in achieving exascale systems. Technical report, DARPA IPTO, Air Force Research Labs, 2008
38. A. Krishnamurthy, D.E. Culler, A. Dusseau, S.C. Goldstein, S. Lumetta, T. von Eicken, K. Yelick, Parallel programming in Split-C, in *Proceedings of the 1993 ACM/IEEE Conference on Supercomputing, Supercomputing '93* (ACM, New York, NY, 1993), pp. 262–273
39. M. Laurenzano, M. Tikir, L. Carrington, A. Snavely, PEBIL: efficient static binary instrumentation for Linux, in *2010 IEEE International Symposium on Performance Analysis of Systems Software (ISPASS)*, March 2010, pp. 175–183
40. J. Leskovec, D. Chakrabarti, J. Kleinberg, C. Faloutsos, Z. Ghahramani, Kronecker graphs: an approach to modeling networks. J. Mach. Learn. Res. 11, 985–1042 (2010)
41. N. Liu, J. Cope, P. Carns, C. Carothers, R. Ross, G. Grider, A. Crume, C. Maltzahn, On the role of burst buffers in leadership-class storage systems, in *2012 IEEE 28th Symposium on Mass Storage Systems and Technologies (MSST)* (IEEE, 2012), pp. 1–11
42. G. Loh, 3D-Stacked memory architectures for multi-core processors, in *Proceedings of the International Symposium on Computer Architecture* (2008), pp. 453–464
43. C.-K. Luk, R. Cohn, R. Muth, H. Patil, A. Klauser, G. Lowney, S. Wallace, V.J. Reddi, K. Hazelwood, Pin: building customized program analysis tools with dynamic instrumentation. SIGPLAN Not. **40**(6), 190–200 (2005)
44. H. Meuer, E. Strohmaier, J. Dongarra, H. Simon, Top500 supercomputing sites, 2011
45. S. Oral, J. Simmons, J. Hill, D. Leverman, F. Wang, M. Ezell, R. Miller, D. Fuller, R. Gunasekaran, Y. Kim et al., Best practices and lessons learned from deploying and operating large-scale data-centric parallel file systems, in *Proceedings of the International Conference for High Performance Computing, Networking, Storage and Analysis* (IEEE Press, 2014), pp. 217–228
46. D.A. Patterson, Latency lags bandwidth. Commun. ACM **47**(10), 71–75 (2004)
47. S.J. Plimpton, K.D. Devine, MapReduce in MPI for large-scale graph algorithms. Parallel Comput. **37**(9), 610–632 (2011). Emerging Programming Paradigms for Large-Scale Scientific Computing
48. G. Shipman, D. Dillow, S. Oral, F. Wang, The spider center wide file system: from concept to reality, in *Proceedings, Cray User Group (CUG) Conference*, Atlanta, GA, 2009
49. M. Taufer, M. Crowley, D. Price, A. Chien, C. Brooks III, Study of a highly accurate and fast protein-ligand docking based on molecular dynamics, in *Parallel and Distributed Processing Symposium, 2004. Proceedings. 18th International*, April 2004, p. 188
50. M. Taufer, R. Armen, J. Chen, P. Teller, C. Brooks, Computational multiscale modeling in protein–ligand docking. Eng. Med. Biol. Mag. IEEE **28**(2), 58–69 (2009)
51. J. Towns, T. Cockerill, M. Dahan, I. Foster, K. Gaither, A. Grimshaw, V. Hazlewood, S. Lathrop, D. Lifka, G. D. Peterson, R. Roskies, J.R. Scott, N. Wilkens-Diehr, Xsede: accelerating scientific discovery. Comput. Sci. Eng. **16**(5), 62–74 (2014)
52. F. Wang, S. Oral, G. Shipman, O. Drokin, T. Wang, I. Huang, Understanding Lustre filesystem internals. Oak Ridge National Laboratory, National Center for Computational Sciences, Tech. Rep, 2009
53. W.A. Wulf, S.A. McKee, Hitting the memory wall: implications of the obvious. SIGARCH Comput. Archit. News **23**(1), 20–24 (1995)
54. W. Xu, Y. Lu, Q. Li, E. Zhou, Z. Song, Y. Dong, W. Zhang, D. Wei, X. Zhang, H. Chen et al., Hybrid hierarchy storage system in milkyway-2 supercomputer. Front. Comput. Sci. **8**(3), 367–377 (2014)

55. B. Zhang, T. Estrada, P. Cicotti, M. Taufer, On efficiently capturing scientific properties in distributed big data without moving the data: a case study in distributed structural biology using mapreduce, in *Proceedings of the 2013 IEEE 16th International Conference on Computational Science and Engineering, CSE '13* (IEEE Computer Society, Washington, DC, 2013), pp. 117–124
56. B. Zhang, T. Estrada, P. Cicotti, M. Taufer, Enabling in-situ data analysis for large protein-folding trajectory datasets, in *Proceedings of the 2014 IEEE 28th International Parallel and Distributed Processing Symposium, IPDPS '14* (IEEE Computer Society, Washington, DC, 2014), pp. 221–230
57. B. Zhang, T. Estrada, P. Cicotti, P. Balaji, M. Taufer, Accurate scoring of drug conformations at the extreme scale, in *Proceedings of 8th IEEE International Scalable Computing Challenge - Co-located with IEEE/ACM CCGrid*, 2015

Chapter 4
Using Managed High Performance Computing Systems for High-Throughput Computing

Lucas A. Wilson

Abstract This chapter will explore the issue of executing High-Throughput Computing (HTC) workflows on managed High Performance Computing (HPC) systems that have been tailored for the execution of "traditional" HPC applications. We will first define data-oriented workflows and HTC, and then highlight some of the common hurdles that exist to executing these workflows on shared HPC resources. Then we will look at Launcher, which is a tool for making large HTC workflows appear—from the HPC system's perspective—to be a "traditional" simulation workflow. Launcher's various features are described, including scheduling modes and extensions for use with Intel®Xeon Phi™ coprocessor cards.

4.1 Introduction

High Performance Computing (HPC) applications traditionally consist of simulation and modeling applications designed for a small set of scientific disciplines for which predictions can be made by the application of known equations and laws. Applications in these scientific disciplines developed alongside the technologies of HPC in an almost symbiotic relationship; the newest computational techniques and models were incorporated into the applications, and the needs of the applications guided the development on new computational techniques and models. The result is a tool chain tailor-made for these domain applications.

Today, more scientific disciplines than ever are moving towards digital experimentation and analysis. Many researchers in these disciplines may have originally been unaware of the existence of the HPC community, or felt that the learning curve was too steep. In either case, they have developed their own applications and tool chains—sometimes on department clusters, but more typically on their personal computers. Additionally, the workflow demands of these communities are different. Instead of solving known equations of state to predict future events, these disciplines comb through vast amounts of experimental data, hoping to make some sense of

L.A. Wilson (✉)
Texas Advanced Computing Center, The University of Texas at Austin, Austin, TX, USA
e-mail: lucaswilson@acm.org

© Springer International Publishing Switzerland 2016   61
R. Arora (ed.), *Conquering Big Data with High Performance Computing*,
DOI 10.1007/978-3-319-33742-5_4

it all. Now, the computational demands of these communities are exceeding the capabilities of a single workstation or small department cluster, and the logical place to seek more capability is in HPC datacenters. Unfortunately, these systems are rarely tailored for the data-oriented workflows that these disciplines require.

This chapter will explore the issue of executing data-oriented workflows on managed HPC systems that have been tailored for the execution of "traditional" HPC applications. We will first define data-oriented workflows, and then highlight some of the common hurdles that exist to executing these workflows on shared HPC resources. Then we will look at Launcher, which is a tool for making large data-oriented workflows appear—from the HPC system's perspective—to be a "traditional" simulation workflow. We discuss in detail Launcher's various features, including startup mechanisms, available environment variables for runtime customization, and scheduling modes for internal jobs. We also discuss extensions to Launcher which allow it to execute Bag of Task (BoT) workloads on Intel®Xeon Phi™ coprocessor cards, allowing for increased throughput on these accelerated systems.

4.2 What Are We Trying to Do?

The computational community has several fuzzy terms for categorizing computational workflows—speaking in terms such as *High Performance Computing, High-Throughput Computing, Big Data*, and so on. While everyone asked will supply a slightly different definition of what these terms mean, we can categorize the computations that modern scientists typically wish to perform into two groups inspired by logical reasoning: *deductive computation* and *inductive computation*.

4.2.1 Deductive Computation

In logic, *deductive reasoning* is the process of reasoning a conclusion from known assumptions using well-established logical rules and transformations. If the initial assumptions are correct and the logical rules are applied correctly, then the resulting conclusion is guaranteed to be correct.

In computation we apply the same concept. *Deductive computation* is the application of well-formed mathematical and physical rules to a given set of initial conditions or initial state some number of times, with the assumption that the resulting conclusion (i.e., the state of the system after each application of the rules) is correct. Simulation problems in physics, cosmology, meteorology, and aerospace, mechanical, and structural engineering all fall into this category—first principle equations and laws are well-established, and the correct application of these laws to a known correct initial condition will result in an assumed correct conclusion about the future state of the system.

Deductive computation is where supercomputers have traditionally excelled, since computers were designed with this specific purpose in mind from the beginning. Parallel computers are no exception; their hardware and software frameworks were originally designed with these problems in mind, and their continued evolution is still influenced by these problems.

4.2.2   Inductive Computation

Inductive reasoning, in contrast to deductive reasoning, is the process of using vast amounts of existing data in order to derive some generalized observation or rule which applies to all cases. Essentially, inductive reasoning attempts to start with the conclusions and produce the rules, rather than start with the rules and produce the conclusion.

Inductive computation, like inductive reasoning, is the process of analyzing recorded conclusions (e.g., data gathered from physical experiments) and trying to determine some underlying rule or pattern. In these cases, patterns do not always emerge from relatively minimal amounts of data. Rather, a large amount of data resulting from a large number of independent experiments are needed to garner any useful insight. The results of these independent experiments are then analyzed—first independently, then together—using statistical or probabilistic methods to attempt to recover patterns. Biology (via genomics, proteomics, and phylogeny), traffic research, sociology, economics, and many other disciplines rely heavily on these approaches. Big Data, as these types of computations are routinely called, is really the application of inductive computation to very large data sets.

4.2.2.1   High-Throughput Computing

One parallel model which is regularly used for inductive computation is *High-Throughput Computing* (HTC), where many independent jobs need to be executed as quickly as possible. HTC goes by other names, including bag-of-tasks (BoT) parallel, pleasantly parallel, and embarrassingly parallel. Each job—which may take minutes, hours, or days—must be executed on a separate input set, and produces a separate output. And while many different execution platforms have been created to execute these workloads, including grids [3, 5–7, 11, 18] and volunteer computing systems [1, 13], researchers who need to do HTC often turn to shared cyberinfrastructure in the form of managed HPC systems to get their work done.

4.3   Hurdles to Using HPC Systems for HTC

Attempting to run HTC workloads on HPC systems can sometimes be a frustrating exercise. Managed HPC systems typically enforce restrictions on user actions in order to ensure fairness and stability for the many hundreds or thousands of users of a particular shared resource. While restrictions can vary from system to system, depending on the site hosting the resource or the particular funding agency responsible for it, resource managers and batch schedulers on these systems all employ some combination of runtime limits, job-in-queue limits, deprioritizing of serial applications, and restrictions on dynamic job submission. In many cases, researchers attempt to jump each of these hurdles one-by-one as they are encountered. We will discuss each of these hurdles in detail before looking at some potential solutions.

4.3.1   Runtime Limits

Many shared cyberinfrastructure resources employ hard runtime limits in order to give all users an opportunity to take advantage of the system. On HPC systems, runtime limits for a job are typically in the 24–48 h range. On some systems, runtime limits for serial jobs can be as short as 6–12 h, as a way of prioritizing parallel jobs for which these systems are tailored.

For a researcher who wishes to run a large set of independent jobs, their first thought may be to script a loop to iterate through each input file. Even if each iteration only takes a few minutes, having hundreds or thousands of input files can quickly put you over the runtime limits. This leaves only two options: either ask the system administrators to relax the runtime limit (a possible but unlikely solution), or attempt to parallelize by submitting more than one job at a time.

4.3.2   Jobs-in-Queue Limits

Once the runtime limits have been overcome as a roadblock to executing an HTC workflow, the next option is to do job-level parallelization by submitting multiple jobs, each with some subset of the tasks you wish to perform. The ideal would be to have each job submitted to the batch scheduler setup in such a way that it can complete within the runtime limit, and then submit as many jobs as is necessary to complete the workload. In this way, a researcher can complete their HTC workload in a parallel fashion (since each job is dispatched to a different compute node) while ensuring that submitted jobs will not be terminated by the runtime limit.

However most shared HPC systems—again in a completely legitimate attempt to ensure fairness for all users of a resource—impose limits on the number of jobs any single user may have in the queues. In some cases the limit is between 40 and 50 jobs, depending on the resource. While many workloads would be able to fit within this limit, very large workloads would run into both the runtime limit and the jobs-in-queue limit.

At this point, a researcher with a large HTC workload may conclude that the next obvious choice is to make the workload dynamic. That is, have each job submit a new job to the batch system upon completion, that way hundreds of jobs can be run while staying underneath the jobs-in-queue limit since by the time a job performs the next submission, it has already been de-queued and opened a new job slot.

4.3.3 Dynamic Job Submission Restrictions

With the runtime limit hurdle overcome, and a potential solution found for the jobs-in-queue limit, researchers with HTC workloads may find themselves confronted with another restriction, this time on dynamic job submission. On many shared HPC systems, dynamic job submission—the act of submitting a new job to the queue from within a currently running job—is prohibited. Why? Again, the answer is fairness. If a user can submit new jobs from every job they run, then it is conceivable that they can saturate the system, leaving other users' jobs to starve in the queue.

4.3.4 Solutions from Resource Managers and Big Data Research

Many existing resource managers provide a workaround for these problems called job arrays [7, 17, 19]. These job arrays allow the user to create a single job out of many smaller, independent jobs, and run them on multiple nodes and processors. However, administrators for many shared HPC resources also disable job arrays, because they provide a way to circumvent other fair use limits placed on the system such as jobs-in-queue and dynamic submission restrictions.

Additionally, BigData tools such as Apache YARN [14] and Mesos [9] are well suited to systems devoted to analytic processing using tools like Hadoop/Spark, which use the MapReduce [4] computational model. However, when the primary concern is running on shared cyberinfrastructure in the form of managed HPC systems, these particular resource brokering tools are not necessarily available, and may require significant re-engineering on the part of the user in order to be of use.

4.3.5   A Better Solution for Managed HPC Systems

A better potential solution would be to create a small cluster within a cluster. A single parallel batch submission to a managed HPC system which acts, internally, as a resource manager tasked with scheduling all of the sequential jobs which need to be executed. This process, which we call *bundling*, allows HTC workflows—which are dominated by many hundreds or thousands of sequential tasks to execute—to run as single, long-running multi-node parallel jobs: Exactly what managed HPC systems are configured to execute.

4.4   Launcher

Launcher is a simple, shell script-based framework for bundling large numbers of small, independent jobs into a single batch submission suitable for running on HPC systems whose policies have been tailored for large parallel applications [16]. Launcher is specifically designed for executing jobs in the HTC model, where many independent data sets are independently analyzed, with the task of further analysis left to other tools. This particular tool has been used on systems at the Texas Advanced Computing Center (TACC) at the University of Texas at Austin for the last 10 years, and has undergone numerous updates in that time to increase functionality, improve performance, and become more useful to the TACC user community. It has since been generalized and released as an open source tool for users to deploy on their own clusters, workgroups, and workstations.

Launcher uses several cooperating shell scripts to kick start multi-node execution, manage number of processes per node, efficiently schedule individual jobs, and even make use of Many Integrated Core (MIC) coprocessor cards. Users can customize the launcher by setting various environment variables.

4.4.1   How Launcher Works

Launcher consists of four major scripts which work together to run HTC workloads on managed HPC systems. The scripts are responsible for kick starting multi-node execution, managing multi-core execution, and executing and scheduling individual jobs:

- `paramrun`: Top-level script responsible for interfacing with the system's resource manager, ensuring appropriate environment variables are set, and kick-starting multi-node execution,
- `tskserver`: Python-based TCP/IP dynamic scheduling service,
- `init_launcher`: Script responsible for on-node process management for multi-core and many-core processors, and

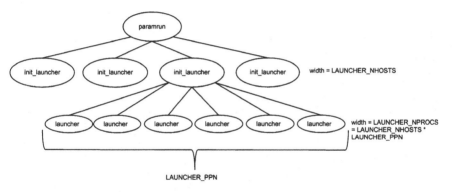

Fig. 4.1 Process hierarchy for launcher with corresponding environment variables

Table 4.1 List of environment variables for use in control file

Variable name	Meaning
LAUNCHER_NHOSTS	The number of hosts on which this particular launcher instance is executing
LAUNCHER_PPN	The number of processes per node/host with which this particular launcher instance is executing
LAUNCHER_NPROCS	The total number of processes on which this launcher instance is executing (NHOSTS * PPN)
LAUNCHER_TSK_ID	The particular launcher task (0..NPROCS-1) on which this job is executing
LAUNCHER_NJOBS	The number of jobs for this particular launcher bundle (NJOBS = wc -l control_file)
LAUNCHER_JID	The particular launcher job that is being executed. This corresponds to a particular line in the control file (1..NJOBS)

- `launcher`: Leaf script responsible for executing appropriate jobs from the job file, timing individual jobs, and providing stdout/stderr content.

Figure 4.1 shows the hierarchy of shell scripts used by the launcher to efficiently execute across large numbers of multi-core and many-core servers, as well as the environment variables used/defined by the launcher which are available to the user (see Table 4.1).

Any of the provided variables in Table 4.1 can be referenced in the *job file*. The job file can contain any shell-executable commands, including referencing external shell scripts, using bash for loops and pipes, and stdin/stdout/stderr redirection. The job file can consist of any number of commands, placed one-per-line, so

Listing 4.1 Examples of Valid Job File Entries

```
./a.out $LAUNCHER_TSK_ID
./a.out $LAUNCHER_JID
echo $LAUNCHER_PPN
echo $LAUNCHER_NHOSTS
grep "bar" foo | wc -l > baz.o$LAUNCHER_JID
```

long as there are no blank lines in the file. Listing 4.1 shows several examples of valid job file entries. Launcher can be directed to this job file by exporting the LAUNCHER_JOB_FILE environment variable prior to calling paramrun.

4.4.2 Guided Example: A Simple Launcher Bundle

With all of the pieces of the launcher explained, we can now put together a complete launcher bundle. Launcher can execute on workstations and work groups of computers, as well as on HPC systems. For this example, we will build a bundle to be run on a cluster which is managed with the SLURM resource manager, although other resource managers are easily supported.

4.4.2.1 Step 1: Create a Job File

As a first step, we will create a job file which prints a variant of "Hello, World!" to the screen as many times as we wish. To start, we can create a text file (helloworld) which contains some number of copies of this line, remembering to remove any blank lines:

```
echo "Hello from $LAUNCHER_JID, task $LAUNCHER_TSK_ID!"
```

4.4.2.2 Step 2: Build a SLURM Batch Script

Once we have built a job file, we can construct a simple SLURM batch script which will run the launcher on whatever nodes SLURM allocates for this particular batch job. An example job script, which assumes 4 cores per node and requests 4 nodes, is given in Listing 4.2.

4.4.3 Using Various Scheduling Methods

Launcher can schedule jobs within a bundle using three different methods: a basic *dynamic* scheduling method, and two different static scheduling methods. The scheduling method used can be changed by altering the value of the LAUNCHER_SCHED environment variable prior to executing paramrun.

Listing 4.2 Example SLURM batch script
```
#!/bin/bash
#$SBATCH -n 16
#$SBATCH -N 4
#$SBATCH -t 00:05:00
#$SBATCH -p normal

export LAUNCHER_JOB_FILE=jobfile
$LAUNCHER_DIR/paramrun
```

Algorithm 1: Dynamic scheduling client

---
retries ← 3
LAUNCHER_JID ← ⊥   ▷ Start with non-numeric value
while LAUNCHER_JID ∉ $\mathbb{N}^+$ ∧ retries> 0 **do**
    LAUNCHER_JID ← i ∈ $(\mathbb{N}^+ \cup \bot)$ ▷ Response from tskserver
    if LAUNCHER_JID = ⊥ **then**   ▷ Handle non-numeric case
        retries←retries−1   ▷ Decrement remaining retries
    else
        retries ← 3   ▷ Reset the retry counter if numeric value received
    end if
end while

4.4.3.1 Dynamic Scheduling

By default, the launcher uses a dynamic scheduling mode which has two components: a *client* piece within the launcher script which is responsible for extracting the command associated with line LAUNCHER_JID from the job file (see Algorithm 1), and a *server* component called tskserver, which is responsible for generating monotonically increasing natural numbers served on a first come, first served basis to whichever clients are actively requesting (see Algorithm 2). A illustrative example of dynamic scheduling is given in Fig. 4.3c.

Dynamic scheduling is most efficient when the execution time per job in a bundle is variable. By being able to begin the next task whenever the current task is completed, the amount on wait time per processor is reduced, and the overall turnaround time is reduced in kind.

Performance

Dynamic scheduling for the launcher incurs minimal overhead, even at large scales. Strong scaling tests [16] using Autodock Vina [12] to analyze more than 600,000 ligands show only minimal deviation from the ideal schedule for the bundle out to 65,536 compute cores (see Fig. 4.2a), while weak scaling tests performed on an artificially generated workload show good scaling out to 65,536 cores (see Fig. 4.2b).

Algorithm 2: Dynamic scheduling server

MAX_N ← **count lines** LAUNCHER_JOB_FILE
n ← 1   ▷ This number is 1-indexed, rather than 0-indexed
while receiving new connection requests **do**
    if *n* ≤ MAX_N **then**
        Client ← *n*   ▷ Transmit *n* to client
    else
        Client ← ⊥   ▷ Transmit non-numeric value to client
    end if
end while

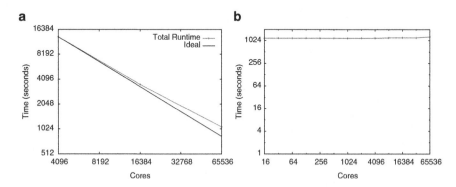

Fig. 4.2 Performance of launcher using dynamic scheduler. (**a**) Strong scaling using Autodock Vina. (**b**) Weak scaling for artificial workload (40 jobs/core)

4.4.3.2 Static Scheduling

For situations where the execution time of each job in a bundle is nearly identical, a static scheduling method may be more efficient. Static schedules are calculable before execution begins, meaning that minimal execution time overhead costs are incurred using these approaches. The two static scheduling methods that are implemented in Launcher are *interleaved* and *block* scheduling.

Interleaved Scheduling

Interleaved scheduling uses a simple recurrence-relation based allocation method for mapping jobs to tasks (see Algorithm 3 and Fig. 4.3a). Interleaved scheduling is a round-robin approach, meaning the distribution most closely resembles dealing cards to multiple players. The calculation, while performed at execution time, has minimal overhead cost (only a few arithmetic operations) and requires no intervening service to function (such as `tskserver`).

Algorithm 3: Interleaved scheduling

$j \leftarrow 0$
while LAUNCHER_JID $\leq$ LAUNCHER_NJOBS **do**
   if $j = 0$ **then**
      LAUNCHER_JID $\leftarrow$ LAUNCHER_TSK_ID $+1$
      $j \leftarrow 1$
   else
      LAUNCHER_JID $\leftarrow$ LAUNCHER_JID $+$ LAUNCHER_NPROCS
   end if
end while

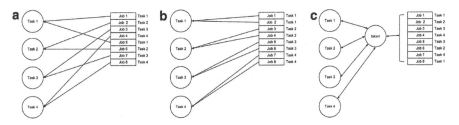

Fig. 4.3 Three scheduling methods provided with launcher. (**a**) Interleaved. (**b**) Block. (**c**) Dynamic

Algorithm 4: Block scheduling

JPT $\leftarrow$ $\lceil$LAUNCHER_NJOBS / LAUNCHER_NPROCS$\rceil$ ▷ Determine jobs per task
LAUNCHER_JID $\leftarrow$ (LAUNCHER_TSK_ID×JPT)$+1$
LAUNCHER_SJID $\leftarrow$ LAUNCHER_JID   ▷ Retain starting job id
while (LAUNCHER_JID$\leq$LAUNCHER_NJOBS) $\wedge$
(LAUNCHER_JID$\leq$LAUNCHER_SJID$+$JPT) **do**
   LAUNCHER_JID $\leftarrow$ LAUNCHER_JID$+1$
end while

Block Scheduling

Block scheduling is very similar to interleaved scheduling, except that a division-based approach is used rather than a recurrence relation (see Algorithm 4 and Fig. 4.3b). Block scheduling, as opposed to interleaved, more closely resembles passing handouts to students sitting in different rows, where a set of handouts is given to the student sitting closest to the isle. As with interleaved scheduling, the calculation is performed at execution time, but the overhead of a such a small number of arithmetic operations is negligible.

Table 4.2 User-definable Phi-related environment variables for launcher

Variable	Meaning
LAUNCHER_NPHI	The number of coprocessor cards per host
LAUNCHER_PHI_PPN	The number of processes per coprocessor card with which this particular launcher instance is executing
LAUNCHER_PHI_MODEL	The Xeon Phi useage model. Options are none, offload, independent, and symmetric

Table 4.3 Xeon Phi-related environment variables provided by launcher

Variable	Meaning
LAUNCHER_PHI_NPROCS	The total number of coprocessor tasks for this launcher instance (NHOSTS * NPHI * PHI_PPN; independent and symmetric models)
LAUNCHER_PHI_TSK_ID	The particular launcher task (0..PHI_NPROCS-1) on which this job is executing (indepdenent model only)
LAUNCHER_PHI_NJOBS	The number of jobs for this particular launcher instance (independent model only)
LAUNCHER_PHI_JID	The particular launcher job that is being executed. This corresponds to a particular line in the control file (1..PHI_NJOBS; independent model only)

4.4.4 Launcher with Intel®Xeon Phi™ Coprocessors

By default, Launcher assumes that there are no coprocessor cards available for use. In order to enable the use of coprocessors in an HTC or BoT workload, the environment variable LAUNCHER_NPHI must be set to the number of coprocessor cards per host (Table 4.2). Being unset (which is the default) or set to zero will disable coprocessor scheduling.

Three potential usage models for the Xeon Phi as a BoT processor are enabled, and can be selected using the LAUNCHER_PHI_MODEL environment variable (Table 4.2). The first is to use the Xeon Phi as an accelerator for codes which are capable of offloading computations directly (offload). The second is to use the Xeon Phi to execute its own BoT workload, independent of the host (independent). The third is to use the Xeon Phi and the host together to complete the same workload (symmetric). If LAUNCHER_PHI_MODEL is set to none or is not set (default), then coprocessor scheduling will be disabled (Table 4.3).

4.4.4.1 Offload

In the offload usage model, the primary application is initiated on the host and contains offload regions which are computed on the coprocessor (see Fig. 4.4a). Within this use case, two different possibilities were considered: (1) Only 1 application is being executed on a host (LAUNCHER_PPN=1), or (2) multiple applications are being executed per host.

Single Application Instance per Host

In the case of a single application being executed per host, offload to the attached Xeon Phi is seamless. Any code which contains offload capable regions will have access to the entire card. No other applications instances will be competing for resources.

Multiple Application Instances per Host

The case of multiple applications executing on the same host provides a more interesting challenge. What should be done if more than one application wishes to offload to the Xeon Phi? How can we ensure that the two applications to not offload to the same set of cores on the Xeon Phi, as would happen by default? To address this, Launcher automatically partitions the cores on the coprocessor into separate, distinct regions.

Automatic Core Partitioning

Launcher makes use of the Intel®OpenMP runtime [2] to manage thread place-ment on the Intel®Xeon Phi™ when multiple applications are going to use the coprocessor(s) simultaneously. Each Launcher *task* (see Sect. 4.4.1) receives a portion of the cores on a coprocessor, using a simple partitioning strategy that ensures two applications do not overlap on the same physical core. Using the MIC_KMP_PLACE_THREADS environment variable (the MIC prefix is necessary because this will be set on the host, not on the coprocessor directly), Launcher can set the number of cores and the core offset for all offloading applications initiated from each launcher task.

Because offload codes need a core to be set aside to handle data transmission via the Coprocessor Offload Infrastructure (COI) [10], only cores 1 through 60 will be used for computational work. We can therefore view any particular coprocessor card as a sequence of cores:

$$\Phi^k = \left(c_1^k, c_2^k, \ldots, c_{60}^k \right)$$

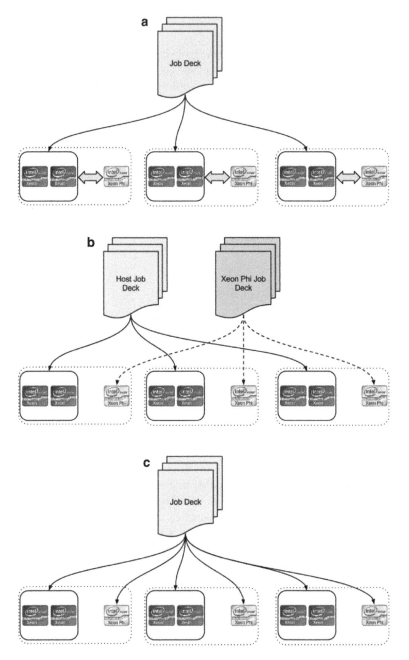

Fig. 4.4 Execution models for Intel®Xeon Phi™ on the Stampede HPC Cluster at TACC. (**a**) Offload. (**b**) Independent. (**c**) Symmetric

---

Algorithm 5: Automatic core partitioning (ACP)

```
tasks_per_card ← ⌈LAUNCHER_PPN / LAUNCHER_NPHI⌉
cores_per_task ← 60 ÷ tasks_per_card
card ← LAUNCHER_TSK_ID ÷ tasks_per_card
offset ← (LAUNCHER_TSK_ID × cores_per_task) + 1
```

Using `MIC_KMP_PLACE_THREADS` (for an explanation, see [8]), Launcher partitions the coprocessor based on the values of `LAUNCHER_PPN` and `LAUNCHER_NPHI`. For example, if a host contains two coprocessors (Φ^1 and Φ^2), and is running 12 applications ($A^1, \ldots, A^{12}$) simultaneously on the host (`LAUNCHER_PPN=12`), then each process will be given ten cores on a single coprocessor card:

$$A^1 \rightarrow \left(c_1^1, c_2^1, \ldots, c_{10}^1\right)$$

$$A^2 \rightarrow \left(c_{11}^1, c_{12}^1, \ldots, c_{20}^1\right)$$

$$\vdots$$

$$A^{12} \rightarrow \left(c_{51}^2, c_{52}^2, \ldots, c_{60}^2\right)$$

The automatic core partitioning strategy (see Algorithm 5) will always assign an equivalent number of cores to each application, even if that means leaving cores idle on the coprocessor. Applications are not permitted to span coprocessor cards. In Algorithm 5, the operator ÷ is an integer division.

4.4.4.2   Independent Workloads for Host and Coprocessor

If the application(s) for an HTC or BoT workload can be compiled natively for the coprocessor, then the coprocessor can be used as an additional standalone computational resource. In this usage model, Launcher *tasks* are initiated directly on the coprocessor, and draw from an independent set of jobs from the jobs being processed by the host. The reason for this is because of the discrepancy in performance between the coprocessor and typical host processors, especially for codes which are not easily vectorized. As a result, the coprocessor(s) can be given a set of jobs which are either smaller or larger, so that the total runtime on the coprocessor(s) can be balanced with the total runtime on the host (see Fig. 4.4b).

Table 4.4 contains a list of the additional environment variables that can be used to setup an additional, independent workload on the coprocessors.

For independent workloads, `LAUNCHER_PHI_MODEL` should be set to `independent`. Once Launcher has determined that the coprocessor(s) will be used and the environment variables `LAUNCHER_NPHI` and `LAUNCHER_PHI_PPN` are set to valid values, Launcher will use the same method for partitioning the

Table 4.4 User-definable variables for independent coprocessor workload

Variable	Meaning
LAUNCHER_NPHI	The number of coprocessor cards per host on which this particular Launcher instance is executing
LAUNCHER_PHI_PPN	The number of processes per coprocessor card
LAUNCHER_PHI_MODEL	The usage model for the coprocessor cards
LAUNCHER_PHI_SCHED	The scheduling method to be used for the coprocessor tasks. Options are interleaved (default), block, and dynamic. This is independent of the scheduling method selected for the hosts

coprocessor cores among independent processes as in the offload model (see Algorithm 5). Although primary processes will be started on logical context 0 (where the shell is executing), use of KMP_PLACE_THREADS will force thread migration to appropriate logical contexts when applications are executing (use of the MIC_ prefix is unnecessary due to initialization directly on the coprocessor, rather than on the host). Table 4.4 provides a description of the environment variables that are used for an independent workload on the coprocessor.

4.4.4.3 Symmetric Execution on Host and Phi

In the independent usage model, expected discrepancies between running time of host and coprocessor jobs means that a separate set of jobs is used for each processor class in order to maintain overall load balance. In cases where an application can execute in similar time for both processor classes, Launcher can execute independent tasks on both the host and the coprocessor which share the same job bag. This symmetric model treats both classes of processors in the machine as essentially equivalent, and the addition of the coprocessor simply means a larger pool of processors to complete the provided job deck (see Fig. 4.4c).

As with the two previous usage models, Launcher can be told to use symmetric execution by setting LAUNCHER_PHI_MODEL=symmetric. In this case, scheduling of jobs on both host and coprocessor use the same facility, so the LAUNCHER_PHI_SCHED environment variable used for independent workloads (see Table 4.4) has no effect. Instead, both host and coprocessor tasks will reference the LAUNCHER_SCHED environment variable for determining the scheduling method. As with independent workload execution, the symmetric model makes use of the LAUNCHER_NPHI and LAUNCHER_PHI_PPN environment variables for determining number of coprocessor cards per host and number of tasks per coprocessor, respectively.

4.4.5 Use Case: Molecular Docking and Virtual Screening

High-Throughput Computing, enabled on managed HPC clusters using Launcher, is a common form of data analysis for performing comparisons of hundreds of thousands of different possibilities. These space search problems require large amounts of computational time, and the data parallelism is easily exploited on large distributed-memory clusters.

One such example is molecular docking. Molecular docking software such as Autodock Vina [12] is used to virtually screen for best fit protein bindings. When searching for binding configurations for a particular target (e.g., searching for new drugs), a reference "target" protein may be compared against hundreds, thousands, or millions of potential companions (the drug to be designed). The better the fit between the target and the potential companion, the better chance that particular option has of being an effective drug delivery mechanism.

Launcher has been used extensively for this purpose for several years. One large project, DrugDiscovery@TACC [15] used the Launcher to analyze thousands of potential protein candidates in search of a favorable target for treating dengue fever. Launcher gives DrugDiscovery@TACC the ability to bundle many thousands of protein combinations into a single batch job, converting it into a candidate job on TACC's managed HPC systems. Without Launcher's ability to bundle small sequential jobs into a single parallel batch job, the DrugDiscovery workflow would be impossible to execute on TACC systems, given administrative restrictions.

4.5 Conclusion

This chapter has explored the issue of executing data-oriented workflows on managed HPC systems that have been tailored for the execution of "traditional" HPC applications. We first defined data-oriented workflows, and then highlighted some of the common hurdles that exist to executing these workflows on shared HPC resources. We then looked at Launcher, which is a tool for making large data-oriented workflows appear—from the HPC system's perspective—to be a "traditional" simulation workflow. Not only was the underlying structure of Launcher described, but example use cases for simple bundles, varying scheduler methods, and integration of Intel®Xeon Phi™ coprocessor cards were discussed.

Moving forward, the Launcher will continue to see improvements which improve overall performance without additional user overhead. Future plans include better process and memory pinning support for many-core architectures, as well as better statistics collection and aggregation so that users can get a better sense of the overall performance of their Launcher bundles.

Acknowledgements The authors acknowledge the Texas Advanced Computing Center (TACC) at The University of Texas at Austin for providing HPC resources that have contributed to the research reported within this paper. The Launcher is available for download on GitHub: https://github.com/TACC/launcher.

References

1. D.P. Anderson, Boinc: a system for public-resource computing and storage, in *Proceedings. Fifth IEEE/ACM International Workshop on Grid Computing, 2004* (IEEE, New York, 2004), pp. 4–10
2. F. Broquedis, T. Gautier, V. Danjean, libkomp, an efficient openmp runtime system for both fork-join and data flow paradigms, in *OpenMP in a Heterogeneous World*, ed. by B. Chapman, F. Massaioli, M.S. Müller, M. Rorro. Lecture Notes in Computer Science, vol. 7312 (Springer, Berlin/Heidelberg, 2012), pp. 102–115. doi:10.1007/978-3-642-30961-8_8. http://dx.doi.org/10.1007/978-3-642-30961-8_8
3. J. Cao, S. Jarvis, S. Saini, G.R. Nudd et al., Gridflow: workflow management for grid computing, in *Proceedings of the 3rd IEEE/ACM International Symposium on Cluster Computing and the Grid, CCGrid 2003* (IEEE, New York, 2003), pp. 198–205
4. J. Dean, S. Ghemawat, Mapreduce: simplified data processing on large clusters. Commun. ACM **51**(1), 107–113 (2008)
5. E. Deelman, J. Blythe, Y. Gil, C. Kesselman, G. Mehta, S. Patil, M.H. Su, K. Vahi, M. Livny, Pegasus: mapping scientific workflows onto the grid, in *Grid Computing* (Springer, Berlin, 2004), pp. 11–20
6. D.W. Erwin, D.F. Snelling, Unicore: a grid computing environment, in *Euro-Par 2001 Parallel Processing* (Springer, Heidelberg, 2001), pp. 825–834
7. W. Gentzsch, Sun grid engine: towards creating a compute power grid, in *Proceedings. First IEEE/ACM International Symposium on Cluster Computing and the Grid, 2001* (IEEE, New York, 2001), pp. 35–36
8. R.W. Green, OpenMP* thread affinity control (2012), https://software.intel.com/en-us/articles/openmp-thread-affinity-control
9. B. Hindman, A. Konwinski, M. Zaharia, A. Ghodsi, A.D. Joseph, R.H. Katz, S. Shenker, I. Stoica, Mesos: a platform for fine-grained resource sharing in the data center, in *NSDI*, vol. 11 (2011), pp. 22–22
10. C. Newburn, C. Dmitriev, R. Narayanaswamy, J. Wiegert, R. Murty, F. Chinchilla, R. Deodhar, R. McGuire, Offload compiler runtime for the Intel Xeon Phi coprocessor, in *2013 IEEE 27th International Parallel and Distributed Processing Symposium Workshops PhD Forum (IPDPSW)* (2013), pp. 1213–1225. doi:10.1109/IPDPSW.2013.251
11. K. Seymour, H. Nakada, S. Matsuoka, J. Dongarra, C. Lee, H. Casanova, Overview of GridRPC: a remote procedure call API for grid computing, in *Grid Computing—GRID 2002* (Springer, Berlin, 2002), pp. 274–278
12. O. Trott, A.J. Olson, Autodock Vina: improving the speed and accuracy of docking with a new scoring function, efficient optimization, and multithreading. J. Comput. Chem. **31**(2), 455–461 (2010)
13. A. Tsaregorodtsev, M. Bargiotti, N. Brook, A.C. Ramo, G. Castellani, P. Charpentier, C. Cioffi, J. Closier, R.G. Diaz, G. Kuznetsov et al., Dirac: a community grid solution. J. Phys. Conf. Ser. **119**, 062048 (2008)
14. V.K. Vavilapalli, A.C. Murthy, C. Douglas, S. Agarwal, M. Konar, R. Evans, T. Graves, J. Lowe, H. Shah, S. Seth et al., Apache Hadoop yarn: yet another resource negotiator, in *Proceedings of the 4th Annual Symposium on Cloud Computing* (ACM, New York, 2013), p. 5

15. U. Viswanathan, S.M. Tomlinson, J.M. Fonner, S.A. Mock, S.J. Watowich, Identification of a novel inhibitor of dengue virus protease through use of a virtual screening drug discovery web portal. J. Chem. Inform. Model. **54**(10), 2816–2825 (2014)
16. L.A. Wilson, J.M. Fonner, Launcher: a shell-based framework for rapid development of parallel parametric studies, in *Proceedings of the 2014 Annual Conference on Extreme Science and Engineering Discovery Environment, XSEDE '14* (ACM, New York, 2014), pp. 40:1–40:8. doi:10.1145/2616498.2616534. http://doi.acm.org/10.1145/2616498.2616534
17. A.B. Yoo, M.A. Jette, M. Grondona, Slurm: simple linux utility for resource management, in *Job Scheduling Strategies for Parallel Processing* (Springer, Berlin, 2003), pp. 44–60
18. J. Yu, R. Buyya, A taxonomy of workflow management systems for grid computing. J. Grid Comput. **3**(3–4), 171–200 (2005)
19. S. Zhou, LSF: load sharing in large heterogeneous distributed systems, in *Proceedings of the Workshop on Cluster Computing* (1992)

Chapter 5
Accelerating Big Data Processing on Modern HPC Clusters

Xiaoyi Lu, Md. Wasi-ur-Rahman, Nusrat Islam, Dipti Shankar, and
Dhabaleswar K. (DK) Panda

Abstract Modern HPC systems and the associated middleware (such as MPI
and parallel file systems) have been exploiting the advances in HPC technologies
(multi-/many-core architecture, RDMA-enabled networking, and SSD) for many
years. However, Big Data processing and management middleware have not fully
taken advantage of such technologies. These disparities are taking HPC and Big
Data processing into *divergent trajectories*. This chapter provides an overview
of popular Big Data processing middleware, high-performance interconnects and
storage architectures, and discusses the challenges in accelerating Big Data processing middleware by leveraging emerging technologies on modern HPC clusters.
This chapter presents case studies of advanced designs based on RDMA and
heterogeneous storage architecture, that were proposed to address these challenges
for multiple components of Hadoop (HDFS and MapReduce) and Spark. The
advanced designs presented in the case studies are publicly available as a part of
the High-Performance Big Data (HiBD) project. An overview of the HiBD project
is also provided in this chapter. All these works aim to bring HPC and Big Data
processing into a *convergent trajectory*.

5.1 Introduction

The International Data Corporation (IDC) study in 2011 [16] on Digital Universe
indicated the beginning of "Information Age", where the foundation of economic
value is largely derived from information vs. physical things. The digital universe is
doubling in size every 2 years and is expected to multiply tenfold between 2013
and 2020—from 4.4 trillion gigabytes to 44 trillion gigabytes [7]. The rate of
information growth appears to be exceeding Moore's Law. The availability of a
huge number of diverse and high-resolution data sets, i.e., "Big Data", provides

X. Lu (✉) • Md. Wasi-ur-Rahman • N. Islam • D. Shankar • D.K. (DK) Panda
Department of Computer Science and Engineering, The Ohio State University,
Columbus, OH, USA
e-mail: luxi@cse.ohio-state.edu; rahmanmd@cse.ohio-state.edu; islamn@cse.ohio-state.edu;
shankard@cse.ohio-state.edu; panda@cse.ohio-state.edu

© Springer International Publishing Switzerland 2016   81
R. Arora (ed.), *Conquering Big Data with High Performance Computing*,
DOI 10.1007/978-3-319-33742-5_5

groundbreaking opportunities for enterprise information management. Big Data is fundamentally changing the way decisions are being made in a wide range of domains. As data acquisition technologies and data sources witness an explosion in the amount of input data, it is expected that many IT companies in the fields of e-commerce, financial services, search engines, social networking sites and many others, will increasingly need to process massive quantities of data in the order of hundreds or thousands of petabytes to gain *insights* into patterns and trends. In addition to IT companies, the High-Performance Computing (HPC) world appears to be also bearing the brunt of this transition. A study by IDC in 2013 [19] on the latest trends of HPC usage and spending indicated that 67 % of HPC sites were running High-Performance Data Analysis (HPDA) workloads. IDC forecasts HPDA revenues will experience robust growth from 2012 to 2017, reaching almost $1.4 billion in 2017, versus $743.8 million in 2012.

To meet the growing demands of Big Data applications, IT organizations are relying on the capabilities of data-intensive computing middleware to process and analyze data. For instance, many of them have deployed the Hadoop MapReduce [1] framework with the underlying distributed file system, Hadoop Distributed File System (HDFS) [47], to perform HPDA computations in a scalable and fault-tolerant manner. MapReduce [6] has been proven as a viable model for processing hundreds or thousands of petabytes of data. This model enables developers to write highly parallel applications without dealing with many of the intricate details of data analytics and fault tolerance. The Apache Hadoop project [1] is a popular open source implementation of the MapReduce model from the Apache Software Foundation that has gained widespread acceptance, and is used in organizations world-wide. Hadoop relies on HDFS for data distribution and fault tolerance. HDFS is also the underlying file system for many other components, such as Hadoop database (HBase), an open-source implementation of Google's BigTable [4] and Apache Spark [2, 60], a fast and general in-memory cluster computing system for Big Data. While MapReduce has been highly successful in implementing large-scale batch jobs, it is a poor fit for low-latency interactive and iterative computations, such as machine learning and graph algorithms. As a result, the more recently designed in-memory high-speed and Directed Acyclic Graph (DAG) based data-processing framework, Apache Spark, has been stealing the limelight.

In order to process and analyze such large quantities of data in a timely and cost-efficient manner, thousands of servers with modern processing, networking, and storage architectures are required. Hence, efficient data-intensive processing middleware need to be designed to take full advantage of the advances in modern system architectures to deliver high performance. While Hadoop and Spark are gaining popularity for processing Big Data, their performance and scalability can still be improved significantly. At the same time, these middleware and the associated Big Data applications are not able to leverage the advanced features on modern HPC systems, which haven been deployed all over the world.

The design and deployment of HPC systems during the last decade has largely been fueled by the following three factors: (1) advances in multi-/many-core technologies and accelerators, (2) Remote Direct Memory Access

(RDMA)-enabled networking, and (3) Enterprise-grade Non-volatile Random-Access Memory (NVRAM) and Solid State Drives (SSDs). Modern HPC clusters with high compute-densities are being fueled by the use of multi-/many-core and accelerator technologies. The continued reduction in costs of hardware and the use of accelerators/co-processors (e.g., Intel Many Integrated Core (MIC) [18] and GPGPUs [10]) make it possible to design highly capable systems. Networking technology has also made rapid advances during recent years. RDMA-enabled commodity networking technologies like InfiniBand [17], RDMA over Converged Enhanced Ethernet (RoCE) [50], and 10/40-Gigabit Ethernet with Internet Wide Area RDMA Protocol (iWARP) [44] are allowing petascale systems to be designed with commodity cluster configurations at relatively modest costs. The RDMA technology allows a process to directly access remote memory locations without any involvement from the remote CPU, resulting in a much lower (practically zero) CPU load on the remote process for communication. The latest InfiniBand technology with RDMA provides less than 1.0 μs latency and 100 Gbps bandwidth between two nodes. Based on the November 2015 TOP500 [55] ranking, there are 235 InfiniBand clusters (47 %) in the top 500 supercomputers. Not only for host-to-host communication, the recently proposed GPUDirect RDMA (GDR) [37] technology can enable a direct path for data exchange between the GPU and a third-party peer device (e.g., network interfaces) using RDMA as well. Storage technology has also been rapidly growing during recent years. Enterprise-grade NVRAM and SSDs using the PCIe/NVMe (NVM Express) protocol which provide high data reliability and excellent performance [38] are beginning to be deployed in large-scale clusters and servers [30]. NVRAM and NVMe-SSDs far outperform hard disks due to their high bandwidth and fast random access. Compared to RAM, NVRAMs and SSDs provide a much larger capacity at a very low cost with substantially less power consumption. The above-mentioned advances in multi-/many-core, networking and storage technologies are providing novel features to design communication and I/O subsystems for modern and next-generation HPC systems. Middleware for HPC such as Message Passing Interface (MPI) [36] and Parallel File Systems (such as PVFS [39], Lustre [5] etc.) have been able to take advantage of the features of the modern technologies to push the envelope of high-performance computing to the multi-petaflop era.

However, the performance of current generation Big Data middleware remains unsatisfactory because several fundamental bottlenecks exist in current software designs. First of all, the use of the traditional BSD Sockets interface with two-sided (send/recv) communication semantics prevents the use of RDMA and associated advanced features of modern networking and I/O technologies. Second, the current internal designs for Big Data middleware are based on the traditional slow hard disk drive-based storage systems that can not exploit high-performance networks and protocols, unless used together with high-performance storage, such as NVRAMs and SSDs [52]. Besides, these systems do not exploit the modern trends of multi-/many-core architectures and accelerators. Furthermore, executing the current Big Data middleware on modern HPC systems leads to sub-optimal performance because of inability of the middleware to leverage high-throughput and large capacity parallel file systems, such as Lustre [5, 42]. All of the above-mentioned disparities are taking HPC and Big Data processing into *divergent trajectories*. This is leading to two different kinds of systems in the community—HPC systems for scientific computing and Hadoop systems for Big Data processing. Such an approach is neither economical nor productive. This situation has created the following fundamental research opportunities and challenges:

- Novel and high-performance communication and I/O runtimes need to be designed for Big Data processing while exploiting the features of modern multi-/many-core, networking, and storage technologies.
- Accelerate Big Data middleware (such as Apache Hadoop and Spark) by taking advantage of such runtimes to deliver performance and scalability on modern and next-generation HPC systems.
- All these enhanced designs should be done in a transparent manner so that Big Data applications can leverage the enhanced designs without any code changes.

Solving all of the above-mentioned fundamental challenges can put HPC and Big Data processing into a *convergent trajectory*. Such an approach has an immense potential to run Big Data applications on current and next-generation multi-Petaflop/Exaflop HPC systems with high performance and scalability. Big Data communities will directly benefit through this approach.

5.2 Overview of Apache Hadoop and Spark

5.2.1 Overview of Apache Hadoop Distributed File System

The Hadoop Distributed File System (HDFS) is a distributed file system which is used as the primary storage for Hadoop cluster. HDFS cluster consists of two types of nodes: NameNode and DataNode. The NameNode manages the file system namespace, maintains the file system tree and stores all the meta data. The DataNodes, on the other hand, act as the storage system for the HDFS files. HDFS divides files into blocks (e.g., 128 MB/block). Each block is stored as an independent file in the local file system of the DataNodes. HDFS usually replicates each block to three (default replication factor) DataNodes to guarantee data availability and fault-tolerance.

The HDFS client contacts the NameNode during file system operations. When the client wants to write a file to HDFS, it gets the block IDs and a list of DataNodes for each block from the NameNode. Each block is split into smaller packets and sent to the first DataNode in the pipeline. The first DataNode then replicates each of the packets to the subsequent DataNodes. A DataNode can receive packets from the previous DataNode while it is replicating data to the next DataNode. If the client is running on a DataNode, then the block will be first written to the local file system. When a client reads an HDFS file, it first contacts the NameNode to check its access permission and gets the block IDs and locations for each of the blocks. For each block belonging to the file, the client connects with the nearest DataNode and reads the block.

5.2.2 Overview of Apache Hadoop MapReduce

In a typical first generation Apache Hadoop MapReduce (MRv1) cluster, the NameNode has a JobTracker process, and all the DataNodes run one or more Task-Tracker processes. These processes, together, act as a master-slave architecture for a MapReduce job. A MapReduce job usually consists of three basic stages: map, shuffle/merge/sort and reduce. A single JobTracker and a number of TaskTrackers are responsible for successful completion of a MapReduce job. Each TaskTracker can launch several MapTasks, one per split of data. The map () function converts the original records into intermediate results and stores them onto the local file system. Each of these files is sorted into many data partitions, one per ReduceTask. The JobTracker then launches the ReduceTasks as soon as the map outputs are available from the MapTasks. TaskTracker can spawn several concurrent MapTasks or ReduceTasks. Each ReduceTask starts fetching the map outputs from the map output locations that are already completed. This stage is the shuffle/merge period, where the data from various map output locations are sent and received via HTTP requests and responses. A merge algorithm is run to merge these data to be used as an input for the reduce operation. The reduce tasks load and process the merged outputs using the user defined reduce () function, and the final results are stored in HDFS.

In a typical Hadoop-1.x (MRv1) cluster, the master (i.e., JobTracker) is responsible for accepting jobs from clients, job scheduling and resource management. On the other hand, Hadoop-2.x introduces YARN (Yet Another Resource Negotiator) [56], that decouples the resource management and scheduling functionality of the JobTracker in Hadoop-1.x, to improve scalability. There is a global Resource Manager (RM) responsible for assigning resources to all the jobs running on the Hadoop cluster. The Node Manager (NM) is similar to the TaskTracker in MRv1 with one NM running per node. For each application, the Application Master (AM) coordinates with the RM and NMs to execute the corresponding tasks.

5.2.3 Overview of Apache Spark

Apache Spark [2, 60, 61] is an open source data analytics cluster computing framework originally developed in the AMPLab at UC Berkeley. It was designed for iterative workloads such as machine learning algorithms that reuse a working set of data across parallel operations and interactive data mining. To optimize for these types of workloads, Spark employs the concept of in-memory cluster computing, where datasets can be cached in memory to reduce their access latency. Spark's architecture revolves around the concept of a Resilient Distributed Dataset (RDD) [61], which is a fault-tolerant collection of objects distributed across a set of nodes that can be operated on in parallel. These collections are resilient as they can be rebuilt if a portion of the dataset is lost. The tasks run by the executor are made up of two types of operations, supported by the RDDs: an *action* which performs a computation on a dataset and returns a value to the main program and a *transformation*, which defines a new dataset from an existing dataset. The *transformation* operation specifies the processing dependency Directed Acyclic Graph (DAG) among RDDs. These dependencies come in two forms [61]: *narrow* dependencies (e.g., Map, Filter), where each partition of the parent RDD is used by at most one partition of the child RDD and *wide* dependencies (e.g., GroupByKey, Join), where multiple child partitions may depend on the same partition of the parent RDD. Evidently, *wide* dependencies involve data shuffle across the network. Thus, *wide* dependencies are communication-intensive and can turn out to be a performance bottleneck for Spark applications.

Spark applications run as independent sets of processes on a cluster, coordinated by the *SparkContext* object in your main program called the *driver program*. On a cluster, *SparkContext* can connect to several types of cluster managers, either Standalone Cluster Manager, Apache Mesos or Hadoop YARN. In stand-alone mode, the environment consists of one Spark Master and several Spark Worker processes. Once the cluster manager allocates resources across applications, executors on the worker nodes are acquired to run computations and store data for the application. Finally, *SparkContext* sends tasks for the executors to run. At the end of the execution, actions are executed at the workers and results are returned to the *driver program*. Currently, Spark already has API support for programming with Scala, Java, Python, and R. It also has many higher-level tools including Spark SQL [62] for SQL and DataFrames, MLlib [2] for machine learning, GraphX [13] for graph processing, and Spark Streaming [3] for stream processing.

5.3 Overview of High-Performance Interconnects and Storage Architecture on Modern HPC Clusters

HPC has found enormous applications in the scientific domain, industrial and business analytics. The design and deployment of HPC systems comprises of two important aspects: network and storage.

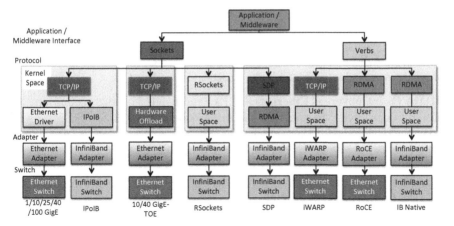

Fig. 5.1 Overview of high-performance interconnects and protocols

5.3.1 Overview of High-Performance Interconnects and Protocols

During the past decade, the HPC field has witnessed a transition to commodity clusters connected with modern interconnects such as InfiniBand and 10/40 Gigabit Ethernet/RoCE/iWARP. Figure 5.1 illustrates the various high-performance interconnects and protocols.

5.3.1.1 Overview of High Speed Ethernet

1/10/25/40/100 GigE Traditionally, server connections in data centers used 1 GigE interconnects. With recent enhancements in CPU performance and I/O, the 1 GigE network has increasingly become the application and workload performance bottleneck. Recently, data center architectures are upgrading to a combination of 10 GigE connections. Low latency is critical for HPC applications and financial trading environments, and 10 GigE offers a compelling improvement in end-to-end latency. While 10 GigE is still paving its way into the data centers, the demand for higher bandwidth and faster data transfer rates have made way for 40 GigE and 100 GigE. Hardware accelerated versions of TCP/IP are available. These are called TCP Offload Engines (TOE), which use hardware offload. The benefits of TOE are to maintain full socket streaming semantics and implement them efficiently in hardware. Recently, 25 GigE was introduced to provide 2.5X the performance of 10 GigE Ethernet, making it a cost-effective upgrade to the 10 GigE infrastructure.

iWARP (Internet Wide Area RDMA Protocol) In an effort to improve bandwidth in data-center environments that widely use 10/40 GigE, 10 GigE was standardized. To support increasing speeds of network hardware, it was not completely feasible to only offer traditional sockets interface and there was a need to reduce memory copies while transferring messages. Towards that effort, iWARP [44] standard was introduced. iWARP is very similar to the verbs layer used by InfiniBand, with the exception of requiring a connection manager. The OpenFabrics network stack provides an unified interface for both iWARP and InfiniBand.

RDMA Over Converged Ethernet (RoCE) InfiniBand has started making inroads into the commercial domain with the recent convergence around RDMA over Converged Enhanced Ethernet (RoCE) [50]. RoCE is a network protocol that allows remote direct memory access over an Ethernet network.

5.3.1.2   Overview of InfiniBand

InfiniBand [17] is an industry standard switched fabric that is designed for interconnecting nodes in HPC clusters. Available as low-cost PCI-Express devices, these interconnects provide not only high bandwidth (up to 100 Gbps) and low latencies (<1 μs), but also help server scalability by using very little CPU and reduced memory copies for network intensive operations. In addition, they provide advanced features, such as RDMA, that enable the design of novel communication protocols and libraries. This feature allows software to remotely read memory contents of another remote process without any software involvement at the remote side. This feature is very powerful and can be used to implement high-performance communication protocols. The InfiniBand specification clearly marks the duties of hardware (such as Host Channel Adapters or HCAs) and the software. The interaction between the software and the HCA is carried out by the verbs layer, which is described in the following section.

Infiniband Verbs Layer Upper-level software uses an interface called Verbs to access the functionality provided by HCAs and other network equipment (such as switches). This is illustrated in Fig. 5.1 (right-most column). Verbs that are used to transfer data are completely OS-bypassed. The verbs interface is a low-level communication interface that follows the Queue Pair model. Communication end-points are required to establish a queue pair between themselves. Each queue pair has a certain number of work queue elements. Upper-level software places a work request on the queue pair that is then processed by the HCA. When a work element is completed, it is placed in the completion queue. Upper-level software can detect completion by polling the completion queue. There are Reliably Connected (RC) queue pairs that provide reliable transmission (retransmissions after packet losses are performed by the HCA). These RC queue pairs need to be established uniquely for each communicating pair. The Unreliable Datagram (UD) queue pair does not provide reliable transmission although it has a significant memory advantage—only one UD QP is capable of communicating with all remote processes. Additionally there are other types of InfiniBand transport protocols such as Extended Reliable Connected (XRC), Dynamic Connected (DC) [51], etc. Applications can achieve the best communication performance through RDMA operations at the verbs-level.

InfiniBand IP Layer InfiniBand also provides a driver for implementing the IP layer. This exposes the InfiniBand device as just another network interface available from the system with an IP address. Typically, these IB devices are presented as ib0, ib1, and so on. This interface is presented in Fig. 5.1 (second column from the left, named IPoIB). It does not provide OS-bypass. This layer is often called "IP-over-IB" or IPoIB in short. There are two modes available for IPoIB. One is the datagram mode, implemented over UD, and the other is connected mode, implemented over RC. The connected mode offers better performance since it leverages reliability from the hardware.

InfiniBand Sockets Direct Protocol Sockets Direct Protocol (SDP) [12] is a byte-stream transport protocol that closely mimics TCP socket's stream semantics. It is an industry-standard specification that utilizes advanced capabilities provided by the network stacks to achieve high performance without requiring modifications to existing sockets-based applications. SDP is layered on top of IB message-oriented transfer model. The mapping of the byte-stream protocol to the underlying message-oriented semantics was designed to transfer application data by one of two methods: through intermediate private buffers (using buffer copy) or directly between application buffers (zero-copy) using RDMA. Typically, there is a threshold of message size above which zero-copy is used. Using SDP, complete OS-bypass can be achieved. SDP can also be used in the buffered mode.

RSockets RSockets is a protocol over RDMA that supports a socket-level API for applications. RSockets APIs are intended to match the behavior of corresponding socket calls. RSockets are contained as a wrapper library in the OFED Infiniband software stack, with near optimal speed over InfiniBand networks. The wrapper library method can in principle be used on any system with dynamic linking. The performance improvements gained by scaling out to increase parallelism using RSockets over Infiniband is significantly higher than what can be achieved using regular Ethernet networks.

InfiniBand has been widely used in TOP500 supercomputers [55]. Majority of HPC applications and middleware (such as MPI [36]) take advantage of InfiniBand either via native IB verbs, RoCE, or iWARP, while traditionally, Big Data middleware run over clusters with 10 GigE, TCP/IP TOE, or leverage InfiniBand via IPoIB. With the rise of high-performance data analytics, several efforts are being made to bridge the gap between HPC and Big Data by leveraging advanced features like RDMA to enhance communication.

5.3.2 Overview of High-Performance Storage

Most modern HPC clusters such as TACC Stampede [53], SDSC Comet [45], etc. are equipped with heterogeneous storage devices such as, RAM, SSD, HDD, and high-performance parallel file systems such as Lustre. Moreover, the traditional Beowulf architecture model [48, 49] has been followed for building these clusters, where the compute nodes are provisioned with either a disk-less or a limited-capacity local storage, and a sub-cluster of dedicated I/O nodes with parallel file systems.

Solid State Drives (SSDs) Storage technology has been rapidly growing over the recent years. Conventional hard drives (HDDs) are constrained by the mechanical rotating disk, which results in poor random access performance and excessively high power consumption [8, 11]. This has led flash memory (electronic-erasable non-volatile memory) to pave its way into HPC clusters, due to its compact factor and low power consumption. SATA SSDs are being widely used due to their low cost, and high-performance as compared to HDDs. While they are low cost, the SATA-based interface limits the capacity of the bus that transfers data from the SSDs to the processor. The current generation of PCIe flash SSDs have thus become very popular in modern HPC clusters due to their high bandwidth and fast random access. While they provide unmatchable performance, the adoption of PCIe SSDs is inhibited by different implementations and unique drivers. This has led to the definition of the NVM Express standard (NVMe) [38] to enable faster adoption and interoperability of PCIe SSDs. The benefits of NVMe SSDs are reduced latency, increased Input/Output Operations Per Second (IOPS), lower power consumption, and durability.

Non-volatile Random-Access Memory (NVRAM) NVRAM is random-access memory that retains its information even when power is turned off (non-volatile). It provides high data reliability and byte addressability, which makes them excellent contenders to co-exist with RAM and SSDs in large-scale clusters and server deployments.

Shared Parallel File Systems Parallel file systems are a type of clustered file system that spread data across multiple storage nodes, usually for redundancy or performance. Data is distributed across multiple servers and can be concurrently accessed by multiple tasks. Lustre [5], PVFS [39], etc. are shared file systems that provide fast and scalable data storage. The Lustre file system is an open-source, parallel file system that supports many requirements of leadership class HPC environments. The Parallel Virtual File System (PVFS) is an open source parallel file system designed for large-scale cluster computing.

5.4 Challenges in Accelerating Big Data Processing on Modern HPC Clusters

As indicated in Sects. 5.1 and 5.3, technology advances in multi-/many-core, accelerator, networking, and storage architecture on modern HPC clusters are providing novel features to design communication and I/O subsystems for accelerating Big Data applications and middleware. These features and the associated performance and scalability benefits are already being harnessed by high-performance computing

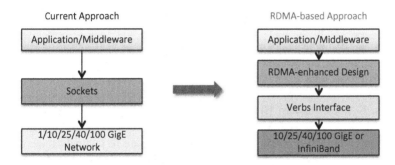

Fig. 5.2 Accelerating big data processing through RDMA

middleware (such as the MPI and Parallel File Systems). However, Big Data processing middleware have not been able to take advantage of the capabilities of these technologies in a significant manner, even though these technologies have been available in the market for a long time as commodity components at low cost.

Most of the current generation Big Data processing middleware and applications, including the driving ones (like Apache Hadoop and Spark) mentioned in Sect. 5.2, use the traditional BSD Sockets interface with two-sided (send/recv) communication, as shown in the left-hand side in Fig. 5.2. The TCP/IP-based sockets communication incurs overheads on both the sender and the receiver side. They can run on high-performance networks like InfiniBand using the IPoIB [20] interface, as introduced in Sect. 5.3. However, this approach has a significant overhead and exploits only a fraction of the maximum performance of the underlying networks. This interface cannot use the RDMA features of modern InfiniBand and iWARP/RoCE networks to achieve one-sided communication with low CPU overhead and overlap of computation with communication. There have been attempts to design intermediate protocols (such as Sockets Direct Protocol) and accelerated sockets [28] to use RDMA. However, these protocols and interfaces still do not fully exploit the *bare-metal* performance of the modern 56/100 Gbps networks. These interfaces do not have the flexibility to exploit the use of additional features (such as overlap, atomics and virtual lanes for QoS, etc.) to enhance the capabilities of the next-generation Big Data processing middleware and applications. Alternatively, recent studies [22, 25, 32, 34, 40, 41] have shed light on the possible performance improvements for different Big Data processing middleware using RDMA-enhanced designs with native InfiniBand and RoCE support at the verbs-level. Such an approach, as shown in the right-hand side in Fig. 5.2, has been emerging and is seen to be an effective way to design high-performance Big Data processing middleware and applications on modern HPC clusters.

Looking from the storage angle, most of the modern HPC clusters follow a hybrid topological solution of the traditional Beowulf architecture [48, 49] with separate I/O service nodes. The architecture of these clusters opens up the possibility of keeping lean compute nodes, with a lightweight operating system and limited storage capacity [9], connected to a sub-cluster of dedicated I/O nodes with enhanced parallel file systems, such as Lustre, to provide fast and scalable solutions. Each of the compute nodes has small local storage as well as Lustre client to read/write data to Lustre. Due to the limited amount of local disk-space per node, default Big Data middleware that rely heavily on local storage cannot be efficiently deployed on HPC clusters, leading to sub-optimal solutions in leadership-class HPC systems. Besides, modern HPC clusters are often equipped with heterogeneous storage devices such as RAM, NVRAM, SATA-/PCIe-/NVMe-SSD, and HDD. It becomes a critical problem for Big Data middleware to take advantage of the heterogeneous storage options in the most optimized manner for data-intensive applications running over HPC Clusters. All these fundamental issues facing in the Big Data community lead to the following broad challenges:

1. What are the requirements and bottlenecks of current Big Data middleware for using the emerging technologies available on modern HPC clusters?
2. Can the bottlenecks be alleviated with new designs by taking advantage of modern HPC technologies?
3. What are the communication and I/O characteristics of driving Big Data applications and benchmarks and how they can be extracted and utilized to enhance Big Data middleware?
4. Can RDMA-enabled high-performance interconnects benefit Big Data processing?
5. Can modern HPC Clusters with high-performance storage systems (e.g., SSD and parallel file systems) benefit Big Data applications?
6. Can current Big Data middleware be re-designed and enhanced with the advanced communication and I/O runtime?
7. What kind of benefits (in terms of performance and scalability) can be achieved by the enhanced designs for Big Data middleware and applications on modern HPC clusters?

To address these challenges, many novel research work and designs have been proposed in the literature recently. This chapter will briefly introduce case studies related to accelerating Big Data processing on modern HPC clusters in next section. These case studies focus on enhancing the three most popular Big Data middleware (HDFS, MapReduce, and Spark) by leveraging HPC technologies.

5.5 Case Studies of Accelerating Big Data Processing on Modern HPC Clusters

5.5.1 Accelerating HDFS with RDMA

Hadoop Distributed File System (HDFS) is a communication-intensive framework because of its distributed nature. All existing communication protocols [1] of HDFS are layered on top of sockets over TCP/IP. Due to the byte stream communication nature of TCP/IP, multiple data copies are required, which results in poor performance in terms of both latency and throughput. Consequently, even though the underlying system is equipped with high performance interconnects such as InfiniBand, HDFS cannot fully utilize the hardware capability and obtain peak performance. Therefore, the high performance HDFS design [22, 23, 25] incorporates the following features:

RDMA-Based Communication The high performance HDFS design [22] uses RDMA for HDFS write and replication via the Java Native Interface (JNI) mechanism, whereas all other HDFS operations go over Java-Socket. The JNI layer bridges Java-based HDFS with communication library written in native C for RDMA operations. This design supports dynamic connection creation along with connection sharing for ensuring low overhead in connection management. In this design, the existing HDFS architecture is kept intact.

Parallel Replication By default, HDFS supports pipelined replication to maximize throughput. HDFS was designed to run on commodity hardware over slow networks. In the presence of high performance interconnects, the network bandwidth is no longer a limitation. Therefore, the high performance HDFS design incorporates parallel replication [23] that can send all three replicas in parallel from the client to the DataNodes.

SEDA-Based Overlapping in Different Stages of HDFS Write HDFS write operation can be divided into four stages: (1) Read, (2) Packet Processing, (3) Replication, and (4) I/O. After data is received via RDMA, the data is first read into a Java I/O stream. The received packet is then replicated after some processing operations. The data packet is also written to the disk file. In the default architecture of HDFS, all these stages are handled sequentially by a single thread per block. Whereas, SOR-HDFS [25] incorporates a Staged Event-Driven Architecture (SEDA) [59] based approach to maximize overlapping among different stages of HDFS write operation. In this design, each of the stages is handled by different thread pools and thus the operations among different stages can overlap at packet level as well as block level. SOR-HDFS provides overalpping among data read, processing, replication, and I/O phases for the same block. The proposed design also preserves overlapping among communication and other phases of HDFS write via back-to-back data transfer. In this way, in addition to providing task-level parallelism, SOR-HDFS achieves overlapping among various stages of the same block.

5.5.2 Accelerating HDFS with Heterogeneous Storage

In modern HPC clusters, each node may be equipped with different types of storage devices like RAM Disk, SSD, and HDD. A high-performance HDFS design should be able to fully take advantage of these available storage resources in the most efficient manner. In the Triple-H [26] design, each HDFS DataNode runs a RAM

Disk and SSD-based buffer-cache on top of the disk-based storage system. It also uses the parallel file system (i.e., Lustre) installation in HPC clusters for storing data from Hadoop applications. Triple-H can run in two different modes: Default and Lustre-Integrated. The main features of this design are:

Buffering and Caching Through Hybrid Buffer-Cache In the Triple-H design, the data written to (read from) HDFS is buffered (cached) in RAM Disk which is the primary buffer-cache in Triple-H. The size of the buffer-cache is enlarged by using SSD. Triple-H hides the cost of disk access during HDFS Write and Read by placing the data in this buffer-cache.

Storage Volume Selection and Data Placement through On-Demand Weight Adjustment Triple-H calculates the available space in the storage layer based on the placement policy selection. If there is sufficient space available for the file, it is stored in the requested medium. Otherwise, the weight of the replica is adjusted and placed in the next level of the storage hierarchy. However, for each replica, it remembers the weight assigned by the Placement Policy Selector so that whenever there is space available in the requested level, the file can be moved there.

Fault-Tolerance of RAM Disk Data Through SSD-Based Staging Data stored in RAM Disk cannot sustain power/node failures. Therefore, each data placed into the RAM Disk is asynchronously flushed to an SSD-based staging layer.

Data Movement Through Eviction/Promotion Manager This module is responsible for evicting cold data and making space for hot data in the buffer-cache. It also promotes the hot data from SSD/HDD/Lustre to RAM Disk/SSD/HDD. Since the DFSClient reads each file sequentially, blocks of the same file are moved during the same window of data movement.

Efficient Data Placement Policies Data placement policies play a very important role in achieving high performance for HDFS. Triple-H has three types of placement policies; these are:

- **Greedy Placement**: In this policy, the incoming data is placed in the high-performance storage layer in a greedy manner by the DataNodes. So, as long as there is space available in the RAM Disk-based primary buffer-cache, the DataNode writes all the data there. Then it switches to the next level of storage based on SSD and so on. Triple-H follows a hybrid replication scheme through which the first replica of a file is placed in the RAM Disk-based buffer-cache in a greedy manner while the other two are stored in the SSD-based secondary buffer-cache. Alternatively, two replicas can be placed to RAM Disk and the other one in SSD.
- **Load-Balanced Placement**: This policy spreads the amount of I/O across multiple storage devices in a balanced manner. The I/O load is balanced between RAM Disk and SSD. Both greedy placement and load-balanced placement are performance-sensitive policies.

- **Storage-Sensitive Placement**: With this policy, one replica is stored in local storage (RAM Disk or SSD) and one copy is written to Lustre through the parallel file system. This policy reduces local storage requirements.

5.5.3 Accelerating HDFS with Lustre Through Key-Value Store-Based Burst Buffer System

Although parallel file systems are optimized for concurrent access by large-scale applications, write overheads can still dominate the run times of data-intensive applications. Besides, there are applications that require significant amount of reads from the underlying file system. The performances of such applications are highly influenced by the data locality in the Hadoop cluster [26, 58]. As a result, applications that have equal amounts of reads and writes suffer from poor write performance when run on top of HDFS; whereas, because of inadequate locality, read performs sub-optimally while these applications run entirely on top of Lustre. Such applications need a new design that efficiently integrates these two file systems and can offer the combined benefits from both of these architectures. In order to address these issues, a Memcached-based burst buffer system that can be integrated with HDFS and parallel file systems like Lustre was proposed in [24, 27].

Key-Value Store-Based Burst Buffer System RDMA-based Memcached [15] is used to design a burst buffer system. HDFS sends data in the form of key-value pairs to RDMA-based Memcached servers through RDMA-based libMemcached client library. The key is formed by appending the packet sequence number with the corresponding block name and the value is the data packet. Thus, all the packets belonging to the same block have the same key prefix (block name). The concept of HDFS blocks is maintained in the Memcached layer by modifying the libMemcached hash function. Instead of hashing on the entire key, it hashes based on the block name prefix of the key. In this way, all the data packets belonging to the same block go to the same Memcached server. The Memcached server side stores the data sent from the HDFS layer in the in-memory slabs. Data can also be read by the HDFS clients from the server. The burst buffer functionalities are introduced in the Memcached server by persisting the incoming data to SSD and sending the data to the parallel file system.

Schemes to Integrate HDFS with Lustre Through Burst Buffer System HDFS is integrated with Luster through the burst buffer layer. Considering the aspects of data locality and fault-tolerance, this design supports three different modes:

- **Asynchronous Lustre Write (ALW)**: In this scheme, HDFS client writes one copy of data to the local storage on the DataNode and the other copy is transferred to the Memcached server. The DataNode forwards the data to the parallel file system in an asynchronous manner to hide the latency of shared file system access. The burst buffer server ensures data persistence by synchronously writing each data to SSD. The map and reduce tasks of a MapReduce job, read data from the local storage whenever possible to achieve good locality. Otherwise, data is read from the in-memory slabs of the Memcached servers.

- **Asynchronous Disk Write (ADW):** In this scheme, HDFS client writes one copy of data to the local disks on the DataNode asynchronously. The second copy of data is sent to the Memcached server. This scheme assumes that the Memcached servers do not have any local SSD. Also, this scheme prioritizes data fault-tolerance over write performance. Therefore, the Memcached based burst buffer layer writes data synchronously to Lustre. The map and reduce tasks of a MapReduce job, read data from the local storage or Memcached.

- **Bypass Local Disk (BLD):** This scheme places one copy of data to RAM Disks on the compute nodes in a greedy manner. When RAM Disk usage threshold is reached, data is forwarded to the Memcached server and stored to the in-memory slabs. The other copy of data is synchronously written to Lustre. In this scheme, the key-value store is used as a buffer so that the stored data can be read at memory speed.

5.5.4 Accelerating Hadoop MapReduce with RDMA

The default MapReduce framework employs bulk data transmission over the underlying interconnect and also a large number of disk operations during shuffle and merge phases, that introduce performance bottlenecks on modern HPC clusters. Different enhancements have been proposed in the literature [40, 57] that address these issues and present RDMA-based shuffle inside MapReduce. However, without an efficient execution pipeline among different job phases in MapReduce, the RDMA-based shuffle design cannot extract the full performance potential from modern HPC clusters. To overcome this, a high-performance design of MapReduce has been proposed. This design is named as *HOMR* [41] (*H*ybrid *O*verlapping in *M*ap*R*educe), which not only brings RDMA-based data transmission into the framework, but also incorporates advanced features.

RDMA-Based Shuffle In the default MapReduce framework, shuffle uses HTTP for map output data transmission. In HOMR, this shuffling of data is implemented over RDMA. RDMA Copiers send requests to TaskTrackers for recently completed map output data. RDMA Responders in TaskTrackers receive those requests and respond back to ReduceTasks.

In-Memory Merge In HOMR, entire merge operation can take place in-memory, which reduces significant number of disk operations in the ReduceTask. As in RDMA, data can be retrieved much faster, it creates the opportunity to transfer one map output file in multiple communication steps instead of one. By doing this, the merge phase can start as soon as some key-value pairs from all map output files reach at the reducer side.

Overlapping of Map, Shuffle, and Merge Unlike initial RDMA-based designs [40, 57], HOMR employs bulk data transfer during early shuffle stage. Because of this reason, merge also starts with shuffle and keeps building up the priority queue as well as merges newly shuffled data to the queue. In this way, as soon as maps complete their executions, merge phase almost has entire shuffled data merged and ready for reduce. This helps to start reduce immediately after the last map's first data packet is merged to the priority queue.

Overlapping of Shuffle, Merge and Reduce For default MapReduce, merge starts immediately with shuffle. But reduce cannot start until all data has been merged and kept in disk. However, HOMR can start reduce operation as soon as first merge process generates a sorted output. Thus, it can overlap shuffle, merge, and reduce operations through efficient pipelining among these phases.

Prefetching and Caching of Map Output HOMR implements an efficient caching technique for the intermediate data residing in map output files. For a large number of ReduceTasks, more requests for map output files arrive to a single TaskTracker, that can take over the I/O bandwidth in TaskTracker side. So, an efficient cache implementation can avoid massive disk read operations in TaskTracker.

Advanced Shuffle Algorithms In addition to the default shuffle strategy, HOMR also supports advanced shuffle algorithms. Through these algorithms, each map output file is assigned a weight that signifies the importance of this data for performing an in-memory merge. Based on the weight value, the algorithm either chooses to shuffle the entire map output file at once or a fraction of the output file after dividing it into multiple packets.

Dynamic Adjustment of Shuffle HOMR can dynamically adjust the weights statically assigned by the shuffle algorithms. As soon as it detects some priority map outputs based on the merge progress, it quickly adjusts the weights of those map locations. During subsequent shuffle for these map locations, TaskTracker sends more packets according to the adjusted weight assigned by ReduceTask.

With all these features, HOMR can achieve maximum possible overlapping across different phases of job execution. Figure 5.3 differentiates the overlapping in different phases for default MapReduce and HOMR. The implicit barrier presented in the figure highlights the fact that the map and reduce phases cannot overlap with

Fig. 5.3 Overlapping of different phases for default MapReduce (*left*) and HOMR (*right*)

each other because of the inherent design choices of the framework. With all the design enhancements, HOMR can execute much faster than default MapReduce framework on modern HPC clusters.

5.5.5 Accelerating MapReduce with Lustre

As indicated in Sect. 5.4, the compute nodes on most modern HPC clusters only have a limited-capacity local storage. At the same time, they are often connected to a sub-cluster of dedicated I/O nodes with enhanced parallel file systems, such as Lustre, which can provide fast and scalable data storage solutions. This architecture is not naively conducive for default MapReduce. In this perspective, advanced designs [42, 43] for MapReduce have been proposed that introduce Lustre as the underlying file system. MapReduce can be deployed in two different ways to run on top of parallel file systems based on the intermediate data directories. The intermediate data directories can be configured with the local disks similar to a MapReduce cluster on top of HDFS. In the other way, Lustre can provide both the intermediate data directory space as well as the underlying distributed file system space. For the first one, advanced MapReduce designs, such as HOMR [41] can exploit the benefits from HPC systems in a similar fashion as outlined in Sect. 5.5.4. For the second deployment, advanced shuffle strategies are proposed in [43] and they are described as follows:

Lustre Read-Based Shuffle This shuffle strategy is based on Lustre file system read/write operations. Since the data generated from completed maps reside in the underlying global file system, direct read operations from the file system necessarily complete the shuffle process for the ReduceTask. To facilitate this, the design proposed in [43] can use the Lustre client in the local node to read a particular file residing in the underlying global file system. However, since HOMR can assign weights for each completed map output, it maintains a limit of how much data can be read from a particular map output file. This ensures the availability of data from each completed map location during the merge process as well as minimizes the possibility of swapping out of memory. Since each ReduceTask reads the data from the global file system by itself in this shuffle strategy, the pre-fetch and caching mechanism for these map outputs is kept disabled.

RDMA-Based Shuffle This shuffle strategy is based on RDMA-based communication among the NodeManagers and the containers running ReduceTasks, as outlined in Sect. 5.5.4. For fast response during shuffle, pre-fetching and caching of data is kept enabled in this approach.

Dynamic Adaptation Between Shuffle Strategies Both the shuffle strategies employ a static way to choose between RDMA and Lustre Read based shuffle. However, it may not be an intelligent solution to specifically choose one over the other for all submitted jobs in a typical HPC cluster. For example, if several jobs are running concurrently, the Lustre read and write throughput may vary significantly. Also, depending on the Lustre read size granularity, each read operation may provide variable performance. Similarly, if all jobs are trying to utilize RDMA for shuffle, it may saturate the network bandwidth very fast. To overcome this by utilizing both RDMA and Lustre in the most efficient manner, authors in [43] introduce dynamic adaptation in choosing shuffle policy. Through this approach, the shuffle policy is adapted based on the underlying Lustre performance at run time and it can achieve significant benefits in different HPC environments.

5.5.6 Accelerating Apache Spark with RDMA

As mentioned in Sect. 5.2.3, when wide dependencies exist between RDDs, it will cause a global many-to-many data shuffle process in Spark, which is a communication-intensive process. The default Apache Spark design provides two approaches to perform data shuffle. The first is Java NIO based data shuffle, and the second is based on the Netty [54] communication substrate. In the latest Apache Spark [2], the Netty based shuffle is the default approach. Both Java NIO and Netty still rely on sockets-based send/receive two-sided communication model, which could not fully take advantage of the performance benefits provided by high-performance interconnects [34]. This has become the major performance bottleneck for Apache Spark on modern HPC clusters. In order to address this, a high-performance RDMA-based shuffle design has been proposed in [34]. However, without an efficient buffer and connection management and communication optimization in Spark, the RDMA-based shuffle design cannot extract the full performance potential from modern HPC clusters. A high-performance design of RDMA-based Apache Spark in [34] mainly involves advanced features as follows:

SEDA-Based Data Shuffle Architecture High-throughput is one of the major goals in designing data shuffle systems. Staged Event-Driven Architecture (SEDA) [59] is widely used for achieving high throughput. The basic principle of SEDA is to decompose a complex processing logic into a set of stages connected by queues. A dedicated thread pool will be in charge of processing events on the corresponding queue for each stage. By performing admission controls on these event queues, the whole system achieves high throughput through maximally overlapping different processing stages. Efforts on improving Hadoop components (e.g., HDFS, RPC) [25, 32] have also shown the SEDA approach is applicable for RDMA-based data processing systems. Using SEDA, the whole shuffle process can be divided into multiple stages and each stage can overlap with the others by using events and thread pools. In this manner, the design can achieve the default task-level parallelism in Apache Spark, as well as overlapping within block processing with SEDA shuffle engine.

Efficient RDMA Connection Management and Sharing As shown in RDMA-based designs for Hadoop [22, 40], the overhead of the RDMA connection establishment is a little higher than that of connection establishment with sockets. In order to alleviate this overhead, an advanced connection management scheme is needed to reduce the number of connections. Apache Spark uses multi-threading approach to support multi-task execution in a single JVM, by default, which provides a good opportunity to share resources. This inspires an interesting idea to share the RDMA connection among different tasks as long as they want to transfer data to the same destination. The connection sharing mechanism will help to significantly reduce the number of total connections, which further reduces the resource usage overall. In this way, a good trade-off between resource utilization and performance can be achieved.

Non-blocking Data Transfer With connection sharing, each connection may be used by multiple tasks (threads) to transfer data concurrently. In this case, packets over the same communication lane will go to different entities in both server and client sides. In order to achieve high throughput, a large data block can be divided into a sequence of chunks and be sent out in a non-blocking fashion. This can improve the network bandwidth utilization by offloading more packets to the NIC. Through non-blocking chunk-based data transfer, the design can efficiently work with the connection sharing mechanism.

Off-JVM-Heap Buffer Management In RDMA-based data shuffle engine, a pool of buffers will be used for both sending and receiving data, at any end-point. The buffer pool is constructed from off-JVM-heap buffers that are also mapped to the Java/Scala layer as shadow buffers. These buffers are registered for RDMA communication. Having a pool of off-JVM-heap buffers is reasonable for high-performance and robust handling of data packets in event-driven communication architecture, while providing scope for more advanced communication features. Furthermore, off-JVM-heap based buffer management also has the potential to reduce Java Garbage Collection (GC) overhead compared to the scheme that has all these buffers inside JVM heap.

5.6 High-Performance Big Data (HiBD) Project

The High-Performance Big Data (HiBD) project [15] is designed and developed by the Network-Based Computing Laboratory of The Ohio State University. As of Feb '16, the HiBD packages are being used by more than 145 organizations worldwide across 20 countries to accelerate Big Data applications. More than 14,900 downloads have taken place from this project's site. The main objective of the HiBD project is to design high-performance Big Data middleware that can leverage HPC technologies. The HiBD project currently contains the following packages:

- **RDMA-based Apache Spark (RDMA-Spark)**: This is a high performance design with native InfiniBand and RoCE support at the verbs level for Apache

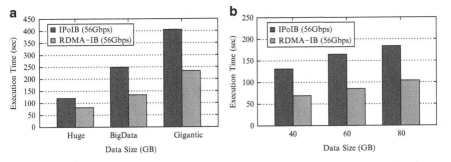

Fig. 5.4 Performance improvement of RDMA-based designs for Apache Spark and Hadoop on SDSC Comet cluster. (**a**) PageRank with RDMA-Spark. (**b**) Sort with RDMA-Hadoop-2.x

Spark. It supports multiple advanced features such as RDMA-based data shuffle, SEDA-based shuffle architecture, efficient connection management and sharing, non-blocking and chunk-based data transferring, off-JVM-heap buffer management, etc. The plug-in based approach with SEDA-/RDMA-based designs provides both high performance and high productivity. As shown in Fig. 5.4a, the RDMA-based design for Apache Spark (denoted by "RDMA-IB") improves the average job execution time of HiBench [14] PageRank on 64 SDSC Comet [45] worker nodes by 40–46 % compared to IPoIB (56 Gbps). These experiments are performed with full subscription of cores, so that 64-node jobs run with a total of 1536 maps and 1536 reduces. Spark is run in Standalone mode. SSD is used for Spark local and work data. More detailed configurations and numbers can be found in [15].

- **RDMA-based Apache Hadoop 2.x (RDMA-Hadoop-2.x):** This is a high-performance design with native InfiniBand and RoCE support at the verbs level for Apache Hadoop 2.x. This software is a derivative of Apache Hadoop 2.x and is compliant with Apache Hadoop 2.x and Hortonworks Data Platform (HDP) APIs and applications. Figure 5.5 presents a high-level architecture of RDMA for Apache Hadoop. In this package, many different modes have been designed that can be enabled/disabled to obtain performance benefits for different kinds of applications in different Hadoop environments. This package can be configured to run MapReduce jobs on top of HDFS as well as Lustre.

Following are the different modes that are included in RDMA-Hadoop-2.x package.

HHH: Heterogeneous storage devices with hybrid replication schemes are supported in this mode of operation to have better fault-tolerance as well as performance. This mode is enabled by **default** in the package.

HHH-M: A high-performance in-memory based setup has been introduced in this package that can be utilized to perform all I/O operations in-memory and obtain as much performance benefit as possible.

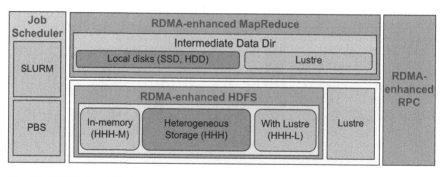

Fig. 5.5 RDMA-based Hadoop architecture and its different modes

HHH-L: With parallel file systems integrated, HHH-L mode can take advantage of the Lustre available in the cluster.

MapReduce over Lustre, with/without local disks: In addition to HDFS based solutions, this package also provides support to run MapReduce jobs on top of Lustre alone. Here, two different modes are introduced: with local disks and without local disks.

Running with Slurm and PBS: Provides built-in scripts to support deploying RDMA for Apache Hadoop 2.x package with Slurm and PBS in different running modes (HHH, HHH-M, HHH-L, and MapReduce over Lustre).

With above-mentioned advanced designs, the performance of Apache Hadoop 2.x is improved significantly. The package is also easy-to-use on HPC clusters. As shown in Fig. 5.4b, the RDMA-based design for Apache Hadoop 2.x (denoted by "RDMA-IB") improves the job execution time of Sort on 16 SDSC Comet worker nodes by up to 48 % compared to IPoIB (56 Gbps). These experiments are performed with a total of 64 maps and 28 reduces. HDFS block size is kept to 256 MB. The NameNode runs in a different node of the Hadoop cluster. 70 % of the RAM disk is used for HHH data storage. More detailed configurations and numbers can be found in [15]. RDMA-based Apache Hadoop 2.x package has been deployed on SDSC Comet cluster, where users can either use built-in scripts as mentioned above or myHadoop [29] scripts to launch Hadoop jobs.

• **RDMA-Based Apache Hadoop 1.x (RDMA-Hadoop-1.x):** This is a high-performance design with native InfiniBand and RoCE support at the verbs level for Apache Hadoop 1.x. This software is a derivative of Apache Hadoop 1.x and is compliant with Apache Hadoop 1.x APIs and applications. It supports multiple advanced features such as RDMA-based HDFS write, RDMA-based HDFS replication, parallel replication support in HDFS, RDMA-based shuffle in MapReduce, in-memory merge, advanced optimization in overlapping among different phases, RDMA-based Hadoop RPC, etc. Through all these advanced designs, the performance of Apache Hadoop 1.x is improved significantly.

• **RDMA-based Memcached (RDMA-Memcached):** This is a high-performance design with native InfiniBand and RoCE support at the verbs level for

Memcached [35] and libMemcached [31]. This software is a derivative of Memcached and libMemcached and is compliant with libMemcached APIs and applications. It supports multiple advanced features such as RDMA-based key-value pair operations, SSD-assisted hybrid memory, etc. Through RDMA-based design, the performance of key-value pair operations gets significantly improved, while the SSD-assisted hybrid memory provides increased cache capacity.

- **OSU HiBD-Benchmarks (OHB):** Typically researchers use traditional benchmarks such as Sort, TeraSort, etc., to evaluate new designs for the Hadoop ecosystem. However, all these benchmarks need to require the involvement of several components such as HDFS, RPC, MapReduce framework etc., thus making it hard to isolate problems and evaluate performance of individual components that are vital to the functioning of the entire system. In order to address this need for designing effective micro-benchmarks, to evaluate the performance of Big Data middleware, the HiBD project proposes OHB Micro-benchmarks to support stand-alone evaluations of HDFS [21], MapReduce [46], Hadoop RPC [33] and Memcached [15]. Similarly, micro-benchmarks for Apache Spark are in the works.

5.7   Conclusion

Advances in technology have enabled us to collect large amounts of data from all walks of life. Efficiently processing such large volumes of data, or "Big Data", and gaining meaningful insights is a significant challenge facing the Big Data community. It is critical that the Big Data middleware processing such data are diligently designed, with high performance and scalability, in order to meet the growing demands of Big Data applications. Current generation Big Data processing middleware (such as Apache Hadoop and Spark) have not yet taken full advantage of emerging technologies on modern HPC clusters. While this is necessary to meet the increasing demands of Big Data applications, there are several critical challenges that need to be addressed in order to achieve optimal performance. This chapter presents an overview of Apache Hadoop and Spark, as well as high-performance interconnects and storage architecture on modern HPC clusters. It showcases several case studies in the HiBD project that propose advanced designs based on RDMA and heterogeneous storage architecture for popular Big Data middleware. Based on these, this chapter gives the following main conclusions:

- **RDMA and high-performance interconnects (such as InfiniBand) can benefit Big Data processing middleware and applications**. Through case studies of RDMA-enhanced designs for HDFS, MapReduce, and Spark, significant performance benefits can be achieved by using RDMA.
- **The performance of Big Data processing middleware and applications can be significantly improved by using high-performance storage and parallel file systems (such as SSD and Lustre)**. Through case studies of Triple-H

and MapReduce over Lustre, the advanced designs on heterogeneous high-performance storage architecture have been discussed, and these designs have shown large performance benefits.

- **Big Data applications based on Apache Hadoop and Spark can benefit from all these RDMA and I/O enhanced designs transparently**. All the available designs in the HiBD project keep the default Big Data middleware APIs intact, which can provide performance benefits to end-user applications without any code changes.

All of these studies are pushing the envelope of converging HPC and Big Data processing technologies. By taking advantage of high-performance interconnects/protocols (especially RDMA) and storage architecture available on modern HPC clusters, the novel enhanced designs for popular Big Data middleware will play an important role in Big Data processing on current and next-generation Multi-Petaflop/Exaflop HPC systems.

Acknowledgements This research is supported in part by National Science Foundation grants #CNS-1419123, #IIS-1447804, and #ACI-1450440.

References

1. Apache Software Foundation (2016) Apache Hadoop. http://hadoop.apache.org/
2. Apache Software Foundation (2016) Apache Spark. http://spark.apache.org/
3. M. Armbrust, R.S. Xin, C. Lian, Y. Huai, D. Liu, J.K. Bradley, X. Meng, T. Kaftan, M.J. Franklin, A. Ghodsi, M. Zaharia, Spark SQL: relational data processing in spark, in *Proceedings of the 2015 ACM SIGMOD International Conference on Management of Data, SIGMOD '15* (ACM, New York, 2015), pp. 1383–1394
4. F. Chang, J. Dean, S. Ghemawat, W.C. Hsieh, D.A. Wallach, M. Burrows, T. Chandra, A. Fikes, R.E. Gruber, Bigtable: a distributed storage system for structured data, in *7th Conference on Usenix Symposium on Operating Systems Design and Implementation*, vol. 7 (2006), pp. 205–218
5. Cluster File System Inc., Lustre: scalable clustered object storage (2016), http://www.lustre.org/
6. J. Dean, S. Ghemawat, MapReduce: simplified data processing on large clusters, in *OSDI'04: Proceedings of the 6th conference on Symposium on Operating Systems Design and Implementation* (USENIX Association, Berkeley, CA, 2004)
7. Digital Universe Invaded By Sensors (2014), http://www.emc.com/about/news/press/2014/20140409-01.htm
8. X. Ding, S. Jiang, F. Chen, K. Davis, X. Zhang, DiskSeen: exploiting disk layout and access history to enhance I/O prefetch, in *2007 USENIX Annual Technical Conference on Proceedings of the USENIX Annual Technical Conference, ATC'07* (USENIX Association, Berkeley, CA, 2007), pp. 20:1–20:14
9. C. Engelmann, H. Ong, S.L. Scott, Middleware in modern high performance computing system architectures, in *Proceedings of ICCS*, Beijing (2007)
10. General-Purpose Computation on Graphics Processing Units (GPGPU) (2016), http://gpgpu.org
11. C. Gniady, Y. Hu, Y.H. Lu, Program counter based techniques for dynamic power management, in *IEEE Proceedings-Software* (2004), pp. 24–35

12. D. Goldenberg, M. Kagan, R. Ravid, M.S. Tsirkin, Transparently achieving superior socket performance using zero copy socket direct protocol over 20 Gb/s InfiniBand links, in *2005 IEEE Int'l Conference on Cluster Computing (Cluster)* (2005), pp. 1–10
13. J.E. Gonzalez, R.S. Xin, A. Dave, D. Crankshaw, M.J. Franklin, I. Stoica, GraphX: Graph processing in a distributed dataflow framework, in *11th USENIX Symposium on Operating Systems Design and Implementation (OSDI 14)* (USENIX Association, Broomfield, CO, 2014), pp. 599–613
14. HiBench Suite: The BigData Micro Benchmark Suite (2016), https://github.com/intel-hadoop/HiBench
15. High-Performance Big Data (HiBD) (2016), http://hibd.cse.ohio-state.edu
16. IDC Digital Universe Study (2011), http://www.emc.com/leadership/programs/digital-universe.htm
17. Infiniband Trade Association (2016), http://www.infinibandta.org
18. Intel Many Integrated Core Architecture (2016), http://www.intel.com/technology/architecture-silicon/mic/index.htm
19. International Data Corporation (IDC): New IDC Worldwide HPC end-user study identifies latest trends in high performance computing usage and spending (2013), http://www.idc.com/getdoc.jsp?containerId=prUS24409313
20. IP over InfiniBand Working Group (2016), http://www.ietf.org/html.charters/ipoib-charter.html
21. N.S. Islam, X. Lu, M.W. Rahman, J. Jose, D.K. Panda, A micro-benchmark suite for evaluating HDFS operations on modern clusters, in *Proceedings of the 2nd Workshop on Big Data Benchmarking, WBDB* (2012)
22. N.S. Islam, M.W. Rahman, J. Jose, R. Rajachandrasekar, H. Wang, H. Subramoni, C. Murthy, D.K. Panda, High performance RDMA-based design of HDFS over InfiniBand, in *The International Conference for High Performance Computing, Networking, Storage and Analysis (SC)* (2012)
23. N.S. Islam, X. Lu, M.W. Rahman, D.K. Panda, Can parallel replication benefit Hadoop distributed file system for high performance interconnects?, in *The Proceedings of IEEE 21st Annual Symposium on High-Performance Interconnects (HOTI)*, San Jose, CA (2013)
24. N. Islam, X. Lu, M. Wasi-ur Rahman, R. Rajachandrasekar, D. Panda, In-memory I/O and replication for HDFS with memcached: early experiences, in *IEEE International Conference on Big Data (Big Data'14)* (2014), pp. 213–218
25. N.S. Islam, X. Lu, M.Wu. Rahman, D.K.D. Panda, SOR-HDFS: a SEDA-based approach to maximize overlapping in RDMA-enhanced HDFS, in *Proceedings of the 23rd International Symposium on High-performance Parallel and Distributed Computing, HPDC '14* (ACM, New York, 2014), pp. 261–264
26. N.S. Islam, X. Lu, M.W. Rahman, D. Shankar, D.K. Panda, Triple-H: a hybrid approach to accelerate HDFS on HPC clusters with heterogeneous storage architecture, in *15th IEEE/ACM International Symposium on Cluster, Cloud and Grid Computing* (2015)
27. N.S. Islam, D. Shankar, X. Lu, M. Wasi-Ur-Rahman, D.K. Panda, Accelerating I/O performance of big data analytics on HPC clusters through RDMA-based key-value store, in *44th International Conference on Parallel Processing (ICPP)* (2015), pp. 280–289
28. M. Itoh, T. Ishizaki, M. Kishimoto, Accelerated socket communications in system area networks, in *IEEE International Conference on Cluster Computing, Cluster '00* (IEEE Computer Society, Los Alamitos, CA, 2000), p. 357
29. S. Krishnan, M. Tatineni, C. Baru, myHadoop - Hadoop-on-Demand on traditional HPC resources. Tech. rep., Chapter in 'Contemporary HPC Architectures' [KV04] Vassiliki Koutsonikola and Athena Vakali. Ldap: Framework, Practices, and Trends (2004)
30. S.W. Lee, B. Moon, C. Park, Advances in flash memory SSD technology for enterprise database applications, in *Proceedings of the 2009 ACM SIGMOD International Conference on Management of Data, SIGMOD '09* (ACM, New York, 2009), pp. 863–870
31. libmemcached: Open Source C/C++ Client Library and Tools for Memcached (2016), http://libmemcached.org/

32. X. Lu, N.S. Islam, M.W. Rahman, J. Jose, H. Subramoni, H. Wang, D.K. Panda, High-performance design of Hadoop RPC with RDMA over InfiniBand, in *The Proceedings of IEEE 42nd International Conference on Parallel Processing (ICPP)* (2013)
33. X. Lu, M. Wasi-ur Rahman, N. Islam, D. Panda, A micro-benchmark suite for evaluating Hadoop RPC on high-performance networks, in *Advancing Big Data Benchmarks*. Lecture Notes in Computer Science, vol. 8585 (Springer, Heidelberg, 2014), pp. 32–42
34. X. Lu, M. Rahman, N. Islam, D. Shankar, D. Panda, Accelerating spark with RDMA for big data processing: early experiences, in *2014 IEEE 22nd Annual Symposium on High-Performance Interconnects (HOTI)* (2014), pp. 9–16
35. Memcached: High-Performance, Distributed Memory Object Caching System (2016), http://memcached.org/
36. MVAPICH: MPI over InfiniBand, 10GigE/iWARP and RoCE. Network Based Computing Lab, The Ohio State University (2016), http://mvapich.cse.ohio-state.edu/
37. NVIDIA: GPUDirect RDMA (2016), http://docs.nvidia.com/cuda/gpudirect-rdma
38. NVM Express (NVMe) (2016), http://www.enterprisetech.com/2014/08/06/flashtec-nvram-15-million-iops-sub-microsecond-latency/
39. Parallel Virtual File System (2016), http://www.pvfs.org
40. M.W. Rahman, N.S. Islam, X. Lu, J. Jose, H. Subramoni, H. Wang, D.K. Panda, High-performance RDMA-based design of Hadoop MapReduce over InfiniBand, in *The Proceedings of International Workshop on High Performance Data Intensive Computing (HPDIC), in conjunction with IEEE International Parallel and Distributed Processing Symposium (IPDPS)*, Boston (2013)
41. M.W. Rahman, X. Lu, N.S. Islam, D.K. Panda, HOMR: a hybrid approach to exploit maximum overlapping in MapReduce over high performance interconnects, in *International Conference on Supercomputing (ICS)*, Munich (2014)
42. M.W. Rahman, X. Lu, N.S. Islam, R. Rajachandrasekar, D.K. Panda, MapReduce over lustre: can RDMA-based approach benefit?, in *20th International European Conference on Parallel Processing*, Porto, Euro-Par (2014)
43. M.W. Rahman, X. Lu, N.S. Islam, R. Rajachandrasekar, D.K. Panda, High-performance design of YARN MapReduce on modern HPC clusters with lustre and RDMA, in *29th IEEE International Parallel and Distributed Processing Symposium (IPDPS)* (2015)
44. RDMA Consortium: Architectural Specifications for RDMA over TCP/IP (2016), http://www.rdmaconsortium.org/
45. SDSC Comet (2016), http://www.sdsc.edu/services/hpc/hpc_systems.html
46. D. Shankar, X. Lu, M.W. Rahman, N. Islam, D.K. Panda, A micro-benchmark suite for evaluating Hadoop MapReduce on high-performance networks, in *Proceedings of the Fifth workshop on Big Data Benchmarks, Performance Optimization, and Emerging Hardware, BPOE-5*, vol. 8807 (Springer International Publishing, Hangzhou, 2014), pp. 19–33
47. K. Shvachko, H. Kuang, S. Radia, R. Chansler, The Hadoop distributed file system, in *The Proceedings of the IEEE 26th Symposium on Mass Storage Systems and Technologies (MSST)*, Washington, DC (2010)
48. T.L. Sterling, J. Salmon, D.J. Becker, D.F. Savarese, *How to Build a Beowulf: A Guide to the Implementation and Application of PC Clusters* (MIT Press, Cambridge, MA, 1999)
49. T. Sterling, E. Lusk, W. Gropp, *Beowulf Cluster Computing with Linux* (MIT Press, Cambridge, MA, 2003)
50. H. Subramoni, P. Lai, M. Luo, D.K. Panda, RDMA over ethernet - a preliminary study, in *Proceedings of the 2009 Workshop on High Performance Interconnects for Distributed Computing (HPIDC'09)* (2009)
51. H. Subramoni, K. Hamidouche, A. Venkatesh, S. Chakraborty, D. Panda, Designing MPI library with dynamic connected transport (DCT) of InfiniBand: early experiences, in *Super-computing*, ed. by J. Kunkel, T. Ludwig, H. Meuer. Lecture Notes in Computer Science, vol. 8488 (Springer, Berlin, 2014), pp. 278–295

52. S. Sur, H. Wang, J. Huang, X. Ouyang, D.K. Panda (2010) Can high performance interconnects benefit Hadoop distributed file system?, in *Workshop on Micro Architectural Support for Virtualization, Data Center Computing, and Clouds, in Conjunction with MICRO 2010*, Atlanta, GA
53. TACC Stampede (2016), https://www.tacc.utexas.edu/stampede/
54. The Netty Project (2016), http://netty.io
55. Top500 Supercomputing System (2016), http://www.top500.org
56. V.K. Vavilapalli, A.C. Murthy, C. Douglas, S. Agarwal, M. Konar, R. Evans, T. Graves, J. Lowe, H. Shah, S. Seth, B. Saha, C. Curino, O. O'Malley, S. Radia, B. Reed, E. Baldeschwieler, Apache Hadoop YARN: yet another resource negotiator, in *Proceedings of the 4th Annual Symposium on Cloud Computing, SOCC '13* (ACM, New York, 2013), pp 5:1–5:16
57. Y. Wang, X. Que, W. Yu, D. Goldenberg, D. Sehgal, Hadoop acceleration through network levitated merge, in *Proceedings of International Conference for High Performance Computing, Networking, Storage and Analysis (SC)*, Seattle, WA (2011)
58. Y. Wang, R. Goldstone, W. Yu, T. Wang, Characterization and optimization of memory-resident MapReduce on HPC systems, in *28th IEEE International Parallel and Distributed Processing Symposium (IPDPS)* (2014)
59. M. Welsh, D. Culler, E. Brewer, SEDA: an architecture for well-conditioned, scalable Internet services, in *Proceedings of the 18th ACM Symposium on Operating Systems Principles (SOSP)*, Banff, Alberta (2001)
60. M. Zaharia, M. Chowdhury, M.J. Franklin, S. Shenker, I. Stoica, Spark: cluster computing with working sets, in *Proceedings of the 2nd USENIX Conference on Hot Topics in Cloud Computing (HotCloud)*, Boston, MA (2010)
61. M. Zaharia, M. Chowdhury, T. Das, A. Dave, J. Ma, M. McCauly, M.J. Franklin, S. Shenker, I. Stoica, Resilient distributed datasets: a fault-tolerant abstraction for in-memory cluster computing. Presented as part of the 9th USENIX symposium on networked systems design and implementation (NSDI 12) (USENIX, San Jose, CA, 2012), pp. 15–28
62. M. Zaharia, T. Das, H. Li, T. Hunter, S. Shenker, I. Stoica, Discretized streams: fault-tolerant streaming computation at scale, in *Proceedings of the Twenty-Fourth ACM Symposium on Operating Systems Principles, SOSP '13* (ACM, New York, 2013), pp. 423–438

Chapter 6
dispel4py: Agility and Scalability for Data-Intensive Methods Using HPC

Rosa Filgueira, Malcolm P. Atkinson, and Amrey Krause

Abstract Today's data bonanza and increasing computational power provide many new opportunities for combining observations with sophisticated simulation results to improve complex models and make forecasts by analyzing their relationships. This should lead to well-presented actionable information that can support decisions and contribute trustworthy knowledge. Practitioners in all disciplines: computational scientists, data scientists and decision makers need improved tools to realize such potential. The library dispel4py is such a tool. dispel4py is a Python library for describing abstract workflows for distributed data-intensive applications. It delivers a simple abstract model in familiar development environments with a fluent path to production use that automatically addresses scale without its users having to reformulate their methods. This depends on optimal mappings to many current HPC and data-intensive platforms.

6.1 Introduction

Virtually every domain is enjoying an increasing wealth of data, e.g., from observing natural phenomena, experiments, societal behavior, or business transactions. The complexity of today's challenges and the increases in computational power lead to simulations which yield large volumes of data. Models and understanding are improved by comparing such results with observations—a demanding data-intensive stage in many scientific methods. The aim is to present information on which decision makers may act, e.g., publish, make management decisions, alert responders, compile knowledge as validated models, or make forecasts. There is a commensurate growth in expectations about what can be achieved with this wealth of data and computational power. To meet these expectations with available expertise requires much better tools for data-driven methods.

R. Filgueira (✉) • M.P. Atkinson
School of Informatics, University of Edinburgh, Edinburgh, UK
e-mail: rosa.filgueira@ed.ac.uk; Malcolm.Atkinson@ed.ac.uk

A. Krause
EPCC, University of Edinburgh, Edinburgh EH8 9LE, UK
e-mail: a.krause@epcc.ed.ac.uk

© Springer International Publishing Switzerland 2016   109
R. Arora (ed.), *Conquering Big Data with High Performance Computing*,
DOI 10.1007/978-3-319-33742-5_6

Advances in our ability to use data depend on the creativity of individuals and teams, inventing and refining methods for extracting knowledge from data. Those methods typically involve many steps and stages, to progress from multiple heterogeneous data sources, through data preparation and integration, to analysis, distillation and visualization. The principles guiding such methods have recently been termed *"data science"*. We focus on the means of describing, refining and using such methods.

The `dispel4py` system is a new tool for formulating and executing data-intensive methods. It is based on a simple and abstract model of the logic required. That abstract model carefully eliminates details of target platforms and data-handling steps that can be provided automatically. This abstraction is needed for three reasons:

1. so that domain experts formulating and using data-intensive methods are not distracted and do not have to understand target platforms;
2. so that methods are not locked to platforms, but can be moved to suitable new platforms without human intervention and with the encoded method's semantics unchanged; and
3. so that data-intensive engineers have the scope to develop optimal mappings to suitable platforms.

This model was devised for `Dispel` [47] and has been reformulated in Python as `dispel4py` to reach the extensive community of Python users, who include the seismologists we worked with on the VERCE project [13]. The model comprises nodes, called *Processing Elements* (PEs), connected together by *data streams*. The PEs process *units of data* from each of their inputs and emit units of data on each of their outputs. Each data stream carries a sequence of data units from its source, normally a PE's output port, to all of the input ports to which it is connected. A data stream will use the lowest cost transport mechanism available, e.g., copying via shared memory for co-located PEs, avoiding unnecessary I/O. The PEs may be *composite*, i.e. a logical unit that is in fact an instance of a `dispel4py` graph, or *primitive* implemented as a Python class that may wrap code in other languages, e.g., to incorporate legacy method elements. They normally auto-iterate over their input data streams.

The Python scripts using the `dispel4py` library construct the graph of PEs interconnected by data streams ducted through *connections*. In a development context this is interpreted in a single process. Production runs choose a target platform, and optimally map the graph onto that platform taking account of performance, data volumes, and locality issues. The resulting set of distributed processes are then started. Using Python brings the following advantages:

- A large number of the data-driven research communities already use Python productively.
- The library mechanisms are easily used and support sharing of the basic `dispel4py` system, of domain-specific PE libraries, and of PEs and workflows within a group.

- The library mechanism also encourages productive interplay between data-science experts, data-intensive engineers and domain experts as they collaborate to build and exploit effective methods [9].
- Python has a very rich repertoire of general purpose, statistical and presentational libraries and some discipline-specific libraries.
- The object-orientation enables us to provide `class` definitions that can easily be used by domain specialists when they want to define and introduce a new PE into their data-driven methods. This independence from computing experts is critical when they are exploring potential innovations. Depending on such (often scarce) experts introduces delays, a need to communicate requirements not yet well understood, and inhibits the development of intuitions about what has become feasible.
- It is straightforward for data scientists and data-intensive engineers to provide functions that generate frequently recurring patterns.
- Python is ubiquitous across platforms, facilitating installation, deployment and method mobility.
- Python delivers high productivity through its succinct and consistent style and via an excellent set of development and diagnostic tools [40].

In summary, the dispel4py system embedded in Python empowers domain scientists, who have the key understanding of the data and the systems under investigation, to experimentally develop and to use data-intensive methods. They understand their field's issues, phenomena and challenges well enough to create and refine both the key questions and the paths to definitive answers. The description needs to facilitate collaborative working with experts in data analysis, machine learning and data management. It often has to support the synthesis of parts of data-science methods contributed by specialists in different stages of the data lifecycle, in multiple sub-disciplines or with particular statistical skills. Their combined intellectual investment in creating, refining and steering data-science methods is very substantial; it is therefore imperative that it retains its value as the digital ecosystem supplying computation, storage, processing, communication, and human-machine interaction evolves, which it does much more rapidly than the useful lifetime of data-driven methods.

Data-driven method descriptions need to be executable; that is, they need to (a) fetch their input data from wherever they may be, (b) move data between stages when necessary, (c) perform computations for simulation, data preparation, for analyses and for presentation, (d) store final results together with user-selected intermediates, and (e) provide a framework for diagnosis, validation, and the use of end-results. The methods need to be quickly and conveniently executed for modest data volumes, so that method creation and refinement is straightforward using local resources, such as a researcher's laptop or local machine. This convenience allows experimentation to develop a specialist's intuitions about possible methods and to facilitate diagnostics. But data-science methods need to scale to large data volumes, high data rates and high request rates. The transition between development and production should be fluent, i.e. involve *no* changes to the method descriptions. This is consistent with the above target of intellectual-investment longevity, as the ability to automatically transfer from a simple development context to a sophisticated architecture for production also means that transferring between today's versions of distributed and high-performance computing to next year's or next decade's architectures will be handled by the same automatic mapping.

Production-scale capabilities are achieved by mapping their methods *completely unchanged* to a variety of middleware systems that exploit many different distributed computing infrastructures (DCIs). The target may be chosen by users or by enactment-management systems. The mappings exploit data from prior runs and other information to optimize production work. The mapping transforms the graph into one where PE instances are distributed across nodes in the platform and data stream connections use mechanisms available for their given source and origin. Nodes may be replicated to achieve scalability. PE deployment, data movement, distributed shut-down and clean-up, are all handled implicitly, and parallelization is implemented during mapping. The mapping may include translation to exploit mechanisms offered by a target middleware. Systematic provenance collection and diagnostic data gathering allow members of the teams to verify and control method executions.

An overview of the architecture of the `dispel4py` system is shown in Fig. 6.1. The tools used by domain experts present the system in abstract terms, whereas those used by data-intensive engineers access the implementation and mapping details. Five target platforms are supported by today's mappings.

This chapter is structured as follows. Section 6.2 further examines the requirements of the different categories of experts involved and introduces the best strategy for meeting those requirements in the context of practical and contemporary

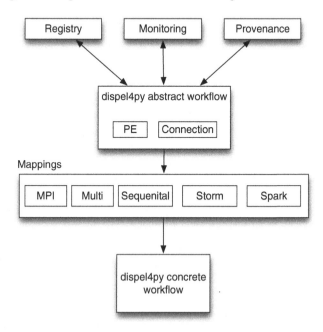

Fig. 6.1 Overview of the architecture that supports `dispel4py`

collaborative environments. Section 6.3 reviews prior work and other influences shaping our approach. Section 6.4 defines more precisely the permitted forms of data-science method that may be coded in dispel4py and illustrates these with examples and tutorials. The implementors of dispel4py try to handle all the underlying complexity, deliver scalability and reliability, and exploit sophisticated specialized data-intensive systems. Section 6.5 summarizes the different dispel4py tools available to make data-intensive methods more reproducible and open. Section 6.6 outlines the engineering needed to achieve this. Section 6.7 presents measurements to show how well this engineering works. Section 6.8 concludes, drawing together the ideas presented and tentatively explores future directions.

6.2 Motivation

In most data-driven contexts three categories of experts combine their skills, insights and efforts to push forward the exploitation of data in their field [9]. These are:

1. *The domain specialists* who have considerable expertise and training in understanding and addressing the particular issues in their domain. They understand which sources of data are relevant, how to obtain access rights to those data, how those data relate to the challenges and opportunities in their field, the relevant phenomena and mechanisms operating in their field, and the preferred presentation of actionable result information. They have been inducted into the culture of their field and interact with its community.
2. *The data scientists* who have expertise in handling the data and extracting significant information from them. They often have statistical expertise and are able to create, select or deploy the relevant algorithms and machine learning strategies. They may have data-integration expertise to transform and link heterogeneous data. They may be generalists or may develop specific approaches for a particular field, which may draw on long-term alliances with domain specialists in that field.
3. *The data-intensive engineers* who choose target distributed computing infrastructures or architectures, and develop the optimized and automated mappings onto them. This includes transforming the methods to highly parallel forms, and organizing that authority to access data is established, data queries and transfers are coupled, software is deployed, storage and computational resources are allocated, and clean-up after the methods is completed. They establish mechanisms for handling failures—inevitable at production scales. They set up an environment to enable the other two categories of expert to develop methods, to improve methods using diagnostics from previous runs, to collect and review provenance data, and to submit runs.

There are of course rare individuals who master more than one of these skill sets, but they are rare. The growing scale and heterogeneity of available data, the growing subtlety of the questions studied, and the immense diversity of available data-analysis platforms makes them an endangered species.

Effective synergy between these three categories of experts is essential. As many such groups are often involved in building the stages of sophisticated data-science methods, coupling their work together is a benefit. `dispel4py` builds an environment that addresses all three viewpoints as explained below. Crucially, it also provides a medium where by they can represent a data-science method and all work using that representation.

6.2.1 Supporting Domain Specialists

Domain specialists require an abstract representation that is conceptually simple so that they can focus on their viewpoint without being distracted by technical details. We use a simple graph of connected processes coupled by data streams—Sect. 6.4. Because we work with specialists who are already adept at Python scripts, e.g., [13], the notation is built using a Python library. This enables those who use Python to use their familiar editing, development and testing tools. It is key to enable the domain specialists to shape their methods, experiment quickly to explore possibilities and to submit these to evaluation and production, without encountering distracting difficulties. The local execution of `dispel4py` scripts and their transfer to other platforms *unchanged* with automated transformation enables this. The methods compose steps, called "*Processing Elements*" (PEs) that draw from Python libraries or from the registry (see Sect. 6.5.1). To extend the repertoire of PEs, the domain specialists often write their own, at least for the simple cases. This is critical to unfettered exploration of ideas. It is often inhibited by complexity in many of today's workflow systems.

Domain specialists want their methods to last. When they have invested much effort in refining them to precisely meet their needs, they want to trust in their continued usability. This is another reason for avoiding technical detail creeping in. Technical detail often reflects underlying systems and current provisioning practices. Those change frequently as providers improve their systems, and as software infrastructures and provider business models evolve. This issue is also addressed by strategies to capture the computational context of a workflow using virtualization [55]. That approach supports re-runs of previous methods but does not support their exploitation of new platforms.

6.2.2 Supporting Data Scientists

Data scientists often work closely with domain scientists, but some work for the larger Python user community by building rich and powerful Python libraries for statistics, visualization, machine learning, data transformation and so on. Python also allows processing in other languages to be wrapped, which can be key to reaching developments in other languages. Other data scientists work for a specific domain, for example, the ObsPy community build Python libraries for seismologists to use [48]. Python's convenient library system enables the domain specialists who choose to write their own PEs to draw on all of these resources.

Data scientists working for the dispel4py context also exploit Python's rich libraries. They produce two categories of extensions for domain specialists and other data scientists to use. The first category provides ready-made PEs, perhaps encapsulating more sophisticated algorithms, widely applicable operations and collections of compatible PEs designed for a particular field. They may exploit knowledge of the ways in which optimized mappings work to improve their performance. It is crucial that these PEs remain straightforward to use from the viewpoint of domain specialists.

The second category of extensions is Python functions that generate graphs, *standard patterns*, of connected PEs. When these functions are used they are parameterized with domain-specific PEs and generic PEs. For example, a function to cross-correlate an arbitrary number of source data streams, might be parameterized with pipelines of PEs for data preparation, PEs for sorting and grouping data units prior to correlation, with a PE performing correlation, and with integrating PEs that act on correlation outputs. These functions enable the data scientists to encapsulate regular patterns that scale and that are recognizable by the optimizers performing mappings—see Sect. 6.6. The data scientists can explain each parameter separately, so that the domain specialists do not need to think about the scalability mechanisms, and the complex graph that the function generates. This frees the domain scientists from iteratively constructing graph topologies. The graph produced can be wrapped as a PE class that takes the same parameters when it is instantiated, so that it can be used without domain experts being aware that it is complex and composite.

6.2.3 Supporting Data-Intensive Engineers

Data-intensive engineering becomes ever more important as more data is addressed. Today it is a major undertaking on cloud and HPC systems. Many technology providers and computational resource providers are investing in new architectures and new middleware infrastructures, such as MPI, Spark™ and Storm, to accelerate processes, improve throughput, scalability and efficiency. This effort is amortized over very large communities and often driven by commercial goals. Data-driven R&D needs to exploit such engineering effort, to give the dispel4py access to its advantages and ubiquity, but taking care not to lock in to one particular middleware model. Thus our own data-intensive engineering works on simple architectures, advanced architectures and maps to these distributed data infrastructures. The key requirement is to sustain the existing semantics as the target infrastructures evolve and as workloads are moved between different infrastructures. This needs to be done with reasonable optimization, which depends on operational data from the monitoring system—see Sect. 6.6.

6.2.4 Communication Between Experts

It is crucially important to enable effective communication among experts. Often they are geographically dispersed or contributing at different times. The library mechanisms of Python provide a convenient way for data scientists and domain experts to leave elements for others to use. The registry provides more explicit description of the data flows and handles sharing within groups, versions of collections and access controls. The dispel4py system offers convenient mechanisms to visualize methods as graphs of PEs (nodes) connected by data streams (directed arcs). These visualizations facilitate communication among domain experts and between domain experts and data scientists. This abstract view proves important in sharing ideas. However, for domain experts to be really innovative they need intuitions about what is feasible; these are often triggered by the functionally packaged patterns. Many domain experts, particularly those embarking into new territory, have little access to technical help and to data scientists. It is vital that the dispel4py system encourages their innovative drive.

Communication with data engineering begins with the submission of a dispel4py script for enactment. This is made simple for the domain expert by providing consistent submission arrangements. Introspection over the submitted graphs, combined with process-monitoring data helps data engineers identify targets for improvement,

6.3 Background and Related Work

There are many scientific workflow systems, including: Pegasus [28], Kepler [45], Swift [66], KNIME [16, 20], Taverna [67], Galaxy [21], Trident [58] and Triana [24]. These are task-oriented, that is their predominant model has stages that correspond to tasks, and they organise their enactment on a wide range of distributed computing infrastructures (DCI) [42], normally arranging data transfer between stages using files [63]. These systems have achieved substantial progress in handling data-intensive scientific computations; e.g., in astrophysics [18, 19, 57], in climate physics and meteorology [35], in biochemistry [5], in geosciences and geo-engineering [46] and in environmental sciences [15, 39].

Despite the undoubted success of the task-oriented scientific workflow systems, dispel4py adopts a data-streaming approach in order to be efficient on diverse targets by reducing I/O activity, e.g., avoiding disk reads and writes. This mirrors the shared-nothing composition of operators in database queries and in distributed query processing [22] that has been developed and refined in the database context [60]. Data streaming was latent in the auto-iteration of Taverna [26], has been developed as an option for Kepler [41], is the model used by Meandre [1], and motivated the design of Dispel [10, 11]. Dispel was proposed as a means of enabling the specification of scientific methods assuming a stream-based conceptual model that allows users to define abstract, machine-agnostic, fine-grained data-intensive workflows. The dispel4py system implements many of the original Dispel concepts, but presents them as Python constructs.

Bobolang, a relative new workflow system based on data streaming, has linguistic forms based on C++ and focuses on automatic parallelisation [33]. It also supports multiple inputs and outputs, meaning that a single node can have as many inputs or outputs as a user requires. Currently, it does not support automatic mapping to different DCIs.

A data-streaming system, such as dispel4py, typically passes small data units along its streams compared with the volume of each data unit (file) passed between stages in task-oriented workflows. In principle, at least, the units passed in a data stream can be arbitrarily large, e.g., multi-dimensional arrays denoting successive states in a finite element model (FEM) of a dynamic system [23], though they are typically time-stamped tuples often encoding time and a small number of scalars in a highly compressed form. The data-streaming model can also pass file names in its data units and thereby draw on the facilities task-oriented systems use.

The optimisation of data-streaming workflows has been investigated recently [2–4, 37]. Ultimately this needs to avoid any focus that becomes a bottleneck [68]. For example, Kryder [65] has identified disk I/O as an increasing challenge as disk capacity outgrows CPU capacity.

Mechanisms to improve sharing and reuse of workflows have proved important in the task-oriented context, e.g., myExperiment [27] and Wf4Ever [17]. It is unclear whether these will need extension to accommodate data-streaming workflows [43], and the scale of data handled precludes simple bundling of data with workflows to ensure reproducibility as is appropriate for computationally intensive task-oriented workflows [56].

6.4 Semantics, Examples and Tutorial

The dispel4py data-streaming workflow library is a contribution to a greater vision for formalizing and automating both data-intensive and compute-intensive methods. We posit that workflow tools and languages will play increasingly significant roles due to the modularity they encourage, to their independence from low-level implementations, to their user-friendly properties, to their accommodation of method refinement from rapid prototyping to optimized production, and to their intuitive visualization properties; graphs appear to be a natural way to visualize logical relationships. Data streaming is a technological discipline and abstraction which will have a significant impact in the way scientists think and carry out their data-analysis and computation tasks, due to its divide-and-conquer properties.

We now present a summary of the main dispel4py concepts and terminology:

Table 6.1 Predefined categories of PEs—subclasses of `GenericPE`

Type	Inputs	Outputs	When to use it
GenericPE	*n* inputs	*m* outputs	Zero or more inputs and zero or more outputs
IterativePE	1 input named *input*	1 output named *output*	Process one and produce one data unit per iteration
ConsumerPE	1 input named *input*	No output	No output and one input
ProducerPE	No input	1 output named *output*	No inputs and one output; usually the root in a graph
Simple FunctionPE	1 input named *input*	1 output named *output*	Only implement *process* method; it can not store state between calls automatically
Create _iterative _chain	1 input named *input*	1 output named *output*	Pipeline of functions processing sequentially; creates a composite PE

- A *processing element* (PE) is a computational activity, corresponding to a step in a scientific method or a data-transforming operator. PEs encapsulate an algorithm or a service. They are the computational blocks of any `dispel4py` workflow, and are instantiated as nodes in a workflow graph. `dispel4py` offers a variety of PEs, as shown in Table 6.1. The code in Listing 6.1 belongs to the first PE, from the `dispel4py` workflow in Fig. 6.2. `FilterTweet` has no input data streams and reads from a file, called `tweets.json` produced by the Tweet API containing one tweet per line. `FilterTweet` emits two data streams: one with each tweets' `hash_tag` and the other with its `language` as output data streams. The PE's `init` method defines the inputs and outputs, and the data-processing logic is implemented in the PE's `process` method. When a PE has input streams, the `process` method is called once per incoming data unit. In this case, where there are no inputs, it is called once, when the workflow is started. When there are inputs, it is called when the first data unit arrives on any input stream, and is called again for each subsequent data unit. This choreographs overlapping execution of PEs.
- An *instance* is the executable copy of a PE with its input and output ports that runs in a process as a node in the data-streaming graph. During enactment and prior to execution each PE is translated into one or more instances. Multiple instances may occur because the same action is required in more than one part of the encoded scientific method or to parallelize to increase throughput.

Listing 6.1 A dispel4py example showing a primitive PE definition

```
class FilterTweet(GenericPE): #FilterTweet subclass of GenericPE
    def __init__(self):                    #set up two output ports
        GenericPE.__init__(self)
        self._add_output('hashtags')
        self._add_output('language')

    def process(self, inputs): #define process for each tweet

        twitterDataFile= inputs['input']
        tweet_file = open(twitterDataFile)
        for line in tweet_file:
            tweet = json.loads(line)
            language  = ' '
            hashtags=[]
            language = tweet[u'lang'].encode('utf-8')
            text = tweet[u'text'].encode('utf-8')
            hashtags = re.findall(r"#(\w+)", text)
            self.write('hash_tag', hashtags)
            self.write('language', language)
```

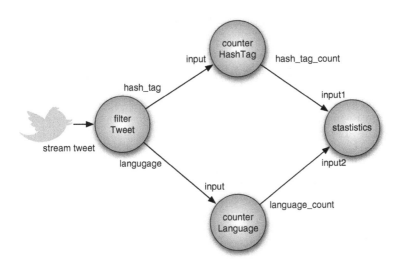

Fig. 6.2 Example dispel4py workflow mining_tweets

- A *connection* streams data from one output of a PE instance to one or more input ports on other PE instances. The rate of data consumption and production depends on the behavior of the source and destination PEs. Consequently a connection needs to provide adequate buffering. Distributed choreography is achieved: when a buffer is full the data generating process pauses, and when the buffer is empty the consuming processes are suspended. Connections also provide signaling pathways to achieve the first two forms of termination (see below).
- A *composite processing element* is a PE that wraps a dispel4py sub-workflow. Composite processing elements allow for synthesis of increasingly complex workflows by composing previously defined sub-workflows. In the code in Listing 6.2 creates a composite PE given a list of functions: add_value,

subtract_value, and multiply_value, and their corresponding parameters. The functions will be applied in the specified order. The use of Python functions to provide users with re-usable patterns is illustrated here by applying create_iterative_chain. It forms a pipeline of PE instances, where successive PEs have their process method apply the corresponding function in the supplied list with the corresponding parameter.

Listing 6.2 A dispel4py example of a composite PE definition

```
def add_value(data, value):    # define first function
    data += value
    return data

def subtract_value(data, value): # define second function
    data -= value
    return data

def multiply_value(data, value): # define third function
    data *= value
    return num
                # create PE pipeline applying each function in turn
compositePE = create_iterative_chain([(add_value,{'num'=5}),\
    (subtract_value,{'num'=3}), (multiply_value,{'num'=2})])
```

- A *partition* is a number of PEs co-located within the same process; it is used when they have relatively low CPU and RAM demands, but high data-flows between them. It corresponds to task-clustering in the task-oriented workflow systems, and will also occur automatically in dispel4py. For example, in the code in Listing 6.3 defines three partitions; the first and third partitions each have one PE; however, the second partition has three PEs, which will be run in a single process.

Listing 6.3 A dispel4py example showing partition specification

```
producer = ProducerStream()   # new instance of PE ProducerStream
filterStream = FilterStream()      # ditto FilterStream
fillGap = FillGap()                # ditto FillGap
processStream = ProcessStream()    # ditto ProcessStream
streamToFile = StreamToFile()      # ditto StreamToFile
graph.partitions = [[producer], \ # group instances in partitions
    [filterStream, fillGap, processStream],[streamToFile]]
```

- A *graph* defines the ways in which PEs are connected and hence the paths taken by data, i.e. the topology of the workflow. There are no limitations on the type of graphs that can be designed with dispel4py. Figure 6.2 is an example graph involving four PEs.

    FilterTweet emits the tweets' hash_tags and language as outputs, which are sent to different PEs: CounterHashTag and CounterLanguage, which count the number of different hash_tags, and of different languages respectively. The outputs from those PEs are then merged in StatisticsPE that displays the five most popular hash_tags and the language most used. More examples can be found in the dispel4py documentation [30]
- A *grouping* specifies for an input connection the communication pattern between PEs. There are four patterns available: shuffle, group_by, one_to_all and all_to_one. Each pattern arranges that there are a set of receiving

PE instances. The shuffle grouping randomly distributes data units to the instances, whereas group_by ensures that each value that occurs in the specified elements of each data unit is sent to the same PE instance. one_to_all means that all PE instances send copies of their output data to all the connected PE instances and all_to_one means that all data is merged and delivered to a single PE instance. In the mining_tweets dispel4py workflow, CounterHashTag and CounterLanguage apply a grouping_by based upon the field hash_tag and language respectively, and Statistics applies an all_to_one grouping.

To construct dispel4py workflows, users employ PEs from the dispel4py libraries and registry, or implement PEs (in Python) if they require new ones. They connect them as they desire in graphs. We show the code for creating the mining_tweets dispel4py workflow represented in Fig. 6.2. The code in Listing 6.4 assumes that the logic within PEs has already been implemented.

Listing 6.4 A dispel4py example producing the mining_tweets graph

```
from dispel4py.workflow_graph import WorkflowGraph
pe1 = FilterTweet()      # create instances of PEs
pe2 = CounterHashTag()
pe3 = CounterLanguage()
pe4 = Statistics()

graph = WorkflowGraph() # start a new graph
graph.connect(pe1,'hash_tag',pe2,'input') # establish connections
graph.connect(pe1,'language',pe3,'input') # along which data flows
graph.connect(pe2,'hash_tag_count',pe4,'input1')
graph.connect(pe3,'language_count',pe4,'input2')
```

Once the dispel4py workflow has been built, it can be executed in several distributed computing infrastructures exploiting the mappings explained in Sect. 6.6.

Hence dispel4py workflows can be executed anywhere Python is available and without any adaptation by users. If a dispel4py workflow is executed using MPI or Multiprocess with several processes, then the PEs are equally distributed among the processes, except for the first PE, which is assigned one process by default. If users want to change the default topology, they write the following instruction in the script before connecting their PEs in the graph.

    <name_of_PE>.numprocesses = Number

If the number of processes is not specified the enactment system attempts to allocate an optimal number.

The command parameters offered by dispel4py are summarized below:

- -h help: Help message with all the dispel4py commands.
- -n number processes: Number of processes to run the dispel4py workflow.
- -a attribute: Name of a variable in the dispel4py workflow.
- -f inputfile: File containing input dataset in JSON format.
- -d inputdata: Input dataset in JSON format.
- -i iterations: Number of iterations to execute the dispel4py workflow.

6.5 dispel4py Tools

In addition to its modeling and programming constructs, dispel4py comes with
an information registry, and provenance and diagnosis tools.

6.5.1 Registry

The modularity of workflow approaches, and in particular the data-centric, fine-
grained design of dispel4py, leads to extensive reusability. In dispel4py
users can store, share and reuse workflow entities, such as PEs and functions, via
the dispel4py information registry [34]. The registry, part of the dispel4py
framework, implements a data schema able to describe dispel4py entities at a
level of abstraction usable by the dispel4py enactment engine. Researchers can
import into their workspace or their group's workspace in the registry their own or
third-party PE specifications for inclusion in their workflows. A prototype version
of the information registry has been released as an open-source project [31]. This
has been used to explore its integration with a prototype workflow editor.

6.5.2 Provenance Management

The provenance mechanism [59] allows users to analyze at runtime the provenance information collected. Tools exploiting provenance provide user-steered
visualizations of the relationships between data products and the performance
of multi-faceted queries over the provenance data extended with user-controlled
metadata. These tools facilitate bulk data and job-management operations, e.g.,
visualization or download of sets of data so selected, and triggering of actions
when conditions specified in terms of the provenance data are satisfied. It adopts the
W3C-PROV recommendation. It is accessible via a prototypical browser interface
and a web API. It fosters rapid diagnosis of logical failures thanks to a flexible
metadata structure and error capturing.

6.5.3 Diagnosis Tool

The diagnosis tool monitors the workflows' characteristics (i.e. timings, parameters,
stream properties, topology of workflow) in real-time as they are executed on
different DCI with different mappings. The information extracted is stored in a
database, pooled and analyzed to optimize mappings and targets for later runs. This
information can be accessed via a web-GUI.

6.6   Engineering Effective Mappings

One of dispel4py's strengths is that it allows the construction of workflows without knowledge of the hardware or middleware context in which they will be executed. Users can therefore focus on designing their workflows at an abstract level, describing actions, input and output streams, and how they are connected. The dispel4py system then maps these descriptions to the enactment platforms. Since the abstract workflows are independent from the underlying mechanisms these workflows are portable across different computing platforms without any migration cost imposed on users. Data-intensive engineers have to have prepared the mappings. Currently we have prepared mappings for Apache Storm, MPI, Multiprocessing and Spark DCIs, as well as a Sequential mapping for development and small applications. Descriptions of these mappings follow.

6.6.1   Apache Storm

The dispel4py system was initially designed to use Apache Storm [8]. This was motivated by similarities between dispel4py's and Storm's streaming models, and because Storm delivered dynamic scaling and recovery, and had been well-proven notably in the context of Twitter.

Apache Storm executes graphs, called *topologies*, that are like workflows; they consume and process streams of data items when data arrive, typically running continuously until killed. The Storm system handles load balancing and recovers from failures of worker nodes by restarting crucial services. Workers can be added to the cluster at runtime, building on the Apache Zookeeper technology [7]. However, Storm is not normally deployed on HPC resources, on which most large-scale scientific computing runs. Instead, it requires installation on a dedicated cluster.

The dispel4py system maps to Storm by translating its graph description to a Storm topology. As dispel4py allows its users to define data types for each PE in a workflow graph, types are deduced and propagated from the data sources throughout the graph when the topology is created. Each Python PE is mapped to either a Storm bolt or spout, depending on whether the PE has inputs (a bolt), i.e. is an internal stage, or is a data source (a spout), i.e. is a point where data flows into the graph from external sources. The data streams in the dispel4py graph are mapped to Storm streams. The dispel4py PEs may declare how a data stream is partitioned across processing instances. By default these instructions map directly to built-in Storm stream groupings. The source code of all dispel4py mappings is available in the github [29].

There are two execution modes for Storm: a topology can be executed in local mode using a multi-threaded framework (for development and testing), or it can be submitted to a production cluster. The user chooses the mode when executing a dispel4py graph in Storm. Both modes require the availability of the Storm package on the client machine. The following command submits the mining_tweets dispel4py graph (Fig. 6.2) as a Storm topology in local mode or to a remote cluster.

```
dispel4py storm mining_tweets -m <local|remote> \
  -d '{"ReadData" : [ {"input" : "tweets.json"} ]}'
```

6.6.2 MPI

MPI is a standard, portable message-passing system for parallel programming, whose goals are high performance, scalability and portability [51]. MPI, in contrast to Storm, is very well known and widely supported in HPC environments. For this mapping, dispel4py uses mpi4py [25], which is a full-featured Python binding for MPI based on the MPI-2 standard. The dispel4py system maps PEs to a collection of MPI processes. Depending on the number of targeted processes, specified when requesting the mapping, multiple instances of each PE are created to make use of all available processes. Input PEs, i.e. at the root of the dispel4py graph, only ever execute in one instance to avoid the generation of duplicate data units.

Data units to be shipped along streams are converted into generic pickle-based Python objects and transferred using MPI asynchronous calls. Groupings are mapped to communication patterns, which assign the destination of a stream according to the grouping (e.g., shuffle grouping is mapped to a round-robin pattern, for group-by the hash of the data block determines the destination).

To use the MPI mapping, the mpi4py library and any MPI interface need to be installed, such as mpich [50] or openmpi [52]. To execute the mining_tweets dispel4py graph using the MPI mapping issue the following command:

```
mpiexec -n <number mpi_processes> dispel4py mpi
  mining_tweets -d '{"ReadData" : [ {"input" :
  "tweets.json"} ]}'
```

6.6.3 Multiprocessing

The Python library multiprocessing is a package that supports spawning subprocesses to leverage multicore shared-memory resources. It is available as part of standard Python distributions on many platforms without further dependencies, and hence is ideal for small jobs on desktop machines. The Multiprocessing mapping of dispel4py creates a pool of processes and assigns each PE instance to its own process. Messages are passed between PEs using multiprocessing.Queue objects. Depending on the number of targeted processes that the user specifies, multiple instances of each PE are created to exploit all available processes.

As for the MPI mapping, dispel4py maps PEs to a collection of processes. Each PE instance reads from its own private input queue on which its input blocks arrive. Each data block triggers the execution of the process() method which may or may not produce output blocks. Output from a PE is distributed to the connected PEs depending on the grouping pattern that the destination PE has requested. The distribution of data is managed by a Communication class for each connection. The default is ShuffleCommunication which implements a round-robin pattern; the use case below also uses GroupByCommunication which groups the output by certain attributes.

The Multiprocessing mapping also allows partitioning of the graph to support handling several PEs together in one process. Users can specify partitions of the graph and the mapping distributes these across processes in the same way as single PEs. The following shows the command to execute the mining_tweets dispel4py graph, using the Multiprocessing mapping:

```
dispel4py multi -n <number processes> mining_tweets \
-d '{"ReadData" : [ {"input" : "tweets.json"} ]}'
```

6.6.4 Spark

Apache Spark™ is a popular platform that leverages Hadoop® YARN and HDFS taking advantage of many properties such as dynamic scaling and fault tolerance [62]. It has also been used on HPC platforms by distributing Spark worker nodes at runtime to the available processors for a job on an HPC cluster and managing Spark tasks. The Spark mapping of dispel4py is a prototype and is targeted at users who are not familiar with the Hadoop®/MapReduce environment but would like to take advantage of the rich functionality provided by that platform.

The dispel4py system maps to Spark™ by translating a graph description to PySpark actions and transformations on Spark's resilient distributed datasets (RDDs). RDDs can be created from any storage source supported by Hadoop®, such as text files in HDFS, HBase tables, or Hadoop sequence files. Root PEs in the dispel4py graph are mapped to RDD creators, and each PE with inputs is mapped to an action or a transformation of an RDD. At the leaves of the dispel4py graph a call to *foreach()* is inserted in order to trigger the execution of a complete pipeline of actions. In the future we envisage mapping a set of reserved PE names (possibly supported by the registry) to access all of the available actions and transformations in Spark™and thereby take full advantage of the power of the Spark™ platform.

```
dispel4py spark mining_tweets \
-d '{"ReadData" : [ {"input" : "tweets.json"} ]}'
```

6.6.5 Sequential Mode

The sequential mode (simple) is a simple standalone mode that is ideal for testing workflow execution during development. It executes a dispel4py graph within a single process without optimization. When executing a dispel4py graph in sequential mode, the dependencies of each PE are determined and the PEs in the graph are executed in a depth-first fashion starting from the roots of the graph (data sources). The source PEs process a number of iterations as specified by the user. All data is processed and messages are passed in-memory within a single process.

```
dispel4py simple mining_tweets \
-d '{"ReadData" : [ {"input" : "tweets.json"} ]}'
```

6.7 Performance

The dispel4py system is currently being developed as part of the VERCE project [64], which is developing a virtual research environment to enable siesmologists to exploit their growing wealth of data [13]. Several seismic workflows have been developed using dispel4py, including the Seismic Ambient Noise Cross-Correlation workflow, the xcorr workflow for short, which we have selected to evaluate the performance of dispel4py because it represents a common data-intensive analysis pattern and is used by many seismologists. It preprocesses and cross-correlates traces (sequences of measurements of acceleration in three dimensions) from multiple seismic stations. The xcorr workflow has two phases:

- *Phase 1—Preprocess*: Each time series from a seismic station (each *trace*), is subject to a series of data-preparation treatments chosen and parameterized by seismologists. These are varied to explore different strategies for statistically extracting information from the noise. The processing of each trace is independent from other traces, making this phase "pleasingly" parallel (complexity $O(n)$, where n is the number of stations).
- *Phase 2—Cross-Correlation*: For all pairs of stations calculate the correlation, essentially identifying the time for signals to travel between that pair, and hence infer some, as it turns out time varying, properties of the intervening rock. The complexity is $O(n^2)$.

Figure 6.3 shows the dispel4py xcorr workflow, which has five PEs. Note that the tracePrep PE is a compositePE, where data preparation takes place. Each of those PEs, from decim to calc_fft, performs processing on the data stream. The design and formalization of the scientific method (the PE composition and the cross-correlation function) are easily modified by seismologists to meet revised goals, by selecting a different sequence of PEs and their parameters coded as simple Python functions—see Listing 6.2. The scientists do not worry about

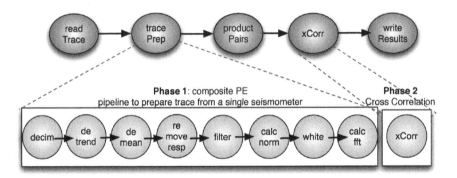

Fig. 6.3 A simplified dispel4py abstract workflow for seismic cross-correlation

how to parallelize the workflow nor choose on which platform it will run because dispel4py performs the parallelization automatically. The source code of the PE implementations in the example above is 350 lines of Python, while the definition of the graph is only 60 lines long.

6.7.1 Experiments

Five platforms have been used for our experiments: Terracorrelator, the SuperMUC cluster (LRZ – Munich), Amazon EC2, the Open Science Data Cloud cluster (OSDC sullivan), and the Edinburgh Data-Intensive Machine (EDIM1); these are described below and summarized in Table 6.3.

The Terracorrelator [49] is configured for massive data assimilation in environmental sciences at the University of Edinburgh. The machine has four nodes, each with 32 cores. Two nodes are Dell R910 servers with 4 Intel® Xeon® E7-4830 8 processors, each with 2 TB RAM, 12 TB SAS storage and 8 Gbps fibre-channel to storage arrays. We used one 32-core node for our measurements.

SuperMUC [44] is a supercomputer at the Leibniz Supercomputing Centre (LRZ) in Munich, with 155,656 processor cores in 9400 nodes. SuperMUC is based on the Intel® Xeon® architecture consisting of 18 Thin Node Islands and one Fat Node Island. We used two Thin (Sandy Bridge) Nodes, each with 16 cores and 32 GB of memory, for the measurements. SuperMUC has >300 TB RAM and InfiniBand ® FDR10 interconnect.

On the Amazon EC2 the Storm deployment used an 18-worker node setup. We chose Amazon's T2.medium instances [6], provisioned with 2 VCPUs and 4 GB of RAM. Amazon instances are built on Intel® Xeon® processors operating at 2.5 GHz, with Turbo up to 3.3 GHz. The MPI measurements on Amazon EC2 used the same resources.

Table 6.2 Test loads used for measurements in cross-correlation experiments

Scenario	Seismic traces	Sampling period	Input data size	Output data size
X_2^{90d}	2	90 days	1.75 GB	25 MB
X_2^{180d}	2	180 days	3.5 GB	51 MB
X_{1000}^{1h}	1000	1 h	150 MB	39 GB

OSDC sullivan [54] is an OpenStack® cluster with GlusterFS. Each node is an m1.xlarge with 8 VCPUS, 20 GB VM disk, and 16 GB RAM. Four nodes were used, providing 32 cores, for our measurements.

EDIM1[32] is an Open Nebula[53] linux cloud designed for data-intensive workloads. Backend nodes use mini ITX motherboards with low-powered Intel® Atom™ processors with plenty of space for hard disks. Our experiments on EDIM1 used a 15-node Apache Storm cluster, on a one-to-one setup with the hosting nodes. Each VM in our cluster had four virtual cores—using the processor's hyperthreading mode, 3 GB of RAM and 2.1 TB of disk space on three local disks. Data were streamed to and from a virtual cluster with the same specifications and number of nodes, implementing Apache Hadoop® HDFS.

Table 6.2 summarizes the test loads used in our experiments for evaluating the xcorr workflow, taking into account the number of seismic traces, the sampling period, the input and the output data sizes.

Measurements were repeated five times. As Storm could not be installed on all resources the set of measurements varies with target DCI as shown in Table 6.3.

6.7.2 Experimental Results

The experimental results are ordered according to Table 6.3, traversing the X_2^{90d} in order of DCI and then the X_2^{180d} and X_{1000}^{1h} in a similar order. Two types of experiments have been performed for evaluating dispel4py: Scalability and Performance.

6.7.2.1 Scalability Experiments

For each measurement we varied the number of cores, except for the simple mapping, which always uses one core to run a dispel4py workflow.

Figure 6.4 (Terracorrelator) shows that MPI and Multiprocess mappings scale well when the number of cores is increased for both X_2^{90d} and X_2^{180d}. As the Terracorrelator is a shared memory machine, the Multiprocess mapping slightly outperforms MPI.

Table 6.3 Coverage of computational platforms by cross-correlation experiments

Load	`Terra-correlator`	`SuperMUC`	`Amazon EC2`	`OSDC sullivan`	`EDIM1`
DCI type	Shared-memory	Cluster	Cloud	Cloud	Cloud
Nodes	1	16	18	4	14
Cores per node	32	16	2	8	4
Total cores	32	256	36	32	14
Memory	2 TB	32 GB	4 GB	20 GB	3 GB
X_2^{90d}	`MPI, multiprocessing &` `simple`	`MPI, multiprocessing` `& simple`		`MPI & multiprocessing`	`MPI & multiprocessing`
X_2^{180d}	`MPI, multiprocessing &` `simple`	`MPI, multiprocessing` `& simple`		`MPI & multiprocessing`	
X_{1000}^{1h}	`MPI & multiprocessing`	`MPI`	`Storm & MPI`		`MPI & Storm`

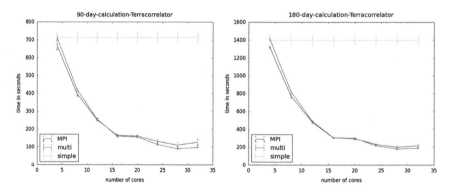

Fig. 6.4 Cross-correlation experiments running dispel4py on the Terracorrelator cluster

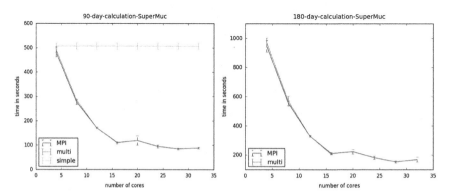

Fig. 6.5 Cross-correlation experiments running dispel4py on part of SuperMUC

Figure 6.5 shows that the MPI and the Multiprocess mappings scale well on SuperMUC, which is very fast, so our mappings perform extremely well. The MPI implementation used is optimized to a degree that it performs as fast as the multiprocessing library within shared memory. As the number of cores per node is 16, we only tested the Multiprocess mapping up to that number, because as we have shown in Fig. 6.6, that this scale of problem the mapping does not improve when there are more processes than cores.

Figure 6.6 (OSDC cloud) shows that the Multiprocess mapping scales for 8 cores, but then levels off for more as this cluster only has 8 cores per node. For the MPI mapping, it scales well for X_2^{180d}, but shows some variation for X_2^{90d}, probably due to the increase of messages for the same input data.

The simple mode is a sequential mapping that keeps all the intermediate data in memory and does not make use of multiple cores, which explains its constant performance regardless of the number of cores allocated. As an HPC platform, Super-MUC shows better performance than the others for simple. Only Terracorrelator had sufficient RAM per node for X_2^{180d} using the simple mode.

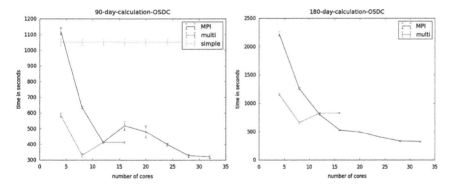

Fig. 6.6 Cross-correlation experiments running dispel4py on an OSDC cluster

6.7.2.2 Performance Experiments

To evaluate exhaustively the performance of dispel4py's parallel mappings (MPI, Multiprocessing, and Storm), we ran the X_{1000}^{1h} use case in four DCI, which have very different features using two mappings on each platform, except SuperMUC, where only the MPI mapping was tested. The Terracorrelator was selected because it is an example of a shared memory (SMP) DCI, allowing us to test Multiprocessing and MPI mappings up to 32 cores. For popularity and freedom to adjust the environment we chose Amazon EC2 Cloud, where we installed Storm and MPI.

The Storm mapping was not tested on the Terracorrelator or the SuperMUC as it required a Storm Cluster, which is not allowed on either platform. We used EDIM1 as we have control of this DCI and we had the same freedom as on Amazon EC2 to use Storm and MPI. However, the processor and network speed that EDIM1 offers are the lowest of all the DCI we tried as it was designed to minimize energy and component costs while maximizing channels to backing store per node (1 SSD and 3 HD).

The measurements on the SuperMUC, Terracorrelator, Amazon EC2, and EDIM1 have been performed with the maximum number of cores available in each DCI (256, 32, 36 and 14 respectively), as we want to evaluate the performance for each mapping under the best conditions for each DCI. Measurements were run several times for each mapping and DCI, and the results reported in Table 6.4 are the average, except for Amazon EC2, where the measures shown in the table are the fastest, because the EC2 performance suffers substantial variations (greater than a factor of 5), as a result of external factors [14].

The results show that the performance of X_{1000}^{1h} (see Table 6.4) demonstrate that dispel4py can be applied to diverse DCI targets and adapt to variations among them. For example, if we focus on MPI mapping, we observe that it performs very differently on each DCI. For example, the best results in terms of performance were achieved on the SuperMUC machine with MPI followed by

Table 6.4 Measures (in seconds) for X_{1000}^{1h} on four DCI with the maximum number of cores available

Mode	Terracorrelator	Amazon EC2	EDIM1	SuperMUC
MPI	3066	16,863	38,657	1093
multi	3144			
Storm		27,899	120,077	

Table 6.5 Highlights from measured (in seconds) performance on multiple DCI

Load	Mode	Terra-correlator	SuperMUC	Amazon EC2	OSDC sullivan	EDIM1
X_2^{180d}	simple	1420				
	MPI	242	173		613	
	multi	218	203		325	
X_{1000}^{1h}	MPI	3066	1093	16,863		38,657
	multi	3144				
	Storm			27,899		120,077

the `Terracorrelator` machine with `MPI` and `multi` mappings. The `Storm` mapping proved to be the least suitable in this case. Yet it is the best mapping in terms of fault-tolerance for any case and DCI, as `Storm` delivers automatic fault recovery and reliability. It may be those features that make it the slowest mapping.

We have demonstrated that `dispel4py` is able to map to diverse DCI targets adapting to their variations, and have shown how the performance depends on the DCI selected, and how the same use case can run faster or slower depending on the selection made (currently by the user) of DCI and `dispel4py` mapping. In future work, we plan to automate those choices, enabling `dispel4py` to identify which is the best DCI and mapping for each application.

To illustrate the way a scientist would use `Simple_process` to develop a workflow for X_{1000}^{1h} we obtained timings for X_5^{1h}; these are 88 s on a Mac OS X 10.9.5 laptop, with processor 1.7 GHz Intel® Core™ i5 and 8 GB RAM.

6.7.3 Analysis of Measurements

The major features of the measured results are summarized in Table 6.5.

To assess `dispel4py`'s automatic parallelization, we calculated the efficiency of the `MPI` mapping by using Eq. (6.1) below, which is a common method in HPC for measuring the scalability of an application. As shown in Table 6.6, for large datasets the efficiency is at over 70 % on all platforms.

$$\frac{Time\_32\ processes}{Time\_4\ processes * \frac{32}{4}} \tag{6.1}$$

Table 6.6 Efficiency values
with MPI mapping

Machine	X_2^{90d}	X_2^{180d}
Terracorrelator	0.664	0.774
Super-MUC	0.681	0.702
EC2		
OSDC	0.437	0.860

The results overall show that: (a) the *same* dispel4py workflow can be used unchanged with different mappings, (b) the scalability achieved demonstrates the power of data streaming for data-intensive workloads, (c) that the dispel4py Python library provides access to this power for scientists, both when they are developing and when they are running in production mode their automated scientific methods, and (d) mapping to different target DCIs is essential to handle the variety of workloads—exploiting effectively the features of the target DCIs.

6.8 Summary and Future Work

In this chapter we presented dispel4py, a novel data-intensive and high-performance computing middleware that is made available via a standard Python library for describing stream-based workflows. It allows its users to develop their scientific applications locally and then to run them on a wide range of HPC infrastructures without any changes to their code. Moreover, it provides automated and efficient parallel mappings to MPI, multiprocessing, Storm and Spark frameworks, gaining the benefits of their engineering for big data applications. Though it gains access to the full power and ubiquity of Python, it retains and visualizes a simple conceptual model so that users specializing in any field of R&D can use it easily, from the stages of experimenting with new ideas, through data-driven method development to sustained production use. It facilitates collaboration between those domain specialists and data scientists, and invests in its own data-intensive engineering to map flexibly onto traditional and emerging platforms with unchanged semantics but improved performance.

We demonstrate using an application from the field of seismology how dispel4py can be used to design and formalize scientific methods (the PE compositions and their connectivity). This illustrates how easy dispel4py is to use as it has a simple conceptual model and requires very few lines of Python code to define a workflow. The processing elements (PEs) that manipulate data units flowing along data streams are easily reused in a well-defined and modular way by different users, in different workflows, on different platforms via different mappings.

To help make data-intensive methods more understandable, reproducible and open, and to aid diagnosis of faults, dispel4py comes with a data provenance functionality, and with an information registry that can be accessed transparently by workflows. By using the registry, users store their workflows (and their components) with their relevant annotations, for further runs and/or for sharing them with others. The provenance mechanism allows users to analyze at runtime the provenance information collected and offers combined operations and triggers to access and download data, which may be selectively stored at runtime, into dedicated data archives. There is also an interactive tool that lets users view provenance graphs and initiate such operations. The diagnostic tool monitors each workflow's performance and computes the most efficient parallel parameters to use. Currently, we are developing a run-time adaptive compression strategy to reduce the volume of data streamed between the storage and compute systems or between a workflow's components.

As an open-source project dispel4py's development will be driven by its users and contributors. The engineering for consistency, stability and sustainability across diverse and evolving platforms will continue as a focus of attention with particular concern for minimizing data traffic and dynamically choosing appropriate platforms. As in all workflow systems, building a well-designed and well-explained repository of ready-made processing elements and reusable patterns is key to adoption. We are fortunate in that this often only requires simple wrapping of existing Python libraries. Usability, particularly for the data-driven domain specialists, will remain a key concern. This requires that we keep the conceptual model simple both for the data-flow graphs and the PEs, so that the many domain experts who don't have technical support close at hand can still flourish; indeed we believe that it should be simpler than it is today. In addition, data-intensive methods are limited if they are marooned on a dispel4py island, as many of today's sophisticated methods are compositions of methods developed by different communities using different technologies. This should be accommodated by multi-workflow systems [61] frontended by adaptive and intuitive method composition tools [36].

The growth and importance of data-driven methods will continue for the foreseeable future. Investment in engineering for these systems is already vigorous. The corresponding investment in making them usable, understandable and trustworthy is lagging behind. dispel4py is a small step on the route to addressing this.

References

1. B. Ács, X. Llorà, L. Auvil, B. Capitanu, D. Tcheng, M. Haberman, L. Dong, T. Wentling, M. Welge, A general approach to data-intensive computing using the Meandre component-based framework, in *Proceedings of 1st International Workshop on Workflow Approaches to New Data-centric Science, WANDS '10* (ACM, New York, 2010), pp. 8:1–8:12
2. B. Agarwalla et al., Streamline: scheduling streaming applications in a wide area environment. J. Multimedia Syst. **13**, 69–85 (2007)
3. K. Agrawal et al., Mapping filtering streaming applications. Algorithmica **62**(1–2), 258–308 (2012)
4. S.G. Ahmad et al., Data-intensive workflow optimization based on application task graph partitioning in heterogeneous computing systems, in *4th IEEE International Conference on Big Data and Cloud Computing* (2014)
5. S. Aiche et al., Workflows for automated downstream data analysis and visualization in large-scale computational mass spectrometry. Proteomics **15**(8), 1443–1447 (2015)

6. Amazon web services, http://aws.amazon (2016)
7. Apache, http://zookeeper.apache.org (2016)
8. Apache, storm.apache.org/ (2016)
9. M.P. Atkinson, M. Parsons, The digital-data challenge, in *The DATA Bonanza – Improving Knowledge Discovery for Science, Engineering and Business*, Chap. 1, ed. by M.P. Atkinson et al. (Wiley, Hoboken, 2013), pp. 5–13
10. M.P. Atkinson, C.S. Liew, M. Galea, P. Martin, A. Krause, A. Mouat, Ó. Corcho, D. Snelling, Data-intensive architecture for scientific knowledge discovery. Distrib. Parallel Databases **30**(5–6), 307–324 (2012)
11. M.P. Atkinson et al., Data-Intensive thinking with Dispel, in *THE DATA BONANZA: Improving Knowledge Discovery for Science, Engineering and Business*, Chap. 4 (Wiley, Hoboken, 2013), pp. 61–122
12. M.P. Atkinson, R. Baxter, P. Besana, M. Galea, M. Parsons, P. Brezany, O. Corcho, J. van Hemert, D. Snelling, *The DATA Bonanza – Improving Knowledge Discovery for Science, Engineering and Business* (Wiley, Hoboken, 2013)
13. M.P. Atkinson, M. Carpené, E. Casarotti, S. Claus, R. Filgueira, A. Frank, M. Galea, T. Garth, A. Gemünd, H. Igel, I. Klampanos, A. Krause, L. Krischer, S.H. Leong, F. Magnoni, J. Matser, A. Michelini, A. Rietbrock, H. Schwichtenberg, A. Spinuso, J.-P. Vilotte, VERCE delivers a productive e-Science environment for seismology research, in *Proceedings of 11th IEEE eScience Conference* (2015)
14. AWS EC2, The top 5 AWS EC2 performance problems (2013), http://www.datadoghq.com/wp-content/uploads/2013/07/top_5_aws_ec2_performance_problems_ebook.pdf
15. D. Barseghian et al., Workflows and extensions to the Kepler scientific workflow system to support environmental sensor data access and analysis. Ecol. Inform. **5**, 42–50 (2010)
16. S. Beisken et al., KNIME-CDK: workflow-driven cheminformatics. BMC Bioinform. **14**(1), 257 (2013)
17. K. Belhajjame, J. Zhao, D. Garijo, M. Gamble, K. Hettne, R. Palma, E. Mina, O. Corcho, J.-M. Gómez-Pérez, S. Bechhofer, G. Klyne, C. Goble, Using a suite of ontologies for preserving workflow-centric research objects, in *Web Semantics: Science, Services and Agents on the World Wide Web*, vol. 32 (2015), pp. 16–42. ISSN:1570-8268
18. G.B. Berriman et al., Generating complex astronomy workflows, in *Workflows for e-Science* (Springer, London, 2007)
19. G.B. Berriman, E. Deelman, P.T. Groth, G. Juve, The application of cloud computing to the creation of image mosaics and management of their provenance, in *Software and Cyberinfrastructure for Astronomy*, vol. 7740, ed. by N.M. Radziwill, A. Bridger (SPIE, Bellingham, 2010), p. 77401F
20. M.R. Berthold, N. Cebron, F. Dill, T.R. Gabriel, T. Kötter, T. Meinl, P. Ohl, K. Thiel, B. Wiswedel, Knime - the konstanz information miner. SIGKDD Explor. **11**, 26–31 (2009)
21. D. Blankenberg, G.V. Kuster, N. Coraor, G. Ananda, R. Lazarus, M. Mangan, A. Nekrutenko, J. Taylor, Galaxy: a web-based genome analysis tool for experimentalists, in *Current Protocols in Molecular Biology* (Wiley, New York, 2010)
22. C. Buil-Aranda, M. Arenas, O. Corcho, A. Polleres, Federating queries in {SPARQL} 1.1: syntax, semantics and evaluation. Web Semant. Sci. Serv. Agents World Wide Web **18**(1), 1–17 (2013). Special section on the semantic and social web
23. M. Carpené, I. Klampanos, S. Leong, E. Casarotti, P. Danecek, G. Ferini, A. Gemünd, A. Krause, L. Krischer, F. Magnoni, M. Simon, A. Spinuso, L. Trani, M.P. Atkinson, G. Erbacci, A. Frank, H. Igel, A. Rietbrock, H. Schwichtenberg, J.-P. Vilotte, Towards addressing cpu-intensive seismological applications in europe, in *Supercomputing*, vol. 7905, ed. by J. Kunkel, T. Ludwig, H. Meuer. Lecture Notes in Computer Science (Springer, Berlin/Heidelberg, 2013), pp. 55–66
24. D. Churches et al., Programming scientific and distributed workflow with Triana services. Concurr. Comput. Pract. Exp. **18**(10), 1021–1037 (2006)
25. L. Dalcin, https://pypi.python.org/pypi/mpi4py (2016)

26. D. De Roure, C. Goble, Software design for empowering scientists. IEEE Softw. **26**(1), 88–95 (2009)
27. D. De Roure et al., The design and realisation of the myexperiment virtual research environment for social sharing of workflows. Futur. Gener. Comput. Syst. **25**, 561–567 (2009)
28. E. Deelman, K. Vahi, G. Juve, M. Rynge, S. Callaghan, P.J. Maechling, R. Mayani, W. Chen, R.F. da Silva, M. Livny, K. Wenger, Pegasus, a workflow management system for science automation. Futur. Gener. Comput. Syst. **46**, 17–35 (2015)
29. DIR group, https://github.com/dispel4py/dispel4py/ (2016)
30. DIR group, https://github.com/dispel4py/dispel4py/tree/master/dispel4py/examples (2016)
31. DIR group, https://github.com/iaklampanos/dj-vercereg (2015)
32. DIR group, https://www.wiki.ed.ac.uk/display/dirc (2015)
33. Z. Falt, D. Bednárek, M. Kruliš, J. Yaghob, F. Zavoral, Bobolang: a language for parallel streaming applications, in *Proceedings of HPDC '14* (ACM, New York, 2014), pp. 311–314
34. R. Filgueira, A. Krause, M.P. Atkinson, I. Klampanos, A. Spinuso, S. Sanchez-Exposito, dispel4py: an agile framework for data-intensive escience, in *Proceedings of IEEE eScience 2015* (2015)
35. D. Gannon, B. Plale, S. Marru, G. Kandaswamy, Y. Simmhan, S. Shirasuna, Dynamic, adaptive workflows for mesoscale meteorology, in *Workflows for e-Science: Scientific Workflows for Grids*, ed. by Taylor et al. (Springer, London, 2007), pp. 126–142
36. S. Gesing, M.P. Atkinson, R. Filgueira, I. Taylor, A. Jones, V. Stankovski, C.S. Liew, A. Spinuso, G. Terstyanszky, P. Kacsuk, Workflows in a dashboard: a new generation of usability, in *Proceedings of WORKS '14* (IEEE Press, Piscataway, 2014), pp. 82–93
37. F. Guirado et al., Enhancing throughput for streaming applications running on cluster systems. J. Parallel Distrib. Comput. **73**(8), 1092–1105 (2013)
38. P. Kacsuk (ed.), *Science Gateways for Distributed Computing Infrastructures: Development Framework and Exploitation by Scientific User Communities* (Springer, Cham, 2014)
39. S. Kelling, D. Fink, W. Hochachka, K. Rosenberg, R. Cook, T. Damoulas, C. Silva, W. Michener, Estimating species distributions – across space, through time and with features of the environment, in *The DATA Bonanza – Improving Knowledge Discovery for Science, Engineering and Business*, Chap. 22, ed. by M.P. Atkinson et al. (Wiley, Hoboken, 2013), pp. 441–458
40. H. Koepke, Why Python rocks for research. Technical report, University of Washington (2014)
41. S. Kohler, S. Gulati, G. Cao, Q. Hart, B. Ludascher, Sliding window calculations on streaming data using the kepler scientific workflow system. Proc. Comput. Sci. **9**, 1639–1646 (2012)
42. M. Kozlovszky, K. Karóczkai, I. Márton, P. Kacsuk, T. Gottdank, DCI bridge: executing WS-PGRADE workflows in distributed computing infrastructures, in *Science Gateways for Distributed Computing Infrastructures: Development Framework and Exploitation by Scientific User Communities*, Chap. 4, ed. by P. Kacsuk (Springer, Cham, 2014), pp. 51–67
43. L. Lefort et al., W3C Incubator Group Report – review of Sensor and Observation ontologies. Technical report, W3C (2010)
44. LRZ, http://www.lrz.de/services/compute/supermuc/systemdescription/ (2015)
45. B. Ludäscher, I. Altintas, C. Berkley, D. Higgins, E. Jaeger, M. Jones, E.A. Lee, J. Tao, Y. Zhao, Scientific workflow management and the Kepler system. Concurr. Comput. Pract. Exp. **18**(10), 1039–1065 (2006)
46. P. Maechling, E. Deelman, L. Zhao, R. Graves, G. Mehta, N. Gupta, J. Mehringer, C. Kesselman, S. Callaghan, D. Okaya, H. Francoeur, V. Gupta, Y. Cui, K. Vahi, T. Jordan, E. Field, SCEC CyberShake workflows—automating probabilistic seismic hazard analysis calculations, in *Workflows for e-Science: Scientific Workflows for Grids*, ed. by I.J. Taylor et al. (Springer London, 2007), pp. 143–163
47. P. Martin, G. Yaikhom, Definition of the DISPEL language, in *THE DATA BONANZA: Improving Knowledge Discovery for Science, Engineering and Business*, Chap. 10 (Wiley, Hoboken, 2013), pp. 203–236

48. T. Megies, M. Beyreuther, R. Barsch, L. Krischer, J. Wassermann, ObsPy—What can it do for data centers and observatories? Ann. Geophys. **54**(1), 47–58 (2011)
49. M. Mineter, http://gtr.rcuk.ac.uk/project/f8c52878-0385-42e1-820d-d0463968b3c0 (2015)
50. MPI Forum, http://www.mpich.org/ (2016)
51. MPI Forum, MPI: a message-passing interface standard. Int. J. Supercomput. Appl. **8**, 165–414 (1994)
52. Open MPI Team, http://www.open-mpi.org/ (2016)
53. Open Nebula, http://opennebula.org
54. OSDC, https://www.opensciencedatacloud.org/ (2015)
55. I.S. Pérez, M.S. Pérez-Hernández, Towards reproducibility in scientific workflows: an infrastructure-based approach. Sci. Program. **2015**, 243180:1–243180:11 (2015)
56. D. Rogers, I. Harvey, T.T. Huu, K. Evans, T. Glatard, I. Kallel, I. Taylor, J. Montagnat, A. Jones, A. Harrison, Bundle and pool architecture for multi-language, robust, scalable workflow executions. J. Grid Comput. **11**(3), 457–480 (2013)
57. M. Rynge et al., Producing an infrared multiwavelength galactic plane atlas using montage, pegasus and Amazon web services, in *ADASS Conference* (2013)
58. Y. Simmhan et al., Building the trident scientific workflow workbench for data management in the cloud, in *ADVCOMP* (IEEE, Sliema, 2009)
59. A. Spinuso et al., Provenance for seismological processing pipelines in a distributed streaming workflow, in *Proceedings of EDBT '13* (ACM, New York, 2013), pp. 307–312
60. M. Stonebraker, P. Brown, D. Zhang, J. Becla, SciDB: a database management system for applications with complex analytics. Comput. Sci. Eng. **15**(3), 54–62 (2013)
61. G. Terstyanszky, T. Kukla, T. Kiss, P. Kacsuk, A. Balasko, Z. Farkas, Enabling scientific workflow sharing through coarse-grained interoperability. Futur. Gener. Comput. Syst. **37**, 46–59 (2014)
62. UC Berkeley AMPLab, http://spark.apache.org/ (2016)
63. K. Vahi, M. Rynge, G. Juve, R. Mayani, E. Deelman, Rethinking data management for big data scientific workflows, in *Workshop on Big Data and Science: Infrastructure and Services* (2013)
64. VERCE project, http://www.verce.eu (2015)
65. C. Walter, Kryder's law: the doubling of processor speed every 18 months is a snail's pace compared with rising hard-disk capacity, and Mark Kryder plans to squeeze in even more bits. Sci. Am. **293**(2), 32–33 (2005)
66. M. Wilde, M. Hategan, J.M. Wozniak, B. Clifford, D.S. Katz, I. Foster, Swift: a language for distributed parallel scripting. Parallel Comput. **37**(9), 633–652 (2011)
67. K. Wolstencroft, R. Haines, D. Fellows, A. Williams, D. Withers, S. Owen, S. Soiland-Reyes, I. Dunlop, A. Nenadic, P. Fisher, J. Bhagat, K. Belhajjame, F. Bacall, A. Hardisty, A. Nieva de la Hidalga, M.P. Balcazar Vargas, S. Sufi, C. Goble, The taverna workflow suite: designing and executing workflows of web services on the desktop, web or in the cloud. Nucleic Acids Res. **41**(W1), W557–W561 (2013)
68. J.M. Wozniak, T.G. Armstrong, K. Maheshwari, E.L. Lusk, D.S. Katz, M. Wilde, I.T. Foster, Turbine: a distributed-memory dataflow engine for high performance many-task applications. Fundam. Inform. **128**(3), 337–366, 01 (2013)

Chapter 7
Performance Analysis Tool for HPC and Big Data Applications on Scientific Clusters

Wucherl Yoo, Michelle Koo, Yi Cao, Alex Sim, Peter Nugent, and Kesheng Wu

Abstract Big data is prevalent in HPC computing. Many HPC projects rely on complex workflows to analyze terabytes or petabytes of data. These workflows often require running over thousands of CPU cores and performing simultaneous data accesses, data movements, and computation. It is challenging to analyze the performance involving terabytes or petabytes of workflow data or measurement data of the executions, from complex workflows over a large number of nodes and multiple parallel task executions. To help identify performance bottlenecks or debug the performance issues in large-scale scientific applications and scientific clusters, we have developed a performance analysis framework, using state-of-the-art open-source big data processing tools. Our tool can ingest system logs and application performance measurements to extract key performance features, and apply the most sophisticated statistical tools and data mining methods on the performance data. It utilizes an efficient data processing engine to allow users to interactively analyze a large amount of different types of logs and measurements. To illustrate the functionality of the big data analysis framework, we conduct case studies on the workflows from an astronomy project known as the Palomar Transient Factory (PTF) and the job logs from the genome analysis scientific cluster.

W. Yoo (✉) • A. Sim • K. Wu
Lawrence Berkeley National Laboratory, Berkeley, CA, USA
e-mail: wyoo@lbl.gov; ASim@lbl.gov; kwu@lbl.gov

M. Koo
University of California at Berkeley, Berkeley, CA, USA
e-mail: michellekoo@berkeley.edu

Y. Cao
California Institute of Technology, Pasadena, CA, USA
e-mail: ycao@astro.caltech.edu

P. Nugent
Lawrence Berkeley National Laboratory, Berkeley, CA, USA
University of California at Berkeley, Berkeley, CA, USA
e-mail: penugent@lbl.gov

© Springer International Publishing Switzerland 2016
R. Arora (ed.), *Conquering Big Data with High Performance Computing*,
DOI 10.1007/978-3-319-33742-5_7

139

Our study processed many terabytes of system logs and application performance measurements collected on the HPC systems at NERSC. The implementation of our tool is generic enough to be used for analyzing the performance of other HPC systems and Big Data workflows.

7.1 Introduction

Large science projects have been relying on thousands of CPUs to compute terabytes or petabytes of data [17, 31]. This chapter studies the challenges of analysis on large amount of monitored performance measurement data from the cluster system, and tackles the challenges by providing a performance analysis tool. Many HPC applications are built to generate and analyze terabytes or petabytes of data, and they often require running over thousands of CPU cores and large amount of data accesses, data movements, and computations. HPC applications running on HPC platforms include parallel applications or high-throughput computing applications, and these applications could involve Big Data workflows. The job executions from the complex workflows generate a large volume of measurement data over time. Due to the complexities of the job executions on the large number of machines and large amount of data, it is challenging to identify bottlenecks or to debug the performance issues in HPC applications and scientific clusters. Understanding the performance characteristics of the complex scientific workflows managing thousands of concurrent operations and debugging their performance issues are challenging for various reasons. The concurrent data accesses may compete for shared data storage and networking resources with each other on the system. The performance characteristics on the current generation of the storage hardware and memory hierarchies are sometimes unexpected due to the complexities. Unexpected delays can be introduced by the temperature-based throttling mechanisms on the modern CPUs, which reduce the clock rate to decrease heat production. It is common for large parallel jobs to experience mysterious performance fluctuations. To address these challenges and to help understand these performance fluctuations and diagnose performance bottlenecks, we have developed PATHA (Performance Analysis Tool for HPC Applications) [41] for HPC applications and scientific clusters using a state-of-art big data processing tools .

Our tool can ingest system logs and application performance measurements to extract key performance measures, and apply the most sophisticated statistical tools and data mining methods on the performance data. It utilizes an efficient data processing engine to allow users to interactively analyze large amounts of different types of logs and measurements. Using PATHA, an interactive exploration of the performance measurement data is enabled for the user's understanding about the performance of their own applications. A big data processing framework, Apache Spark^{TM} [43] is employed in the backend to distribute and parallelize computational workloads for analyzing large amounts of performance data. Spark^{TM} can utilize in-memory processing to reduce an overhead of loading data from disk. Compared with other big processing frameworks such as Hadoop, Spark^{TM} fits better for PATHA to conduct performance analysis combined with in-memory computations by reducing loads and stores of intermediate results on disk. PATHA can identify performance bottlenecks through outlier detection and other data mining techniques through the extensive analysis capability of Spark^{TM}. PATHA further provides interactive visualization of these bottlenecks and their dependencies, and allows quick integration of the new performance information as it gathers from the newly generated log files.

For case studies, we have worked with the Palomar Transient Factory (PTF) [22, 28] application and job logs collected from Genepool cluster [15] for genome analysis. We have used PATHA to analyze application performance of the PTF application with the measurements collected on the NERSC Edison cluster. We have also analyzed system performance to identify job performance outliers from the logs of Genepool cluster. We believe that PATHA is applicable to other analysis cases for conducting performance analysis and bottleneck detection, and these example case studies are representative use cases. It is generally applicable to the combined multiple data sources such as application logs and cluster logs from schedulers, sub systems of clusters, or monitoring tools.

The PTF application is a wide-field automated survey that records images of variable and transient objects in the sky [22, 28]. Images from these cameras are sent and stored to the NERSC Edison cluster for processing through the near real-time image subtraction data analysis pipeline. In each processing step, the timestamps of the execution were recorded in the database. As the PTF analysis processing pipeline has been optimized, its performance analysis to find hidden performance bottlenecks is particularly challenging. In addition, queries on the database need to be minimized for severe overhead on the production database shared by many users. Through our study with PATHA, we were able to identify and to optimize hidden performance bottlenecks and inefficient operational steps, without incurring large database overhead.

The Genepool scientific cluster produces large job logs from a large number of nodes and multiple parallel task executions, and it is challenging to analyze and extract meaningful information from the job logs due to the complexities. Many performance-related fields in the logs are correlated to each other, and jobs interact in the task executions. Using PATHA, we were able to analyze system performance in an efficient and user-friendly way, to extract interesting information about system performance, and to identify performance outliers. We believe that PATHA can analyze the performance of other scientific workflows as well as cluster systems using the application logs and cluster system logs.

The contributions are:

- the design of bottleneck detection methods in PATHA, e.g., execution time analysis and data dependency performance analysis
- the development of PATHA to handle different types of measurements from scientific applications and HPC cluster systems

- the evaluation of PATHA using a big data application such as PTF and large-size job logs of a scientific cluster

The rest of the chapter is organized as follows. Section 7.2 presents related work. Section 7.3 demonstrates the design and implementation of PATHA. Sections 7.4 and 7.5 present case studies for experimental evaluations. The conclusion and future work are in Sect. 7.6.

7.2 Related Work

Several performance modeling works were proposed as follows. For scientific workflows, the following works were proposed; for example, on a CPU node [37], in the Grid environment [9, 14], and in the cloud environment [24, 25]. However, the large scientific workflows are frequently running on a large computer with sophisticated storage and networking resources that are not easily captured by the existing models. Williams et al. [37] proposed the Roofline model about a theoretical model for analyzing upper bounds of performance with given computational bottlenecks and memory bottlenecks. Tikir et al. [34] proposed to use genetic algorithms to predict achievable bandwidth from cache hit rates for memory-bound HPC applications. Duan et al. [14] proposed to use a hybrid Bayesian-neural network to predict the execution time of scientific workflow in the Grid environment. In addition, performance models have been proposed in other domains. Cohen et al. [12] proposed to learn an ensemble of models using a tree-augmented Bayesian network on a system trace, and cluster the signatures to identify different regions of normality as well as recurrent performance problems. Ironmodel [32] employed a decision tree to build the performance model based on the queuing theory of expected behavior from end-to-end traces. Ganesha [27] adopted a clustering mechanism to learn the initial parameters to model Hadoop performance behavior as a mixture of k Gaussians. These performance models are based on the simplified models or assumptions about the executions on the underlying hardwares and cluster. Our performance analysis is based on the empirical model without sacrificing the complex interactions in the executions.

Researchers have proposed mechanisms to identify performance problems in the cluster environment. Barham et al. [3] proposed to use clustering to identify anomalous requests. Xu et al. [38] proposed to find erroneous execution paths using the PCA [18] on console logs. Bod et al. [4] used logistic regression with L1 regularization on the vector of metric quantiles to fingerprint performance crisis. They used online sampling to estimate quantiles from hundreds of machines. Vento et al. proposed to use floating point operations per seconds (flops) as an indicator of poor performance jobs [36]. Yoo et al. [40] adapted machine learning mechanisms to identify performance bottlenecks using fingerprints generated from micro-benchmarks. Yadwadkar et al. [39] proposed to use the Support Vector Machine (SVM) [13] to proactively predict stragglers from cluster resource utilization counters. Browne et al. [6] proposed a comprehensive resource management tool by combining data from event logs, schedulers, and performance counters. In addition, Chuah et al. [11] proposed to link resource usage anomalies with system failures. These works can help our work differentiate performance bottlenecks at cluster level and those at application level. However, they also lack support to analyze large size logs from scientific workflows.

Several mechanisms have been proposed to find the causes of performance bottlenecks. Chen et al. [10] proposed to use change point detection on the latency of TCP request using conventional statistical mechanism, CUSUM and BCP. It built a causal graph using pc-algorithm. Kim et al. [20] proposed to periodically generate service dependencies and rank root cause candidates using conditional clustering. Killian et al. [19] proposed to find performance affecting changes (per-machine differences) in logs. T-tests were used to compare the two distributions and determine whether the observed differences of variances are significantly different. Sambasivan et al. [29] proposed a mechanism to diagnose the causes of performance changes in a distributed system by extending call path analysis to request flow analysis. They claim that it can find performance affecting changes in flows by comparing to the previous runtime traces. While these proposed mechanisms were not designed to analyze large size of data, they can complement our work by providing automation to identify data dependency of performance bottlenecks.

Yuan et al. [42] used signatures constructed from n-grams of system-call invocations observed during a problem occurrence. They used the Support Vector Machine (SVM) [13] to detect whether a new signature is representative of a previously observed problem. It builds a regression tree showing the low-level parameters such as function parameters, configuration values, or client-sent parameters that best separate requests in these categories. Oliner et al. [26] proposed to identify correlations in anomalies across components. Their mechanism calculates anomaly scores for discrete time-intervals by comparing the distribution of some counters such as average latency. Attariyan et al. [2] proposed performance cost evaluation using information flow analysis. Kundu et al. [21] presented performance modeling of VM-hosted applications as resource allocation and contention using machine learning mechanisms.

Several performance tools have been proposed to improve the performance of HPC applications. Shende et al. [30] designed Tau to support monitoring parallel applications by automatically inserting instrumentation routines. Böhme et al. [5] presented an automatic mechanism which performs instrumentation during compilation in order to identify the causes of waiting periods for MPI applications. Burtscher et al. [8] designed Perfexpert to automate identifying the performance bottlenecks of HPC applications with predefined rules. Adhianto et al. [1] designed HPCToolkit to measure hardware events and to correlate the events with source code to identify performance bottlenecks of parallel applications. The detection mechanisms of these tools were heavily dependent on manually created metrics and rules. Vampir [7] uses MPI workers to parallelize performance analysis computations. However, it lacks supporting distributing the computations to multiple nodes. These performance tools lack distributing and parallelizing the computations of the analysis to large number of machines. Some tools such as Tau [30] and Vampir [7] can parallelize computational loads MPI processes, and potentially these MPI processes can be extended to distribute multiple loads. However, this extension involves significant implementation challenges due to synchronization and inter-process communication complexities and lack of fault tolerance support. Instead, PATHA can interactively analyze the large size application and system logs of scientific workflows requiring large computation within user-tolerable latency. Furthermore, PATHA can complement these tools by providing mechanisms to distribute and parallelize the computational loads in addition to fault tolerance feature from read-only characteristics of RDDs.

Depending on job-specified resource requirements and the current system load, the queuing system may assign one or multiple nodes to the job, and the system captures performance information such as memory usage, CPU time, and elapsed time. However, such information is generally about the whole job, and more fine-grained information would be helpful to understand the individual steps of a large parallel workflow. Alternatively, the workflow management system could record the performance information of each step of a workflow [23], a profiler may be used to automatically capture detailed performance information [30], or the user may instrument selected operations with some library functions [33]. In these cases, the performance data is typically captured into log files. Our tool leverages these measuring mechanisms for the performance analysis.

7.3 Design and Implementation

PATHA is implemented over a big-data processing framework, Apache Spark^{TM} [43] that distributes and parallelizes computational workloads at the parser and the analyzer levels. The PATHA supports:

- execution time analysis to find performance bottlenecks and time consuming routines in applications
- data dependency analysis to identify the possible causes of performance bottlenecks
- interactive visualization synched with performance measurements

Using PATHA, performance analyses can be conducted on different types of logs and measurements in scientific clusters in addition to application logs. As shown in Fig. 7.1, each parser is implemented to parse different types of logs such as application logs, file system logs, job logs, and cluster monitoring logs. At the parser level, the different types of logs stored in parallel file system or database can be loaded into distributed memory of the multiple nodes, as a form of Resilient Distributed Datasets (RDDs). RDDs are the partitioned fault-tolerant (immutable) collection of elements that can be operated in a distributed and parallel manner on Apache Spark^{TM}. The computations of RDDs for parsing and loading multiple files or separate partitions in each file are distributed and computed in parallel in multiple

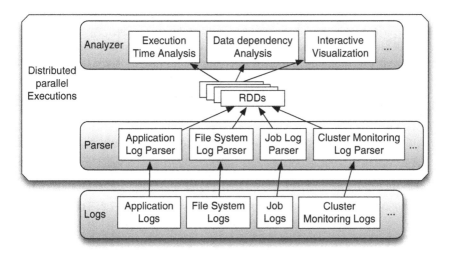

Fig. 7.1 The overview of PATHA

cores and multiple nodes. Then, these parsed results are loaded into memories in multiple nodes or saved in multiple files. These loaded RDDs from the different types of logs can be analyzed separately or together in PATHA. PATHA provides the components of execution time analysis, data dependency performance analysis, and interactive visualization framework. It provides the predefined set of functions to enable users to conduct the performance analysis.

RDDs loaded as a form of rows of tuples can be computed in parallel by using the functional programming operators such as map, reduce, 'group by key', or 'and sort by key'. The executions are implemented by combining these functional programming operators. In addition, computations between RDDs such as join are supported so that different types of logs can be analyzed in a combined way. This enables discovering uncovered performance issues that were difficult to be identified when the logs are separately analyzed. Users can interactively conduct performance analysis with either querying results or generating graphs by combining with grouping, aggregation, and filtering operations with the interesting fields or variables. This is to pinpoint the bottleneck locations from the execution time analysis and to identify the most significant field related to the discovered bottleneck from the data dependency analysis. In addition, it provides the platform that users can use the existing libraries of machine learning and statistics in popular programming languages, such as Java and Python, so that they can easily conduct feature selection, clustering, classification, or regression analysis. Not only conducting the PATHA-provided predefined performance analysis, but users also can implement their customized analysis by combining libraries on the loaded RDDs without consuming much time on the implementation of distributed and parallel programming.

The computations at the analyzer level are distributed and computed in parallel on multiple cores and multiple nodes similarly at the parser level. Apache Spark^{TM} can be deployed in a separate cluster with several hundred nodes so that users can interactively execute analyses after connecting to the cluster.[1] While there is cost of loading data from disk and distributing data into different nodes, the analysis can be conducted on the loaded data from the memory. PATHA utilizes this memory cache of data as much as possible so that the loading overhead can be minimized. The crucial point is that underlying parallel execution of PATHA is dispatched in multiple nodes and multiple cores in each node without the user intervention. Therefore, PATHA can handle the large amount of different types of performance logs and measurements.

The performance analyses in Sects. 7.4 and 7.5 were conducted using the visualization tools and figure outputs of PATHA shown in Fig. 7.2. The interactive framework is implemented with iPython and web browser, which allows users to integrate performance analysis with the web browser front-end. As it uses web browser as front-end, the requirement of installation is much reduced, users can interactively conduct performance analysis by creating the different types of plots with different time window or conditions. The computations on data as RDDs behind this interactive analysis are distributed and executed in parallel. In addition, users can conduct execution time analysis by querying different types of graphs such as histograms, bar graphs, box plots and scatter plots. This analysis framework not only allows users to uncover performance bottlenecks in terms of execution time, but also allows them to further query and to study the possible sources of additional performance bottlenecks related to the data dependency. The case study of the PTF application shows the steps and procedures to use PATHA, and we currently work on to release PATHA as a software package along with the instructional manual. We believe that these example of use cases can generally applicable to other performance analyses for systems and applications. We plan to conduct user studies to improve the user interface and to reduce the learning curve on using PATHA. The development of this tool will continue to advance the future research of characterizing performance behavior and building performance model.

7.4   Case Study—PTF Application

The evaluations of PATHA using the Apache Spark^{TM} [43] were conducted on a part of the NERSC Edison clusters with several hundred machines with two 8-core CPUs, Intel$^{®}$ Xeon$^{®}$ E5-2670 and 64 GB memory. The Palomar Transient Factory

---

[1]The current version of Apache Spark^{TM} is optimized when using local disk as an intermediate data storage instead of accessing data from a parallel file system in scientific clusters. However, the lack of local disk in scientific clusters did not impact much on performance. This was because the most of the performance analyses in PATHA were compute bound as the most of the data movement was happened in parsing and loading time.

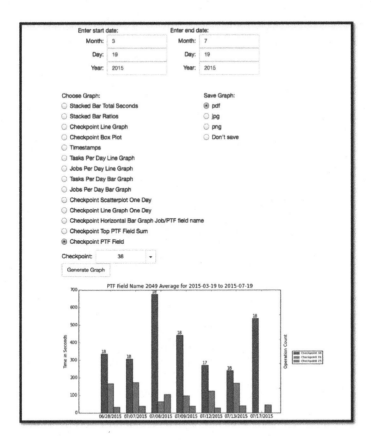

Fig. 7.2 The interactive visualization framework

(PTF) application was used as a case study to evaluate PATHA. We have used the PTF application logs collected on the NERSC Edison cluster system from March 19, 2015 to July 18, 2015 (PST). The PTF application was executed on the compute nodes of the NERSC Edison cluster system assigned for regular applications with two 12-core CPUs, Intel® Xeon® E5-2695 and 64 GB memory.[2] We used Apache Spark™ to distribute and parallelize computational loads for PATHA. PATHA allowed more thorough investigation on the PTF application measurements and derived values from the measurements such as the average execution time by averaging differences of the measured timestamps in multiple tasks in each job. While we were able to select the number of machines up to several hundreds for our experiments, the executions were not exclusive in the allocated machines. We plan to set up exclusive executions on the allocated machines to analyze the scalability of

---

[2]The Edison cluster system for PATHA has different configurations with that of the Edison cluster system for the PTF.

PATHA. Due to our effort to reduce the overhead of data loading and distribution, our initial observations confirmed that PATHA was scalable in several hundred machines without degradation even with the interferences from other job executions.

7.4.1 PTF Application

The PTF application focuses on expanding our knowledge of transient phenomena such as supernova explosions and massive star eruptions [22]. There are four large-scale photometric and spectroscopic surveys that generate and/or utilize hundreds of gigabytes of data per day, and the PTF application is one of them. The transient detection survey component of the PTF has been performed at the automated Palomar Samuel Oschin 48-in. Schmidt telescope equipped with a camera that covers a sky area of 7.3 square degrees in a single snapshot. Data taken with the camera are transferred to NERSC Edison where running a real-time reduction pipeline. The pipeline matches images taken at different nights under different observing conditions and performs image subtraction to search for transients. The transient candidates out of this pipeline then pass through machine-learning classifiers to be prioritized for real transients over artifacts. The final output is then displayed through a web portal for visual inspection by human. This pipeline has achieved the goal of identifying optical transients within minutes of images being taken.

For the case study with the PTF application, we used its measurement logs that were collected in the database. The size of entire database is 1.6 TB. Timestamps, job id, task id, and checkpoint id were loaded into RDDs for execution time analysis. The execution time at each checkpoint was computed for each job and task. Then, the execution times were grouped by different keys, e.g., job or task, and the average execution times were computed with the keys. For this grouping, RDDs were needed to include columns with distinctive values to be used as keys such as job id, task id, and checkpoint id. During computation for the average, missing timestamps or unordered timestamps were filtered out. These irregularities were caused by various reasons, e.g., failures in the executions at application level or system level. To implement filtering out these using database query or customized user application can be challenging and costly. For data dependency performance analysis, the execution times were computed with multiple associated variables or fields that were potentially related to the identified performance bottlenecks.

Figure 7.3 depicts the average amount of time in seconds that the PTF analysis pipeline took on each day to execute all jobs and tasks, which were executed from May 18, 2015 to June 15, 2015. The execution of PTF application involves the executions of multiple jobs computing different areas. Each job consists of ten tasks whose checkpoints are stored in database when each processing step is conducted. As shown in Fig. 7.3a, the PTF analysis pipeline consists of 38 checkpoints, with each color representing a different checkpoint. The top five checkpoints with the longest execution time taken over a span of 64 days were checkpoints 8, 25, 29,

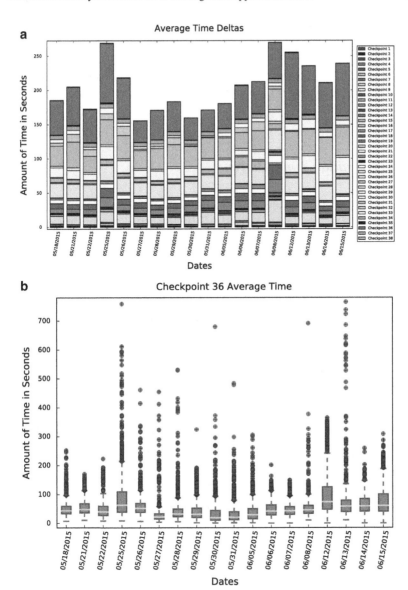

Fig. 7.3 The average amount of time in seconds for checkpoint operations, which was executed from May 18, 2015 to June 15, 2015. (**a**) The average amount of time in seconds for jobs with checkpoints. Each *color* represents one of the 38 checkpoints. (**b**) The amount of time in seconds for jobs with checkpoint 36, where each vertical line is for 1 day. The line in the middle of a box marks the median time, the brackets of a box mark the interquartile ranges (IQRs), the high whisker is at $Q3 + 1.5 \times IQR$, and the circles mark the instances with extra long execution time (Color figure online)

31, and 36 in Fig. 7.3a. The average daily percentage calculations revealed that checkpoint 8 took on average 7.29 %, checkpoint 25 takes 11.16 %, checkpoint 29 takes 6.22 %, checkpoint 31 takes 14.79 %, and most notably, checkpoint 36 takes 23.72 % on average. The three checkpoints with the longest average execution times were further investigated for a potential bottleneck where performance could be improved.

7.4.2 Execution Time Analysis

Using PATHA, we conducted execution time analysis on checkpoint 36 specifically. The Transients in the Local Universe (TILU) query—a geometric query that correlates the incoming candidates with the table of known galaxies with their elliptical shapes and orientations. Figure 7.3b shows the box plot of average execution time of this query together with the performance outliers as circles. We see that many jobs took much longer than the average time. Based on this observation, we focused on certain days, such as June 13, 2015 that has larger variance and many outliers. Further study about this day will be presented next paragraphs.

Figure 7.4a shows the scatter plot of the amount of time in seconds for each job throughout the day starting at approximately 04:30, when the first task of checkpoint 25, 31, and 36 was executed on June 13, 2015. Figure 7.4b shows the scatter plot for checkpoint 36, which shows the spikes of an execution time during the time period from 08:20 to 08:45 on June 13, 2015. This particular time window would need further investigation.

Figure 7.4c shows the time spent by each instance of TILU query in the time window from 08:20 to 08:45. By focusing on the executions in this specific time duration with significantly higher execution times, we can discern whether bottlenecks are caused by cluster load competing system resources or caused by application-specific reasons. The length of each bar in Fig. 7.4c shows the total execution time of each job, and its corresponding job IDs for the checkpoint operation 36. The jobs with longest execution time had job IDs 16339, 16340, and 16342. Interestingly, the other job, 16353 that was executed in the similar time window showed much smaller execution times. These instances of long execution time were interspersed with normal looking instance showing much smaller execution time. Therefore, we speculate that system loads due to competing for shared resources did not cause their long execution times. Additional possibility would be studied in the next section about whether these long execution times had data dependencies in user data.

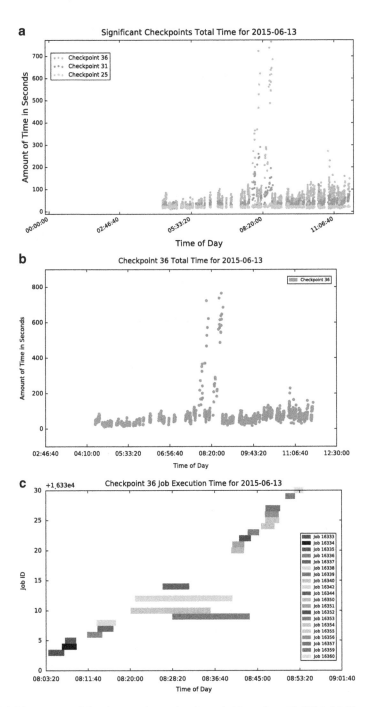

Fig. 7.4 The amount of time in seconds per day for each job on June 13, 2015. (**a**) The average amount of checkpoint time for checkpoint 25, 31, and 36. (**b**) The average amount of time for checkpoint 36. (**c**) The execution times of all jobs with their corresponding job IDs during the time period 12:20 to 13:06 on June 13, 2015

7.4.3   Data Dependency Performance Analysis

We studied two attributes in the PTF application to see how they affected the execution time and how the performance of the PTF application depended on them, based on the suggestions from application scientists. These attributes were: the number of saved objects and the galactic latitude.

7.4.3.1   Analysis of Saved Objects

In the PTF application, a fragmentation algorithm is performed on the subtraction images to identify variable stars and transient candidates over the noisy background and to measure their shape parameters such as the length and angle of its major axis and ellipticity. Then, a simple shape cut is applied to remove elongated candidates that are probably artifacts. The candidates that pass the shape cut are saved for further examination, i.e., checkpoints after the checkpoint 25. The reason of having different numbers of saved objects is that the total number of candidates for further examination is determined by the number of variable stars (since real transients are rare), which in turn correlates with the total number of stars in a given field. Figure 7.5a, c, e show the average execution time of checkpoints 25, 31 and 36 for the number of saved objects, and the linear relation between the average execution time and the number of saved objects.[3] It shows the performance bottleneck in these checkpoints when computed with the large number of stored objects. This is because the large number of saved objects requires more comparisons and computation. This identified bottleneck would lead to reduce the computation time when computing with the large number of stored objects.

7.4.3.2   Analysis of Galactic Latitude

Figure 7.5b, d, f illustrate a correlation between the execution times of three checkpoints (25, 31, and 36) and the absolute galactic latitude (zero degree corresponds to the Milky Way plane), and the performance bottlenecks is shown at low galactic latitudes. The physical reason behind it is that the closer a field is to the Milky Way, the more celestial objects, the more transient/variable candidates, and the longer execution time for these checkpoints. At low galactic latitudes, i.e., close to the Milky Way plane, the stellar density is higher, and so is the density of variable stars. Therefore, images taken at low galactic latitudes in general generate more candidates than those at high galactic latitudes.

With the identified data dependencies, we optimized the application pipeline for the checkpoint 31, where we parallelized the most time consuming routines when

---

[3]The linear regression coefficients are 5.673×10^{-3} for checkpoint 31 and 8.515×10^{-4} for checkpoint 36.

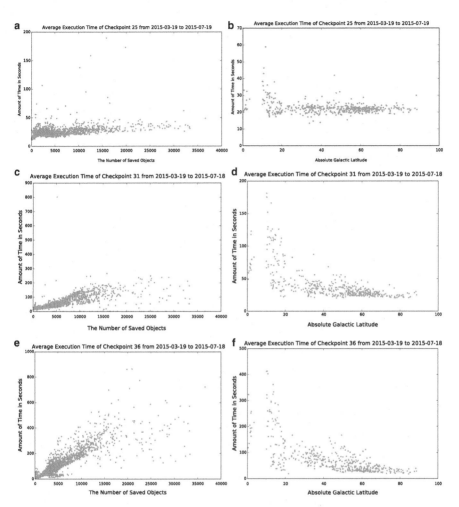

Fig. 7.5 The average execution time of checkpoints 25, 31, and 36 for number of saved objects and absolute galactic latitude. (**a**) Saved objects—checkpoint 25. (**b**) Absolute galactic latitude—checkpoint 25. (**c**) Saved objects—checkpoint 31. (**d**) Absolute galactic latitude—checkpoint 31. (**e**) Saved objects—checkpoint 36. (**f**) Absolute galactic latitude—checkpoint 36

computing the larger number of saved objects and at low absolute galactic latitudes. The optimization showed the reduced execution time up to 2.05 times. We can further improve overall performance of the checkpoint 31 by applying the parallel executions more intelligently. Instead of making all executions in parallel including small execution times, we can only make executions in parallel that supposedly take much larger execution time with larger number of saved objects and at low absolute galactic latitudes. For this purpose, we plan to analyze how to adjust parallelism depending on the number of saved objects and absolute galactic latitudes.

7.5   Case Study: Job Log Analysis

7.5.1   Job Logs

Scientific clusters generally consist of a job scheduling engine, compute nodes for assigned jobs, storage nodes for a parallel file system, data transfer nodes for network accesses, and special purpose nodes for database or web services. Scientific clusters contain sufficiently large number of nodes and multiple parallel executions from the tasks that incur complexity challenges for analysis from developers and system administrators. Due to the complexity and the size of the job logs, it is challenging for developers and system administrators to analyze and extract meaningful information from the logs. For example, one can attempt to select jobs with the top-most resource usage to analyze whether they experience performance anomalies, and this task can be a challenge because of the large amount of job logs and the concurrent data accesses on the shared resources.

7.5.2   Test Setup

In our experiments, we have used the job logs collected on the Genepool cluster at NERSC, consisting of 774 nodes [15]. The logs were written by the Univa Grid Engine [35] when each job was finished. The size of the logs from the Genepool cluster from July 29, 2014 to February 28, 2016 was 4.5 TB that can incur significant computational challenges for an analysis. To generate plots in later sections, we have used the part of the job logs from January 1, 2015 to January 31, 2015 (GMT) with 2.4 million records or 1.1 GB. It contains 45 fields such as host name, job name, failed code, exit code, and resource usages. We selected 13 performance-related fields: wall clock, user/system CPU time, soft/hard page faults, file block input/output, voluntary/involuntary context switches, aggregated memory usage, aggregated I/O, maximum resident set size, and maximum virtual memory. Table 7.1 describes these fields.

7.5.3   Job Log Analysis

Scientific clusters have encountered technical advances that involve increasing scales of data volumes, number of machines, and exploited parallelism in software executions. This leads to unforeseen scales of interactions in software executions between hardware components and nodes. Developers often encounter difficulties to gather information about the details of underlying hardwares and runtime information of a cluster containing large number of nodes. On the other hand, system administrators are overwhelmed by large-scale performance-related logs and

Table 7.1 The description of performance-related fields

Feature	Description
Wall clock	The duration between start and end of a task
User CPU time	The sum of time spent on CPU cores at the user level
System CPU time	The sum of time spent on CPU cores at the system level
CPU time	The sum of the user CPU time and system CPU time
Maximum resident set size	Maximum value of utilized memory size during job execution
Page reclaims	Soft page faults without involving I/O
Page faults	Hard page faults with involving I/O
Block input operations	The number of times that the file system had to perform input
Block output operations	The number of times that the file system had to perform output
Voluntary context switches	The number of times for voluntary context switches
Involuntary context switches	The number of times for involuntary context switches
Memory	The integral memory usage in Gbytes $*$ CPU time in seconds
IO	The amount of data transferred in input/output operations

noises from interactions and interferences in the executions of a cluster. Due to these reasons, it is challenging to analyze system performance on scientific clusters. For these challenges, PATHA provides big-data-ready performance analysis features with much less developmental costs.

Figure 7.6 shows the aggregated CPU time(s) from top four frequently executed applications on Genepool cluster at NERSC between January 1, 2015 and January 31, 2015 (GMT). The most frequently executed applications need to be selected. Then the job executions from these selected top jobs (top four jobs in Fig. 7.6) need to be selected. CPU times of each job execution also need to be aggregated as one job can have multiple sub-job (task) executions. The aggregated CPU times can be plotted as box plots, and application developers can analyze whether the executed jobs spend unexpectedly large CPU time. In addition, the frequently executed top applications can be analyzed for expected performance, and PATHA makes these analyses easier.

7.5.4   Clustering Analysis

Clustering analysis groups task executions represented as points of features sharing similar performance characteristics. In our case, the features correspond to the selected fields of the job logs. The points as the target of clustering correspond to each record of the job logs representing a completed execution. The scales of the features differ by multiple orders of magnitude as they show the different types of fields of the job logs. The scale of each field is adjusted by *L1-norm* scaling of each field.

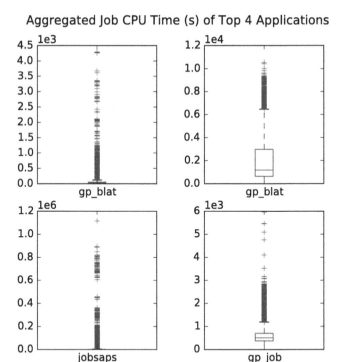

Fig. 7.6 The aggregated CPU time (s) from top four applications

Table 7.2 The size of clustering results with different scalings and k: C_i is the ith cluster

k	C_1	C_2	C_3	C_4	C_5	C_6	C_7	C_8
2	79	2.40M						
4	1	67	78	2.4M				
8	1	1	22	78	78	115	1456	2.4M

We applied K-means clustering algorithm [16], which makes clusters with a specified k as a number of clusters. Using clustering analysis, we can identify the minor clusters containing small number of points, and these minor clusters have different characteristics from other major clusters containing large number of points. When the centroids of these minor clusters are separated from the centroid of the major clusters with significant distances, this can mean that the minor clusters have significantly different characteristics. Therefore, these minor clusters can be good targets for further performance analysis where significantly different characteristics are resulted from.

Table 7.2 shows the size of clustering results with different k. For instance, in Table 7.2 with L1-*norm* scaling, C_1 (size 79) with $k = 2$ is divided into C_1 (size 1) and C_3 (size 78) with $k = 4$. In addition, C_1 and C_3 with $k = 4$ are repeatedly identified with the same size in C_1 and C_4 wit $k = 8$. We inspected these two clusters, and discovered that they contain extraordinarily high values of integrated

Fig. 7.7 PCA-transformed clustering results. (**a**) Original, $L1$-*norm*, $k = 2$. (**b**) Original, $L1$-*norm*, $k = 4$. (**c**) Original, $L1$-*norm*, $k = 8$

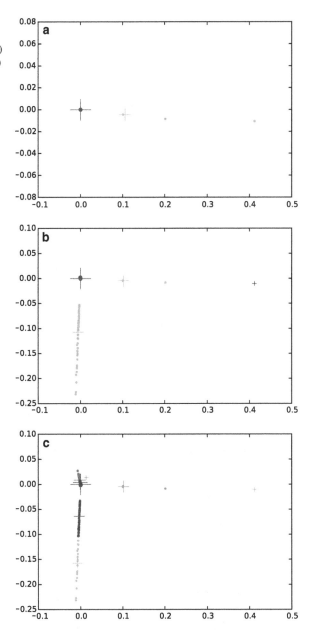

memory usage above the theoretically possible value. We speculated that this was a system glitch and required further investigation of its causes. We believe that this example shows the usage of the tool towards the identification of the performance outliers from the clustering results.

Plotting results from the clustering algorithm help validate fitting results. As the size of features is 13, it is not possible to directly plot on 2D or 3D space. To enable plotting, we applied dimensionality reduction method, PCA [18]. Figure 7.7 shows that the PCA-transformed plot of clustering results for the original $L1$-*norm* scaled data in Table 7.2. Each cluster is colored in a different color. The centers of the clusters are represented with cross marks with the same color of the cluster. The points in clusters are randomly selected in log-log scale of the size of the clusters. This is to reduce the number of points that are most likely redundant in large clusters. However, this selection may cause an underestimation of large clusters. In addition, the sizes of cross marks of centers are increased in log-log scale to represent the size of clusters. Figure 7.7 shows the identified performance outliers. Figure 7.7a, b, c show significantly distant minor clusters near (0.1,0), (0.2,0), and (0.4,0). They were the clusters, C_1 (size 79) with $k = 2$ and C_1 (size 1) and C_3 (size 78) with $k = 4$ in Table 7.2.[4]

7.6 Conclusion

As the computations and analyses of large datasets are distributed and parallelized on multiple compute-nodes, it becomes challenging to analyze the performance issues related to the applications and hardware platforms due to the large collection of performance measurements. In order to tackle this challenge, we have developed PATHA (Performance Analysis Tool for HPC Applications) using an open-source big data processing framework. The HPC applications as referred to here include parallel applications, high-throughput computing applications, and other applications for Big Data processing.

Users can use PATHA to identify performance characteristics and performance bottlenecks in their science applications and scientific clusters. PATHA can analyze large volume of performance measurement data from large science projects. It provides the execution time analysis to find performance bottlenecks and time-consuming routines in applications, data dependency performance analysis to identify possible data dependencies of discovered performance bottlenecks. These analyses can be interactively conducted by using different types of performance measurements from scientific clusters.

We have conducted two case studies to evaluate PATHA. With the PTF application, we identified performance bottlenecks in checkpoint operations 25, 31, and 36. We also identified their direct data dependencies on the number of saved objects and the absolute galactic latitude. Developers of the PTF application have been working on optimizing identified performance bottlenecks, and the execution time has been reduced up to 2.05 times. In the other case study with the job logs, we have analyzed system performance in a large scientific cluster. We were also able to identify system performance outliers using clustering analysis and dimensionality reduction method.

---

[4]Please note that the points in Fig. 7.7b, c near (0,[−0.05, −0.25]) are not shown in Fig. 7.7a as they are the part of the major cluster near (0,0).

For the future work, we plan to use the PATHA in the extended analysis combining the measurements of hardware executions in scientific clusters and the measurements from the applications. In addition, we plan to automate the process of bottleneck identification. These will help identify the performance bottlenecks due to the system related issues along with the application related issues.

Acknowledgements This work was supported by the Office of Advanced Scientific Computing Research, Office of Science, the U.S. Dept. of Energy, under Contract No. DE-AC02-05CH11231. This work used resources of NERSC. The authors would like to thank Douglas Jacobson, Jay Srinivasan, and Richard Gerber at NERSC, Bryce Foster and Alex Copeland at JGI, and Arie Shoshani at LBNL.

References

1. L. Adhianto, S. Banerjee, M. Fagan, M. Krentel, G. Marin, J. Mellor-Crummey, N.R. Tallent, HPCTOOLKIT: tools for performance analysis of optimized parallel programs. Concurr. Comput. Pract. Exp. **22**(6), 685–701 (2010)
2. M. Attariyan, M. Chow, J. Flinn, X-ray: automating root-cause diagnosis of performance anomalies in production software, in *OSDI '12: Proceedings of the 10th USENIX Conference on Operating Systems Design and Implementation* (2012), pp. 307–320
3. P. Barham, A. Donnelly, R. Isaacs, R. Mortier, Using magpie for request extraction and workload modelling, in *OSDI'04: Proceedings of the 6th Conference on Symposium on Operating Systems Design & Implementation* (2004), pp. 259–272
4. P. Bod, U.C. Berkeley, M. Goldszmidt, A. Fox, U.C. Berkeley, D.B. Woodard, H. Andersen, P. Bodik, M. Goldszmidt, A. Fox, D.B. Woodard, H. Andersen, Fingerprinting the datacenter, in *EuroSys'10: Proceedings of the 5th European Conference on Computer Systems* (ACM, New York, 2010), pp. 111–124. doi:10.1145/1755913.1755926
5. D. Bohme, M. Geimer, F. Wolf, L. Arnold, Identifying the root causes of wait states in large-scale parallel applications, in *Proceedings of the 2010 39th International Conference on Parallel Processing* (IEEE, San Diego, 2010), pp. 90–100
6. J.C. Browne, R.L. DeLeon, C.D. Lu, M.D. Jones, S.M. Gallo, A. Ghadersohi, A.K. Patra, W.L. Barth, J. Hammond, T.R. Furlani, R.T. McLay, Enabling comprehensive data-driven system management for large computational facilities, in *2013 International Conference for High Performance Computing, Networking, Storage and Analysis (SC)* (2013), pp. 1–11. doi:10.1145/2503210.2503230
7. H. Brunst, M. Winkler, W.E. Nagel, H.C. Hoppe, Performance optimization for large scale computing: the scalable vampir approach, in *Computational Science-ICCS 2001* (Springer, Heidelberg, 2001), pp. 751–760
8. M. Burtscher, B.D. Kim, J. Diamond, J. McCalpin, L. Koesterke, J. Browne, PerfExpert: an easy-to-use performance diagnosis tool for HPC applications, in *Proceedings of the 2010 ACM/IEEE International Conference for High Performance Computing, Networking, Storage and Analysis* (2010), pp. 1–11
9. J. Cao, D. Kerbyson, E. Papaefstathiou, G.R. Nudd, Performance modeling of parallel and distributed computing using pace, in *Conference Proceeding of the IEEE International Performance, Computing, and Communications Conference, 2000. IPCCC '00* (2000), pp. 485–492. doi:10.1109/PCCC.2000.830354
10. P. Chen, Y. Qi, P. Zheng, D. Hou, CauseInfer: automatic and distributed performance diagnosis with hierarchical causality graph in large distributed systems, in *INFOCOM'14: Proceedings IEEE International Conference of Computer Communications* (IEEE, Toronto, 2014), pp. 1887–1895. doi:10.1109/INFOCOM.2014.6848128

11. E. Chuah, A. Jhumka, S. Narasimhamurthy, J. Hammond, J.C. Browne, B. Barth, Linking resource usage anomalies with system failures from cluster log data, in *IEEE 32nd International Symposium on Reliable Distributed Systems (SRDS)* (2013), pp. 111–120. doi:10.1109/SRDS.2013.20

12. I. Cohen, J.S. Chase, M. Goldszmidt, T. Kelly, J. Symons, Correlating instrumentation data to system states: a building block for automated diagnosis and control, in *OSDI*, vol. 6 (USENIX, Berkeley, 2004), pp. 231–244

13. C. Cortes, V. Vapnik, Support-vector networks. Mach. Learn. **20**(3), 273–297 (1995). doi:10.1007/BF00994018

14. R. Duan, F. Nadeem, J. Wang, Y. Zhang, R. Prodan, T. Fahringer, A hybrid intelligent method for performance modeling and prediction of workflow activities in grids, in *Proceedings of the 2009 9th IEEE/ACM International Symposium on Cluster Computing and the Grid, CCGRID '09* (IEEE Computer Society, Washington, 2009), pp. 339–347. doi:10.1109/CC-GRID.2009.58

15. Genepool cluster, http://www.nersc.gov/users/computational-systems/genepool (2015)

16. J.A. Hartigan, M.A. Wong, Algorithm AS 136: a K-means clustering algorithm. J. R. Stat. Soc. Ser. C Appl. Stat. **28**(1), 100–108 (1979). doi:10.2307/2346830

17. T. Hey, S. Tansley, K. Tolle (eds.), *The Fourth Paradigm: Data-Intensive Scientific Discovery* (Microsoft, Redmond, 2009)

18. I. Jolliffe, Principal component analysis, in *Wiley StatsRef: Statistics Reference Online* (Wiley, New York, 2014)

19. C. Killian, K. Nagaraj, C. Killian, J. Neville, Structured comparative analysis of systems logs to diagnose performance problems, in *NSDI'12: Proceedings of the 9th USENIX Conference on Networked Systems Design and Implementation* (USENIX, Berkeley, 2012)

20. Kim, M., Sumbaly, R., Shah, S., Root cause detection in a service-oriented architecture. ACM SIGMETRICS Perform. Eval. Rev. **41**(1), 93–104 (2013). doi:10.1145/2465529.2465753

21. S. Kundu, R. Rangaswami, A. Gulati, M. Zhao, K. Dutta, Modeling virtualized applications using machine learning techniques. ACM SIGPLAN Not. **47**(7), 3–14 (2012)

22. N.M. Law, S.R. Kulkarni, R.G. Dekany, E.O. Ofek, R.M. Quimby, P.E. Nugent, J. Surace, C.C. Grillmair, J.S. Bloom, M.M. Kasliwal, L. Bildsten, T. Brown, S.B. Cenko, D. Ciardi, E. Croner, S.G. Djorgovski, J.V. Eyken, A.V. Filippenko, D.B. Fox, A. Gal-Yam, D. Hale, N. Hamam, G. Helou, J. Henning, D.A. Howell, J. Jacobsen, R. Laher, S. Mattingly, D. McKenna, A. Pickles, D. Poznanski, G. Rahmer, A. Rau, W. Rosing, M. Shara, R. Smith, D. Starr, M. Sullivan, V. Velur, R. Walters, J. Zolkower, The palomar transient factory: system overview, performance, and first results. Publ. Astron. Soc. Pac. **121**(886), 1395–1408 (2009)

23. B. Ludäscher, I. Altintas, C. Berkley, D. Higgins, E. Jaeger, M.B. Jones, E.A. Lee, J. Tao, Y. Zhao, Scientific workflow management and the kepler system. Concurr. Comput. Pract. Exp. **18**(10), 1039–1065 (2006)

24. M. Malawski, G. Juve, E. Deelman, J. Nabrzyski, Cost- and deadline-constrained provisioning for scientific workflow ensembles in iaas clouds, in *Proceedings of the International Conference on High Performance Computing, Networking, Storage and Analysis, SC '12* (IEEE Computer Society Press, Los Alamitos, 2012), pp. 22:1–22:11

25. A. Matsunaga, J.A.B. Fortes, On the use of machine learning to predict the time and resources consumed by applications, in *Proceedings of the 2010 10th IEEE/ACM International Conference on Cluster, Cloud and Grid Computing, CCGRID '10* (IEEE Computer Society, Washington, 2010), pp. 495–504. doi:10.1109/CCGRID.2010.98

26. A.J. Oliner, A.V. Kulkarni, A. Aiken, Using correlated surprise to infer shared influence, in *DSN'10: IEEE/IFIP International Conference on Dependable Systems & Networks* (IEEE, Chicago, 2010), pp. 191–200. doi:10.1109/DSN.2010.5544921

27. X. Pan, J. Tan, S. Kavulya, R. Gandhi, P. Narasimhan, Ganesha: blackBox diagnosis of MapReduce systems. ACM SIGMETRICS Perform. Eval. Rev. **37**(3), 8–13 (2009). doi:10.1145/1710115.1710118

28. F. Rusu, P. Nugent, K. Wu, Implementing the palomar transient factory real-time detection pipeline in GLADE: results and observations, in *Databases in Networked Information Systems*. Lecture Notes in Computer Science, vol. 8381 (Springer, Heidelberg, 2014), pp. 53–66

29. R.R. Sambasivan, A.X. Zheng, M.D. Rosa, E. Krevat, S. Whitman, M. Stroucken, W. Wang, L. Xu, G.R. Ganger, M. De Rosa, E. Krevat, S. Whitman, M. Stroucken, W. Wang, L. Xu, G.R. Ganger, Diagnosing performance changes by comparing request flows, in *NSDI'11: Proceedings of the 8th USENIX Conference on Networked Systems Design and Implementation* (USENIX, Berkeley, 2011)
30. S.S. Shende, A.D. Malony, The TAU parallel performance system. Int. J. High Perform. Comput. Appl. **20**(2), 287–311 (2006)
31. A. Shoshani, D. Rotem, (eds.), *Scientific Data Management: Challenges, Technology, and Deployment* (Chapman & Hall/CRC Press, Boca Raton, 2010)
32. E. Thereska, G.R. Ganger, Ironmodel: robust performance models in the wild. ACM SIGMETRICS Perform. Eval. Rev. **36**(1), 253–264 (2008). doi:10.1145/1375457.1375486
33. B. Tierney, W. Johnston, B. Crowley, G. Hoo, C. Brooks, D. Gunter, The netlogger methodology for high performance distributed systems performance analysis, in *The Seventh International Symposium on High Performance Distributed Computing, 1998. Proceedings* (1998), pp. 260–267. doi:10.1109/HPDC.1998.709980
34. M. Tikir, L. Carrington, E. Strohmaier, A. Snavely, A genetic algorithms approach to modeling the performance of memory-bound computations, in *Proceedings of the 2007 ACM/IEEE Conference on Supercomputing* (ACM, New York, 2007), p. 47
35. Univa grid engine, http://www.univa.com/products/grid-engine.php (2015)
36. D.D. Vento, D.L. Hart, T. Engel, R. Kelly, R. Valent, S.S. Ghosh, S. Liu, System-level monitoring of floating-point performance to improve effective system utilization, in *2011 International Conference for High Performance Computing, Networking, Storage and Analysis (SC)*, pp. 1–6
37. S. Williams, A. Waterman, D. Patterson, Roofline: an insightful visual performance model for multicore architectures. Commun. ACM **52**(4), 65–76 (2009). doi:10.1145/1498765.1498785
38. W. Xu, L. Huang, A. Fox, D. Patterson, M.I. Jordan, Detecting large-scale system problems by mining console logs, in *SOSP'09: Proceedings of the ACM SIGOPS 22nd Symposium on Operating Systems Principles* (ACM, New York, 2009), pp. 117–131. doi:10.1145/1629575.1629587
39. N.J. Yadwadkar, G. Ananthanarayanan, R. Katz, Wrangler: predictable and faster jobs using fewer resources, in *Proceedings of the ACM Symposium on Cloud Computing, SOCC '14* (ACM, New York, 2014), pp. 26:1–26:14. doi:10.1145/2670979.2671005. http://doi.acm.org/10.1145/2670979.2671005
40. W. Yoo, K. Larson, L. Baugh, S. Kim, R.H. Campbell, ADP: automated diagnosis of performance pathologies using hardware events, in *Proceedings of the 12th ACM SIGMETRICS/PERFORMANCE*, vol. 40 (ACM, New York, 2012), pp. 283–294. doi:10.1145/2254756.2254791
41. W. Yoo, M. Koo, Y. Cao, A. Sim, P. Nugent, K. Wu, Patha: performance analysis tool for hpc applications, in *IPCCC'15: Proceedings of the 34st IEEE International Performance Computing and Communications Conference* (2015)
42. C. Yuan, N. Lao, J.R. Wen, J. Li, Z. Zhang, Y.M. Wang, W.Y. Ma, Automated known problem diagnosis with event traces, in *EuroSys'06: Proceedings of the 1st ACM SIGOPS/EuroSys European Conference on Computer Systems*, vol. 40 (ACM, New York, 2006), pp. 375–388. doi:10.1145/1218063.1217972
43. M. Zaharia, M. Chowdhury, M.J. Franklin, S. Shenker, I. Stoica, Spark: cluster computing with working sets, in *Proceedings of the 2Nd USENIX Conference on Hot Topics in Cloud Computing, HotCloud'10* (USENIX, Berkeley, 2010)

Chapter 8
Big Data Behind Big Data

Elizabeth Bautista, Cary Whitney, and Thomas Davis

Abstract There is data related to the collection and management of big data that is as relevant as the primary datasets being collected, and can itself be very large. In this chapter, we will examine two aspects of High Performance Computing (HPC) data that fall under the category of big data. The first is the collection of HPC environmental data and its analysis. The second is the collection of information on how large datasets are produced by scientific research on HPC systems so that the datasets can be processed efficiently. A team within the computational facility at NERSC created an infrastructure solution to manage and analyze the data related to monitoring of HPC systems. This solution provides a single location for storing the data, which is backed by a scalable and parallel, time-series database. This database is flexible enough such that maintenance on the system does not disrupt the data collection activity.

8.1 Background and Goals of the Project

As more complex computational resources are needed to process, analyze, and simulate large datasets, we need to monitor how these resources are being used; however, the collected monitoring data can also be large and complicated, producing large datasets in itself. Depending on the industry, the monitoring process could be implemented with computers and their associated infrastructure, for example, in robotic systems in the manufacturing lines, in office building facility management systems, and even in wide area network performance or bandwidth monitoring. When the data being collected starts to expand beyond a single device to incorporate information from the surrounding environment and other devices, its complexity increases, leading into the big data realm.

The 4 V's are used to describe big data [1]. This is how the 4 V's map into our problem and the extra element we have to deal with.

E. Bautista (✉) • C. Whitney • T. Davis
National Energy Research Scientific Computing Center (NERSC), Lawrence Berkeley National Laboratory (LBNL), USA
e-mail: ejbautista@lbl.gov; clwhitney@lbl.gov; tadavis@lbl.gov

© Springer International Publishing Switzerland 2016   163
R. Arora (ed.), *Conquering Big Data with High Performance Computing*,
DOI 10.1007/978-3-319-33742-5_8

- Variety (Different forms of data): With the growing concerns with the environment, energy efficiency is becoming a much bigger issue. This data added to computer host and user job data gives a variety of data types, locations and formats that need to be gathered.
- Volume (Scale of data): With the addition of the environmental data and other external considerations have caused the volume of data to increase beyond the basic well-understood issues of computer host monitoring.
- Velocity (Analysis of streaming data): The interplay between a running computer, a global filesystem, which serves the data, and the electrical/mechanical environment that the computer runs in have caused the data collection rates to be increased to help better understand how changes in one system affects the others.
- Veracity (Uncertainty of data): Much of the data collected is uncertain in how it interacts with the data center as a whole. Research work is needed here to determine if the data is needed and at what collection rate.
- Extra element: Our unique element is the different types of consumers desiring knowledge from the data. Each consumer has their own requirements and sometimes, conflict with other consumers. Allowing each individual to gain insights from the same data without too much reconfiguration is a major goal of the project.

In the process of collecting this data, we focused on using open source [2] software in order to provide a framework of a more general scope rather than using software that was more specific in what was being accumulated. As a result, some of the analysis functionality is still in early development. We are providing package names as a reference and starting point to help the reader understand the principles behind this work.

The primary requirements of our collection system came from the needs of our environmental monitoring data and how this information can correlate to the functionality of NERSC's (National Energy Research Scientific Computing Center) new building where the goal is a Power Usage Effectiveness (PUE) [3, 4] under 1.1. (As background information, our computing facility was relocated to a new building where the computation floor that houses the supercomputers and infrastructure systems is cooled by a series of circulating air and water.) PUE is the total power provided to the facility over the power consumed by the computing resources. We wanted to efficiently circulate hot air generated by the computational floor to heat other areas of the building, such as the office floors, and be cooled by air coming from outside the building. This is in addition to the cool water system being circulated through the computational systems. This method and many of these tools could be used in any industry, especially in plant management and services.

8.1.1 The Many Faces of Data

This environmental data collect structure lend to its expansion to the greater NERSC data center serving the Lawrence Berkeley National Laboratory (LBNL), staff, groups of collaborators, project teams, and collaborators in multi-organizational structures needing data collected to answer specific questions, such as the following:

- How efficiently does the system complete jobs?
- How will the system be affected if we lower the chiller temperature?
- How can we improve the data transfer from one storage library to the computational system?
- How did the power sag affect the processing of long jobs?
- What is the energy efficiency of the facility?
- What is our power utilization on a warm day?
- How does the weather affect a system's job processing?

8.1.2 Data Variety and Location

Some of the data was being collected in areas accessible only for the data owner, while some data was not being collected at all. Because other groups did not have access to this data, and because there was no index of available data, it was possible for another group to duplicate this effort. In addition, the data is in whatever format established by the data owner, which makes it difficult if not impossible for anyone else to reformat the data. We wanted to provide a centralized location and standardized format for this data. This became the primary goal of this project.

At the start of the project, we determined what data was being collected "out there," where they were located, and in what format. As demonstrated by the sample questions above, we learned that the data collected was varied and diverse. It was necessary to provide a dataset that is expandable, adaptable and with a standardized format that one user can use in its original state yet could be reformatted easily by another user for their purpose.

8.1.3 The Different Consumers of the Data

We also considered how the consumers of this data, mainly the management team, the systems administrator, various research experts who assisted in processing the data, the scientific researchers themselves, and our funding agency, would need to interact with the data. Each of these consumers approach data in a different way, and their roles can be illustrated by metaphors of industry. For example, system administrators like plant or facility managers and manufacturing managers, need to know what is happening on the system or computing environment on a moment-by-moment basis. They need information quickly and for a short time. They use this information for fault monitoring, predictive failure, if possible, and performance characteristics.

The management team, like business managers in industry, may need quick and efficient access to the data and any correlations for their various reports to their management or even funding agencies. The research systems analyst wants the immediate view of the data to anticipate issues that may cause researchers any problems when running their jobs or to verify whether a problem may be system-related or not. This individual also needs a longer view of the data to determine if the issues are recurring or if known problems have resurfaced from prior instances. Furthermore, both the system administrator and research systems analyst constantly need to determine if the latest software upgrade has slowed the system's processing speed or has caused some other detrimental effect on the system or if the researcher needs to port his code to sync with the upgrade. If they observe a new outcome that could mean recalculating a new baseline analysis to which new results can be compared.

The scientific researchers are similar to efficiency managers and are interested in system efficiency and performance. The researchers may have written large and complex code to perform computation, to analyze their data, to perform computer simulations or to visualize their data in areas such as climate modeling, fusion research, astrophysics, and genetic research. The models that this code produces tend to be very complex; therefore, optimizing that code could be intricate. In this situation, we want to provide an environment where the researcher can inject messages or statements into their data stream to allow them to measure what is occurring during the computing run to improve speed and performance. These messages should be time-stamped with the same bases as the running job so that the researcher can do correlations. Furthermore, these messages should be easy for the researcher to access but hidden from other users.

Another consumer we had to consider is the system researcher. These individuals usually want the ability to measure how the system environment, such as the filesystem and computing resources, are being used in order to project what the future codes will need. They usually need long-term data so that they can develop or observe trend analysis in both the scientific codes and the computing hardware or software. For example, if software code developers continue to use more computation resources with a smaller memory footprint and to rely more heavily upon the network infrastructure, system architects can incorporate this specification in the next system to purchase. On the other hand, if less computing but more memory resources are needed, the ability to do remote direct memory access (RDMA [5]) in the network may be a required feature. Regardless, we need to provide this data so that these researchers can make a more informed purchase decision on their technical specification and product requirements.

Likewise, the facilities manager needs to know information like whether the new system is using more power or more cooling or if the installed system is using the full rated power draw so that they can make required changes to the building, to capacity planning or plan to correct inefficiencies in the next upgrade. For example, should they choose to spend more money to install 1.5 MW of power because the power supplies indicate that is what is needed when in comparison, the maximum draw of the system is only 0.75 MW? Could this additional expense have been used at other areas of the facility now? Should that extra power capability be installed now to make future power expansions cheaper? These changes to facility capability can be as drastic as software changes to the scientific researchers.

Lastly, we also examined the needs of the non-consumers—regular users of data whose requirements continued to evolve over time and included the ability to duplicate data to different destinations depending on their usage, move data from one location to another, and save their data in different formats.

8.2   What Big Data Did We Have?

At our organization, we have a diverse research community who has a diverse workload for our computational systems. We have categorized data according to the following five types of data patterns and resources we had observed:

• Collected data
• Data-in-flight
• Data-at-rest
• Data-in-growth
• Event data

8.2.1   Collected Data

Collected data is almost all of the general time-series data. Most of this data will be the environmental data for our new computing facility. This data becomes more important since our center will rely upon the external temperature for the heating and cooling and we need a better understanding of the computing room temperature, especially air circulation. There are five temperature sensors on the front and rear of all the racks, on the floor, including one that goes up the hot chimney that nearly reaches the ceiling. There were also sensors that measured humidity and dust particle count in the air. The new facility uses cooling towers, instead of mechanical cooling, which is a more efficient way of cooling our systems but now we need to measure the flow and temperature of water around the center. The last major data collected in this category is the power flow that included power use measurements and any losses at each step along the way throughout the data center. We measured the power flow from the main transformer through the distribution panels to the Power Distribution Unit (PDU) [6] on the floor and the individual compute nodes, observing that at each of these steps, there was some power loss. We can determine where the major losses have occurred and then devise possible ways to mitigate those losses.

8.2.2 Data-in-Flight

Data-in-flight are datasets created by large experiments and transmitted to various locations for processing. A good example of data-in-flight are the data generated by the Large Hadron Collider (LHC) [7] at the Conseil Européen pour la Recherche Nucléaire (CERN) [8], in Geneva, Switzerland. The CERN beamline can generate up to one petabyte of data per day and send that out to as many as 170 different research institutions for processing. This requires knowledge of how the wide area networks function and, more important, of the filesystem where the data will come to rest. An important aspect of transferring these large datasets is knowing the filesystem's write characteristics and expected performance. This helps to determine if the filesystem is sufficient to accept the data and if it has the ability to recover should there be any interruptions in the data flow across the wide area network. For example, while this data is being transferred "in flight," we need to collect data on network speeds, latency, and packet loss all along the wide area network to ensure a clear path from starting point to destination. In addition, as data is being received by the filesystem, we are collecting data on the disk write speeds, I/O, CRC errors [9], etc., to ensure a successful receipt.

8.2.3 Data-at-Rest

Data-at-rest are large datasets that researchers conduct searches against. This type of data will experience many reads from many different systems that could result in data hot spots. A hot spot occurs when many processes want to access the same data and all these processes could be slightly out of sync with each other, causing the physical disk head to seek around the disk, thus causing performance problems for all the processes. There are strategies to mitigate this problem, ranging from caching to data duplication, but first one needs to know where, when, and to what extent the problem is happening.

8.2.4 Data-in-growth

Another data type we have is data-in-growth where we observe many processes generating data from an initial set. This is slightly different from data-in-flight where we have to ensure the filesystem write capability is able to accept the data. In the case of data-in-growth, we need to collect data to ensure that writes can be processed rapidly from multiple compute hosts so that they do not impact the application's performance.

8.2.5   Event Data

The last data type we have is event data. Events need to be correlated with the running jobs since many of them will affect jobs in either a good or bad way. Some of this data comes from data normally collected by the system such as the following:

- Syslog
- Console logs
- Program checkpoints
- Hardware failure events
- Power events
- Anything that has a start and end time

8.2.6   Data Types to Collect

With the five defined data types and their resource requirements, we are now able to determine a set of data points to be gathered for the collector.

- Computing performance and system health data on the host(s): This included data about CPUs, memory, networking counters, user and some system processes, filesystem counters, and overall node health.
- Network performance: Data may be collected from the hosts but we also need to collect data and statistics from the switches to find oversubscribed network links and to determine the health of the switches themselves.
- Filesystem data: the biggest and most diverse type. Depending on the filesystem type, we collect the used and maximum size of the partitions to monitor for filled disk partitions or servers. We also collect data on the filesystem server load: Is one system being used more heavily than the others? If yes, why and where is it coming from? We use the read and write performance data to tune the filesystem to read/write block size, stream characteristics, and to determine applicable file sizes. Each of the above data types tends to have different filesystem needs.
- Environmental data: ambient temperature, humidity, particle counts, power, or water flow temperature. These sensors may require additional networking and infrastructure to bring the data back to the central collector.
- Event data: This type of collected data can be one of the trickiest to manage because most event data logs are easily accessible but difficult because it contains private information.

8.3   The Old Method Prompts a New Solution

Given that some of this data was already there, we wanted to know how the users at NERSC were collecting it, and what process was used to interact with this data. We had to implement many different tools over time to get the data we needed. Although many of these tools were very good at doing a specific task, they could not be expanded to a more general role. Like a beloved car that you grew up with, you eventually outgrew it or your needs changed. That was the case for most of our old monitoring and data collection system.

8.3.1   Environmental Data

The environmental data consisted of a mired of protocols and very old software with many custom data collections methods. In addition, one software package had a limitation of only functioning on a Windows 98 system using obsolete hardware, where the collection rate was one data point every 5 min. This method did not give us the resolution or the response time we needed for the new facility. Examples of the protocols used are the following:

- SEAbus™ [10]—The Siemens Energy & Automation, Inc two-wire communication protocol over RS485 for power management.
- Modbus™ [11]—The Modbus Organization serial communication protocol between electronic devices.
- Modbus™/RTU—Modbus™ protocol over serial communication like RS485 or RS232.
- Modbus™/TCP—Modbus™ protocol over TCP/IP.
- SNMP [12]—Simple Network Management Protocol. Used to collect data and program devices over TCP/IP.
- BACnet® [13]—An American Society of Heating, Refrigerating and Air-Conditioning Engineers standards protocol for building automation and control networks.
- Metasys® [14]—A Johnson Controls protocol for building automation and control.
- Johnson Controls—A building automation system.
- Metasys2—Allows non-Johnson Control devices to participate in a Metasys® network.
- Incom™ [15]—Eaton Corporation two-way INdustrial COMmunications between a network master and Cutler-Hammer breakers and switches.

We tried to create a common datastore in MySQL™ [16], of the Oracle Corporation for the environmental data. MySQL™ offered an easy to install and configure solution, and thus offered a low barrier to entry while still providing a powerful mechanism to data access. The problems that we started to encounter were when the database became very large, in excess of six billion items. At this point, malformed queries caused the database server to become unresponsive and hang. We alleviated these issues by upgrading MySQL™, getting a bigger system, and tuning the configuration, but again we soon hit the limit. We realized at that point that MySQL™ was not an easy solution, and we soon required a full-time Database Administrator (DBA) to manage the database. However, even maintaining the database became a chore. Backups either took too long or could not be completed because of table-locking issues. When the hardware failed, we lost hours of uncollected data because it took too long to restore. The process of pruning the database involved creating a new table and dropping the old, which is a quick but inefficient approach when you are trying to recover the old data and transferring it to a different machine.

In summary, MySQL™ met some of the desired goals of the project, such as developing a database that offered a single location, a standard format, and ease of use for multiple users but it did not meet our other goals to achieve a resilient, interchangeable, composable [17], and easy-to-maintain system. At this point, we decided we needed a fresh and innovative solution and relocating to the new building offered a clean break from the old processes.

8.3.2   Host Based Data

Our staple monitoring tool, Nagios® [18], has served us well. With its updated user interface and refreshed data collection methodology, we expect to continue to use Nagios® in other areas of the facility. However, the package is unable to collect data over a period of time. For example, Nagios® alerts us about a filesystem being full but not about how fast the disk partition filled up over time.

The second tool we used was Ganglia [19], which collected many of the host-based metrics that we required and offered the ability to add additional metrics via a plugin environment. However, its default datastore—Round Robin Datastore (RRD) [20]—emphasized speed and size over data volume, which did not lend itself to long-term analysis. High-resolution data was summarized into lower-resolution data over time. While Ganglia's Graphical User Interface (GUI) provided some correlation functionality, it is actually optimized for the system administrator, not necessarily for any other user.

We also used the Lustre® [21] Management Tool (LMT [22]), a specialized monitoring application. LMT's default datastore, MySQL™, gave us some difficulty that we experienced with our other MySQL™ databases. We also needed to collect additional information from these nodes, and doing so meant we would have to run two or more data collectors, a process we had no desire to implement.

Homegrown scripts are another group of monitoring tools that needed to be replaced. These scripts directly addressed needs that came about during the operation of the systems. Most of these scripts suffer from both the consistent storage of data as well as the problematic display of the results. Most of the time, only the author and some other initiate knew how to use and interpret the data.

8.3.3 Refinement of the Goal

To overcome the challenges of our old methods, we propose a new collection system that:

• Is centrally located outside of any computational system. One previous method was to collect the data on one of the compute nodes. Managing this as a separate entity means the hardware can be retired and upgraded when needed.
• Is in a common storage format for all data to ensure that future data analysis can function seamlessly.

  • Enables individual monitoring components to be changed out when new or better solutions become available.
  • Is flexible enough to add new data collections and processing as we learn more about the data we are collecting.
  • Is secure enough to protect system data while allowing researchers access to discover new interactions in this ecosystem.
  • Allows private data associated with a single job and intended for one particular researcher.

8.4 Out with the Old, in with the New Design

In the new facility, we wanted to address limiting the number of protocols in the environmental data collection area. To do this, we standardized on a common PDU in the computing rack setup, and built a monitoring network into the infrastructure that allowed the collection of the environmental data to be more consistent and on a reliable timescale.

From the data collection point of view, we needed to break this problem into its primary parts:

• Data collection
• Data transport components
• Data storage
• Visualization and analysis

An all-encompassing program that would carry out all parts of the monitoring process would not work. We knew that such programs start out well, but over time, grow to be overwhelming to maintain, and that all system flexibility would be lost. We therefore settled on an Advanced Message Queuing Protocol (AMQP)

[23] solution used by RabbitMQ® of Pivotal Software, Inc. [24]. The overall result is a scheme that allows any component to be swapped out or replaced when better or more appropriate solutions become available. By achieving modularity, the packages that we selected to use in our solution could be replaced with other similar packages to achieve the same results.

8.4.1   *Elastic*

The ELK stack by Elastic [25] stands for Elasticsearch, Logstash, and Kibana, an integrated solution that helps analyze the data in real time. Each of these products is open source and well supported. Used together, it provided us the tools we needed to search through and analyze our data. Elastic provides the ELK stack as a commercially supported product with some extra features, which we are evaluating at this time. Elastic has now provided Beats, which is a collection method for system metrics and logs.

With Elastic providing some form of the each of our requirement, we still needed to supplement their offering.

Elastic, Beats and Filebeat are trademarks of Elasticsearch BV.

Elasticsearch, Logstash and Kibana are trademarks of Elasticsearch BV, registered in the U.S. and in other countries.

8.4.2   *Data Collection*

8.4.2.1   Collectd

The major data collecting component of the framework is Collectd [26]. Like other data collection tools, Collectd has plugins for reading and writing the data and allows many different configurations to choose from. The design goal is if Collectd needs to run on a node to collect data, it should be the only thing running to collect data. We sometimes found that special purpose gateways may run data collection methods needed for a specific environment, and that those methods would send their data directly into the monitoring framework. Collectd offers the following benefits:

- A consistent data structure and definition to the information being collected.
- Since the data is sent via UDP, problems in the network or infrastructure do not take out computing resources. We do not want the monitoring to cause a job to fail. Thus the aggregation point takes most of the brunt of the monitoring process.
- Plugins can be written in C [27], even though there are Perl and PHP hooks.
- Data collection rates and plugins can be configured independently.

8.4.2.2   Custom Scripts

Our search for open source solutions did not always work, thus many of the environmental sensors required a custom solution. We tried to keep it simple by creating a common framework for the collection framework and this framework fed into RabbitMQ®.

8.4.2.3   Filebeats

Filebeats is the Elastic offering that follows log files and forwards them to a different destination. We are using it to capture much of our event data, sending it into data collect structure.

8.4.3   Data Transport Components

8.4.3.1   RabbitMQ®

RabbitMQ® provided the NERSC facility the following benefits:

- A fault-tolerant distribution setup.
- A rich number of plugins to connect to other applications.
- Accepts a good number of input applications.
- Offers a buffering capacity if segments of the infrastructure go down through the use of durable queues.
- Smooths out the bursty [28] profile of the collection process.
- Easily add data readers to a stream.
- Adds security via encrypted channels.

8.4.3.2   Logstash

We had considered using Logstash as the main connectivity between components, but RabbitMQ® has a few more benefits, and both applications work very well together. Logstash is used as the feeder into Elastic and is also the link between the remote systems. A diagram of the overall layout is shown in Fig. 8.1.

Logstash, when used as the local system aggregation point, gives us some very important functions:

- Reduces the number of network connections that the central logging clusters need to manage. The system's local server takes the local connections and forwards a single connection to the center logger.

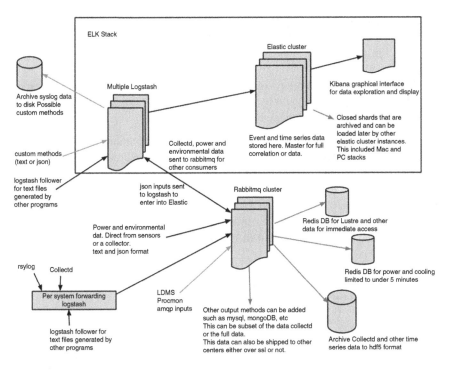

Fig. 8.1 Central Data Collect data flow

- Provides the encryption point so non-encrypted data is only present on the local system or within the local system where the data may be protected by other methods.
- In conjunction with the Collectd method, converts the UDP [29] packets that Collectd uses to TCP as a way to keep from dropping packets and loosing data. Collectd is further explained in its own section.

Logstash is also used for these applications:

- The collection and forwarding of text logs. These include syslog, console logs, and other text-based logs. Logstash has the ability to follow hard-to-forward text files, which allows us to scrape files like the torque accounting record file, console output files, etc. This file data is also forwarded to the central logger over a single stream.
- To provide a method for user applications to insert data into the collection path. Having the application write a JSON [30] output line and sending it to logstash to accomplish this.

8.4.4   Data Storage

8.4.4.1   Elasticsearch

Elasticsearch is the datastore for the ELK stack. Elasticsearch is easily clustered, has a nice shard structure, and has many different add-on applications available. Elasticsearch offers the following benefits:

- New nodes can be added to the Elasticsearch cluster without downtime to the entire cluster, and the datastore will begin to rebalance and reallocate seamlessly.
- Add-on applications for shard management and archiving.
- Add-on to allow datastore access to look similar to a SQL database.
- Since Elasticsearch is written in Java® of Oracle Corporation, it can run almost anywhere, meaning researchers who would like to analyze long-term data correlations could get individual shards and load them onto their laptops.

8.4.5   Visualization and Analysis

8.4.5.1   Kibana

The last component of the ELK stack is Kibana, the visualization tool of the stack that provides the ability to generate dashboards of the data. Kibana offers the following features:

- Integrated access to Elasticsearch datastore.
- Intelligent data delivery to the browser. For example, if the graph shows 5-min data increments and the data was collected at 1-s increments, an average will be sent to the browser instead of the full raw data stream.
- Other types of data visualization beyond the standard bar, line, and pie charts.

Another major design component of our framework is the stream processing. RabbitMQ® can write a copy of a subset of the data directly to the consumer. This is accomplished via the STOMP [31] protocol and will forward to different applications for display purposes. This allows the following:

- On-the-fly processing of the data. The only load time would be the data collection interval of the longest data point.
- Stream anomaly detection via applications such as Heka [32].
- Display dashboard such as Freeboard [33].

8.4.6   Future Growth and Enhancements

Lastly, with the ability of RabbitMQ® to republish copies and subsets of the data stream, we can load that data into other applications that can answer the questions some of our researchers have of the system. These include:

- A stream of data to a consumer to archive all data to HDF5 [34] format, which allows researchers to use a language such as R [35] effectively in correlating events.
- Streaming a subset of data to MySQL™ to populate an existing database with the same data that was gathered by different means so websites and other portals continue to function seamlessly.
- A subset of data could be streamed to a process that could mimic writing to the RRD files of a Ganglia setup to allow the GUI to be viewed by those who find it useful.
- A Redis® a trademark of Salvatore Sanfilippo [36] datastore could be populated with filesystem data for a month, allowing support staff fast access to the latest performance data and thus helping system troubleshooting.
- A second Redis® datastore with tombstone data: With only one value stored, the old value is dropped once a new value is added. This allows applications such as Nagios® to query this datastore for some of its check information instead of connecting to a host and running a program.

8.5   Data Collected

The largest part of any monitoring project is the data being collected. We are collecting from sensors in different areas of the center to perform correlations between all types of events that could affect the running of the center and the jobs running on the computing resources. We collect the following types of data:

- Electrical
- Environment
- Building automation
- Host
- Application
- Events

8.5.1 Environmental

Electrical
We are collecting data from sensors at the substation, through the different levels of PDU's available in the building, down to the node level if possible. This also includes the UPS/generator setup. Figure 8.2 below shows how data is collected from the subpanels and passed to the central monitoring cluster via a Power Over Ethernet (PoE) [37] network setup. The PoE setup is needed since many of these switches and panels are located far away from the traditional network infrastructure.

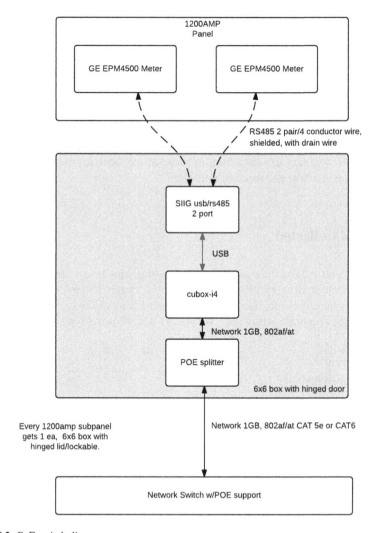

Fig. 8.2 PoE switch diagram

For example, the substation might not include normal 110 power for the sensors and hardware, which is why PoE is an easy way to get both networking and power to these remote locations. We estimate we will need 3000+ sensors with each sensor collecting 10 data points with a frequency of 1 s.

Environment
These are the sensors that collect water flows and humidity readings, and measure temperatures in different areas of the racks and center. Many of these sensors are used to ensure that the computing floor is functioning correctly to keep the systems from experiencing an issue. For example, on each rack door, there is a one-wire [38] network of 12 temperature sensors per rack, with four on each door and two on top. There are also 22 sensors in the ceiling and several under the floor. The 5000+ sensors will collect a single data point every 20 s.

Building Automation
These sensors tend to be everywhere except the HPC floor. This is primarily the lights and heating/cooling in which the latter is controlled by the workload on the computing floor. This is the smallest sensor suite but probably an interesting component to measure how the systems operate. Here we are planning for 500+ sensors collecting over 50 data points per sensor at a frequency of 2 s.

Most of the electrical, environmental, and building automation are sent into the monitoring cluster via glue code and gateways into RabbitMQ®.

8.5.2 Computational

Host
This is data we collect from the computational and support systems. The computation pool is over 11,000 nodes and may only get a summary treatment for data collection. This is one area that is still under discussion since the collection of data can slow the computation of an application. Our primary function is to serve the scientific research community, not hinder it. The computing arena is one area where computation power is at its premium.

The second type of hosts is the filesystem servers, login nodes, gateway nodes, and other types of support nodes. These nodes will have a base collection of network statistics, mounted filesystem size, memory usage, process count, users logged in, and some other general items. With a minimum of 3500+ sensors and upwards of 150 data points per sensor, this is one of the largest single sources of data. This data will be collected at a frequency of 5 s but will change to 1 s for research purposes.

A sample listing of data collected would be:

- 1-, 5- and 15-min load average
- CPU utilization
- df, diskstats of the local filesystems

- The IP network interface statistics
- The InfiniBand® from the InfiniBand Trade Association network statistics
- Processes running on the system
- Users who are logged in
- Swap and memory usage.
- Uptime

Application
One of the major applications that run on all systems is the filesystem. Here we are measuring the two global filesystems at the facility: Lustre® and GPFS™ of International Business Machine Corporation (IBM) [39]. Most of these filesystems have two different components: the server side and the clients. There will be some collection of data from both sides, but primarily the server side will be targeted first. Since the filesystems are very complicated, they tend have much more data per collection cycle. For example, the Lustre® filesystem has 500+ sensors collecting data points at 5-s collection intervals and 3500 data points per sensor. We are not measuring GPFS™ since it is still in development.

The collected data is gathered from the proc [40] filesystem and includes all the MDS [41] and OSS [42] servers:

- filesfree, filestotal
- kbytesavail, kbytesfree, kbytestotal
- md_stats
- stats
- job_stats
- brw_stats

One aspect of the collection environment allows us to enable collection of data when needed. The Lustre® client data can be collected, but we are not doing so at this time. This would require 100+ sensors collecting data at 5-s intervals and equivalent to 2500 data points per sensor. This could include the 11,000 compute nodes and much of the same data being collected in the paragraph above but from the client's point of view.

8.5.3 Event

Events
Another major datastore is syslog and other types of log data. This is slightly different from the time series performance data that is always considered but very important in determining the health and events of the system and center. This data gives us the start and stop time of jobs; critical and sometimes nonfatal errors from hardware; security data for incident detection; and other events to annotate the time-series data. This can add up to 200–300+ events per second.

The last data component for applications is the researcher-generated data, which include items such as library usage, modules loaded, license checkouts, different events that may be desired to help diagnose issues that may arise on the systems, and user-defined program checkpoints to help measure the job's progress. These events are inserted or converted to the JSON format for easy insertion into Elastic.

Since all the sensors have not been installed yet, we have tested this layout in other ways. We have loaded filesystem metadata into the system at rates upward of 350,000 inserts per second from a single process along with the three or four other input streams and three output streams without the database being affected. We have also had over six billion items in the Elasticsearch datastore. Dashboard accesses have been rather fast, and with further tuning, we do not see any issue there. Lastly, this process uses less physical storage than in our old method, approximately 1 terabyte.

8.6 The Analytics of It All: It Just Works!

Let's start by watching a data flow. In this particular case, we will start with Collectd and the paths that its data will take.

Collectd is running on our system "X," which is a Lustre® MDS for one of our systems. This filesystem is named "scratch." To start Collectd, run the following command as shown in Table 8.1.

Inside the configuration file (collectd.conf) we have something that looks like the paragraph in Table 8.2.

Things to note here is that the types.db file that contains all the data definitions for the data Collectd gathers is also shared by Logstash, which decodes the binary Collectd data stream and converts it to JSON.

Table 8.1 Running Collectd from the command line

./collectd -C collectd.conf

Table 8.2 Beginning of the collectd's configuration file collectd.conf

BaseDir	"/opt/collectd"
PIDFile	"/tmp/collectd.pid"
PluginDir	"/opt/collectd/lib/collectd"
TypesDB	"/etc/logstash/types.db"
Include	"/opt/collectd/etc/collectd.d/base.conf"
Include	"/opt/collectd/etc/collectd.d/mds.conf"
Interval	10
ReadThreads	25
WriteThreads	25

Table 8.3 Common elements of the collectd.conf file. These will be read from the base.conf file

base.conf
LoadPlugin cpu
LoadPlugin df
LoadPlugin disk
LoadPlugin interface
LoadPlugin load
LoadPlugin memory
LoadPlugin network
LoadPlugin processes
LoadPlugin swap
LoadPlugin uptime
LoadPlugin users
LoadPlugin vmem
\<Plugin df\>
MountPoint "/global"
IgnoreSelected true
ReportInodes true
\</Plugin\>
\<Plugin network\>
Server "logstash-local.domain.com" "25826"
MaxPacketSize 1024
\</Plugin\>

Table 8.4 Environment specific configuration for the collectd.conf file. Read from the mds.conf file

mds.conf
LoadPlugin mds
LoadPlugin ib

The two included configuration files in Table 8.3 (base.conf) and Table 8.4 (mds.conf), contain the needed plugins and are specialized based on node function.

When we load all of our plugins, the df plugin tells Collectd not to collect df information for the filesystem mounted at /global and to report inode information. While the mds.conf file tells Collectd to load the two special plugins: one for the Lustre® MDS, which collects the Lustre® MDS statistics and the other, collects Infiniband® network statistics.

The network plugin is used to send binary data from this Collectd instance to "logstash-local.domain.com," which is the local instance of Logstash. It is then Logstash's job to forward the data into the center-wide monitoring environment.

Now we move the local Logstash. Its job is to forward local data to the center-wide collector. Thus it is started on the host with a sample name of 'logstash-local.domain.com' that has a configuration file similar to Table 8.5:

What does all this do? First, when it receives a Collectd packet, it decodes it with the associated types.db files and then adds some tagging information to give Elastic and downstream processors a bit more information (see Table 8.6). Then it adds two

Table 8.5   The logstash configuration file

```
input {
  udp {
    port => 25826
    buffer_size => 1452
    workers => 3
    queue_size => 3000
    codec => collectd {
      typesdb => [ "/etc/logstash/types.db", "/etc/logstash/local-types.db" ]
    }
    tags => [ "collectd", "X" ]
    add_field => { "system" => "X" }
    add_field => { "function" => "scratch" }
    type => "collectd"
  }
}
input {
  tcp {
    port => 1514
    type => "syslog-X"
    tags => [ "syslogd", "tcp", "X", "internal" ]
    add_field => { "system" => "X" }
  }
  udp {
    port => 1514
    type => "syslog-X"
    tags => [ "syslogd", "udp", "X", "internal" ]
    add_field => { "system" => "X" }
  }
}
output {
  if [type] == "collectd" {
    rabbitmq {
      host => "rabbit-host.domain.com"
      port => 5671
      ssl => true
      verify_ssl => false
      exchange => "ha-metric"
      exchange_type => "topic"
      durable => true
      persistent => false
      user => "<RabbitMQ user>"
      password => "<Password>"
      key => "%{system}.%{function}.%{host}.%{type}.%{plugin}"
    }
  } else {
```

Table 8.5 (continued)

rabbitmq {
host => "rabbit-host.domain.com"
port => 5671
ssl => true
verify_ssl => false
exchange => "ha-log"
exchange_type => "topic"
durable => true
persistent => false
user => "<RabbitMQ user>"
password => "<Password>"
key => "%{system}.%{host}.%{type}"
}
}
}

Table 8.6 Logstash configuration file for the receiving logstash process. This creates the RabbitMQ® exchange

rabbitmq {
host => "rabbit-host.domain.com"
port => 5671
ssl => true
verify_ssl => false
exchange => "ha-metric"
queue => "ha-system-metric2elastic"
user => "<RabbitMQ user>"
password => "<Password>"
key => "system.#"
prefetch_count => 1500
threads => 3
codec => "json"
}

fields that are treated as hard information. This is more than just a tag. These fields are used later on when sending the data to RabbitMQ®. This instance of Logstash will also forward syslog messages.

Once the packet comes in and is processed, Logstash will compare it to the output types. Once it finds a match, it sends the packet using an encrypted connection to the RabbitMQ® cluster. In this case, the Collectd stanza will be used, and the data will be sent with the AMQP key, "%{system}.%{function}.%{host}.%{type}.%{plugin}" or 'X.scratch.mdshost.collectd.{mds,load,user,vmem,..}' This information is sent to the RabbitMQ® queue ha.metric.

From there, RabbitMQ® forwards ha.metric messages based on the %system key. For this data, the system key is "X," and RabbitMQ® will forward this to ha.X.metric. If ha.X.metric exchange has not been create, RabbitMQ® will then create it.

From here, there is a Logstash listening on queue connected to ha.X.metric and forwarding all incoming data to the Elastic cluster. This queue is sectioned off based on the system key passed in from the collection side. If the queue does not exist, it will be created and linked to the listed exchange. The 'key' field will be used to subscribe to the type of data coming from that exchange.

There could also be a Freeboard instance listening in on ha.X.metric via the STOMP protocol, but it could be asking for data only from "X.scratch.*.collectd.load," which would give this Freeboard all the load averaged for all the hosts in the function group scratch.

Lastly, a feed from that same queue could go to a Redis® datastore to keep the MDS data for the next 30 days. However, this would be only a portion of the data and not the full data flow.

Now, we go back to the Logstash listener on ha.X.metric. This process takes the data streaming to it and places it into Elastic for long-term storage and dashboard analysis.

This is how we implemented Elastic and how it is configured:

- All data is collected into location-event shards, which are created on a daily basis. In this example: X.function.collectd.
- The most recent shard of data less than 24 h old is stored on Solid State Drive (SSD) [43] attached locally to each Elasticsearch node.
- Two-day-old shards are migrated from the SSD drive to local drives also on each node. This data is still available to the Elasticsearch datastore.
- At this point, the two-day-old shards are archived to the global filesystem. Researchers now have the ability to load these shards back into their personal copies of the ELK stack.
- This data is copied to our long-term tape storage for archival purposes.
- After 30 days, this data is removed from the local drives and the Elasticsearch database.
- Data index management is performed by the Knapsack [44] Elasticsearch plugin.

The SSD step was needed to help Elasticsearch keep up with the data rates we are approaching. This will also be an "ingest-only" Elasticsearch, meaning that most uses of the data will be on an external Elasticsearch system which would insulate the data collecting cluster from inappropriate queries.

After the data has been ingested into Elasticsearch, Kibana now has access to it. At this point, Kibana dashboards can be created to display parts of the collected data. We set the data source for Kibana to be "X.function.collectd." We then followed the on-screen menus to explore and create graphs. Below are examples of such a dashboards.

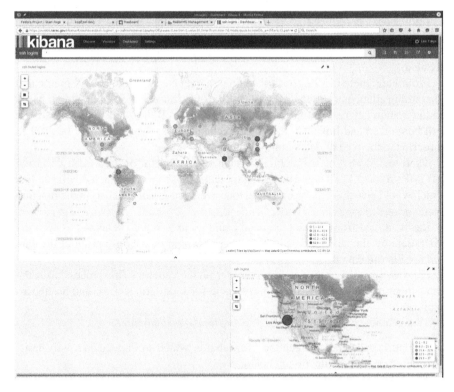

Fig. 8.3 Failed ssh connection locations

This Kibana dashboard (Fig. 8.3) shows the failed ssh [45] connection attempt into some of the cluster nodes. Other visualizations we could show could be the computer room heat map, resource utilization for network bandwidth, disks, computational resources, or other spatial data. The following Kibana dashboard shows typical line graphs of some performance metrics (Fig. 8.4).

The last part of the framework is the cluster management. We are using oVirt™ [46] of Red Hat, Inc to manage the virtual environments. All the Logstash and RabbitMQ® instances are running in oVirt™, which allows us to migrate an instance to another node if we need to perform any cluster maintenance. Another advantage of the virtual environment is we can turn up additional Logstash and RabbitMQ® nodes if we need them for special processing. The Elasticsearch nodes are all running on bare metal [47] since the virtual environment does not give us much benefit. Elasticsearch itself does the replication and failover for its cluster.

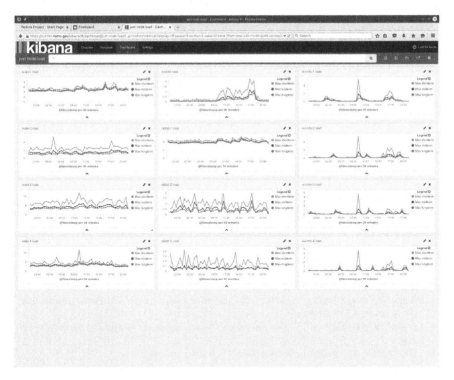

Fig. 8.4 General network statistics graphs

8.7   Conclusion

Building a monitoring infrastructure is exciting, challenging, and a necessity given our computational environment and the growing needs for efficiency and understanding in many other environments. While there is no single way to do this, it still needs to be done. The biggest issue of collecting monitoring data is choosing what data to collect. You need to know what questions can be answered by monitoring; thus if you know the question, you know what to collect. However, you can get into a very complex discussion of what data to collect, what format you can put it in, and how much to collect. This thinking leads to the fear of collecting too much data or data that is not needed. Another thought is to collect everything but that also leads to inefficiencies of collecting too much.

In our scenario, we have taken a hybrid approach that collects the data that was already being collected in some fashion, and supplements it with some data points that we think we will need. A more important consideration for us is to have a solution that allowed us to collect data in a single location was resilient, interchangeable, and composable. As a result, we were able to provide a database that is flexible when inserting new data as well as editing or archiving data, yet flexible enough that we can actually perform maintenance on the system without disrupting the collection activity.

Finally, we have talked about monitoring data in a supporting role for other sciences, but many of the techniques and information presented could be used for primary collections. Data is data: it is our frame of mind that puts meaning to that data.

References

1. IBM Big Data & Analytics Hub (2016), http://www.ibmbigdatahub.com/infographic/four-vs-big-data. Accessed 8 Feb 2016
2. Open Source Initiative (2016), http://opensource.org/. Accessed 8 Feb 2016
3. The Green Grid (2016), http://www.thegreengrid.org. Accessed 8 Feb 2016
4. Wikipedia, Power usage effectiveness (2016), https://en.wikipedia.org/wiki/Power_usage_effectiveness. Accessed 8 Feb 2016
5. Wikipedia, Remote direct memory access (2016), https://en.wikipedia.org/wiki/Remote_direct_memory_access. Accessed 8 Feb 2016
6. Wikipedia, Power Distribution Units (2016), https://en.wikipedia.org/wiki/Power_distribution_unit. Accessed 8 Feb 2016
7. Large Hadron Collider (2016), http://home.cern/topics/large-hadron-collider. Accessed 8 Feb 2016
8. CERN (2016), http://home.cern/. Accessed 8 Feb 2016
9. Wikipedia, Cyclic redundancy check (2016), https://en.wikipedia.org/wiki/Cyclic_redundancy_check. Accessed 8 Feb 2016
10. Siemens Energy & Automation, Inc, 4720 SEAbus protocol reference manual (1995), http://w3.usa.siemens.com/us/internet-dms/btlv/ACCESS/ACCESS/Docs/4720_SEAbusProtocol_Reference.pdf
11. Wikipedia, Modbus (2016), https://en.wikipedia.org/wiki/Modbus. Accessed 8 Feb 2016
12. Wikipedia, Simple network management protocol (2016), https://en.wikipedia.org/wiki/Simple_Network_Management_Protocol. Accessed 8 Feb 2016
13. BACnet (2016), http://www.bacnet.org/. Accessed 8 Feb 2016
14. Johnson Controls, Metasys (2016), http://cgproducts.johnsoncontrols.com/default.aspx?topframe.aspx&0. Accessed 8 Feb 2016
15. D. Loucks, INCOM protocol documentation, EATON (2015), http://pps2.com/smf/index.php?topic=7.0. Accessed 8 Feb 2016
16. MySQL™ (2016), https://www.mysql.com/. Accessed 8 Feb 2016
17. Wikipedia, Composability (2016), https://en.wikipedia.org/wiki/Composability. Accessed 8 Feb 2016
18. Nagios® (2016), https://www.nagios.org/. Accessed 8 Feb 2016
19. Ganglia Monitoring System (2016), http://ganglia.sourceforge.net/. Accessed 8 Feb 2016
20. T. Oetiker, RRDtool (2014), http://oss.oetiker.ch/rrdtool/. Accessed 8 Feb 2016
21. Lustre® (2016), http://lustre.org/. Accessed 8 Feb 2016
22. LMT (2013), https://github.com/chaos/lmt/wiki. Accessed 8 Feb 2016
23. AMQP advanced message queuing protocol (2016), https://www.amqp.org/. Accessed 8 Feb 2016
24. RabbitMQ (2016), https://www.rabbitmq.com/. Accessed 8 Feb 2016
25. Elastic (2016), https://www.elastic.co/. Accessed 8 Feb 2016
26. Collectd (2016), https://collectd.org/. Accessed 8 Feb 2016
27. Wikipedia, Programming language (2016), https://en.wikipedia.org/wiki/Programming_language. Accessed 8 Feb 2016

28. Wikipedia, Burst transmission (2016), https://en.wikipedia.org/wiki/Burst_transmission. Accessed 8 Feb 2016
29. Wikipedia, User datagram protocol (2016), https://en.wikipedia.org/wiki/User_Datagram_Protocol. Accessed 8 Feb 2016
30. JSON (2016), http://www.json.org/. Accessed 8 Feb 2016
31. STOMP (2016), https://stomp.github.io/. Accessed 8 Feb 2016
32. Heka (2016), https://hekad.readthedocs.org/en/v0.10.0b1/. Accessed 8 Feb 2016
33. Freeboard (2016), https://freeboard.io/. Accessed 8 Feb 2016
34. The HDF5 Group (2016), https://www.hdfgroup.org/HDF5/. Accessed 8 Feb 2016
35. Wikipedia, R (programming language) (2016), https://en.wikipedia.org/wiki/R_(programming_language). Accessed 8 Feb 2016
36. Redis® (2016), http://redis.io/. Accessed 8 Feb 2016
37. Wikipedia, Power over Ethernet (2016), https://en.wikipedia.org/wiki/Power_over_Ethernet. Accessed 8 Feb 2016
38. Wikipedia, 1-Wire (2016), https://en.wikipedia.org/wiki/1-Wire. Accessed 8 Feb 2016
39. IBM, IBM Knowledge Center (2016), http://www-01.ibm.com/support/knowledgecenter/SSFKCN/gpfs_welcome.html?lang=en. Accessed 8 Feb 2016
40. Wikipedia, Procfs (2016), https://en.wikipedia.org/wiki/Procfs. Accessed 8 Feb 2016
41. Lustre® MDS (MetaData Server) (2016), https://build.hpdd.intel.com/job/lustre-manual/lastSuccessfulBuild/artifact/lustre_manual.xhtml#understandinglustre.tab.storagerequire. Accessed 8 Feb 2016
42. Lustre® OSS (Object Storage Server) (2016), https://build.hpdd.intel.com/job/lustre-manual/lastSuccessfulBuild/artifact/lustre_manual.xhtml#understandinglustre.tab.storagerequire. Accessed 8 Feb 2016
43. Wikipedia, Solid-state drive (2016), https://en.wikipedia.org/wiki/Solid-state_drive. Accessed 8 Feb 2016
44. Knapsack (2016), https://github.com/jprante/elasticsearch-knapsack. Accessed 8 Feb 2016
45. OpenSSH (2016), http://www.openssh.com/. Accessed 8 Feb 2016
46. oVirt™ (2016), http://www.ovirt.org/Home. Accessed 8 Feb 2016
47. Wikipedia, Bare machine (2016), https://en.wikipedia.org/wiki/Bare_machine. Accessed 8 Feb 2016

Chapter 9
Empowering R with High Performance Computing Resources for Big Data Analytics

Weijia Xu, Ruizhu Huang, Hui Zhang, Yaakoub El-Khamra, and
David Walling

Abstract The software package R is a free, powerful, open source software
package with extensive statistical computing and graphics capabilities. Due to its
high-level expressiveness and multitude of domain specific packages, R has become
the lingua franca for many areas of data analysis, drawing power from its high-
level expressiveness and its multitude of domain specific, community-developed
packages. While R is clearly a "high productivity" language, it has not necessarily
been a "high performance" language. Challenges still remain in developing methods
to effectively scale R to the power of supercomputers, and in deploying support
and enabling access for the end users. In this chapter, we focus on approaches
that are available in R that can adopt high performance computing resources for
providing solutions to Big Data problems. Here we first present an overview
of current approaches and support in R that can enable parallel and distributed
computations in order to improve computation scalability and performance. We
categorize those approaches into two on the basis of the hardware requirement:
single-node parallelism that requires multiple processing cores within a computer
system and multi-node parallelism that requires access to computing cluster. We
present a detail study on performance benefit of using Intel® Xeon Phi coprocessors
(Xeon Phi) with R for improved performance in the case of single-node parallelism.
The performance is also compared with using general-purpose graphic processing
unit through *HiPLAR* package and other *parallel* packages enabling multi-node
parallelism including *SNOW* and *pbdR*. The results show advantages and limitations
of those approaches. We further provide two use cases to demonstrate parallel
computations with R in practice. We also discuss a list of challenges in improving R

W. Xu (✉) • R. Huang • Y. El-Khamra • D. Walling
University of Texas at Austin, Austin, TX, USA
e-mail: xwj@tacc.utexas.edu; rhuang@tacc.utexas.edu; yye00@tacc.utexas.edu;
walling@tacc.utexas.edu

H. Zhang
University of Louisville, Louisville, KY, USA
e-mail: hui.zhang@louisville.edu

© Springer International Publishing Switzerland 2016   191
R. Arora (ed.), *Conquering Big Data with High Performance Computing*,
DOI 10.1007/978-3-319-33742-5_9

performance for the end users. Nevertheless, the chapter shows the potential benefits of exploiting high performance computing with R and recommendations for end users of applying R to big data problems.

9.1 Introduction

In many academic domains, the increasing sheer volume of data presents both exciting opportunities of new scientific discoveries and new challenges in conducting required data analysis workflow. The Big Data problem is not only caused by the absolute number of bits of data, but the mismatch between the availability of the data and the existing analytic methods. The first roadblock the researchers often encounter is that the existing solutions stop working as the data grows. While the Big Data problem will eventually require a fundamental shift in computing models for scientific data analysis, advances in hardware and software tools development could meet immediate needs to scale-up computation of existing solutions. With such advances, the end users may only need minimum changes in the current workflow without costly efforts in developing new sophisticate software tools from scratch.

In this chapter, we focus on how new hardware capable of providing massive parallelism can be utilized with a popular data analysis software tool, R [1]. Here, we first introduce and survey a number of popular packages and libraries that enable parallel computations within R. Those packages are discussed in two categories, packages of supporting parallelism within a single node, packages of supporting parallelism with multiple nodes. We then focus on the case of using Xeon Phi in a single node for parallel processing with R. The performance is also compared with using general-purpose graphic processing unit card and enabling multi-node parallelisms. We then present two use case examples to discuss the usability of those packages.

9.1.1 Introduction of R

R is an open source software package tool that supports a large variety of common statistics analysis and data analysis tasks. Due to its high extensibility and continuous developments by its active user community, R has become a popular analytic environment by many researchers across scientific fields over the past decades. First created as an open-source statistical computing language in 1993, the R ecosystem now has evolved with features to support statistical analysis, data mining and visualizations for both generic and domain specific problems [1]. R enables users to develop domain-focused libraries as packages that can be easily distributed to and shared to the other R users. To date, there are 7036 packages available through the repository maintained by Comprehensive R Archive Network (CRAN [2]). Not to mention there are many more packages that are developed and maintained by individual research groups outside CRAN.

One of the unique features of the R environment is the high reusability of developed R packages. The R packages can provide solutions to practical problems in a wide variety of research domains, such as social science [3], bioinformatics [4, 5], geosciences [6], business analysis [7] and in clinical sciences [8], to just list a few. Some packages focus on generic implementations of a collection of popular data analytic methods. Those packages usually require little additional development works to be adapted to address specific analytic workflows by end users. There are also packages developed to addresses specific domain problems directly. In the latter case, those packages incorporate not just collections of individual analytic functions but also the support for running end-to-end analytic workflows, such as from reading raw data file to visualizing analytic results [5, 9, 10]. Through those packages, complex domain specific analysis workflows are transformed as a chain of function calls and can be easily reused by other users interested in the same problem without significant programming efforts. As a result, those packages quickly become popular among researchers who are tackling similar research questions.

9.1.2 Motivation of Empowering R with HPC

Although R is clearly a "high productivity" language, high performance has not been a development goal of R. On the contrary, R-based analysis solutions often have the reputation of lacking the efficiency required for large-scale computations. As Big Data becomes a norm in almost every scientific field, many inherent issues hindering the programming execution efficiency become real challenges and roadblocks that prevent an existing solution viable with increasing volume of data and increasing complexity of the analysis in practice. It is a common case that the running time of an R solution is often measured in hours, or even in days, for the analysis to finish. However, as the volume of data to be analyzed increases, the required execution time of a solution can become prohibitively long, especially for those cases where computational complexity of the analysis is beyond linear scaling. In other cases, the R solution can simply stop working due to insufficient computational resources, such as system memory.

Unfortunately, several factors contributing to the performance issue in R are tightly related to its design and implementations. Strictly speaking, R is a script programming language specification and requires an implementation of interpreter that translates R scripts into byte code for execution at runtime. Hence, the inefficiency can come both from the programming specification itself and the interpreter environment implementation [11]. Designed as a computing language with high-level expressiveness, R lacks much of the fine-grained control and basic constructs to support highly efficient code development. For example, the data type in R has been simplified and complex data type can be dynamically changed and determined. While this design feature simplifies development process, it also results computing program prone to bugs and inefficient use of memory. In this paper, the R implementation refers to the GNU version that is the most popular R implementation. The R runtime environment enables interactive analysis and simplifies programing development. But it also requires additional time and resources of computation with each command execution. A common dilemma for R users is a choice between either completely re-implementing the existing analytic workflow or spending days for the analysis to finish, assuming the increasing computing requirement will not cause the existing code to fail. Last but not the least, much of the R framework have been designed in 1990s and only utilize a single thread execution mode. So much of the R language specification and implementation is not able to directly take advantage of modern computer infrastructure, such as multiple cores, parallel coprocessors and multi-node computing clusters. Therefore, enabling parallelism and exploiting usage of high performance computing is an effective and required approach of scaling up the processing capability of existing R solution.

While most features in R are implemented as single thread process, efforts have been made in enabling parallelism with R over the past decade. Those approaches include using dynamic libraries written in other programming language for expensive computations and developing R packages as wrappers and utilities to low-level parallel libraries. It is important to review those approaches and conduct performance evaluation to inform R users. The contribution of this chapter including, (1) a survey of the state-of-arts on utilizing R in HPC environment; (2) performance comparisons of selected common R *parallel* packages (3) use case examples to demonstrate the potential of utilizing HPC with R. This chapter is organized in six sections. Section 9.2 introduces the background of high performance computing technologies and their potential and challenges for empowering R computations. Section 9.3 presents a survey on selected commonly used R packages that provide parallel execution support. Section 9.4 presents a comparative study on the performance and usability of those packages in utilizing the parallel resource. The comparison includes packages supporting single-node parallelism, such as utilizing multiple cores, Intel® Xeon Phi coprocessor, General Purpose Graphic Processing Units (GPGPU), and packages supporting multiple node parallelism such as through socket connection and through message passing interface (MPI). The comparison was conducted using an existing R benchmark scripts including a variety tasks as well as several selected tasks. Part of results presented in this section have been presented in a workshop presentation previously [12]. Section 9.5 presents two use case examples of utilizing high performance computing resources with R with practical use cases. We conclude in Sect. 9.6.

9.2   Opportunities in High Performance Computing to Empower R

Driven by the ever-increasing computation demands, significant efforts have been made in parallel and distributed computing technologies over the past decades. In this section, we present an overview on those technologies that are currently utilized by R. We organize our discussions in two parts based on the scope of parallelism. Section 9.2.1 discusses single node parallelism in which computations are executed within a single computer node with shared-memory and multiple processing units. Those processing units include host CPUs, processing cores and co-processing cards. Section 9.2.2 discusses technologies that enable efficient usage of multiple computation nodes.

9.2.1   Parallel Computation Within a Single Compute Node

When a single computer system (hereafter referred as a compute node) has multiple processing units installed, multiple processing threads can be run concurrently for increased performance. There are two common approaches to expand the parallel processing capability within a single node: to increase the number of Central Processing Unit (CPU) within a node; and to include add-on processing devices.

Modern computers can host multiple identical CPUs by adding additional sockets in a single computer system. Within each CPU, there are also multiple processing components (cores) that can read and execute instructions independently from each other. For example, the latest Intel® E7 processor can have 18 cores. A typical commercial computer usually has 8–16 cores available. With the capabilities of installing multiple CPUs, a single system can now have up to 72 total numbers of processing cores. Each processing core has the same hardware specification and can archive the same computation performance. Each core can be used independent from each other. In theory, a computer system can run a number of, up to the total available processing cores in a system, tasks concurrently without performance degradation. However, multiple parallel processes will compete for other shared resources within the same system, such as memory and data access bandwidth. These shared resources set hard limits to the number of parallel worker threads, and at many times the resultant overhead may offset the benefit of running parallel threads.

The other approach to increase concurrent processing threads is to use an accelerator card such as GPGPU or Xeon Phi. These coprocessors contain a large number of (relatively) simple cores running at lower frequency to deliver much higher peak performance per chip than using more traditional multi-core approaches. Another common feature with co-processing card is the availability of on-board memory units. The processing units on the coprocessor card have direct, and usually fast, access to the data stored in on-board memory without the need for competing for the memory resources on the host system.

GPGPU extends parallel functions and technologies traditionally embedded in graphic processing units to handle more generic computations. The development has started since 2001 [13] and was motivated by providing a flexible and programmable interface for graphic card [14]. The traditional graphic processing units will only read the data from main systems and output rendering results on the display devices. In order to meet increasing demands of rendering complex multi-dimensional structure with low-latency, the GPU is gradually developed with the ability to first store and process simple data structure on the card and then transfer the processing result to display device or to the host system for further processing. Since the GPGPU is designed for faster vectorized computations, it is especially suitable for problems involving linear algebra computation such as matrix computations. Computational solutions can utilize the parallel features provided by GPU through programing interface such as OPENCL [15] and CUDA [16]. GPGPU can be utilized to implement high-level machine learning algorithms and implementations in scientific computing and has been used across multiple domains such as in biomedical research, bioinformatics and cheminformatics [17].

The basis of the Xeon Phi is a lightweight x86 core with in-order instruction processing, coupled with 512 bit SIMD registers and instructions. With these two features the Xeon Phi die can support 60+ cores, and can execute eight Double Precision (DP) vector instructions. The core count and vector lengths are basic extensions of an x86 processor, and allow the same programming paradigms (serial, threaded and vector) used on other Xeon (E5) processors. A critical advantage of the Xeon Phi coprocessor is that, unlike GPU-based coprocessors, the processing cores run the Intel® x86 instruction set (with 64-bit extensions), allowing the use of familiar programming models, software, and tools. So unlike the GPGPU accelerator model, the same program code can be used efficiently on the host and the coprocessor. In addition to allowing the host system to offload computing workload partially to the Xeon Phi, it also can run a compatible program independently. The Xeon Phi runs a lightweight BusyBox Operating System (OS), thereby making the Xeon Phi function as a separate Symmetric Multiprocessor (SMP). So, while the Xeon Phi can be used as a work offload engine by the host processors, it is also capable of working as another independent (SMP) processor. In the latter mode Message Passing Interface (MPI) processes can be launched on the Xeon Phi and/or the E5 processors. In this "symmetric" mode the Xeon Phi appears as an extra node for launching MPI tasks. In the case of the Intel® Xeon Phi SE10P Coprocessor used in this chapter, each coprocessor chip has a peak performance of roughly 1070 GFLOPS, approximately six times the peak performance of a single Xeon E5 processor, or three times the aggregate peak performance of the two Xeon E5 processors. Each coprocessor is equipped with 8GB of GDDR5 DRAM with a peak bandwidth of 352GB/s, also significantly higher than the 51.2GB/s peak bandwidth available to each host processor chip.

9.2.2 Multi-Node Parallelism Support

Increasing the parallel processing capabilities within a single node is often less costly and easier for individual users and research groups. However, as the number of parallel processes is ultimately limited by several other hardware factors, analysis work cannot always fit within one computer system. In the latter cases, multiple computing nodes must be used to enable the analysis. There are two major approaches of leveraging multiple nodes for distributing workload.

In a traditional high performance computing clusters, all compute nodes are connected through one or more high performance switch which support high performance communication among any two computing nodes using high bandwidth interconnect such as InfiniBand [18]. In this type of infrastructure, it is often the case that the computation and data are distributed together during the parallel processing. In traditional high performance computing cluster, MPI is one of commonly used libraries that implement the communication among different compute nodes. MPI is a standardized and portable message-passing system designed by a group of researchers from academia and industry to function on a wide variety of parallel computers. The MPI standard defines the syntax and semantics of a core of library routines useful to a wide range of users writing portable message-passing programs in different computer programming languages such as Fortran, C, C++ and Java. The MPI interface provides essential virtual topology, synchronization, and communication functionality between a set of processes that have been mapped to nodes/servers/computer instances in a language-independent way, with language-specific syntax (bindings), plus a few language-specific features. MPI programs always work with processes, commonly referred as tasks as well. Typically, for maximum performance, each core will be assigned a single process at runtime through the agent that starts the MPI program, normally called mpirun or mpiexec [19]. Open source implementations of MPI include MPICH2 [20] and OpenMPI [21]. MPICH is available for most flavors of Unix (include Linux and Mac OS X) and Microsoft Windows. Open MPI is a project combining technologies and resources from several other projects (e.g. LAM/MPI, LA-MPI) and supporting many Unix-like OS.

Recently a new programming paradigm, pioneered by Google, the MapReduce programing model [22], has become increasing popular for Big Data processing. The central idea of this data driven programming paradigm is to store the data distributed across all the nodes and bring the computation to each node. Unlike traditional High Performance Computing jobs, the analysis is carried out with the data locally stored at each node. Upon completion of processing data locally, only the results need to be transferred out and aggregated together. Since the processing results are usually much smaller compared to the raw data set, the data transferred among different nodes are minimized. Two of the popular system implementations following this approach are Hadoop system [23] and Spark [24].

9.3 Support for Parallelism in R

The parallel package development is initially fueled by the increasing computational complexity of the required methodologies. Common examples include matrix-decomposition, linear system solver, Markov Chain Monte Carlo simulation and bootstrapping. Since those solutions typically require linear or even polynomial time in the size of the input data, the increasing volume of big data present can dramatically increase the computational requirement. A common usage model is to rewrite some basic functions or processing workflow with the corresponding parallel version provided by the *parallel* packages. Development of these packages often requires users to have extensive knowledge in both existing R code as well as the parallel mechanism supported by the additional packages.

The development of parallel support in R coincides with the technology advances in parallel system development. For computing clusters, Li and Rossini [25] first introduced a package, *rpvm*, based on Private Virtual Machine (PVM) [26]. Yu created a package *Rmpi* as an interface between R and Message Passing Interface in 2002 [27]. A popular parallel package, *SNOW*: Simple Network and Workstations [28], can utilize several low level communication protocols including MPI, PVM and socket connection [25]. There are over 60 packages that are related in enabling parallelism listed in CRAN Task View for high performance computing. Among them, some are designed to provide explicit parallelism where users control the parallelization (such as *Rmpi* and *SNOW*); some are specially designed to provide implicit parallelism so that the system can abstract parallelization away (such as multi-core); others are high-level wrapper for other packages and intended to ease the use of parallelism, such as *snowfall* and *foreach*. There are also a number of packages developed to utilize a multi-core system including fork, rparallel and multi-core [29, 30]. *Parallel* package is the one now included with CRAN R core package distribution since version 2.14.0. *Pnmath* uses the OPENMP to implement many common mathematic functions to run in parallel. Here we reviewed selected packages that have seen increasing popularity and relevant to our investigations. Reader interested in the packages not reviewed here may refer to other survey papers [31, 32].

9.3.1 Support for Parallel Execution Within a Single Node in R

Many packages supporting parallel executions across multiple nodes can also be used within a single node to utilize the multiple cores available within the computer system. Some of the early efforts to enable efficient usage of multiple cores have been merged into other packages providing more comprehensive functionality. For example, *Multicore* package was one of the popular R package developed to utilize multiple cores available on the system. The package utilizes forking, a system mechanism for creating additional processing threads, to generate additional worker threads running on different cores for processing. The package includes parallel implementation of several common R functions, such as *apply()* function. The parallel version functions often have a prefix attached to their single-threads counterpart. The end users only need to replace the existing version with the parallel version to utilize multiple cores on the system. The functionality of the package is now merged into *parallel* package and distributed with the R core distribution. Those packages will be reviewed in the next subsection. This subsection will focus on packages and approaches supporting usages of co-processing card.

There are several packages in R that support the use of the GPGPU card. *HiPLAR* (High Performance Linear Algebra in R) [33] is one of those packages and shows the best performance and usability during our preliminary testing. *HiPLAR* package supports the usage of both GPU and multiple processing cores in the host system through two low-level libraries *MAGMA* [34] and *PLASMA* [35]. The *PLASMA* library is explicitly developed to utilize the multiple cores within shared memory architectures. The *MAGAMA* library supports hybrid usage of both multi-core CPUs and a GPGPU card compatible with CUDA interface. There are two variants of the package. The *HiPLAM* is implemented to overwrite much of the functions already available in the existing *Matrix* package. The package is also compatible with legacy R code using Matrix package. The *HiPLARb* does not depend on the usage of *Matrix* package and provide support for 26 linear algebra functions in R. Both packages can be used with or without CPU. The user of those packages can get substantial speed-ups without much changing of the existing code.

R also enables linking to other shared mathematics libraries to speed up many basic computation tasks. One option for linear algebra computation is to use Intel® Math Kernel Library (MKL) [36]. MKL includes a wealth of routines to accelerate application performance and reduces development time such as highly vectorized and threaded linear algebra, fast Fourier transforms (FFT), vector math and statistics functions. Furthermore, the MKL has been optimized to utilize multiple processing cores, wider vector units and more varied architectures available in a high-end system. Different from using parallel packages, MKL can provide parallelism transparently and speed up programs with supported math routines without changing code. It has been reported that the compiling R with MKL can provide three times improvements out of box [37].

9.3.2   Support for Parallel Execution Over Multiple Nodes with MPI

There are a number of packages that support parallelism over multiple nodes. Most of these R packages are building upon MPI and support high-level routines for the distributed-memory communication environment of computer clusters. They provide a portable interface for the basic user to use high performance message passing operations available on HPC platforms. Here we reviewed selected popular packages that are directly related to our investigation.

Rmpi is one of the earliest parallel package developed for R and is built upon by other packages [27]. The *Rmpi* package is an interface (wrapper) to port low-level Message Passing Interface (MPI) function for parallel computing using R. It was initially to run under LAM-MPI and was developed on RedHat 9. Over years, It has been ported to work under other implementations of MPI such as MPICH2 and OpenMPI, and can be run under various distributions of Linux, Windows, and Mac OS X. Once the users link the R package with a MPI library installed separately, the package enables the users to develop and execute MPI-like code in R scripts such as using MPI's send function and MPI's receive function. The package also includes limited parallel implementations of existing R functions such as *apply* function family.

In practice, there are a number of other parallel packages in R that are built on top of the *Rmpi* with improved usability for end users and become more widely used than *Rmpi*, such as *SNOW, foreach, doMPI* [38]. For example, the *doMPI* package is built upon *Rmpi* and provides a parallel backend for the *foreach* package. The *foreach* package simplifies the parallel processing development by providing a parallel for-loop construct for R. Those packages also are exemplary for a class of lightweight packages implemented in R. Those packages, still efficient and simple to use, usually only focus on a very limited set of functions and programming supports. Few other packages provide comprehensive usage of multi-node parallelism including *SNOW* and *pbdR*, which are reviewed as follows.

SNOW (Simple Network of Workstations) The *SNOW* package provides support for simple parallel computing on a network of workstations using R. It provides an abstraction layer by hiding the communication details and can use one of four communication mechanisms: sockets, Parallel Virtual Machine (PVM) via *rpmv* package, MPI, or NetWorkSpaces (NWS). A master R process calls *makeCluster* to start a cluster of worker processes; the master process then uses functions such as *clusterCall* and *clusterApply* to execute R code on the worker processes and collect and return the results on the master. The code development can be independent of the communication mechanisms at a cluster or on single multi-core computer. Started with R release 2.14.0, *SNOW* package is incorporated into parallel package. A new package, *snowFT*, was created to as an extension of the *SNOW* package supporting fault tolerant and reproducible applications. The *SNOW* package not only just utilizes *Rmpi* but also several other existing parallel packages to expand the parallel support through a simple interface [10].

pbdR The "Programming with Big Data in R" project (*pbdR*) [39] is a series of R packages and an environment for statistical computing with Big Data by using high-performance statistical computation. The main goal is to empower data scientists by bringing flexibility and a big analytics toolbox to big data challenges, with an emphasis on productivity, portability, and performance. The significant difference between *pbdR* and traditional R code is that the former focuses on distributed memory system while communications between processes are based on MPI. The current list of *pbdR* packages include the follows: The *pbdMPI* package provides S4 classes to directly interface MPI in order to support the Single Program/Multiple Data (SPMD) parallel programming style which is particularly useful for batch parallel execution. The *pbdSLAP* builds on this and uses scalable linear algebra packages (namely *BLACS*, *PBLAS*, and *ScaLAPACK*) in double precision based on *ScaLAPACK* version 2.0.2. The *pbdBASE* builds on these and provides the core classes and methods for distributed data types upon which the *pbdDMAT* builds to provide distributed dense matrices for "Programming with Big Data". The *pbdNCDF4* package permits multiple processes to write to the same file (without manual synchronization) and supports terabyte-sized files. The *pbdDEMO* package provides examples for these packages, and a detailed vignette. The *pbdPROF* package profiles MPI communication SPMD code via MPI profiling libraries, such as *fpmpi*, *mpiP*, or *TAU*.

In terms of performance, the equivalent code in *SNOW* may not be as fast as that of the *Rmpi* because *SNOW* uses MPI via the *Rmpi* package and the for-loop used in *SNOW* has overhead. The package *snowFT* uses the same communications mechanism as *SNOW* and *Rmpi* but includes additional functionality for error handling, so it executes additional checks and decreases performance. The *pbdMPI* package, rewritten from *Rmpi*, provides many performance improvement and a simplified interface. In addition to *pbdMPI*, the *pbdDMAT*, *pbdBASE* and *pbdSLAP* offer high-level syntax to speed up large-scale, distributed matrix algebra and statistics operations and the *pmclust* [40] package offer fast, high-level model-based clustering and an implementation of k-means clustering using the distributed matrix method of *pbdDMAT*.

In term of usability, *Rmpi* offers more control by covering the full functionality of both communication standards and provides a complete API to these standard but needs more involved in code development because it does not provide high-level functionality as *SNOW* package and *pbdMPI*. *SNOW* and *pbdR* provide higher level of abstraction that makes these packages easier for statistical researchers to understand and quickly perform tasks. Particularly, *pbdR* provides operations on dense distributed matrices in parallel in *pbdDMAT* package. *Rmpi* and *pbdMPI* provide better user support and package development and maintenance than *SNOW* package.

9.3.3 Packages Utilizing Other Distributed Systems

In addition to leveraging MPI for parallel computations, recent efforts have been made to adapt R with emerging Big Data processing platforms. Those packages work well with a class of problems, commonly known as *"data parallel problem"*. In this class of problems, a significant portion of the solution can be run independently on different subset of data. A common approach in using R for big data is to break large data sets into chunks and runs each chuck in parallel sessions.

Therefore, more parallel processes can improve the throughput of processing big data problems with R. The solution consists of new programming paradigm widely used for big data processing. There are two main big data analysis systems, Hadoop and Spark. Several packages have been developed to enable R interface with those systems. Readers interested in the performance of R big data packages may refer to the performance evaluation paper [41].

Hadoop is a distributed computing platform written in Java for distributed storage and distributed processing of very large data sets on computer clusters [42]. It was created by Doug Cutting and Mike Cafarella in 2005 and is distributed under the terms of Apache License and therefore free and open source software. All the modules in Hadoop can automatically handle hardware failures of individual machines or racks of machines in the framework. Hadoop streaming is a useful utility that comes with the Hadoop distribution. It allows users to create and run Map/Reduce [43] jobs with any executable or script (e.g., Python, R) as the mapper and/or the reducer. The requirement for Hadoop streaming is that both the mapper and the reducer are executables that read the input from standard input and emit the output to standard output. One R project using this utility is RHadoop, an open source collection of three R packages created by Revolution Analytics that allow users to management and analyze data with Hadoop from an R environment by utilizing the Hadoop streaming. The packages include *rhdfs* that provides file management of the HDFS from with R; *rmr2* that provides Hadoop MapReduce functionality in R and *rhbase* that provides database management for the HBase distributed database within R.

Spark is an open-source cluster computing framework originally developed in the AMPLab at UC Berkeley [24]. One of the distinct differences between Hadoop and Spark is that Spark runs in-memory on the cluster. And Spark does not tie to Hadoop's MapReduce two-stage paradigm. This makes repeated access to the same data much faster. Spark can run as a standalone or on top of a Hadoop cluster, where it can read data directly from the Hadoop cluster and utilize Hadoop cluster for resource management and allocation. In contrast to Hadoop's two-stage disk-based MapReduce paradigm, Spark's in-memory mechanism usually provides better performance for certain applications. By allowing user programs to load data into a cluster's memory and query it repeatedly, Spark is well-suited to machine learning algorithms. *SparkR* is an R package that provides a lightweight frontend to use Apache Spark from R. It provides a distributed data frame implementation that supports operations like selection, filtering, aggregation etc on large datasets. The entry point into *SparkR* is the SparkContext which connects your R program to a Spark cluster. A SparkContext can be created using *sparkR.init* and pass in options such as the application name, any spark packages depended on, etc.

In terms of performance, Apache Spark processes data in-memory while Hadoop MapReduce write/read temporary results to the disk after a map or reduce process. However, if Spark runs on Hadoop YARN with other resource-demanding services, or if the data is too big to fit entirely into the memory, then there could be major performance degradations for Spark. MapReduce, however, kills its processes as soon as a job is done, so it can easily run alongside other services with minor performance differences. Spark would outperform Hadoop MapReduce on iterative computations that need to pass over the same data many times. But when it comes to one-pass ETL-like jobs, for example, data transformation or data integration, then MapReduce is the deal—this is what it was designed for.

In terms of usability, Spark has easy-to-use APIs for Java, Scala and Python, R, and also includes Spark SQL, so it's easy to write user-defined functions. It also includes an interactive mode for running commands with immediate feedback. Hadoop MapReduce doesn't have an interactive mode. Therefore, Hadoop is more difficult to program than Spark. Apache Spark can do more than plain data processing: it can process graphs and use the existing machine-learning libraries. Spark can do real-time processing as well as batch processing. This presents an interesting opportunity to use one platform for everything instead of having to split tasks across different platforms. Compared with spark, Hadoop is great for batch processing.

9.4 Parallel Performance Comparison of Selected Packages

In this section, we present our testing results between single node parallelism and multi parallelism. In particular, we focus on the usage of coprocessors like Intel® Xeon Phi coprocessor. We first present a comprehensive study of Intel® Xeon Phi performance behavior. We then compare its performance with the usage of GPGPU card as well as multi-node parallelisms utilizing Rmpi, SNOW and pbdR.

9.4.1 Performance of Using Intel® Xeon Phi Coprocessor

The primary objective for this investigation is to explore the benefit of using Xeon Phi with R. We test two usage models and compare to a baseline model of running R serially. The first model is to utilize the MKL [36] on the host CPU only. We then experiment using the Xeon Phi processor to co-process with the host process. In the latter model, some of the computation can be passed to the Xeon Phi coprocessor, using workload offloading. Theoretically, with an appropriate library, any computational workload could be offloaded to Xeon Phi for co-processing. Through the usage of MKL, we can run an R script in several different models without changing the script. Specifically, our tests include the following different models of computation.

- (M1) Plain R without any parallelism. In this model, R was compiled and built with MKL, but with available threads set to 1. Therefore, all computations are run in single thread. This serves as a baseline for comparison.
- (M2) R with MKL utilizing host CPU only. In this model, R was compiled and built with MKL as the library for the linear algebra computation. MKL can

automatically utilize the available cores in the host system for parallel processing. In our test, the host-computing node has 16 cores.

- (M3) R with MKL utilizes both host CPU and Xeon Phi coprocessor. In this model, R was compiled and built with MKL as well. However, the offloading to Xeon Phi was enabled. A configurable portion of the workload can be specified to use Xeon Phi, ranging from 0 to 100 %.

For each of the above tests, we tested the factors affecting the performance including, functions affected by MKL, number of threads used, and size of input data. To evaluate how the automatic parallel offloading compares to explicitly parallelism with other packages, batch runs of benchmarks were also conducted. When using with the MKL/Phi, the batch runs were initiated sequentially. While with other parallel packages, the batch runs were distributed out for explicit parallel processing. Lastly, preliminary tests were also conducted with domain application to further evaluate potential benefit in practice.

9.4.1.1 Testing Workloads

We first test using the R-25 benchmark script [43]. The testing script includes 15 common computational tasks grouped into three categories: Matrix Calculation, Matrix function and Programming. The 15 tasks are listed in Table 9.1. In addition to testing the base R-25 benchmark script across the different usage models, we also explore the speed up gained when varying the size of the matrices and number of elements used in the benchmark to compare the results between host only MKL vs. Xeon Phi offloading. We then investigate how parameters controlling offloading computations to Xeon Phi effect speed up of computation heavy matrix based computations. This investigation includes timing DGEMM based calculations while varying work offloading parameters to achieve maximum speed up for these operations.

9.4.1.2 System Specification

To evaluate the applicability of different methods for improving R performance in a high performance compute environment, we used the Texas Advanced Computing Center Stampede cluster. Stampede provides several different techniques for achieving high performance computations, which include using its Xeon Phi coprocessor and/or NVIDIA Kepler 20 GPUs for large matrix calculations. These tests were run on compute nodes that have two Intel® Xeon E5-2680 processors each of which has eight computing cores running @2.7GHz. There is 32GB DDR3 memory in each node for the host CPUs. The Xeon Phi SE10P coprocessor installed on each compute node has 61 cores with 8GB GDDR5 dedicated memory connected by an x16 PCIe bus. The NVIDIA K20 GPUs on each node have 5GB of on-board GDDR5. All compute nodes are running CentOS 6.3. For this study we used the stock R 3.01 package compiled with the Intel® compilers (v.13) and built with Math Kernel Library (MKL v.11).

Table 9.1 Translation of benchmark number to R-25 benchmark description for all R-25 plots

Task number	R25 benchmark description
1	Creation, transp., deformation of a 2500 × 2500 matrix (sec)
2	2400 × 2400 normal distributed random matrix
3	Sorting of 7,000,000 random values
4	2800 × 2800 cross-product matrix
5	Linear regression over a 3000 × 3000 matrix
6	FFT over 2,400,000 random values
7	Eigenvalues of a 640 × 640 random matrix
8	Determinant of a 2500 × 2500 random matrix
9	Cholesky decomposition of a 3000 × 3000 matrix
10	Inverse of a 1600 × 1600 random matrix
11	3,500,000 Fibonacci numbers calculation (vector calculation)
12	Creation of a 3000 × 3000 Hilbert matrix (matrix calculation)
13	Grand common divisors of 400,000 pairs (recursion)
14	Creation of a 500 × 500 Toeplitz matrix (loops)
15	Escoufier's method on a 45 × 45 matrix (mixed)
16	Total time for all 15 tests
17	Overall mean

9.4.1.3 Results and Discussion

Figure 9.1 shows the speed up of three different methods over the single thread execution for tasks listed in Table 9.1. The default R running with single thread is shown in blue as our base line for comparison with a speed up equal to one. The results of using MKL for automatic parallel execution with 16 threads are shown in red. There are five subtasks showing a significant benefit from the automatic parallelization with MKL. Those tasks include cross product between matrices, linear regression, matrix decomposition, computing inverse and determinant of a matrix. Other computing tasks received very little performance gains from parallel execution with MKL. The green column depicts the results when 70 % workload is computed through Xeon Phi. Offloading computation to Xeon Phi can benefit the same set of computing tasks and has about 10 % additional increase over MKL with host CPU alone. In both cases, the maximum speed up we observed is over five times more than single thread. While this is provides significantly faster wall clock times for those computing tasks, the speed up is sub-linear to the additional number of core/processes used. We think this is due to the extra overhead introduced with MKL library for automatic threading.

The percentage of workload assigned to the Xeon Phi coprocessor is an adjustable parameter. We investigated how different sizes and different workload sharing affect performance. Figure 9.2 shows the speed-up factors for different problem sizes at different workload sharing percentages. Note that matrices have to have a minimum size before automatic offloading starts paying off, in this

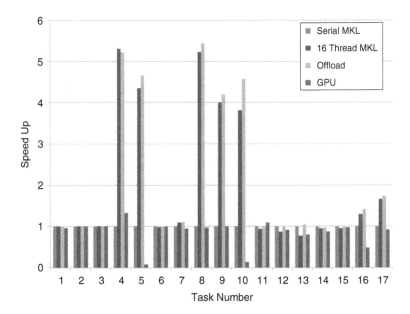

Fig. 9.1 The relative acceleration of the different threading and offloading techniques relative to results for the single threaded MLK benchmark results on the host

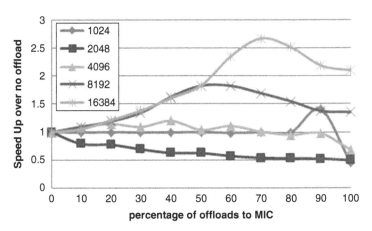

Fig. 9.2 Speedup factor as a function of percentage of work on the coprocessor and matrix size. Note that forced offloading of small matrix operations reduces performance

case 8192×8192. Speedup is highest in the range of 50–70 % workload on the coprocessor. As indicated in Figs. 9.2 and 9.3 the benefit of using parallelism through automatic offloading improves as the input data grows.

There are 60 physical processing cores available on each Intel® Xeon Phi. Each computing core has four hardware threads. We can therefore run with 60–240 parallel threads on each Xeon Phi coprocessor. Furthermore, we can work-share

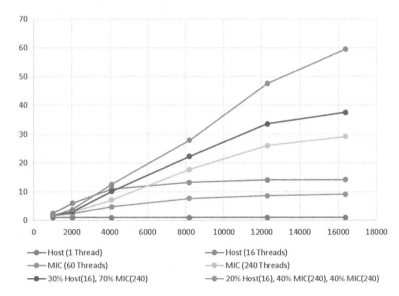

Fig. 9.3 Speedup factors for different configurations. The highest possible speedup is almost 60×
for the largest matrix size (16,384 × 16,384) with two Xeon Phi coprocessors (240 threads) each
with 40 % of the total workload

across the host the Xeon Phi, or across the host and two Xeon Phi coprocessors with
different workloads as shown in Fig. 9.3. Figure 9.3 shows the speedup factors for
a basic matrix multiply in R with one thread on the host, 16 threads on the host, 60
threads on a Xeon Phi, 240 threads on one Xeon Phis with work-sharing at the 30 %
host (16 threads) 70 % coprocessor (240 threads) and with work-sharing at the 20 %
host (16 threads) and 40 % coprocessor for each of the two Xeon Phi's.

9.4.2 Comparison of Parallel Packages in R

To compare the parallelism supported by MKL on Intel® Xeon Phi coprocessor
with other parallel packages, we conducted batch runs with the R-25 benchmark
in parallel using *snowfall* [44] and *multicore* [45] package. The result is shown in
Fig. 9.4. The first five bars show the total running time using *Snowfall* package
(*sfLapply*) with different number of processing cores which scales near linearly to
the number of computing cores used. The bottom four bars compare using multicore
package (*mclapply*) with the serial run (*lapply*) with and without offloading to
Intel® Xeon Phi coprocessors. The comparison indicates that the benefit of using
Xeon Phi coprocessor diminishes when used with other explicit parallelism based
packages. For batch runs, explicit parallelism is more effective than using automatic
parallelization provided through MKL.

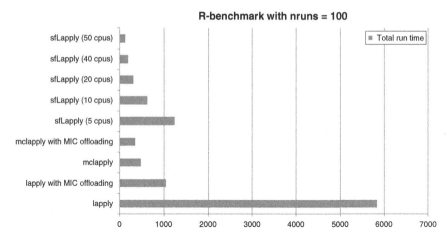

Fig. 9.4 Comparison of computational time over 100 runs on R-benchmark using different parallel packages including Snowfall, multicore, and MKL

In addition, popular R packages for multi-core and multi-node parallelism were tested with high level functions in these packages using three benchmark scripts: (1) approximating using Monte Carlo method, the script has 128 iterations of generating one million points from uniform distribution; (2) Constructing cross product of 2800×2800 matrix; (3) Constructing Covariance Matrix for $10,000 \times 2000$ matrix. The first benchmark was used to test the performance of mclapply function in *parallel*, *dopar* in *foreach* with *doSNOW* for multi-core parallelism, and the performance of MPI connection in *SNOW* and *pbdMPI* packages, and Socket connection via *doSNOW*. The second benchmark was used to test the performance of *HiPLARb* package by using GPU for computations and the performance of R compiled with Intel® compiler which provides Intel® MKL to speed up linear algebra operations by using Xeon Phi SE10P Coprocessor for computation. The third benchmark was used to test the performance of computations with dense, distributed matrices via multi-core and multi-node mechanism.

Table 9.2 lists the runtime in seconds of three benchmarks using R parallel packages. For multi-core mechanism, the performance of parallelizing for-loop is relatively faster by using *dopar* function in *foreach* [38] and *doSNOW* [46] packages than the *mclapply* function in *parallel* [47] package. For the multi-node mechanism, the MPI provides better speed-up than the socket connection, because Mellanox FDR InfiniBand technology used by *RSNOWMPI* has faster network communication than Ethernet by *makeSOCKcluster* function in *SNOW* package. The *pbdMPI* has the best performance among multi-node computation R packages. In terms of linear algebra operations, the R complied with Intel® compiler using Xeon Phi has significant speed up than *HiPLARb* package using GPU. In terms of distributed matrix operations, although the multi-node mechanism has much more cores than the multi-core mechanism (128 vs. 16 cores), the performance of *pbdDMAT* in multi-node is much slower than the one in multi-core because the overhead of transferring data between nodes becomes significant especially for small-scale matrix operations.

9.5 Use Case Examples

The previous sections described a few packages that support parallelism and compared their performance with benchmark tasks. However, practical scientific analysis is much more complex with unique workload. To demonstrate how HPC can be used to improve R in practice, we present two uses of utilizing R solution with high performance computing. The first example is to scale up Gibbs Sampling process, an example for multi-node parallelism. The second example demonstrates how to improve the parallel statistic testing using Intel® Xeon Phi coprocessor and its performance improvement.

9.5.1 Enabling JAGS (Just Another Gibbs Sampler) on Multiple Nodes

Rating of work, performance, and behavior is a critical part of decision making in many fields such as medical diagnosis, psychology and human resource. Hierarchical Rater Model (HRM; Casabianca, Junker, & Patz, [52]) has been widely used to assess the overall proficiencies of individuals on rated tasks, as well as estimates of rater precision, accuracy, and other rater characteristics, under a broad variety of practical rating situations. The HRM is a highly parameterized, complex model that could be fit using Just Another Gibbs Sampler (JAGS), a program for analysis of Bayesian hierarchical models using Markov Chain Monte Carlo (MCMC) simulation. The HRM model is being expanded by a researcher in the college of education at University of Texas Austin. The research focus is to extend the HRM so that it can be applied to ratings from longitudinal and/or complex hierarchical designs and multidimensional assessments (for more information on this work, funded by the NSF, visit: http://nsf.gov/awardsearch/showAward?AWD_ID=1324587). However, the runtime of jags function in R2jags [48], a wrapper function the research uses to implement Bayesian analysis in JAGS, increases dramatically when the number of estimates and the number of iterations increases.

The implementation of R2jags relies on a R library—*rjags* [49] and a C++ library for Gibbs sampling—JAGS [50]. The researcher's goal was to conduct a simulation study in which she had 12 study conditions, or 12 calls to JAGS, each involving the estimation of roughly 1,500 parameters, with 3 chains and 8,000 iterations each. Each of the 12 study conditions were replicated 100 times, leading to a large computational task. With this many iterations and this many parameters

Table 9.2 Comparison of speed-up by parallel packages under multi-core and multi-node mechanism

Parallel mechanism	Package	Monte Carlo simulation of pi (128 iterations with one million random points)		2800×2800 cross-product matrix (b = a'*a)		cov (10,000 by 2000 distributed matrix)	
		Serial	Parallel	Serial	Parallel	Serial	Parallel
Multi-core (16 cores)	Parallel	57.18	5.11	–	–	–	–
	foreach + doSNOW	57.18	4.55	–	–	–	–
	HiPLARb (GPU)	–	–	12.57	4.40	–	–
	Intel compiled R (Xeon Phi)	–	–	12.57	0.21	–	–
	pbdDMAT	–	–	–	–	23.30	3.07
Multi-node (8 nodes × 16 cores)	doSNOW + snow + foreach (MPI)	57.18	1.55	–	–	–	–
	doSNOW + foreach (socket)	57.18	7.68				
	pbdMPI	57.18	1.22	–	–	–	–
	pbdDMAT	–	–	–	–	23.30	6.00

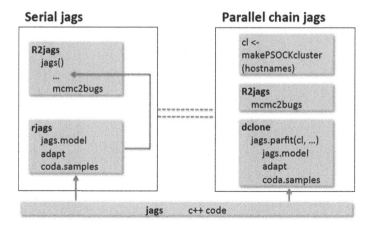

Fig. 9.5 The scheme of parallel chain jags algorithm

to estimate, the simulations become very time consuming, about 120 h for just one of the 12 conditions. Since the *jags.parallel* in *R2jags* package evoked a runtime error that could not be easily identified and fixed, a parallel chain algorithm for Gibbs sampling with multiple Markov Chains (MCs) was implemented by using *jags.parfit* function in *dclone* [51] package and *mcmc2bugs* function in *R2jags* package. The *dclone* package in R provides low-level functions for implementing maximum likelihood estimation procedures for complex models using data cloning and Bayesian Markov chain Monte Carlo methods. The samples returned from *jags.parfit* function are passed to mcmc2bugs to have the estimates fit for the HRM. The simulation time with parallel chain code is decreased to 1/3 (assuming three MCs) compared to the serial codes. After the simulations of all MCs are done, the results are combined and post-analyzed together and the results equivalent to that from the original code can be obtained. The scheme of parallel chain solution (The R package can be downloaded at https://github.com/ruizhuhuang/Stampede) is shown in Fig. 9.5.

The running times using serial and parallel implementations are compared and shown in Fig. 9.6 respectively. The parallel execution runs simulations of three chains in parallel. At lower iteration-number, the parallel implementation is slower than the serial implementation. This is caused by the additional overhead introduced with workload distribution and result collection process. However, as the iteration-number increases, the benefit of parallel execution eventually overcomes the overhead. When the iteration-number becomes large, the speedup of parallel execution can exceed the expected speedup of three times in practice. In serial implementation, the program needs to maintain the results that have been computed and updated them accordingly. The cost associated with those operations also increases as the number of iteration increases. In parallel implementation, the corresponding increasing cost is much lower, resulting in better overall performance.

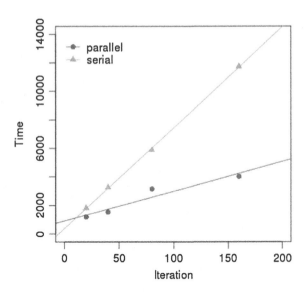

Fig. 9.6 Benchmark of the serial and parallel jags simulations

9.5.2 Exemplar Application Using Coprocessors

Multiple testing is one of the two fundamental statistical issues to address in the tasks of detecting and identifying the "outbreaks" in time series data. This study initiated by a group of researchers in Indiana University Mathematical science department investigates statistical solutions to examine and predict the outbreaks from data streams in Indiana Public Health Emergency Surveillance System, which are collected in an almost-real-time fashion and contain daily counts of ILI, ICD9, patent chief complaints, etc. The compute-intensive component of the project specifically considers the problem of massive data multiple testing under temporal dependence. The observed data is generated from an underlying two-state Hidden Markov model (HMM)—'aberration' or 'usual'. Bayesian methods are applied to develop the independent testing algorithm by optimizing the false negative rate while controlling the false discovery rate. The testing procedures use a length of 1000 as burn-in (the practice of throwing away some iterations at the beginning of an MCMC run) period, with 5000 MCMC iterations. The original implementation was coded using R in a serial fashion and a 20-run procedure roughly took about 5 h on desktop. The parallel solution run on Stampede exploits parallelization with *multicore* package to achieve an approximately threefold speedup, and automatic offloading to Xeon Phi coprocessor indicates another 10 % performance improvement.

As shown in Fig. 9.7, computations are distributed over multiple cores (using *multicore* package) and multiple nodes (using *snowfall* package). Enabling offloading to Phi coprocessors gives us an extra 10 % speedup when using *multicore* package (processing time was decreased from 8347.630 to 7675.636 s). The study runs pairs of such simulations to compare multiple methods including BH

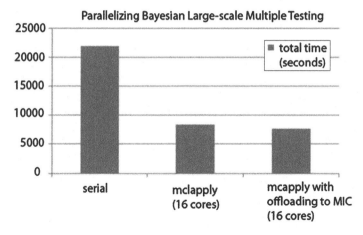

Fig. 9.7 Parallelizing multiple testing tasks. Computations are distributed over multiple cores (using *multicore* package) and multiple nodes (using *snowfall* package). Enabling offloading to Xeon Phi coprocessors gives us an extra 10 % speedup when using *multicore* package (from 8347.630 to 7675.636 s)

(Benjamini and Hochberg), AP (adaptive *p*-value procedure), OR (assume the true parameters are known), LIS (Sun and Cai), FB (full Bayesian method) and NPB (nonparametric Bayesian method) [19].

9.6 Discussions and Conclusion

In this chapter, we presented an overview on how high performance computing can be applied to R to improve its scalability and performance. We categorized the common parallel approach into two categories based on the hardware requirement, single node parallelism and multi-node parallelism. Within a single node, the parallelism utilizes and requires the availability of multiple cores. The number of processing cores within a node can be expanded by utilizing multiple cores within the CPU as well as utilizing co-processing card like GPGPU and Intel® Xeon Phi. The multimode parallelism can also be achieved with a computer cluster-using interface like MPI or on big data system such as Hadoop and Spark. We surveyed selected popular packages and supports available in R to take advantage of those parallel approaches.

We then reported our experience in using new Xeon Phi coprocessor to speed up the R computation. We tested workload offloading potential with a popular R benchmark and a preliminary test on a practical project. The results indicated that the performance improvement varies depending on the type of workload and input data size. We observed significant speed up with linear algebra related operations, such as matrix transformation, inverse matrix and matrices cross product. Our results show a modest additional performance increase when offloading to the Xeon Phi. The performance improvement further increases as the size of the input data increases. However, the speedup does not scale linearly with the number of threads used. This indicates an overhead cost in the process of parallelization. We also found an optimal usage is to offload about 70 % workload with Xeon Phi. We are encouraged by these initial results and feel there is great potential to utilize hybrid parallel models, running across multiple nodes and multiple Xeon Phi coprocessors, in tackling large-scale data problems with R.

The advantage of using single parallelism is that the workload can be executed in parallel automatically and transparent to the end users. Therefore, there is no need to modify the existing R script. However, they are also limited to a number of existing functions, mostly functions associated with linear algebra computations. Future programming efforts are required to enable parallelism manually for other types of computation. The parallelism utilizing multiple nodes provides base programming support to the end user. So the user can develop functions to run in parallel without limitation to vectorized operation only at the cost of additional programming development. We further compared the performance between using Xeon Phi, GPGPU and other popular parallel packages including parallel package, *pbdR* and *SNOW* packages. The purpose of this comparison is not to determine which packages perform the best but to show the potential benefit of the parallelism and their respective pros and cons. We also demonstrated two use case examples in which HPC can improve the execution of practical applications. We hope this chapter can give reader an overview on the potential of enabling high performance computing resources and big data analysis together.

Contrary to one's intuition, the key challenge to this issue is not the shortage of programming support in R to scale up the computations with state-of-the-art computing hardware and/or software models, but to make such support, as well as necessary computing resources, accessible to end users. Despite the availability of high performance support within R and computing resources, the major challenge of scaling up R-based analytics are summarized below accompanied by our proposed solutions: (1) the convolution of the packages and methods availability in R; (2) the complexity and knowledge required for different parallelism; (3) the accessibility of the appropriate computing resources support.

(1) *Convolutions of the methods and packages support in R*: One of the greatest strengths of R, the abundant packages supported by it, also poses the significant challenges to in its usability. Many of such methods and packages in R share similar functionality, the execution performance and suitability to different workload differ greatly. One of the most common examples is between *data frame* package and *data table* package. The authors have worked on several cases, in which analysis can be significantly improved by just replacing the usage of *data frame* with *data table* package. Similar cases are abound in R. There are more than 70 packages related to high performance computations in R. Thus selecting the most suitable packages requires thorough knowledge of R programming packages that is not easy for domain users lacking of training in computing sciences.

(2) *Complexity and knowledge required for different parallelisms*: There are a number of implementations for each mechanism. They differ not only in performance but also in development efforts, suitability towards specific workload, computing resource requirements and limitations. For example, *Single node parallelism* general requires more processing cores and large shared memory pool and/or special co-processing card like GPGPU, Xeon Phi, to speed up the computation. Some *Data parallelism* may depend on support from dedicated Hadoop or Spark cluster to work. To scale up the computation efficiently, additional knowledge of the parallel systems, computing resources specification and optimal settings of the computational resources are often required.

(3) *Accessibility to the appropriate computing resources*: As discussed above, different types of parallelism also require different software and hardware support. To support parallel execution, the corresponding hardware is required which is not commonly accessible to the user. The hardware requirement ranges from nodes with multiple cores and large shared memory pool, to nodes with special GPGPU card; from traditional computing cluster with high performance interconnectivity among nodes, to cluster running Hadoop and Spark. Those state-of-art high performance-computing resources are often expensive and appear remote for the end users who are not familiar with computing jargons.

Many big data problems are no longer just algorithmic problems. The solutions to big data problems therefore require not only new novel algorithms but also appropriate system support that are capable of executing the developed solutions. Unfortunately, the hardware required by those solutions often appears remote to the end users due to their costs and technology sophistication. So it is important now to make the latest technological advances accessible and usable to the domain scientists, who are the driving forces of scientific discovery. Aside of the basic education and training required to achieving this goals, comprehensive analytic software packages and programming environments like R can also help in bringing those new technological advantages to the end user. As we shown in this chapter, many package supports are now available in R to help users to utilize the new hardware transparently. In some cases, the users do not need to be aware of the backend high performance infrastructure at all. We believe such software development is crucial in enabling domain scientists to tackle big data problems with today's most advanced high performance computing resources.

References

1. R Development Core Team, *R: A Language and Environment for Statistical Computing* (R Foundation for Statistical Computing, Vienna, 2005)
2. CRAN [online] (2016), https://cran.r-project.org/web/packages/. Accessed 26 Feb 2016
3. J. Fox, CRAN task view: statistics for the social sciences [online] (2014), https://cran.r-project. org/web/views/SocialSciences.html. Accessed 27 Aug 2015
4. C. Gondro, L.R. Porto-Neto, S.H. Lee, R for genome-wide association studies. Methods Mol. Biol. **1019**, 1–17 (2013)

5. R.C. Gentleman, V.J. Carey, D.M. Bates, B. Bolstad, M. Dettling, S. Dudoit, B. Ellis, L. Gautier, Y. Ge, J. Gentry, K. Hornik, T. Hothorn, W. Huber, S. Iacus, R. Irizarry, F. Leisch, C. Li, M. Maechler, A.J. Rossini, G. Sawitzki, C. Smith, G. Smyth, L. Tierney, J.Y.H. Yang, J. Zhang, Bioconductor: open software development for computational biology and bioinformatics. Genome Biol. 5(10), R80 (2004)

6. E.C. Grunsky, R: a data analysis and statistical programming environment- an emerging tool for the geosciences. Comput. Geosci. 28(10), 1219–1222 (2002)

7. A. Ohri, *R for Business Analytics* (Springer, New York, 2012)

8. S. Pyne, X. Hu, K. Wang, E. Rossin, T.-I. Lin, L.M. Maier, C. Baecher-Allan, G.J. McLachlan, P. Tamayo, D.A. Hafler, P.L. De Jager, J.P. Mesirov, Automated high-dimensional flow cytometric data analysis. Proc. Natl. Acad. Sci. U. S. A. 106(21), 8519–8524 (2009)

9. N. Aghaeepour, G. Finak, H. Hoos, T.R. Mosmann, R. Brinkman, R. Gottardo, R.H. Scheuermann, F. Consortium, D. Consortium, Critical assessment of automated flow cytometry data analysis techniques. Nat. Methods 10(3), 228–238 (2013)

10. R. Ihaka, R. Gentleman, R: a language for data analysis and graphics. J. Comput. Graph. Stat. 5(3), 299–314 (1996)

11. H. Wickham, *Advanced R* (CRC Press, Boca Raton, 2014)

12. Y. El-Khamra, N. Gaffney, D. Walling, E. Wernert, W. Xu, H. Zhang, Performance Evaluation of R with Intel® Xeon Phi Coprocessor, in *Big Data, 2013 IEEE International Conference on*, 2013, pp. 23–30

13. P. Du, R. Weber, P. Luszczek, S. Tomov, G. Peterson, J. Dongarra, From CUDA to OpenCL: towards a performance-portable solution for multi-platform GPU programming. Parallel Comput. 38(8), 391–407 (2012)

14. J. Fung, F. Tang, S. Mann, Mediated Reality Using Computer Graphics Hardware for Computer Vision, in *Proceedings of the Sixth International Symposium on Wearable Computers, 2002 (ISWC 2002)*, 2002, pp. 83–89

15. Khronos Group, The open standard for parallel programming of heterogeneous systems [online] (2015), https://www.khronos.org/opencl/. Accessed 6 Sept 2015

16. J. Nickolls, I. Buck, M. Garland, and K. Skadron, Scalable parallel programming with CUDA. Queue, 6(2), 40–53 (2008)

17. C.Y. Tang, C.-L. Hung, C.-H. Hsu, H. Zheng, C.-Y. Lin, Novel computing technologies for bioinformatics and cheminformatics. Biomed Res. Int. 2014, 392150 (2014)

18. Mellanox, InfiniBand cards—overview [online] (2015), http://www.mellanox.com/page/infiniband_cards_overview. Accessed 6 Sept 2015

19. W. Gropp, E. Lusk, A. Skjellum, *Using MPI: Portable Parallel Programming with the Message-Passing Interface*, vol. 1 (MIT, Cambridge, 1999)

20. D. Buntinas, G. Mercier, W. Gropp, Implementation and evaluation of shared-memory communication and synchronization operations in MPICH2 using the Nemesis communication subsystem. Parallel Comput. 33(9), 634–644 (2007)

21. E. Gabriel, G.E. Fagg, G. Bosilca, T. Angskun, J.J. Dongarra, J.M. Squyres, V. Sahay, P. Kambadur, B. Barrett, A. Lumsdaine, R.H. Castain, D.J. Daniel, R.L. Graham, T.S. Woodall, Open MPI: goals, concept, and design of a next generation MPI implementation, in *Proceedings 11th European PVM/MPI Users' Group Meeting*, 2004, pp. 97–104

22. J. Dean, S. Ghemawat, MapReduce: simplified data processing on large clusters. Commun. ACM 51(1), 1–13 (2008)

23. Apache Hadoop, http://hadoop.apache.org (2009). Access 6 June 2016

24. M. Zaharia, M. Chowdhury, M.J. Franklin, S. Shenker, I. Stoica, Spark□: cluster computing with working sets, in *HotCloud'10 Proceedings of the 2nd USENIX Conference on Hot Topics in Cloud Computing*, 2010, p. 10

25. A.J. Rossini, L. Tierney, N. Li, Simple parallel statistical computing in R. J. Comput. Graph. Stat. 16(2), 399–420 (2007)

26. M.N. Li, A.J. Rossini, RPVM: cluster statistical computing in R. R News 1(3), 4–7 (2001)

27. H. Yu, Rmpi: parallel statistical computing in R. R News 2(2), 10–14 (2002)

28. L. Tierney, A.J. Rossini, N. Li, Snow: a parallel computing framework for the R system. Int. J. Parallel Prog. **37**(1), 78–90 (2009)
29. G. R. Warnes, Fork: R functions for handling multiple processes, CRAN Packag (2007), http:// cran.r-project.org/web/packages/fork
30. G. Vera, R.C. Jansen, R.L. Suppi, R/parallel–speeding up bioinformatics analysis with R. BMC Bioinf. **9**(1), 390 (2008)
31. M. Schmidberger, M. Morgan, D. Eddelbuettel, H. Yu, L. Tierney, U. Mansmann, State-of-the-art in parallel computing with R. J. Stat. Softw. **31**(1), 1–27 (2009)
32. D. Eddelbuettel, CRAN task view: high-performance and parallel computing with R (2015), http://cran.r-project.org/web/views/HighPerformanceComputing.html. Accessed 5 Sept 2014
33. HiPLAR [online] (2016), http://www.hiplar.org/. Accessed 26 Feb 2016
34. J. Dongarra, T. Dong, M. Gates, A. Haidar, S. Tomov, I. Yamazaki, MAGMA: A New Generation of Linear Algebra Library for GPU and Multicore Architectures, in *Supercomputing*, Salt Lake City, UT, 2012
35. E. Agullo, J. Demmel, J. Dongarra, B. Hadri, J. Kurzak, J. Langou, H. Ltaief, P. Luszczek, S. Tomov, Numerical linear algebra on emerging architectures: the PLASMA and MAGMA projects. J. Phys. Conf. Ser. **180**, 012037 (2009)
36. Intel Inc., Intel® Math Kernel Library 11.0 [online] (2015), https://software.intel.com/en-us/intel-mkl. Accessed 27 Aug 2015
37. A.M. Wilson, Speeding up R with Intel®'s Math Kernel Library (MKL) [online] (2015), http:// www.r-bloggers.com/speeding-up-r-with-intels-math-kernel-library-mkl/. Accessed 27 Aug 2015
38. S. Weston, doMPI: foreach parallel adaptor for the Rmpi package (2013), http://CRAN.R-project.org/package=doParallel. R Packag. version 0.2. p. 16
39. D. Schmidt, G. Ostrouchov, Programming with big data in R (2013), http://r-pbd.org
40. W. C. Chen, Ostrouchov G (2012b). "pmclust: Parallel Model-Based Clustering.". R Package, https://cran.r-project.org/web/packages/pmclust/index.html Assess 6 June 2016
41. R. Huang and W. Xu, "Performance Evaluation of Enabling Logistic Regression for Big Data with R," 2015 IEEE Int. Conf. Big Data (2015)
42. T. White, *Hadoop: The Definitive Guide* (O'Reilly Media, Inc., Sebastopol, CA, 2012)
43. J. Dean, S. Ghemawat, MapReduce: a flexible data processing tool. Commun. ACM **53**(1), 72–77 (2010)
44. R benchmarks [online] (2016), http://r.research.att.com/benchmarks/. Accessed 26 Feb 2016
45. J. Knaus, Snowfall: easier cluster computing (based on snow) (2010), http://cran.r-project.org/ package=snowfall. R Packag. version, vol. 1
46. S. Urbanek, Multicore: parallel processing of R code on machines with multiple cores or CPUs (2011), http://cran.r-project.org/package=multicore. R Packag. (v 0.1-7)
47. S. Weston, doSNOW: Foreach parallel adaptor for the snow package R Packag (2011)
48. S. Weston, doParallel: Foreach parallel adaptor for the parallel package. R Packag. version, **1**(8) (2014)
49. Y.-S. Su, M. Yajima, R2jags: a package for running jags from R (2012), http://CRAN.R-project.org/package=R2jags. R Packag. version 0.03-08
50. M. Plummer, *rjags: Bayesian Graphical Models Using MCMC* (R Foundation for Statistical Computing, Vienna, 2013). R package version 3–10
51. M. Plummer, JAGS: just another Gibbs sampler (2004), http://calvin.iarc.fr/-martyn/software/ jags/. Accessed 15 May 2011
52. P. Sólymos, dclone: data cloning in R. R J. **2**(2), 29–37 (2010)
53. Casabianca, J. M., Junker, B. W., & Patz, R. (in press). The hierarchical rater model. Invited chapter for W. J. van der Linden (Ed.), Handbook of modern item response theory. Boca Raton, FL: Chapman & Hall/CRC.

Chapter 10
Big Data Techniques as a Solution to Theory Problems

Richard W. Evans, Kenneth L. Judd, and Kramer Quist

Abstract This chapter proposes a general approach for solving a broad class of difficult optimization problems using big data techniques. We provide a general description of this approach as well as some examples. This approach is ideally suited for solving nonconvex optimization problems, multiobjective programming problems, models with a large degree of heterogeneity, rich policy structure, potential model uncertainty, and potential policy objective uncertainty. In our applications of this algorithm we use Hierarchical Database Format (HDF5) distributed storage and I/O as well as message passing interface (MPI) for parallel computation of a large number of small optimization problems.

10.1 Introduction

Big data refers to any repository of data that is either large enough or complex enough that distributed and parallel input and output approaches must be used (see [9, p. 3]). Liran and Levin [6] discuss the new opportunities in economics using big data, although they focus primarily on searching for important patterns in existing datasets. Varian [8] describes the tools Google uses to address big data questions and provides a mapping to the open source analogues of those proprietary tools. This paper proposes a very different use of big data techniques, using efficient sampling methods to construct a large data set which can then be used to address theoretical questions as well as econometric ones. More specifically, we sample the parameter space of a parametric model and use the large sample to address a research question.

R.W. Evans (✉)
Department of Economics, Brigham Young University, 167 FOB, Provo, UT 84602, USA
e-mail: revans@byu.edu

K.L. Judd
Hoover Institution, Stanford University, Stanford, CA 94305, USA
e-mail: kennethjudd@mac.com

K. Quist
Department of Economics, Brigham Young University, 151 FOB, Provo, UT 84602, USA
e-mail: kramer.quist@gmail.com

© Springer International Publishing Switzerland 2016   219
R. Arora (ed.), *Conquering Big Data with High Performance Computing*,
DOI 10.1007/978-3-319-33742-5_10

Furthermore, constructing the data sample is a large but fixed cost which allows one to use high performance computing to cheaply answer many questions.

Our leading example is an optimal tax application from [2], but we also present an econometric example. The approach described in this chapter is ideally suited for solving nonconvex optimization problems,[1] multi-objective programming problems, models with a large degree of heterogeneity, rich policy structure, potential model uncertainty, and potential policy objective uncertainty.

Our implementation of these methods has used the Python programming language with its integration with the Hierarchical Database Format (HDF5) and its distributed storage and parallel I/O. However, these methods are general across platforms. We will also detail a technique that is new to this area, which is using equidistributed sequences both as an approximation-by-simulation technique as well as an adaptive grid refinement technique by equidistributing a sequence on various hypercubic subspaces.[2]

In Sect. 10.2, we give a general description of the big data approach to solving theoretical problems, a computational description, and a description of our use of equidistributed sequences. In Sect. 10.3, we describe an optimal taxation example of this approach. Section 10.4 describes some other applications of this approach, with a more detailed description of an econometric example. Section 10.5 concludes.

10.2   General Formulation of Big Data Solution Method

In this section, we first formulate a general class of problems that are amenable to our big data solution method. We then outline the computational steps of the method and describe some specific techniques that we use in our implementation. We then describe in more depth one of the key tools we use—equidistributed sequences—to efficiently find the set of solutions using our method. This method is scalable to a large number of processors on a supercomputer and to quickly interface with a large size database of individual behavior.

10.2.1   General Formulation of Class of Models and Solution Method

We first describe a general class of models that are very amenable to big data solution techniques. Let a mathematical model be represented by a general system

---

[1]Nonconvex optimization problems are problems in which the set of possible solutions is a nonconvex set. Androulakis et al. [1] provide a nice introduction and references to general nonconvex optimization problems, as well as common examples. See also [7].

[2]See [5, Chap. 9] on quasi-Monte Carlo methods for an introduction to the uses of equidistributed sequences.

of equations $F(x, \theta)$, where x is a vector of endogenous variables, θ is a vector of model parameters, and F is a vector of functions, each of which operates on some subset of x and θ. Let the solution to that system of equations be a particular vector $\hat{x}(\theta)$ such that,

$$\hat{x}(\theta) \equiv \operatorname{argmin}_x F(x, \theta). \tag{10.1}$$

In other words, $\hat{x}(\theta)$ is a solution to the model given a particular set of model parameters. The specification in (10.1) could also be written as a maximization problem and is general enough to include the solution $\hat{x}$ being the root of the vector of equations F.

Optimal policy problems often take the form of choosing a subset of the parameter vector θ to minimize (or maximize) some scalar-valued function W of a vector of scalar valued functions G of the optimized model equations,

$$\hat{\theta} \equiv \operatorname{argmin}_\theta W\left(G\left(F\left(\hat{x}(\theta), \theta \right) \right) \right) \tag{10.2}$$

where $\hat{x}(\theta)$ is defined in (10.1). If G is vector-valued, then the problem is a multi-objective programming problem. The solution to the policy problem (10.2) is a particular parameterization of the model $\hat{\theta}$ and the model being solved for that particular parameterization $F\left(\hat{x}(\hat{\theta}), \hat{\theta} \right)$.

When both the minimization problem in (10.1) and in (10.2) are convex, the solution $\hat{\theta}$ is straightforward to find with standard computational methods. However, when either (10.1) or (10.2) is a nonconvex optimization problem, finding a solution becomes very difficult and nonstandard computational approaches must be used. Introducing nonconvex structures into the economic model F in (10.1)—such as occasionally binding constraints or nonconvex budget sets—will render the minimization problem in (10.1) nonconvex, thereby making it likely that the minimization problem in (10.2) is not convex. But more subtle model characteristics, such as heterogeneity among the equations in F, can maintain the convexity of the minimization problem in (10.1), but break it in (10.2).

10.2.2 Computational Steps to Big Data Solution Method

Our big data approach to solving theory problems, such as the one described in (10.1) and (10.2), is summarized in Table 10.1. The first step is to make a large database of model solutions and objective realizations $G_n\left(F_n\left(\hat{x}(\theta_n), \theta_n \right) \right)$, where θ_n is the nth realization of the parameter vector θ. The total number of parameter vector realizations N for which the problem is solved is presumably large. One reason why this is a big data solution technique is that the database of model objectives and solutions for each N parameter vectors can be so large that it must be distributed across multiple hard drives. This is step 1 in Table 10.1.

Table 10.1 General summary of big data approach to theory problems

Step description	Output
1. Solve the model for a large number N of parameter vector realizations θ_n.	$G_n\Big(F_n\big(\hat{x}(\theta_n),\theta_n\big)\Big)$
2. Delete all realizations of the objectives vector $G_{n'}$ that are strictly dominated by at least one other realization of the objectives vector G_n.	Frontier of $G_n\Big(F_n\big(\hat{x}(\theta_n),\theta_n\big)\Big)$
3. If the frontier from step (2) is not smooth enough, draw P new realizations of the parameter vector $\theta_{n,p}$ in the neighborhood of each remaining point n on the objective vector frontier.	$G_{n,p}\Big(F_{n,p}\big(\hat{x}(\theta_{n,p}),\theta_{n,p}\big)\Big)$
4. Delete all realizations of the objectives vector $G_{n',p'}$ that are strictly dominated by at least one other realization of the objectives vector $G_{n,p}$	Frontier of $G_{n,p}\Big(F_{n,p}\big(\hat{x}(\theta_{n,p}),\theta_{n,p}\big)\Big)$
5. Repeat refinement steps (3) and (4) until frontier is smooth.	
6. If the objective function W is known, solve for optimal parameter vector $\hat{\theta}$ using Eq. (10.2).	$\hat{\theta} = \operatorname{argmin}_\theta \dots$ $W\Big(G_{n,p}\big(F_{n,p}(\hat{x}(\theta_{n,p}),\theta_{n,p})\big)\Big)$

In generating our database of individual responses $\hat{x}(\theta_n)$ and the corresponding vector of objectives G_n for realization of the parameter vector θ_n, we used the Python programming language. We also use Python's MPI (message passing interface) library `mpi4py` for simultaneously running computations on multiple processors. We ran this code on 12 nodes with a total of 96 processors on the supercomputer at the Fulton Supercomputing Lab at Brigham Young University.[3] In addition to parallel computation, we also exploited Python's library `h5py`, which enables the HDF5 suite of data and file formats and parallel I/O tools.[4] The Python code in Fig. 10.1 shows some of the key operations that generate our database of responses in the Sales Tax example of [2] described in Sect. 10.3. The code in Fig. 10.1 is taken from multiple Python scripts that work together to solve many model solutions simultaneously solve many sets of model equations for carefully load-balanced sections of policy parameter space.

Lines 2 to 4 in Fig. 10.1 import Python's implementation of MPI, define an MPI communicator, and define a barrier that helps in load balancing. The number of processors to be used as well as the wall time allowed for the computation are

---

[3]See https://marylou.byu.edu/ for information about the Fulton Supercomputing Lab at Brigham Young University.

[4]See https://www.hdfgroup.org/HDF5/ for a general description of the HDF5 set of tools, and see http://www.h5py.org/ for a description of the Python library which enables the HDF5 tools.

```
1              ...
2              from mpi4py import MPI
3              comm = MPI.COMM_WORLD
4              comm.Barrier()
5              start = MPI.Wtime()
6              ...
7              import h5py
8              ...
9              def init_database(comm, N, sequence_type, n_policies,
                   type_space, policy_space, tax_rates_same, filename,
                   verbose=True):
10             ...
11             with h5py.File(filename, 'w') as f:
12             ...
```

Fig. 10.1 Python code importing mpi4py and h5py modules

part of a supercomputer-specific job script which tells the supercomputer to start running the job. Once MPI has been enabled for use on multiple processors, we import the HDF5 set of tools with the `import h5py` call. Line 9 of Fig. 10.1 shows one function `init_database()` that is run in parallel for as many Python instances as we have told the supercomputer to create. Each separate instance is designated by the `comm` object in the function. This function computes the solutions to the model $\hat{x}(\theta_n)$ and G_n and then saves those solutions using the HDF5 parallel I/O functionality of store commands after the command in line 11 of code `with h5py.File(filename, 'w') as f:`.

An arguably more important reason for using big data techniques has to do with the manipulation of the database of model objectives and solutions after its creation. Once the database of $G_n\left(F_n\big(\hat{x}(\theta_n),\theta_n\big)\right)$ exists, note that we still have not solved for the optimal parameter vector $\hat{\theta}$. In terms of the database, we want to know what is the θ_n that minimizes some function of the objectives W from (10.2). HDF5 parallel input-output techniques are very efficient at operations across distributed memory such as weighted averages, nonlinear functions, minima, and maxima.

But now assume that you are not sure what the correct objective aggregating function W is. In our approach, we search our database of responses and delete all entries in the database $G_{n'}$ that are strictly dominated by another entry G_n. The first panel in Fig. 10.2 shows the entire database of objective realizations for each θ_n where there are two objectives (each G_n has two elements). In other words, each dot represents $G_{1,n}$ and $G_{2,n}$ for a given vector of parameters θ_n. The second panel in Fig. 10.2 shows the points on the frontier in terms of $G_{1,n}$ and $G_{2,n}$ for all n after deleting all the strictly dominated points.

The execution in our code of this deletion of strictly dominated points, as shown in the first two panels of Fig. 10.2, is something that we have had success in speeding

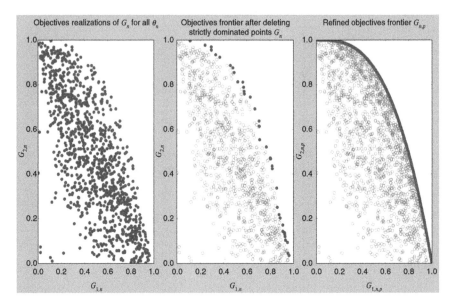

Fig. 10.2 General process of finding the objectives G_n frontier

up and optimizing. We use a parallel quicksort routine in which we sort portions of the points in the first panel along one dimension of objectives $G_{1,n}$ and then delete data points in which the $G_{2,n}$ objective is dominated.

Often times, the frontier traced out in the first deletion of strictly dominated points is too coarse. In that case, we do another step of choosing equidistributed sequences of new realizations of θ_n in the neighborhood of each point on the frontier. We then delete all the strictly dominated objectives from those new realizations to find the refined frontier shown in the third panel of Fig. 10.2.

10.2.3   Virtues of Equidistributed Sequences

In choosing a grid size N of realizations of the parameter vector θ_n and in refining around points on the objective vector frontier $\theta_{n,p}$, it is important to have an efficient method to keep track of all the points that are generated and which points get saved in the database. Using equidistributed sequences provides that efficiency, both in terms of spreading N points uniformly throughout a particular space and in keeping track of those points.

Equidistributed sequences are deterministic sequences of real numbers where the proportion of terms falling in any subinterval is proportional to the length of that interval. A sequence $\{x_j\}_{j=1}^{\infty} \subset D \subset \mathbb{R}^n$ is equidistributed over D if and only if

Table 10.2 Equidistributed sequences in $\mathbb{R}^n$

Name of sequence	Formula for $(x_1, x_2, \ldots, x_n)$
Weyl	$(\{np_1^{1/2}\}, \ldots, \{np_n^{1/2}\})$
Haber	$(\{\frac{n(n+1)}{2}p_1^{1/2}\}, \ldots, \{\frac{n(n+1)}{2}p_n^{1/2}\})$
Niederreiter	$(\{n2^{1/(n+1)}\}, \ldots, \{n2^{n/(n+1)}\})$
Baker	$(\{ne^{r_1}\}, \ldots, \{ne^{r_n}\})$, r_j rational and distinct

$$\lim_{n\to\infty} \frac{\mu(D)}{n} \sum_{j=1}^{n} f(x_j) = \int_D f(x)dx \qquad (10.3)$$

for all Riemann-integrable $f(x) : \mathbb{R}^n \to \mathbb{R}$, where $\mu(D)$ is the Lebesgue measure of D.

There are a number of equidistributed sequences that possess this property. Let $p_1, p_2, \ldots$ denote the sequence of prime numbers $2, 3, 5, \ldots$, and let $\{x\}$ represent the fractional part of x, that is $\{x\} = x - \lfloor x \rfloor$. Table 10.2 contains examples of a number of equidistributed sequences. Figure 10.3 shows the first 10,000 points for two-dimensional Weyl, Haber, Niederreiter, and Baker sequences.

Baker et al. [2] and Bejarano et al. [3] use a scaled Baker sequence. Quasi-Monte Carlo integration is used to integrate over the type space for each point in policy space given the type space distribution. Quasi-Monte Carlo integration is similar to Monte Carlo integration, but chooses points using equidistributed sequences instead of pseudorandom numbers. This allows for a faster rate of convergence for a large number of points. With N points in s dimensions, quasi-Monte Carlo techniques converge in $O\left(\frac{(\log N)^s}{N}\right)$ as opposed to $O\left(\frac{1}{\sqrt{N}}\right)$ for Monte Carlo techniques.[5]

A key distinction between equidistributed sequences and pseudorandom sequences is that equidistributed sequences do not look like random numbers. As can be seen in Fig. 10.3, they generally display substantial serial correlation. From the outset, equidistributed sequences are chosen so as to perform accurate integration, and are not encumbered by any other requirements of random numbers

Another practical advantages of using equidistributed sequences is that it allows one to represent the entire multi-dimensional space of parameters θ in the minimization problem (10.2) as a one-dimensional list, which allows for easy partitioning across computing nodes. Additionally, using equidistributed sequences makes for easy expansion of the database. One has merely to append additional points to the end of the list.

---

[5] See [5, Chap. 9] on quasi-Monte Carlo methods for a more thorough discussion of the advantages of using equidistributed sequences to execute simulation-based methods, Riemann-integrable functions, and Lebesgue measure.

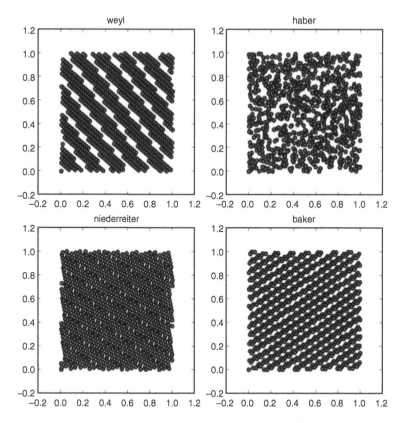

Fig. 10.3 Four two-dimensional equidistributed sequences with $n = 10{,}000$

10.3   Optimal Tax Application

In this section, we highlight an application of the approach presented in Sect. 10.2 to a theory problem related to optimal taxation. This example is described in [2] and solves for an optimal schedule of sales tax rates given a heterogeneous population of consumers. In this sales tax problem, each individual's optimization problem—analogous to the general problem in (10.1)—is convex. However, because of the heterogeneity across individuals, the policy maker's problem in choosing the optimal tax—analogous to the general problem in (10.2)—is not convex.

Baker et al. [2] set up an economic environment in which a policy maker must choose a schedule of sales tax rates on the different types of goods consumed by households and in which the population of households differs in terms of their wage and their elasticity of substitution among eight different types of consumption goods. Total consumption by a given household C is a constant elasticity of substitution (CES) function of all the individual types of consumption c_i the household can choose,

$$C \equiv \left(\sum_{i=1}^{8} \alpha_i (c_i - \bar{c}_i)^{\frac{\eta-1}{\eta}} \right)^{\frac{\eta}{\eta-1}} \quad \forall \eta \geq 1 \qquad (10.4)$$

where $\eta \geq 1$ is the elasticity of substitution among all of the consumption goods, $\alpha_i \in [0, 1]$ is the weight on the consumption of each type of good with $\sum_i \alpha_i = 1$, and $\bar{c}_i \geq 0$ is a minimum level of consumption for each type of good.

Household's face a budget constraint in which their total expenditure on consumption goods must be less-than-or-equal-to their income, which in this case is simply their wage.

$$\sum_{i=1}^{8} (1 + \tau_i) c_i \leq w \qquad (10.5)$$

The household's objective function is a Constant Relative Risk Aversion (CRRA) utility function defined over total consumption from (10.4),

$$u(C) = \frac{C^{1-\gamma} - 1}{1 - \gamma} \qquad (10.6)$$

where $\gamma \geq 1$ is the coefficient of relative risk aversion. The household's optimization problem is to choose a vector of consumptions $c = \{c_1, c_2, \ldots c_8\}$ that maximizes total utility (10.6) subject to the budget constraint (10.5).

Let a household's type be defined by its wage w and its elasticity of substitution η. The household's problem is a convex optimization problem where the solution is a vector of consumption functions $c(w, \eta; \tau)$ that are functions of a household's type (w, η) and the vector of sales tax rates $\tau = \{\tau_1, \tau_2, \ldots \tau_8\}$ as well as a utility function $u\big(c(w, \eta; \tau)\big)$ that is also a function of household type (w, η) and the vector of tax rates τ. This problem is analgous to the problem in (10.1) in Sect. 10.2.

For any given sales tax regime τ, there are as many different household utility levels $u\big(c(w, \eta; \tau)\big)$ and optimal consumption vectors $c(w, \eta; \tau)$ as there are different types of individuals. Baker et al. [2] then choose 57,786 different sales tax policy vectors τ with 5,100 different types of individuals resulting in solving nearly 300 million individual optimization problems.[6] They assume that the policy maker chooses the optimal sale tax schedule τ to maximize some combination of the total utility in the economy (the sum of individual utilities u) and total tax revenue. Each point along the solid curve in Fig. 10.4 represents a sales tax policy τ that is on the frontier in terms of both total utility (x-axis) and total revenue (y-axis).

Figure 10.5 shows how the optimal sales tax policies τ change across the frontier in Fig. 10.4. That is, sales tax rates at the left-hand-side of Fig. 10.5 correspond to

---

[6]Table 3 in [2] details that this computation took 29.5 h of wall time using 96 processors. In serial, this would have taken nearly 3,000 h (about 120 days), which is not feasible.

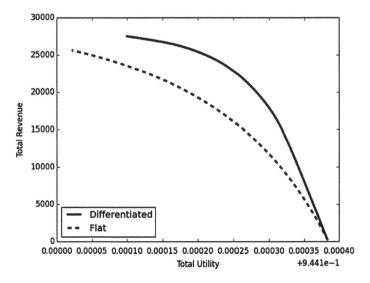

Fig. 10.4 Total utility-revenue frontiers for optimal differentiated tax versus optimal flat tax

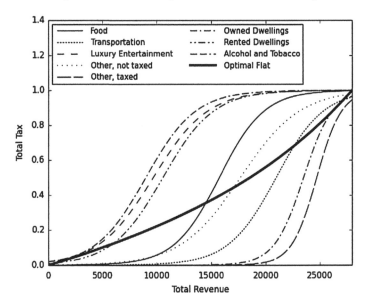

Fig. 10.5 Optimal tax rates for good i for different levels of total revenue

points on the frontier in the lower-right side of Fig. 10.4. Figure 10.5 shows which taxes get increased first in the most optimal sales tax schedule as more total revenue is required. Figure 10.5 represents the entire set of optimal sales tax schedules $\hat{\tau}$ for many different possible policy maker objective functions W over the two objectives of total utility and total revenue.

Baker et al. [2] use this framework to test the welfare and total revenue effects of one optimal sales tax rate on all consumption goods instead of a set of optimal tax rates on each consumption good. They also estimate the loss in revenue from exempting a class of consumptions goods, such as some services are in the U.S. economy. They find that there is only a small loss in total revenue from exempting services from sales taxation. However, that loss is small only because other taxes are higher in order to make up for the exempted category. Further they find a 30 % loss in total tax revenue from a sales tax regime with only one optimally chosen tax rate versus one in which multiple sales tax rates on goods are chosen optimally.

10.4 Other Applications

Multi-objective, nonconvex optimal policy problems abound of the form described in Sect. 10.2. Optimal insurance contracts, political institutions, problems with occasionally binding constraints, auction and mechanism design, and maximum likelihood estimation are a few examples. But the big data approach in this paper is also well-suited for models in which the individual problem from Eq. (10.1) takes a long time to run for any given parameter vector θ_n. The strength of this big data approach to these problems is that the model can be solved independently and in parallel for a grid of points in parameter space θ_n. These solutions can be stored and used by later researchers. These later researchers can either get their solution by interpolating between the stored solutions, or by adding to the database in regions in parameter space θ_n that are too sparse. To describe this class of problems, we define a slightly different version of the model from Sect. 10.2.

Let an econometric model $F(\beta, \theta)$ be defined over a vector of exogenous parameters β, whose values are taken from outside the model, and a vector of endogenous parameters θ, whose values are estimated by the model.

$$\hat{\theta} \equiv \mathrm{argmin}_\theta F(\beta, \theta) \tag{10.7}$$

The solution to the problem (10.7) is an optimal parameter vector $\hat{\theta}(\beta)$ as a function of exogenous parameters and a model solution $F\left(\beta, \hat{\theta}(\beta)\right)$ as a function of exogenous parameters.

One immediate econometric application of this big data approach is when the minimization problem (10.7) is nonconvex, given an exogenous parameter vector β. This is often the case in maximum likelihood estimation. Through a large database of potential endogenous parameter vector θ_n and refinements around the objective function frontier, confidence that $\hat{\theta}$ is the global optimum increases as the size of the database increases. This is simply a non-derivative optimizer that uses an adaptive grid search method.

However, this method becomes very valuable when each computation of a solution $\hat{\theta}(\beta)$ for a given exogenous parameter vector β takes a long time. Many instances of maximum likelihood estimation fit this criterion. Imagine a model that estimates region-r specific parameters θ_r for a given calibration of other parameters β_r for that region. Each estimation for a given region r and its calibrated parameters β_r might take a long time. If we have stored a database of precomputed solutions $\hat{\theta}_r (\beta_r)$, then one can simply interpolate the estimation of a new region rather than computing the solution again.

More generally, maximum likelihood estimation of the problem in (10.7) for one particular realization of the exogenous parameters β might require a long computational time (sometimes days). If one were to precompute once and store in a database the solutions to the problem $\hat{\theta} (\beta)$ for a grid of potential exogenous parameter realizations, solutions on the continuous space of potential exogenous parameter vector realizations β could be quickly computed by interpolating between points saved in the database. One study for which this technique is currently being employed is [4], which describes a difficult maximum likelihood estimation of a quantile regression.

10.5 Conclusion

Computing capability is ever becoming more powerful, less costly, and more broadly available. At the same time, the techniques to store and interact with large datasets are also improving. We have described a novel approach to solving complex minimization problems that combines the tools of MPI for parallel processing the tools of parallel I/O for using big data techniques. This approach allows researchers to solve optimal policy problems that are otherwise too complex. A leading example is the optimal income tax problem from Sect. 10.3. This method has myriad other applications ranging from optimal insurance contracts to maximum likelihood estimation.

Acknowledgements We thank the Hoover Institution and the BYU Macroeconomics and Computational Laboratory for research support. We also thank the Mary Lou Fulton Supercomputing Laboratory at Brigham Young University for use of the supercomputer.

References

1. I.P. Androulakis, C.D. Maranas, C.A. Floudas, αBB: a global optimization method for general constrained nonconvex problems. J. Glob. Optim. **7**(4), 337–363 (1995)
2. C. Baker, J. Bejarano, R.W. Evans, K.L. Judd, K.L. Phillips, A big data approach to optimal sales taxation. NBER Working Paper No. 20130, National Bureau of Economic Research (May 2014)
3. J. Bejarano, R.W. Evans, K.L. Judd, K.L. Phillips, K. Quist, A big data approach to optimal income taxation. Mimeo (2015)

4. B.R. Frandsen, Exact nonparametric inference for a binary endogenous regressor. Mimeo (2015)
5. K.L. Judd, *Numerical Methods in Economics* (MIT, Cambridge, 1998)
6. E. Liran, J.D. Levin, The data revolution and economic analysis. NBER Working Paper No. 19035, National Bureau of Economic Research (2013)
7. S.K. Mishra (ed.), *Topics in Nonconvex Optimization: Theory and Applications*. Nonconvex Optimization and Its Applications (Springer, New York, 2011)
8. H.R. Varian, Big data: new tricks for econometrics. J. Econ. Perspect. **28**(2), 3–28 (2014)
9. T. White, *Hadoop: The Definitive Guide* (O'Reilly Media; Sebastopol, California, 2012)

Chapter 11
High-Frequency Financial Statistics Through High-Performance Computing

Jian Zou and Hui Zhang

Abstract Financial statistics covers a wide array of applications in the financial world, such as (high-frequency) trading, risk management, pricing and valuation of securities and derivatives, and various business and economic analytics. Portfolio allocation is one of the most important problems in financial risk management. One most challenging part in portfolio allocation is the tremendous amount of data and the optimization procedures that require computing power beyond the currently available desktop systems. In this article, we focus on the portfolio allocation problem using high-frequency financial data, and propose a hybrid parallelization solution to carry out efficient asset allocations in a large portfolio via intra-day high-frequency data. We exploit a variety of HPC techniques, including parallel **R**, Intel® Math Kernel Library, and automatic offloading to Intel® Xeon Phi coprocessor in particular to speed up the simulation and optimization procedures in our statistical investigations. Our numerical studies are based on high-frequency price data on stocks traded in New York Stock Exchange in 2011. The analysis results show that portfolios constructed using high-frequency approach generally perform well by pooling together the strengths of regularization and estimation from a risk management perspective. We also investigate the computation aspects of large-scale multiple hypothesis testing for time series data. Using a combination of software and hardware parallelism, we demonstrate a high level of performance on high-frequency financial statistics.

11.1 Introduction

This chapter considers the application of HPC to statistical methods in high-frequency financial analysis. Financial statistics covers a wide array of applications in the financial world, such as (high-frequency) trading, risk management, pricing

J. Zou
Worcester Polytechnic Institute, Worcester, MA, USA
e-mail: jzou@wpi.edu

H. Zhang (✉)
University of Louisville, Louisville, KY, USA
e-mail: hui.zhang@louisville.edu

© Springer International Publishing Switzerland 2016
R. Arora (ed.), *Conquering Big Data with High Performance Computing*,
DOI 10.1007/978-3-319-33742-5_11

233

and valuation of securities and derivatives, and various business and economic analytics. In financial risk management, the question of how to allocate assets in a large portfolio is of utmost interests to most investors. It is necessary to understand the returns to expect from the portfolio, in addition to the volatility the portfolio can experience about that expectation. The portfolio allocation problem typically involves dividing an investment portfolio among different assets based on the volatilities of the asset returns. In the recent decades, it gains popularity to estimate volatilities of asset returns based on high-frequency data in financial economics.

However, the most challenging part in portfolio allocation, especially in high-frequency setting, is the tremendous amount of data and the optimization procedures such as LASSO and SCAD that require very intensive computations. Multiple testing for different return series is another related and more computationally demanding problem. It not only needs to run a large number of Monte Carlo simulations, but also involves calculating the posterior estimates using Markov Chain Monte Carlo (MCMC) [15], which could be a daunting task as the number of simulations (N) and number of MCMC samples (K) go to even moderate values, as the multiplicity is at the order of O(NK). In recent years, a number of computationally demanding financial applications have considered the application of HPC techniques. For example Smelyanskiy et al. investigated the application of modern multi- and many-core IA-based architectures in the analysis and optimization of financial analytics tasks [33]. Creel et al. suggested a GPU based implementation for an estimator based on an indirect likelihood inference method [6]. Bahl et al. developed a parallel aggregate risk analysis algorithm and an engine implemented in C and OpenMP for multi-core CPUs and in C and CUDA for many-core GPUs [2].

Our ultimate goal of this project is to develop an innovative methodology to perform asset allocation using high-frequency financial data. While **R** has been adopted as our major data analysis tool and tremendous amount of data and computations are required in the optimization procedures, we are motivated to investigate a variety of HPC techniques to speed up **R** computations with the utilization of Parallel **R**, the Intel® Math Kernel Library and automatic offloading to Intel® Xeon Phi SE10P Coprocessor. We are mostly interested in massive parallelism for existing **R** solutions with little to no modification.

The rest of this chapter is structured as follows. Section 11.2 elaborates the framework of our methodology of portfolio allocation for high-frequency data. Section 11.3 details our computing environment and our massive parallelism strategies. Section 11.4 presents numerical evidence on the performance comparison of our method under both standard and high-performance computing scenarios. Section 11.5 concludes this chapter.

11.2 Large Portfolio Allocation for High-Frequency Financial Data

11.2.1 Background

Understanding the returns to expect from the portfolio was first explored in a seminal paper [27], which was the original milestone for modern portfolio theory on the mean-variance analysis by solving an unconstrained quadratic optimization problem. This approach has had a profound impact on financial economics. But this model, while appealing in its simplicity, fails to capture some important characteristics of the capital markets. In particular, it assumes that asset expected returns, variances, and covariances remain constant and known. Empirically, this assumption runs counter to the evidence of time-varying expectations, variances, and covariances. For example, asset volatilities and correlations both increase during periods of market stress, and global asset correlations have increased in the recent decades as global capital markets have become increasingly integrated.

The drawback of requiring constant known parameters for this model has led to great interests in novel methods of modeling these parameters and analysis of financial time series. More recently, motivated by wide availability and extra amount of information contained in the high-frequency asset price data, researchers are able to develop more accurate estimators for the volatility matrix. The volatility matrix (or conditional covariance matrix) of daily asset returns is a key input in portfolio allocation, option pricing and risk management. However, the main challenge is that when the number of assets is large, the volatility matrix cannot be estimated accurately. To address this problem, several innovative approaches for volatility matrix estimation were proposed in the past decade. Many estimation methods have been developed for the univariate case [1, 3, 4, 11, 26, 44]. For multiple assets, we face non-synchronization issue, which is referred to as such because high-frequency price data are not aligned properly for different assets, hence are recorded at various mismatched time points. For a pair of assets, [18] and [44] have developed methods based on overlap intervals and previous ticks to estimate co-integrated volatility of the two assets. The development of these new estimators has, in turn, led to investigations into their practical benefits in investment decisions, see e.g., [8, 14, 24].

From a financial risk management perspective, [20] analyzed the impact of weights constraints in large portfolio allocation. They show that solving the global minimum variance portfolio problem with some constraints on weights is equivalent to use a shrinkage estimate of the covariance matrix. Fan et al. [12] studied portfolio allocation with gross-exposure constraint combining vast volatility matrix estimation using different sampling schemes. However, there exists an interesting question as of when and how an investor will benefit from using high-frequency financial data in his/her portfolio allocation decisions.

11.2.2 Our Methods

Our methods adapt the methodology in [46, 47]. Suppose that a portfolio consists of p assets and their log price process $X_t = (X_{1t}, \cdots, X_{pt})^T$ obeys the process governed by

$$dX_t = \mu_t \, dt + \sigma_t \, dW_t, \quad t \in [0, L], \tag{11.1}$$

where W_t is a p-dimensional standard Brownian motion, μ_t is a drift taking values in R^p, and σ_t is a diffusion variance of $p \times p$ matrix. Both μ_t and σ_t are assumed to be continuous in t.

For the portfolio with allocation vector w (i.e., percentage of each asset in the portfolio) and a holding period T, the variance (risk) of the portfolio return is given by $R(w, \Sigma) = w^T \Sigma w$. However, it is well known that the estimation error in the mean vector μ_t could severely affect the portfolio weights and produce suboptimal portfolios. This motivates us to adopt another popular portfolio strategy: the *global minimum variance portfolio*, which is the minimum risk portfolio with weights that sum to one. These weights are usually estimated proportional to the inverse covariance matrix, i.e., $w \propto \Sigma^{-1}$. Following [20] and [13], we consider the following risk optimization with two different constraints:

$$\min w^T \Sigma w, \quad s.t. \, \|w\|_1 \le c \text{ and } w^T \mathbf{1} = 1 \tag{11.2}$$

where c is the gross exposure parameter which specifies the total exposure allowed in the portfolio, and $\| \cdot \|_1$ is the standard vector l_1 norm. The summation to one constraint ensures weight percentages sum to 100 %, inducing a full investment. An additional common requirement is no short selling (e.g., 401k, IRAs, and mutual funds), which adds the non-negative optimization constraint. This corresponds to the case $c = 1$ as in [20]. The second optimization case is the global minimum risk portfolio where the gross exposure constraint $c = \infty$. Note that we only consider these two cases for simplification of the problem. Other cases with varying c can be easily generalized in our methodology.

Then we apply the average realized volatility matrix estimator to estimate the integrated volatility for the ℓ-th day. The integrated volatility for the ℓ-th day is a matrix defined to be

$$\Sigma_x(\ell) = \int_{\ell-1}^{\ell} \sigma_s \sigma_s^\dagger ds, \quad \ell = 1, \cdots, L. \tag{11.3}$$

We consider realized co-volatility based on previous-tick times. Let $n = n_1 + \cdots + n_p$ be the total observations from all p assets and assume that n_i/n are bounded away from zero, and we denote by $Y_i(t_{i,j})$ the observed log price of the i-th asset at time t_{ij}. Take a predetermined sampling frequency $\tau_k, k = 1, \cdots, m$, where m is a fixed integer. One example is to select τ_i be a regular grid. For each $k = 1, \cdots, m$, we choose the corresponding observation time for the i-th asset by

$$\tau_{ik} = \max\{t_{ij} \leq \tau_k, j = 1, \cdots, n_i\}, \qquad i = 1 \cdots, p.$$

The realized co-volatility is defined to be a $p \times p$ matrix $\hat{\Sigma}_y(1)$ whose (i_1, i_2) element is given by

$$\sum_{k=1}^{m} [Y_{i_1}(\tau_{i_1,k}) - Y_{i_1}(\tau_{i_1,k-1})] \, [Y_{i_2}(\tau_{i_2,k}) - Y_{i_2}(\tau_{i_2,k-1})].$$

We estimate $\Sigma_x(1)$ by $\hat{\Sigma}_y(1)$. Zhang [43] proved that with i.i.d. microstructure noise and $m \sim n^{2/3}$,

$$\hat{\Sigma}_y(1) - \Sigma_x(1) = O_P(n^{-1/4}).$$

We apply the realized co-volatility to the price observations on the ℓ-th day and obtain the realized co-volatility estimator $\hat{\Sigma}_y(\ell)$ of integrated volatility $\Sigma_x(\ell)$ on the ℓ-th day.

11.3 Parallelism Considerations

While **R** has been adopted as our major data analysis tool and tremendous amount of data and computations are required in the optimization procedures, we are motivated to investigate a variety of HPC techniques, ideally with little to no modification to existing solutions, to speed up **R** computations with the utilization of Parallel **R**, the Intel® Math Kernel Library (MKL) and automatic offloading to Intel® Xeon Phi SE10P Coprocessor.

11.3.1 Parallel R

R is the major analysis tool in our project. Although **R** is clearly a "high-productivity" language, high-performance has not been a development goal of **R**. Designed as a computing language with high-level expressiveness, **R** lacks much of the fine-grained control and basic constructs to support highly efficient code development. One approach to improve performance of **R** has been using dynamic libraries written in other programming language for expensive computations. While most features in **R** are implemented as single thread processes, efforts have been made in enabling parallelism with **R** over the past decade. Parallel package development coincides with the technology advances in parallel system development.

For computing clusters, Li and Rossini first introduced a package, *rpvm*, based on Private Virtual Machine (*PVM*) [23]. Yu et al. created a package *Rmpi* as an interface between **R** and Message Passing Interface in 2002 [41]. A popular parallel package, *Snow*, can utilize several low-level communication protocols including *MPI*, *PVM* and *socket* connection [30]. There are also a number of packages developed to utilize a multicore system including *fork*, *rparallel* and *multicore* [37]. A common approach in using **R** for large-scale computations is to break large data sets into chunks and runs each chuck in parallel sessions. Therefore, more parallel processes can improve the throughput of processing big data problems with **R**.

11.3.2   Intel® MKL

R enables linking to other shared mathematics libraries to speed up many basic computation tasks. One option for linear algebra computation is to use Intel® Math Kernel Library (MKL) [17]. MKL includes a wealth of routines (e.g., the use of *BLAS* and *LAPACK* libraries) to accelerate application performance and reduce development time such as highly vectorized and threaded linear algebra, fast fourier transforms (FFT), vector math and statistics functions. Furthermore, the MKL has been optimized to utilize multiple processing cores, wider vector units and more varied architectures available in a high-end system. Different from using parallel packages, MKL can provide parallelism transparently and speed up programs with supported math routines without changing the codes. It has been reported that compiling **R** with MKL can provide three times improvements out-of-box [40].

11.3.3   Offloading to Phi Coprocessor

The basis of the Xeon Phi is a light-weight ×86 core with in-order instruction processing, coupled with heavy-weight 512bit SIMD registers and instructions. With these two features the Xeon Phi die can support 60+ cores, and can execute 8 double precision (DP) vector instructions. The core count and vector lengths are basic extensions of an ×86 processor, and allow the same programming paradigms (serial, threaded and vector) used on other Xeon (E5) processors. Unlike the GPGPU accelerator model, the same program code can be used efficiently on the host and the coprocessor. Also, the same Intel® compilers, tools, libraries, etc. that you use on Intel® and AMD systems are available for the Xeon Phi. **R** with MKL can utilize both CPU and Xeon Phi coprocessor. In this model, **R** is compiled and built with MKL. Offloaded to Xeon Phi can be enabled by setting environment variables as opposed to making modifications to existing **R** programs (see e.g., Fig. 11.1 for a sample script to enable 70 % offloaded to Phi.)

Fig. 11.1 Configuring environment variables to enable automatic offloading to Intel® Xeon Phi Coprocessor. In this sample script, 70 % of computation is offloading to Phi, while only 30 % is done on host

```
# enable mkl mic offloading
export MKL_MIC_ENABLE=0

# from 0.0 to 1.0 the work division
export MKL_HOST_WORKDIVISION=0.3
export MKL_MIC_WORKDIVISION=0.7

# Make the offload report big to be visible:
export OFFLOAD_REPORT=2

# now set the number of threads on host
export OMP_NUM_THREADS=16
export MKL_NUM_THREADS=16

# now set the number of threads on the MIC
export MIC_OMP_NUM_THREADS=240
export MIC_MKL_NUM_THREADS=240
```

11.3.4 Our Computing Environment

We use the Stampede supercomputer [19] at the Texas Advanced Computing Center. Stampede provides several different hardware elements for achieving high performance computations which include using its Xeon Phi Coprocessors and/or NVIDIA Kepler 20 GPUs for intensive matrix calculations. In this project, each involved compute node has two Intel® Xeon E5-2680 processors each of which has eight computing cores running @2.7 GHz. There is 32 GB DDR3 memory in each node for the host CPUs. The Xeon Phi SE10P Coprocessor installed on each compute node has 61 cores with 8 GB GDDR5 dedicated memory connected by an ×16 PCIe bus. The NVIDIA K20 GPUs on each node have 5 GB of on-board GDDR5. All compute nodes are running CentOS 6.3. For this study we used the stock R 3.01 package compiled with the Intel® compilers (v.13) and built with Math Kernel Library (MKL v.11). In addition to speed-up by parallel **R** and MKL, our hybrid parallelism strategy also exploits the automatic offloading to Intel® Xeon Phi. A configurable portion of the computational workload can be specified to use Xeon Phi, ranging from 0 % to 100 % (our default configuration enables 30 % offloading to Phi.)

To compare the parallelism supported by MKL and Intel® Xeon Phi processor with other parallel packages, we conducted batch runs with the R-25 benchmark [1] in parallel using *snowfall* and *multicore* package. The first five bars in Fig. 11.2 shows the total running time using *snowfall* package (*sfLapply*) with different number of processing cores which scales near linearly to the number of computing cores used. The bottom four bars compare using *multicore* package (*mclapply*) with the

---

[1]Source code at http://r.research.att.com/benchmarks/R-benchmark-25.R.

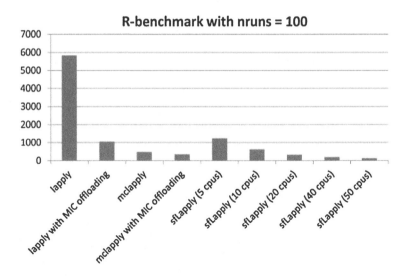

R-benchmark with nruns = 100

Fig. 11.2 Comparison of computational time over 100 runs on R-benchmark using different parallel packages including *snowfall*, *multicore*, and MKL with 30 % offloading to Phi

serial run (*lapply*) with and without offloading to Intel® Xeon Phi Coprocessors. The comparison indicate that explicit parallelism is most effective while automatic parallelization provided through MKL and the benefit of using Xeon Phi processor can potentially provide nearly 30 % performance improvement in addition.

11.4 Numerical Studies

In this section, we focus on the portfolio allocation problem using high-frequency financial data. High-frequency financial data usually refer to intra-day observations. The economic value of analyzing high-frequency financial data is now obvious, both in the academic and financial world. It is the basis of intra-day and daily risk monitoring and forecasting, an input to the portfolio allocation process, and also for the increasingly popular high-frequency trading among investment banks and hedge funds.

11.4.1 Portfolio Optimization with High-Frequency Data

Our first motivating use case concerns the transaction-by-transaction stock prices from the 30 DJIA composite constituents traded in New York Stock Exchange(NYSE). The data set is huge with ultra high-frequency observations since these stocks are highly liquid with vast trading volume. These high-frequency financial data also possess unique features such as price discreteness, unequally spaced time intervals, and non-synchronized trading (see e.g., [38] for some illustrations of these issues).[2] The high-frequency trading data for this study are downloaded from the Wharton Research Data Service (WRDS) Database, which contains transaction-by-transaction stock prices from the 30 DJIA composite constituents traded in New York Stock Exchange(NYSE) in 2011. We found that the high-frequency data possess some unique features such as price discreteness, unequally spaced time intervals, non-synchronized trading, and leverage effect. To demonstrate the features of the realized volatility, we select the most traded stock, Bank of America (BAC), as an example.

The synchronous order of the price is dealt in the following way: for every 5 min start 9:30 to 16:00, the last price at each 5-min interval is recorded as the price for the 5-min interval. Let y_t to represent the 5-min interval prices and the return is expressed as $log(y_t) - log(y_{t-1})$. Then the daily integrated volatility is defined as

$$IV_i = \int_{T_{i-1}}^{T_i} \sigma_t^2 dt, \ where \ T_i - T_{i-1} = 1 \ day$$

and the realized volatility estimate for univariate case is

$$RV_i = \sum_{j=1}^{N} r_{t-j,\Delta}^2 \ , \ where \ \Delta = 1day/N$$

where $N = 78$ for 5-min return interval.

Then we performed portfolio selection procedure based on the methodology in Sect. 11.2. The relationship between the maximum sharpe ratio (risk-to-reward measure, see e.g., [31]) and the number of stocks is shown in Fig. 11.3a, though on someday the maximum sharpe ratio keep increasing or decreasing or stable when changing the number of stocks in the portfolio.

The maximum sharpe ratio across trading days (Fig. 11.3b) also varies a lot since the co-volatilities between stocks are more dynamic. Figure 11.3b also shows volatility clustering, leverage effects and the non-stationary process of the stock price movement. The portfolio based on high-frequency data can achieve high sharpe ratio during the high volatility range of the whole market. This relatively strong performance is universal for the global minimum variance portfolio consisting of 2 stocks to 30 stocks (Fig. 11.3a).

We also checked the composite of the maximum sharpe ratio portfolio. Figure 11.4 shows an example of the maximum sharpe ratio portfolio of five stocks. The composite changes across trading days, indicating rebalance is needed to keep

---

[2]The normal trading hours of the NYSE are from 09:30 until 16:00. Thus, for simplicity, we discarded any transactions beyond these hours from our analysis.

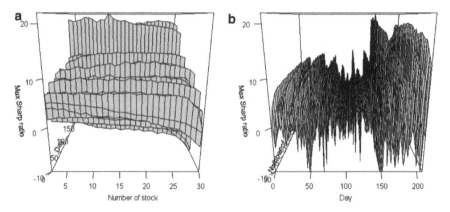

Fig. 11.3 (**a**) Relationship between maximum sharpe ratio and number of stocks. (**b**) Dynamics of maximum sharpe ratio across the whole year

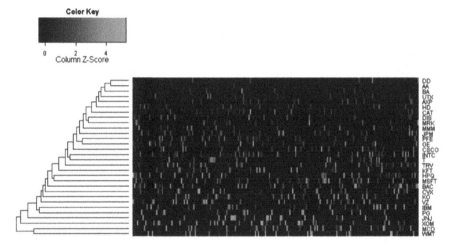

Fig. 11.4 The composite of the maximum sharpe ratio portfolio of five stocks: from *left* to *right* is the trading day at 2011 and from *top* to *bottom* lists the Dow30 stocks. The value of the heat map is scaled value based on the weight of each stock in the portfolio

maximum sharpe ratio. Nevertheless, some interesting patterns conform to our existing knowledge. For example for the technology stocks, GE, CSCO, INTC, and T closely clustered together. Also PG and JNJ, BA and UTX form a cluster implying their similarity in the underlying sector.

11.4.1.1   LASSO Approximation for Risk Minimization Problem

Pertinent to the high dimensionality issues, penalized likelihood methods such as LASSO have been extensively studied for high-dimensional variable selection and considerable amount of research was dedicated recently to development of methods of risk management based on regularization (see e.g., [10, 36]). Although the LASSO estimator can discover the correct sparse representation of the model [7], it is in general a biased estimator especially when the true coefficients are relatively large. Several remedies, including the smoothly clipped absolute deviation (SCAD) [9] and the adaptive LASSO (ALASSO) [45] have been proposed to discover the sparsity of the true models, while producing consistent estimates for non-zero regression coefficients. Other related work include [22, 42], and [16]. In this chapter, we adopt the idea of LASSO/LARS to come up with a regularized version of the estimated ARVM estimator [38] for the daily volatility matrix. Zou and Wu [47] developed a similar approach using a different regularization method.

As we pointed out before, when the number of assets are large, the permutation approach applied in the previous section is not feasible as the complexity of the optimization problem grows exponentially. Recently, [13] proposed that the risk minimization problem (11.2) for portfolio selection can be approximately transformed into a regression model with certain constraints.

$$\text{var}(w^T R) = \min_b \text{E}(w^T R - b)^2 \tag{11.4}$$

$$= \min_b \text{E}(Y - w_1 X_1 - \cdots - w_{p-1} X_{p-1} - b)^2 \tag{11.5}$$

$$\approx \min_{b, \|w\|_1 \leq d} \text{E}(Y - w^T X - b)^2 \tag{11.6}$$

where R is the $n \times p$ return matrix, $Y = R_p$, $X_j = R_p - R_j$, $j = 1, \cdots, p - 1$, and w is the weight vector.

We adopt the methodology to the Dow 30 portfolio allocation problem. The solution is given in Fig. 11.5 with l_1 norm constraint d increasing from 1.5 to 4.0. As the constraint becomes larger, more stocks are selected into the model and when it comes to 2.2, almost all stocks are covered. As the constraint increase and more stocks are allowed to enter the portfolio, the risk decreases and eventually falls close to 0. Note that the LASSO optimized portfolio covariance matrix can be calculated with the following product:

$$cov(w^T R) = \text{diag}(w)^T \Sigma \, \text{diag}(w)$$

where R is the n*p return matrix and w is the weight vector.

The LASSO solution path plot in Fig. 11.6 gives information about the order of the variable which enters the solution and its values. The vertical lines tells about the order of entering, and the right panel marks the index of the variables. The x-axis marks the fraction of sum of the entered weights to the total weight. The left y-axis is the value of the coefficients. Here we applied LASSO risk minimization method to the Dow 30 data with BAC returns as the response. For example, the pink curve at the vertical line marked as 1 represents the index 23, which is PFE, enters the

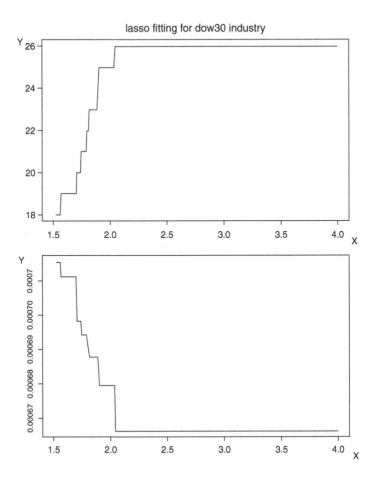

Fig. 11.5 Lasso fitting results for dow30 industry stocks

solution at the first place. Then following stock with index 16, which is JPM, enters
the solution path at the second place.

11.4.1.2 Parallelization

Using our framework of portfolio allocation in high-frequency setting, the most
challenging part is the tremendous amount of data and the optimization procedures
such as LASSO and SCAD involve large-scale computations. Usually the data issue
can be remedied by using some cloud storage and special data management and
processing in SAS (Statistical Analysis System). The computation part is extremely
time consuming if it's done on a personal PC. However, we note that the Monte
Carlo simulation and optimization proceed by generating grids over a certain range

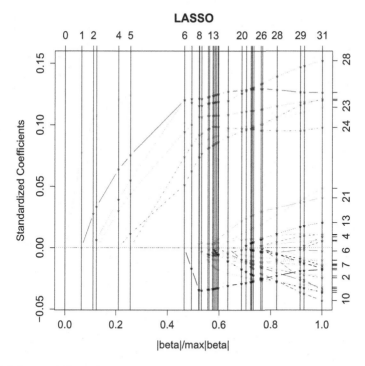

Fig. 11.6 Lasso solution path

of the tuning parameter c and λ over each individual trading day, and then repeat this optimization for K times. Assuming the return level are uncorrelated over time, we can distribute the optimization for each day to different CPUs on different compute-nodes using embarrassingly parallel technique.

Figure 11.7 illustrates the performance rate for our principle test case of repeating optimization for 500 times stepping through 209 trading days. The existing methods are coded in **R** and one run roughly takes about 0.5 h on our desktop. From a computing perspective, we need to run these problems 104,500 (i.e., 209 × 500) combinations of input parameters, hence it will take 50,000 h. Distributing the computations over 209 16-core compute nodes (using *snow*) dramatically reduced the time of the statistical analysis, when each compute node only undertakes the optimization of 500 times over one single trading day. By leveraging Intel® MKL and enabling automatic offloading 30 % computation to Phi coprocessor, we were able to further reduce the processing time by 15 % approximately.

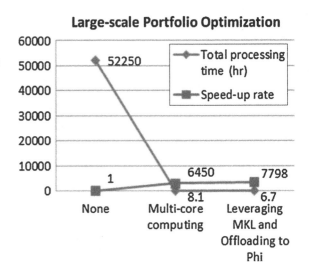

Fig. 11.7 Performance improvement of repeating optimization for 500 times stepping through 209 trading days

11.4.2   Bayesian Large-Scale Multiple Testing for Time Series Data

The issue of multiple testing for different return series is an interesting application in high-frequency finance. For example, an investor may be interested in the question of whether investing the S&P 500 index [25] will generate the same level of return performance over a certain time horizon than to invest on several risky portfolios. Since the risk (volatility) is changing over time, traditional methods such as the t-test will not be accurate as one has to account for potential serial correlation of returns in computing the standard error that appears in the denominator of the test statistic. In this chapter, we follow the framework in [39] and consider the problem of multiple testing under temporal dependence. The observed data is assumed to be generated from an underlying two-state hidden Markov model (to be detailed in Sect. 11.4.2.1). Bayesian methods are applied to develop the testing algorithm by optimizing the false negative rate while controlling the false discovery rate which is comparable to [35]. Simulation studies show the similarity and the difference between the EM approach and the Bayesian approach when the alternative has a simple or a mixture distribution.

There are two main statistical issues involved here: (1) whether the data structure has single or mixture distribution. (2) Whether multiple testing are applied to independent or dependent data. If the data structure only contains a single distribution, then conventional time series analysis such as the ARIMA models are usually sufficient. However, if the data structure is a mixture distribution such as in [34], we can apply the two-state Hidden Markov Model (HMM) to distinguish the 'aberration' or 'usual' state (e.g., in the outbreak detection setting, aberration state represents a disease outbreak). Thus, it can be transformed into a classification or a multiple hypotheses testing problem. In the multiple testing literature, there are a wide range of model-based approaches using independent test statistics. Leek and Storey [21] use dependence kernel to produce conditional independent multiple testing. Morris et al. [28] proposed the Bayesian FDR. In the modeling of mass spectrometry proteomics data observed over time, [32] reduce the number of hypotheses tested by wavelets. When the test statistics are correlated, one cannot ignore the dependence and proceed to p-values and the threshold calculation. Therefore, [5, 29] proposed to control FDR on well-defined clusters or with pre-specified weights.

11.4.2.1 Hidden Markov Model and Multiple Hypothesis Testing

The idea of Hidden Markov Model (HMM) can be best described by the following illustration:

$$
\begin{array}{ccccccc}
\theta_1 & \xrightarrow{A} & \theta_2 & \xrightarrow{A} & \theta_3 & \xrightarrow{A} & \cdots & \xrightarrow{A} & \theta_m \\
\downarrow{\scriptstyle F} & & \downarrow{\scriptstyle F} & & \downarrow{\scriptstyle F} & & & & \downarrow{\scriptstyle F} \\
X_1 & & X_2 & & X_3 & & \cdots & & X_m
\end{array}
$$

Here $x = (x_1, \ldots, x_m)$ are observed values, $\theta = (\theta_1, \ldots, \theta_m)$ are unobservable states. Inference on the unknown and unobservable θ_i's is based on the known and observed X_i's. We also assume the unknown and unobservable θ_i's are stationary, irreducible and aperiodic, and are identically distributed as Bernoulli(π_0). Then we have $X_i | \theta_i \sim (1 - \theta_i)F_0 + \theta_i F_1$. So, the HMM parameters are $\vartheta = (\mathcal{A}, \pi, \mathcal{F})$, where $\mathcal{A} = \{a_{jk}\}$ is the transition matrix, $\pi = (\pi_0, \pi_1)$ is the stationary distribution for the Markov chain, and $\mathcal{F} = \{F_0, F_1\}$ is observation distribution.

Thus, the objective for HMM Hypothesis Testing is to find an optimal false discovery rate (FDR) procedure to minimize the false non-discovery rate (FNR) subject to a constraint on FDR, and also obtain high statistical efficiency. The gains to introduce this method lie in performance improved by adaptively exploiting the dependence structure among hypotheses, and it is especially powerful in identifying clustered non-null cases. Classification of tested hypotheses can be expressed in the following Table.

Hypothesis	Claimed non-significant	Claimed significant	Total
Null	N_{00}	N_{10}	m_0
Non-null	N_{01}	N_{11}	m_1
Total	S	R	m

We are interested in two quantities: FDR

$$E(N_{10}/R|R > 0)Pr(R > 0)$$

and FNR

$$E(N_{01}/S|S > 0)Pr(S > 0)$$

An FDR procedure is *valid* if it controls FDR at a pre-specified level α, and is *optimal* if it has the smallest FNR among all FDR at level α. In our Bayesian Hidden Markov model, the HMM parameters are all estimated using Bayesian approach. We apply Bayesian hierarchical mixture estimation for $x_i|\{\theta_i\}_{i=1}^m = \pi_0 f_0 + \pi_1 f_1$ and $x_i|(\theta_i = 1) = p_{11}f_{11} + p_{12}f_{12} + \cdots + p_{1L}f_{1L}$. Our numerical results show significant improvement in terms controlling both FDR and FNR for the multiple testing problem compared to other existing methods in the literature.

11.4.2.2 Parallelization

For the Bayesian large-scale multiple testing problem mentioned above, the computation is even more demanding since it not only needs to run a large number of Monte Carlo simulations, but also involves calculating the posterior estimates using Markov Chain Monte Carlo (MCMC). This could be a daunting task as the number of simulations N and number of MCMC samples K go to even moderate values, as the multiplicity is at the order of $O(NK)$. This means that for a single PC, if $N = 500$ and $K = 5000$, the program has to generate 2.5 million operations and it costs over 20 days of computing time for each simulation study. Due to the Bayesian structure of the model, within each Markov chain the MCMC samples are not independent. However, the samples across chains are in fact independent. Therefore, we can proceed to carry out parallel computing by separating each Markov chain on different compute-nodes and repeat the sampling process N times. As illustrated in Fig. 11.8, the initial multi-core based Markov chain computation and the further improvement using MKL with offloading to Phi Coprocessor can significantly reduce the computation time on top of each other.

11.5   Discussion and Conclusions

The portfolio optimization under the Markowitz's framework has been applied widely over the years among practitioners. While appealing in its simplicity, the Markowitz's portfolio fails to capture some important characteristics of the capital markets, especially with wide availability of high-frequency financial data nowadays. This work proposed an innovative methodology to perform asset allocation using high-frequency data. The empirical analysis of portfolios allocation using

Fig. 11.8 Performance improvement of Bayesian large-scale multiple testing problem

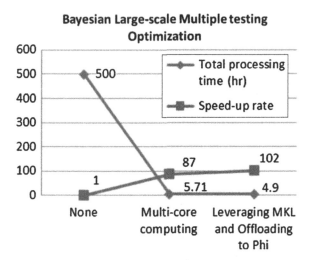

high-frequency data illustrated the efficiency of this method. The penalization based portfolio selection strategy that we proposed offers several advantages. It can significantly reduce the accumulation of small component-wise estimation errors which in turn leads to larger overall portfolio risk. This helps answer questions about performance and risk as part of a broader investment decision-making process. Moreover, our framework can easily accommodate different positions such as short sale constraints. We illustrate the methodology with the high-frequency price data on stocks traded in New York Stock Exchanges in 2011. The numerical results show that our approach performs well in portfolio allocation while pooling together the strengths of regularization and estimation from a high-frequency finance perspective. The benefits of applying the regularization approach is that we avoided looking at all possible combinations as in the permutation approach, which is computationally more attractive in practice. Furthermore, the whole solution path of the optimal portfolio gives insights on the order of dependence of different assets on the whole portfolio with respect to return and risk. This information may be valuable to practitioners when evaluating different hedging strategies.

In this work we also demonstrate two representative financial analysis workload for allocating assets in a large portfolio, an important area of computational finance. We compare and improve our workload's performance on three parallel solutions: Parallel **R**, Intel® MKL, and automatic offloading to Intel® Phi Coprocessor. As the statistical methods in our domain problems significant matrix calculations and function calls, we observed significant speed-up on Parallel **R** with the Intel® Math Kernel library to coordinate usage of Xeon Phi Coprocessor. The workload can be executed in parallel with minimal modification. Enjoying extra performance improvement through MKL and offloading to Phi is done automatically and transparent to end users; there is no need to modify the existing R script.

Further directions include out-of-sample comparisons of the performances of the different allocations derived from different statistical methods of asset allocation strategies.

Acknowledgements We thank XSEDE for awarded SU allocation on Stampede (project number: DMS-130018).

References

1. T.G. Andersen, T. Bollerslev, F.X. Diebold, P. Labys, The distribution of realized exchange rate volatility. J. Am. Stat. Assoc. **96**(453), 42–55 (2001)
2. A. Bahl, O. Baltzer, A. Rau-Chaplin, B. Varghese, Parallel simulations for analysing portfolios of catastrophic event risk, in *2012 SC Companion: High Performance Computing, Networking, Storage and Analysis (SCC)* (2012), pp. 1176–1184
3. O.E. Barndorff-Nielsen, N. Shephard, Econometric analysis of realized volatility and its use in estimating stochastic volatility models. J. R. Stat. Soc. Ser. B Stat. Methodol. **64**(2), 253–280 (2002)
4. O.E. Barndorff-Nielsen, P.R. Hansen, A. Lunde, N. Shephard, Designing realized kernels to measure the ex post variation of equity prices in the presence of noise. Econometrica **76**(6), 1481–1536 (2008)
5. Y. Benjamini, R. Heller, False discovery rates for spatial signals. J. Am. Stat. Assoc. **102**(480), 1272–1281 (2007)
6. M. Creel, M. Zubair, High performance implementation of an econometrics and financial application on GPUs, in *2012 SC Companion: High Performance Computing, Networking, Storage and Analysis (SCC)* (2012), pp. 1147–1153
7. D.L. Donoho, X. Huo, Beamlets and multiscale image analysis, in *Multiscale and Multiresolution Methods*. Lecture Notes in Computational Science and Engineering , vol. 20 (Springer, Berlin, 2002), pp. 149–196
8. R.F. Engle, K.F. Kroner, Multivariate simultaneous generalized ARCH. Econ. Theory **11**(1), 122–150 (1995)
9. J. Fan, R. Li, Variable selection via nonconcave penalized likelihood and its oracle properties. J. Am. Stat. Assoc. **96**(456), 1348–1360 (2001)
10. J. Fan, J. Lv, A selective overview of variable selection in high dimensional feature space. Stat. Sin. **20**(1), 101–148 (2010)
11. J. Fan, Y. Wang, Multi-scale jump and volatility analysis for high-frequency financial data. J. Am. Stat. Assoc. **102**(480), 1349–1362 (2007)
12. J. Fan, Y. Li, K. Yu, Vast volatility matrix estimation using high frequency data for portfolio selection. J. Am. Stat. Assoc. **107**(497), 412–428 (2012)
13. J. Fan, J. Zhang, K. Yu, Asset allocation and risk assessment with gross exposure constraints for vast portfolios. J. Am. Stat. Assoc. **107**(498), 592–606 (2012)
14. J. Fleming, C. Kirby, B. Ostdiek, The economic value of volatility timing using "realized" volatility. J. Financ. Econ. **67**(3), 473–509 (2003)
15. W.R. Gilks, S. Richardson, D. Spiegelhalter, *Markov Chain Monte Carlo in Practice* (Chapman and Hall, London, 1996)
16. J. Guo, E. Levina, G. Michailidis, J. Zhu, Joint estimation of multiple graphical models. Biometrika **98**(1), 1–15 (2011)
17. J.L. Gustafson, B.S. Greer, Clearspeed whitepaper: accelerating the Intel math kernel library (2007)
18. T. Hayashi, N. Yoshida, On covariance estimation of non-synchronously observed diffusion processes. Bernoulli **11**(2), 359–379 (2005)

19. A. Heinecke, A. Breuer, S. Rettenberger, M. Bader, A.-A. Gabriel, C. Pelties, A. Bode, W. Barth, X.-K. Liao, K. Vaidyanathan et al., Petascale high order dynamic rupture earthquake simulations on heterogeneous supercomputers, in *Proceedings of the International Conference for High Performance Computing, Networking, Storage and Analysis* (IEEE, 2014) pp. 3–14
20. R. Jagannathan, T. Ma, Risk reduction in large portfolios: Why imposing the wrong constraints helps. J. Financ. **58**, 1651–1684 (2003)
21. J.T. Leek, J.D. Storey, A general framework for multiple testing dependence. Proc. Natl. Acad. Sci. **48**, 18718–18723 (2008)
22. E. Levina, A. Rothman, J. Zhu, Sparse estimation of large covariance matrices via a nested Lasso penalty. Ann. Appl. Stat. **2**(1), 245–263 (2008)
23. M.N. Li, A. Rossini, Rpvm: cluster statistical computing in R. R News **1**(3), 4–7 (2001)
24. Q. Liu, On portfolio optimization: How and when do we benefit from high-frequency data? J. Appl. Econ. **24**(4), 560–582 (2009)
25. A.W. Lynch, R.R. Mendenhall, New evidence on stock price effects associated with changes in the S&P 500 Index. J. Bus. **70**(3), 351–383 (1997)
26. M.E. Mancino, S. Sanfelici, Robustness of Fourier estimator of integrated volatility in the presence of microstructure noise. Comput. Stat. Data Anal. **52**(6), 2966–2989 (2008)
27. H.M. Markowitz, Portfolio selection. J. Financ. **7**, 77–91 (1952)
28. J. Morris, P.J. Brown, R.C. Herrick, K.A. Baggerly, K. Coombes, Bayesian analysis of mass spectrometry proteomic data using wavelet-based functional mixed models. Biometrics **64**(2), 479–489 (2008)
29. M.P. Pacifico, C. Genovese, I. Verdinelli, L. Wasserman, False discovery control for random fields. J. Am. Stat. Assoc. **99**(468), 1002–1014 (2004)
30. A.J. Rossini, L. Tierney, N. Li, Simple parallel statistical computing in R. J. Comput. Graph. Stat. **16**(2), 399–420 (2007)
31. W.F. Sharpe, The sharpe ratio. J. Portf. Manag. **21**(1), 49–58 (1994)
32. X. Shen, H.-C. Huang, N. Cressie, Nonparametric hypothesis testing for a spatial signal. J. Am. Stat. Assoc. **97**(460), 1122–1140 (2002)
33. M. Smelyanskiy, J. Sewall, D. Kalamkar, N. Satish, P. Dubey, N. Astafiev, I. Burylov, M. Nikolaev, S. Maidanov, S. Li, S. Kulkarni, C. Finan, Analysis and optimization of financial analytics benchmark on modern multi- and many-core ia-based architectures, in *2012 SC Companion: High Performance Computing, Networking, Storage and Analysis (SCC)* (2012), pp. 1154–1162
34. Y. Strat, F. Carrat, Monitoring epidemiologic surveillance data using hidden Markov models. Stat. Med. **1875**, 3463–3478 (1999)
35. W. Sun, T.T. Cai, Large-scale multiple testing under dependence. J. R. Stat. Soc. Ser. B **91**(2), 393–424 (2009)
36. R. Tibshirani, Regression shrinkage and selection via the lasso. J. R. Stat. Soc. Ser. B **58**(1), 267–288 (1996)
37. G. Vera, R.C. Jansen, R.L. Suppi, R/parallel–speeding up bioinformatics analysis with R. BMC bioinf. **9**(1), 390 (2008)
38. Y. Wang, J. Zou, Vast volatility matrix estimation for high-frequency financial data. Ann. Stat. **38**(2), 943–978 (2010)
39. X. Wang, J. Zou, A. Shojaie, Bayesian large-scale multiple testing for time series data (2016), Manuscript
40. A.M. Wilson, Speeding up R with Intel's math kernel library (MKL). Web blog post, R-Bloggers, May 2 (2012), https://www.r-bloggers.com/speeding-up-r-with-intels-math-kernel-library-mkl/
41. H. Yu, Rmpi: Parallel statistical computing in r. R News **2**(2), 10–14 (2002)
42. M. Yuan, Y. Lin, Model election and estimation in the gaussian graphical model. Biometrika **94**, 19–35 (2007)
43. L. Zhang, Efficient estimation of stochastic volatility using noisy observations: a multi-scale approach. Bernoulli **12**(6), 1019–1043 (2006)

44. L. Zhang, P.A. Mykland, Y. Aït-Sahalia, A tale of two time scales: determining integrated volatility with noisy high-frequency data. J. Am. Stat. Assoc. **100**(472), 1394–1411 (2005)
45. H. Zou, The adaptive lasso and its oracle properties. J. Am. Stat. Assoc. **101**(476), 1418–1429 (2006)
46. J. Zou, Y. Wang, Statistical methods for large portfolio risk management. Stat. Interface **6**, 477–485 (2013)
47. J. Zou, Y. Wu, Large portfolio allocation using high-frequency financial data (2016), Manuscript

Chapter 12
Large-Scale Multi-Modal Data Exploration with Human in the Loop

Guangchen Ruan and Hui Zhang

Abstract A new trend in many scientific fields is to conduct data-intensive research by collecting and analyzing a large amount of high-density, high-quality, multi-modal data streams. In this chapter we present a research framework for analyzing and mining such data streams at large-scale; we exploit parallel sequential pattern mining and iterative MapReduce in particular to enable human-in-the-loop large-scale data exploration powered by High Performance Computing (HPC). One basic problem is that, data scientists are now working with datasets so large and complex that it becomes difficult to process using traditional desktop statistics and visualization packages, requiring instead "massively parallel software running on tens, hundreds, or even thousands of servers" (Jacobs, Queue 7(6):10:10–10:19, 2009). Meanwhile, discovering new knowledge requires the means to exploratively analyze datasets of this scale—allowing us to freely "wander" around the data, and make discoveries by combining bottom-up pattern discovery and top-down human knowledge to leverage the power of the human perceptual system. In this work, we first exploit a novel interactive temporal data mining method that allows us to discover reliable sequential patterns and precise timing information of multivariate time series. For our principal test case of detecting and extracting human sequential behavioral patterns over multiple multi-modal data streams, this suggests a quantitative and interactive data-driven way to ground social interactions in a manner that has never been achieved before. After establishing the fundamental analytics algorithms, we proceed to a research framework that can fulfill the task of extracting reliable patterns from large-scale time series using iterative MapReduce tasks. Our work exploits visual-based information technologies to allow scientists to interactively explore, visualize and make sense of their data. For example, the parallel mining algorithm running on HPC is accessible to users through asynchronous web service. In this way, scientists can compare the intermediate data to extract and propose new rounds of analysis for more scientifically meaningful and statistically

G. Ruan (✉)
Indiana University, Bloomington, IN, USA
e-mail: gruan@indiana.edu

H. Zhang
University of Louisville, Louisville, KY, USA
e-mail: hui.zhang@louisville.edu

© Springer International Publishing Switzerland 2016
R. Arora (ed.), *Conquering Big Data with High Performance Computing*,
DOI 10.1007/978-3-319-33742-5_12

G. Ruan and H. Zhang

reliable patterns, and therefore statistical computing and visualization can bootstrap each another. Finally, we show the results from our principal user application that can demonstrate our system's capability of handling massive temporal event sets within just a few minutes. All these combine to reveal an effective and efficient way to support large-scale data exploration with human in the loop.

12.1 Background

A recent trend in many scientific fields is to conduct data-intensive research by collecting a large amount of high-density high-quality multi-modal data [7, 11, 31, 32, 36]. These data, such as video, audio, images, RFID, and motion tracking, are usually multi-faceted, dynamic, and extremely large in size. Yu and Zhang pioneer the use of multi-modal sensing systems to collect, visualize and analyze fine-grained behavioral data in real-time multi-modal communication between autonomous agents (human or robots) [32, 33, 35–37]. Guerri et al. suggest acquiring multimedia data from human bodies by attaching multiple devices and identifying temporal relationships between the data sources to assess the subjects' physical conditions [11]. Other representative efforts include a variety of ways to discover temporal association and their sequential orders from multi-streaming time series (see, e.g., Agrawal [1, 2], Ayres [4], Garofalakis [10], Pinto [25], and Pei [24]), and to extend point-based pattern mining to real valued and interval-based knowledge discovery (see, e.g., [3, 12, 17, 19, 28, 34]).

Due to the complexity of multi-modal streaming data, it has been very challenging to design a useful visual-analytics system. In practice, study of raw multi-modal data streams is often transformed into the statistical investigation of continuous categorical streams using derived measures such as user-defined Areas Of Interest (AOIs), whose complexity may initially suggest that one shall refer to an equally complicated approach for statistical and mathematical analyses. Most often, however, to better accomplish such exploration and analytics tasks researchers should play a critical role in the knowledge discovery by exploring the information visualization, suggesting initial analysis, examining the intermediate analytics result, and directing the research focus for the new round of scientific findings. In this paper we are motivated to develop a hybrid solution—a novel approach to integrate top-down domain knowledge with bottom-up information visualization and temporal pattern discovery. A few key design rules behind our implementation are as follows:

- **Enabling human-in-the-loop knowledge discovery**—we argue that sensible decisions about streams of data analysis cannot be completely pre-determined. Since we cannot specify all of the data analysis details a priori, we need insights from both top-down knowledge and raw data themselves to conduct *interactive data analysis* and *visual data mining* iteratively. In these tasks, researchers play a critical role in this *human-in-the-loop* knowledge discovery by applying statistical techniques to the data, examining visualization results, determining how to chunk the streams of data, and deciding/directing the research focus based on their theoretical knowledge. Redirected bottom-up analytics plays a complementary role in assisting scientists to not only validate their hypothesis but also quantify their scientific findings.

- **Generating bottom-up analysis using machine computation and information visualization**—discovering new knowledge requires the ability to detect unknown, surprising, novel, and unexpected patterns. With fine-grained massive data sets, algorithms and tools are desired to extract temporal properties from multi-modal data streams. Examples include *statistics*, such as the typical duration of a sensory event, *temporal correlations* of derived variables, such as the triggering relationships among events (or sequential association of events), and *visual display* of derived variables or their logical conjunctions.
- **Scalable architecture for data intensive computing**—massive data sets collected from modern instruments impose high demands on both storage and computing powers [14]. Knowledge discovery at terabyte scale is nontrivial as the time cost of simply applying traditional algorithms in a sequential manner can be prohibitive. Thus, distributed parallel processing/visualization at scale becomes a requirement rather than an option.

12.2 Details of Implementation Models

In this section, we introduce an "interactive event-based temporal pattern discovery" paradigm to investigate "moments-of-interest" from multi-modal data streams. To be effective, such a paradigm must meet two goals: on one hand, it must follow the general spirits of information visualization to allow users to interactively explore the visually displayed data streams; on the other hand, machine computation should be applied in a way that can facilitate the identification of statistically reliable patterns, whose visual pictures can then be examined for closer investigation and can trigger a new round of knowledge discovery. Before we detail the logical series of steps, several definitions are in order:

Definition 12.2.1 (Event). An *event* is a tuple $e = (t, s, d)$, where t is the event type (or label), s is the starting time of the event and d indicates its duration. The ending time of the event can be derived from $s + d$.

Definition 12.2.2 (Example). An *example* of length k is a tuple $ex = (id, du, \{e_1, e_2, \cdots, e_k\})$, where id uniquely identifies the *example*, du is the total duration of the *example* and $\{e_1, e_2, \cdots, e_k\}$ is the sequence of events that forms the *example*. We note that events can overlap with each other, namely $overlap(e_i, e_j) = true \iff min(e_i.e, e_j.e) > max(e_i.s, e_j.s)$; where $overlap(e_i, e_j)$ is the predicate to check whether two events e_i, e_j overlaps.

Definition 12.2.3 (Example Set). An *example set* of size n is a set $S = \{ex_1, ex_2, \cdots, ex_n\}$ where ex_i is an example and $1 \leq i \leq n$. Examples in the set should have the same total duration, namely $ex_1.du = ex_2.du =, \cdots, = ex_n.du$.

Definition 12.2.4 (Pattern). A *pattern* of length k is a tuple $p = (du, \{e_1, e_2, \cdots, e_k\})$, definitions of du and e_i, $1 \leq i \leq n$ are the same as those in Definition 12.2.2. Events in a pattern are ordered by beginning times and then by ending times and then by lexicographic order of event types.

12.2.1 Developing Top-Down Knowledge Hypotheses From Visual Analysis of Multi-Modal Data Streams

Information visualization can be effectively exploited to explore *moments-of-interest* in multi-modal data streams (see e.g., [33]). Computational algorithms such as data mining and sequential pattern mining (see e.g., [9, 13, 17, 18, 21, 23, 34] are other variants that have requirement similar to ours. While we of course exploit many techniques of information visualization and interactive data mining that have been widely used in other interfaces, we found that many of the problems we encounter have been fairly unique, and thus requiring customized hybrid approaches.

12.2.1.1 Color-Based Representation of Temporal Events

Multi-modal data streams are first converted to multi-streaming temporal events with categorical type values. We represent an event e as a rectangular bar by assigning the distinct color key to the event type (i.e., *e.t*), with the length corresponding to the event's duration (i.e., *e.d*). The visual display of temporal events themselves in a sequence allows us to examine how frequently each temporal event happens over time, how long each instance of an event takes, how one event relates to other events, and whether an event appears more or less periodically or whether there are other trends over time.

The colored bar representation in principle is sufficient to allow the viewer to examine global temporal patterns by scanning through the event data stream. However, in practice, many interesting temporal pattern discoveries are based on user-defined AOIs, thus oftentimes distinct event types correspond to one AOI in the analytics. We illustrate this point by using an example in which multi-stream behavioral data in real-time multi-modal communication between autonomous agents (human or robots) are recorded and analyzed. Shown in Fig. 12.1a, a human teacher demonstrated how to name a set of shapes to a robot learner who can demonstrate different kinds of social skills and perform actions in the study. Multi-modal interactions between the two agents (speaking, eye contact, pointing, gazing, and hand movement) are monitored and recorded in real time. Figure 12.1b visualizes the three processed streams derived from raw action data from both the human and the robot. The first one is the AOI stream from the robot agent's eye gaze, indicating which object the robot agent attends to (e.g., gazing at one of the three

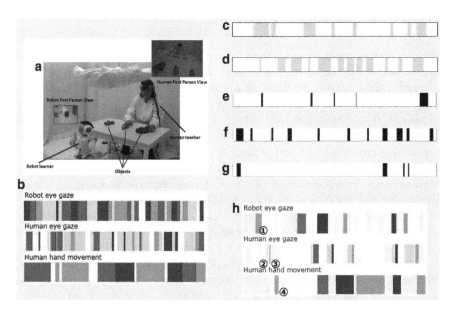

Fig. 12.1 (a)→(b): Using multi-modal sensing systems to collect and analyze fine-grained behavioral data including motion tracking data, eye tracking data, video and audio data. A family of studies using this research paradigm are conducted to collect multi-stream multi-modal data and convert them into multi-streaming time series for further data analysis and knowledge discovery. (c)–(g): Integrating over ROI event streams by overlaying pictures that record individual ROI streams. (c) Robot face-looking event. (d) Human face-looking event. (e) Face-to-face coordination: (Robot face-looking) *XOR* (Human face-looking). (f) Human eye-hand-coordination: (Human eye gaze) *XOR* (Human hand movement). (g) Human-Robot joint attention: (Human eye-hand-coordination) *XOR* (face-to-face coordination). (h) Six instances of momentary interactive behavior highlighted in the AOI streams. This sequential pattern starts with the situation that the robot agent and the human teacher attend to different objects (①), and then the human teacher checks the robot agent's gaze (②) and follows the robot agent attention to the same object (③) and finally reach to that object (④)

virtual objects or looking straight toward the human teacher). The second stream is the AOI stream (three objects and the robot agent's face) from the human teacher's gaze and the third one encodes which object the human teacher is manipulating and moving. Most often, visual attention from both agents was concentrated on either each other's face (represented as yellow bar, as shown in Fig. 12.1c, d or the three objects in the work space (represented in three colors (e.g. red, blue, and green), respectively). Color-based representation of AOIs in temporal events allows us to examine how visual attentions happen over time, how long each instance of an event takes, and how one relates to another.

12.2.1.2   Generating Logical Conjunctions

We can then connect these patterns back to top-down research questions and hypotheses. For example, our color-based representation also allows an end-user to overlay data streams by dragging a rendered data stream on top of another data stream. Our system performs a binary *XOR* operation when two streams are integrated. By *XOR*ing the pixel values of two Region of Interest (ROI) event streams, we can integrate two sensory events to find out the joint attention over these two sensory channels (*XOR* will produce *true* if the two pixels being integrated are of different colors, and *false* if they are of the same color.) For example, in Fig. 12.1e we can overlay the newly derived *robot face-looking* stream (see e.g., Fig. 12.1c) and *human face-looking* stream (see e.g., Fig. 12.1d) to identify the human-robot face-to-face coordination moments. Similarly, in Fig. 12.1f we can integrate *human eye gaze* ROI stream and *human hand movement* ROI stream to obtain a new *eye-hand coordination* stream, which represents two concurrent events: (1) human gazes at an object; and (2) human manipulates with hand the same object. Finally, in Fig. 12.1g we can integrate the *human-robot joint attention* event stream by overlaying *eye-hand coordination* stream (i.e., Fig. 12.1f) and *face-to-face coordination* stream (i.e., Fig. 12.1e). In this way, the color-based event visualization scheme is able to represent various logical conjunctions of those events.

12.2.1.3   Developing Hypotheses From Visual Analysis

Eye-balling the color-based representation of AOI streams helps the viewer to discover momentary interactive behaviors. For example, one such sequential behavioral pattern that seems to frequently happen in those data streams is labeled ①→④ in Fig. 12.1h: this sequential pattern starts with the situation that the robot agent and the human teacher attend to different objects (see e.g., ①, the robot attends to the object indicated by the green bar (i.e. bar marked by ①) while the human doesn't), and then the human teacher checks the robot agent's gaze (e.g., ②, human face-looking indicated by the yellow bar (i.e. bar marked by ②)) and follows the robot agent's attention to the same object (e.g., ③, the human object-looking indicated by the green bar (i.e. bar marked by ③)) and finally reaches to that object (e.g., ④, the human hand-movement indicated by the green bar (i.e. bar marked by ④)).

12.2.2   Complementing Hypotheses with Bottom-Up Quantitative Measures

We next discuss how to employ machine computation to detect and quantify reliable moment-by-moment multi-modal behaviors one could discover by scanning the color-based representation illustrated in Fig. 12.1h. The visual-based knowledge discovery can be complemented and validated by quantitative temporal measures powered by analytics algorithms—e.g., the detection of statistical reliable temporal patterns, the quantification of typical durations and frequencies of repeating temporal phenomena, and the measure of precise timing between associated events.

Our task in this section is to develop bottom-up machine computation methods, to extract two major complementary measures—one focusing on the detection of sequential relationships between events and the other focusing on the precise timing such as duration for a reliable temporal event and the time between events in a sequential pattern. We assume continuous data streams are first pre-processed and chunked into a large sequence of event examples that all have same total duration. These examples are encapsulated into an example set as the input data structure of our machine computation (see Fig. 12.2a). Our basic implementation exploits an Apriori-like "event-based temporal pattern mining algorithm" in 2D event space where each event in the example set is represented as a point. The algorithm is based on the Apriori algorithm [1] for searching frequent patterns, to be discussed shortly in Algorithm 12.1. The logical series of modeling steps, the problems they induce, and the ultimate resolution of the problems are as follows:

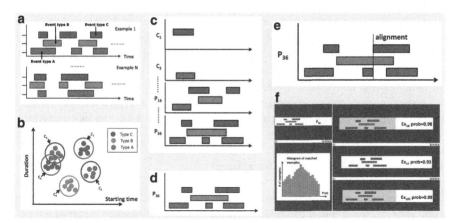

Fig. 12.2 Interactive event-based temporal pattern discovery. (**a**) A subset of example data set, displaying two examples, each with three event types. The example set is the input of the algorithm. (**b**) The algorithm projects each example comprised of events into points in 2D event space (event starting time × event duration) and clustering is performed based on event types. (**c**) Each cluster is used as an initial length-1 candidate pattern for an iterative Apriori-like procedure. (**d**) One potential pattern discovered by the Apriori-like procedure. (**e**) A final adjustment to refine and adjust the temporal relations by removing some potential noise from the data. Whether or not this is used is based on top-down knowledge of the data set, i.e., whether or not you would expect events to be completely synchronous/aligned. (**f**) Pattern query results that visualize the pattern and corresponding matching examples which are sorted in descending order of matching probability, as well as statistical information, e.g., histogram showing the distribution of matching probability of matching examples

- *Project events to 2D event space for clustering.* The algorithm projects examples into an event space and clustering is performed in the event space based on event types (see Fig. 12.2b).
- *Pattern discovery using an Apriori-like algorithm.* These clusters become the first set of candidate patterns for an Apriori-like procedure which then computes representative and frequent sequential pattern prototypes iteratively (see Fig. 12.2c).
- *Refine temporal relationships.* Those prototype patterns are refined by considering their temporal relationships through a pattern adjustment procedure (see Fig. 12.2d, e)
- *Interactive temporal pattern discovery by user query.* Discovered frequent patterns and corresponding matching examples, as well as some statistical information are visualized upon user query (see Fig. 12.2f). Users can trigger and refine new rounds of machine computation to complement their discovery based on the information representation.

12.2.2.1 Clustering in 2D Event Space

Given an example set as input, mining algorithm first projects examples into 2D event space (event starting time × event duration) where each point is an event (see Fig. 12.2a). An Expectation-Maximization (EM) clustering algorithm is then used to find clusters for *each* event type. Several clustering options (centroid-based, distribution-based, density-based and etc) are provided so users can choose based on their domain knowledge or insights obtained from experimental results. Upon convergence of iterative clustering, we take the centroids of the clusters as seed length-1 (single event) candidate patterns for the subsequent Apriori-like procedure.

12.2.2.2 Apriori-Like Pattern Searching

Our customized Apriori-like procedure as shown in Algorithm 12.1 uses centroids in event space as the length-1 candidates. In each iteration, frequent patterns of length-n discovered in previous iteration and frequent length-1 patterns (line 7) are used to generate 1-item longer length-$n + 1$ candidates. Then the algorithm checks the frequency and only sufficiently frequent ones are kept (line 8). Previously mentioned candidate generation and frequency check processes are performed iteratively until there are no new frequent patterns or no candidates can be generated. The final output is a set of frequent patterns.

Our approach to generating longer candidates (line 7 of Algorithm 12.1) is to append length-1 frequent pattern (denoted as p_1) to length-n frequent pattern (denoted as p_n) so long as p_1's starting time is no earlier than that of any events in p_n, i.e., $C_{n+1} = \{c_{n+1} = p_n \oplus p_1 \mid p_1 \in L_1, p_n \in L_n, \forall e \in p_n, p_1.s \geq e.s\}$ ($\oplus$ denotes the concatenation operation on patterns).

We note that Apriori procedure generates redundant patterns (denoted as R) that can actually be derived from longer patterns, i.e., $R = \{r \mid r \in P, \exists p \in P \land p \neq$

Algorithm 12.1: AprioriLikeProcedure

Input : S: example set, M: centroids in event space, f_{min}: frequency threshold, ϵ: pattern
similarity threshold
Output: P: set of frequent candidates

1 $P = \{\}$;
2 $C_1 = M$;
3 $L_1 = $ FindFrequentCandidates $(S, C_1, f_{min}, \epsilon)$;
4 $n = 1$;
5 **while** $L_n \neq \emptyset$ **do**
6     $P = P \bigcup L_n$;
7     $C_{n+1} = $ GenerateCandidates (L_n, L_1);
8     $L_{n+1} = $ FindFrequentCandidates $(S, C_{n+1}, f_{min}, \epsilon)$;
9     $n = n + 1$;
10 $P = $ RemoveRedundantPatterns (P);

Algorithm 12.2: FindFrequentCandidates

Input : S: example set, C: candidate pattern set, f_{min}: frequency threshold, ϵ: pattern
similarity threshold
Output: FP: set of frequent candidates

1 $FP = \{\}$;
2 **foreach** *candidate* $\in C$ **do**
3   *scoretable* $= \{\}$ // a mapping table that maintains mapping between matching example
id and corresponding matching score;
4   **foreach** *example* $\in S$ **do**
5   *score* $= $ GetMatchProbability $(candidate, example)$;
6   **if** *score* $> \epsilon$ **then**
7   *scoretable*.put(*example.id, score*);

8   *normalizedprob* $= \frac{1}{|S|} \sum_{entry \in scoretable} entry.score$;
9   **if** *normalizedprob* $> f_{min}$ **then**
10   FP.put(*candidate*);

$r, \forall e_i \in r, \exists e_{f(i)} \in p \wedge e_i = e_{f(i)}\}$, where f is a monotonically increasing function,
i.e., $f : \mathbb{N}^+ \to \mathbb{N}^+, \forall i, j \in \mathbb{N}^+, i < j \Rightarrow f(i) < f(j)$. After the Apriori-like
procedure is terminated, the algorithm (line 10) removes all redundant patterns.

Algorithm 12.2 outlines the logic of finding frequent candidate patterns and
Algorithm 12.3 shows the logic of calculating similarity score given an example
and a candidate. The method "GetEventMatchScore" invoked in Algorithm 12.3 is
the most crucial part and we use Fig. 12.3 to illustrate this process. We note that
Algorithm 12.3 is fuzzy-matching based since the logic of "GetEventMatchScore"
is able to handle signal interruption (the four events in Fig. 12.3c should effectively
be treated as a single event) we mostly encounter during stream recording process.
User can devise specific matching algorithm based on top-down knowledge and
insight. For detailed implementation of "GetEventMatchScore", readers can refer to
the pseudocode in [27].

Algorithm 12.3: GetMatchProbability

Input : *example*: an example, *candidate*: a candidate pattern
Output: *score*: score that measures the similarity between *example* and *candidate*

1 *score* = 1.0;
2 **foreach** *event* ∈ *candidate* **do**
3   *eventmatchscore* = GetEventMatchScore (*event, example*);
4   **if** *eventmatchscore* > 0 **then**
5   *score* *= *eventmatchscore*;
6   **else**
7   **return** 0.0 // not a match;

8 **return** $score^{1/length(candidate)}$ // normalized score;

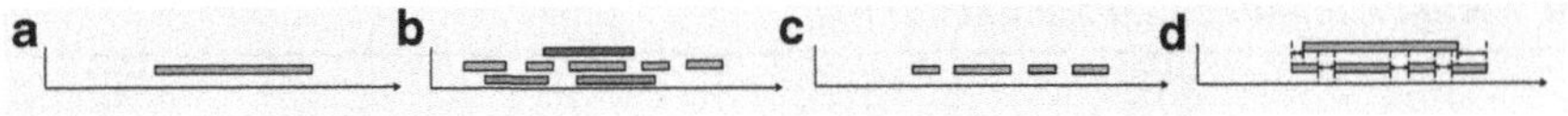

Fig. 12.3 Event matching process. (a) An event of type **B** in candidate. (b) An example. (c) All events in the example of type **B** that overlap with the type **B** event in the candidate. (d) The mismatch (denoted by ↔) calculated by this process

12.2.2.3 Integrating Bottom-Up Machine Computation and Top-Down Domain Knowledge

Aligning Patterns

Statistical analysis always comes with noises, and one important step that requires human in the loop is to apply domain knowledge to align the patterns discovered by machine computation. For example, an event that represents *human gaze at object A* simply should not overlap with another event that represents *human gaze at object B* in time within one pattern; if such patterns are presented from computation they should be synchronized instead. A general probability based adjustment using Gaussian distribution of the events is given in [27].

Validating Hypotheses

In this step user queries patterns by specifying criteria, e.g., length of the pattern (number of events in the pattern), minimum number of matching examples, minimum averaged matching probability, and etc. User also specifies parameters to control visualization, e.g., maximum number of most similar patterns in terms of matching probability to display, number of matching examples to display per page (the bottom of each page displays the pattern), number of bins of the histogram, and whether the histogram represents frequencies or probability densities (see Fig. 12.2f). User visually examines the discovered patterns in this step and gains knowledge of underlying data and in turn guides pattern mining of next round by provisioning top-down knowledge.

12.2.3 Large-Scale Multi-Modal Data Analytics with Iterative MapReduce Tasks

Recently, a vast volume of scientific data is captured by new instruments in various means, and data-driven discovery has already happened in various research and experimentation settings. Oftentimes machine computation needs to work with tens of thousands of data points to generate reliable and meaningful discoveries. The large-scale high-density high-quality multi-modal data make the cost of data processing prohibitively high and aforementioned "human-in-the-loop" interactive data analysis infeasible. Therefore it requires that we use today's state-of-the-art parallelization techniques and peta-scale computing powers to deal with the problem. In this section we first discuss the rationale of our parallel design choice and then describe the parallelization of proposed sequential pattern mining algorithm.

12.2.3.1 Parallelization Choices

Choosing Parallel Computing Model

Both MPI and MapReduce [6] are popular choices when implementing embarrassingly parallel computational tasks where no complicated communication is needed (e.g., our temporal pattern mining algorithm). MPI is a popular parallelization standard which provides a rich set of communication and synchronization constructs from which user can create diverse communication topologies. Although MPI is quite appealing in terms of its diversity in creating communication topologies (great control to the programmer) and high-performance implementations, it requires that programmer explicitly handles the mechanics of the data partitioning/communication/data-flow, exposed via low-level C routines and constructs such as sockets, as well as the higher level algorithm for the analysis. On the contrary, MapReduce operates only at the higher level: the programmer thinks in terms of functions (map and reduce) and the data-flow is implicit [30]. Since several pieces are pluggable in our algorithm, e.g., the logic of event space clustering, event matching and pattern adjustment, we prefer a high-level programming model like MapReduce which allow us to focus on the business logic.

Enabling Iterative Discovery

The original MapReduce framework proposed by Google [6] focuses on fault-tolerance with the assumption that underlying hardware environment is built from heterogeneous and inexpensive commodity machines where component failures are the norm rather than the exception. Therefore, input data are replicated across multiple nodes and intermediate output such as output of map task is stored in file system for fault-tolerance. However, this assumption needs to be reexamined as most researchers run their scientific applications on HPC resources such as XSEDE and FutureGrid which are built from high-performance and homogeneous hardware where failures are actually rare. The second issue is that Google's MapReduce focuses on single step MapReduce job. However, many parallel algorithms in domains such as data clustering, dimension reduction, link analysis, machine learning and computer vision have iterative structures, examples include K-Means [16], deterministic annealing clustering [26], PageRank [20], and dimension reduction algorithm such as SMACOF [15], just to name a few. With MapReduce's open source implementation Hadoop, input data partitions for iterative applications have to be repeatedly loaded from disk (HDFS) into memory and map/reduce tasks need to be initiated in each iteration, which is very inefficient and can degrade performance severely. In-memory MapReduce runtimes such as Twister [8], Haloop [5] and M3R [29], on the contrary, trade fault-tolerance for performance and are particularly designed for iterative data processing. In-memory MapReduce runtime does require larger amount of memory however in HPC environment where 16/32 GB memory is common node configuration this should never be a practical issue. We choose Twister as our runtime which supports long running map/reduce tasks. Moreover, in Twister static input data only need to be loaded once and intermediate map outputs are transferred to reducers through efficient in-memory communication through a publish-subscribe system without touching the disk.

Supporting Human-in-the-Loop Principle

To support interactive data analysis/visual mining we need to provision a user-friendly interface to access the pattern mining algorithm which runs on HPC. We expose the algorithm as *asynchronous* web services which make the algorithm easily accessible from any endpoint outside HPC such as local desktop and mobile device. We currently implement two web services: (1) web service that accepts user input (choices of pluggable components such as event matching algorithm, configurable parameters for algorithm/query/visualization) and downloads visualization results to client by invoking user registered callback; and (2) web service that takes the same input but only notifies completion in the callback. When using the first web service, user employs local tool to display downloaded figures. For the second web service, user leverages advanced visualization tool with client-server architecture. One example is ParaView, in this scenario ParaView server runs on the same HPC as the algorithm and user simply invokes ParaView client for visualization in callback.

12.2.3.2 Parallel Temporal Pattern Mining Using Twister MapReduce Tasks

In Fig. 12.4a we show the overview of our system architecture. Bottom-up machine computation takes place on the HPC, where one master node hosts the job client that submits Twister MapReduce job (pattern mining algorithm in our case), as well

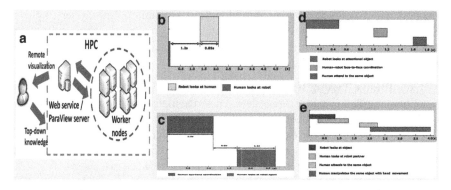

Fig. 12.4 (**a**) System architecture. Interactive exploration of large scale multi-modal data streams consists of three components steps: remote visualization of raw data and intermediate analysis results; applying top-down knowledge to refine pattern and trigger new rounds of pattern discovery; and bottom-up temporal pattern mining powered by parallel computing model and HPC resources. (**b**)–(**c**): The two most reliable sequential patterns found in human's gaze data stream. (**b**) A sequential pattern showing a $0.85s$ human gaze following a robot partner's gaze event, with $1.2s$ statistically detected between the two events. (**c**) A sequential pattern showing a $1.2s$ human eye-hand coordination event followed by a $1.1s$ human gaze (at partner) event, with $0.6s$ between two events. (**d**)–(**e**): two relatively complicated sequential patterns detected from interacting agents' action streams. (**d**) Example pattern showing that one agent's gaze at an attentional object will trigger face-to-face coordination between two interacting agents, and will attract the other agent's visual attention to the same object. (**e**) A more complicated sequential pattern showing that human partner dynamically adapts his/her behavior to reach the same visual and hand attention of his robot partner

as the web service server and an optional visualization server such as ParaView server. A set of worker nodes are deployed for computation. On the client-side, the user at desktop/mobile device receives visual representations of query results and intermediate results through a call-back function, generates the initial hypotheses, invokes the machine computation via web service client or, a ParaView client. (See our github repository [22] for all source code of our algorithms, web service client-server, and PBS scripts for deploying the system are hosted.)

12.3   Preliminary Results

Discovering sequential patterns from multimodal data is an important topic in various research fields. Our use case and principal test data in this work focus on the study of human-human communication, human-agent interactions, and human development and learning, as those fine-grained patterns can advance our understanding of human cognition and learning, and also provide quantitative evidence that we can directly incorporate in designing life-like social robots. The size of the data set is 5.3 GB. We use a 8-node cluster. Each node has two 4-core 2.6 GHz Intel EM64T Xeon E5 processors and 16 GB of DDR3-1333 memory. On average the mining algorithm finishes within 6.2 min. User employs ParaView client at local desktop to examine results. We report some statistically reliable and scientifically meaningful interactive behavioral patterns in our human development and learning study below:

- **Quantitative Timing Information.** Figure 12.4b–c show two reliable patterns of human-robot eye gaze events detected by the algorithm. Figure 12.4b shows a $0.85s$ human gaze (at robot) will reliably follow a robot partner's gaze (at human) event, with a $1.2s$ pause between the these two events. Figure 12.4c illustrates a sequential pattern showing a $1.2s$ human eye-hand coordination event followed by a $1.1s$ human gaze (at partner) event, with $0.6s$ between two events.
- **Sequential Relationships Between Events.** Complicated temporal patterns such as adaptive behavior patterns can be identified with the algorithm as well. Figure 12.4 provide two example of interesting interactive behavioral patterns. The informal meaning of this pattern being identified is when the robot learner is not visually attending to the human teacher, the human will first initiate a face-looking at the robot and expect an eye-contact, followed by a gaze event at the same attentional object (see e.g., Fig. 12.4d); even more complicated, the human partner shows repeat pattern of using hand to manipulate that object with the hope to re-engage the robot's attention (see e.g., Fig. 12.4e).

12.4 Conclusion and Future Work

This chapter presents a novel temporal data mining method focusing on extracting exact timings and durations of sequential patterns extracted from large-scale datasets of multiple temporal events. Our design allows users to use their top-down knowledge of the dataset to supervise the knowledge discovery process and redirect the machine computation. More importantly, we demonstrate a means to exploratively analyze large-scale multi-modal data streams with human in the loop, by integrating interactive visualization, parallel data mining, and information representation. Focusing on multi-source data streams collected from longitudinal multi-modal communication studies, our experimental results demonstrate the capability of detecting and quantifying various kinds of statistically reliable and scientifically meaningful sequential patterns from multi-modal data streams. Starting from this large-scale data exploration framework and the parallel sequential pattern mining algorithm, we plan to proceed to extend and continue our current research in various multi-modal social scenarios and scientific experiment settings.

References

1. R. Agrawal, R. Srikant, Fast algorithms for mining association rules, in *Proceedings of the 20th International Conference on Very Large Data Bases (VLDB'94)* (Santiago, 1994), pp. 487–499

2. R. Agrawal, R. Srikant, Mining sequential patterns, in *Proceedings of the 11th international conference on Data Engineering (ICDE'01)* (1995), pp. 3–14
3. J.F. Allen, Maintaining knowledge about temporal intervals. Commun. ACM **26**(11), 832–843 (1983)
4. J. Ayres, J. Gehrke, T. Yiu, J. Flannick, Sequential pattern mining using a bitmap representation, in *Proceedings of the eighth ACM SIGKDD international conference on Knowledge discovery and data mining (KDD'02)* (Edmonton, 2002), pp. 429–435
5. Y. Bu, B. Howe, M. Balazinska, M.D. Ernst, Haloop: efficient iterative data processing on large clusters. Proc. VLDB Endowment **3**, 285–296 (2010)
6. J. Dean, S. Ghemawat, MapReduce: simplified data processing on large clusters, in *Sixth Symposium on Operating System Design and Implementation (OSDI'04)*, vol. 37 (2004)
7. M. Dolinsky, W. Sherman, E. Wernert, Y.C. Chi, Reordering virtual reality: recording and recreating real-time experiences, in *Proceedings of SPIE The Engineering Reality of Virtual Reality 2012* (2012), pp. 155–162
8. J. Ekanayake, H. Li, B. Zhang, T. Gunarathne, S.-H. Bae, J. Qiu, G. Fox, Twister: a runtime for iterative mapreduce, in *Proceedings of the 19th ACM International Symposium on High Performance Distributed Computing (HPDC'10)* (2010), pp. 810–818
9. D. Fricker, H. Zhang, C. Yu, Sequential pattern mining of multi modal data streams in dyadic interactions, in *Proceedings of 2011 IEEE International Conference on Development and Learning (ICDL'11)*, (2011), pp. 1–6
10. M.N. Garofalakis, R. Rastogi, K. Shim, Spirit: sequential pattern mining with regular expression constraints, in *Proceedings of the 25th International Conference on Very Large Data Bases (VLDB'99)* (Edinburgh, 1999)
11. J.C. Guerri, M. Esteve, C. Palau, M. Monfort, M.A. Sarti, A software tool to acquire, synchronise and playback multimedia data: an application in kinesiology. Comput. Methods Prog. Biomed. **62**(1), 51–58 (2000)
12. T. Guyet, R. Quiniou, Mining temporal patterns with quantitative intervals, in *Proceedings of IEEE International Conference on Data Mining Workshops (ICDMW'08)* (2008), pp. 218–227
13. J. Han, J. Pei, B. Mortazavi-Asl, Q. Chen, U. Dayal, M.-C. Hsu, Freespan: frequent pattern-projected sequential pattern mining, in *Proceedings of the Sixth ACM SIGKDD International Conference on Knowledge Discovery and Data Mining (KDD'00)* (Boston, 2000), pp. 355–359
14. A. Jacobs, The pathologies of big data. Queue **7**(6), 10:10–10:19 (2009)
15. J.D. Leeuw, Applications of convex analysis to multidimensional scaling, in *Proceedings of the European Meeting of Statisticians* (Grenoble, France, 1976), pp. 6–11.
16. J. MacQueen, Some methods for classification and analysis of multivariate observations, in *Proceedings of the fifth Berkeley Symposium on Mathematical Statistics and Probability* (1967)
17. F. Moerchen, D. Fradkin, Robust mining of time intervals with semi-interval partial order patterns, in *Proceedings of SIAM Conference on Data Mining (SDM'10)* (2010)
18. M. Mouhoub, J. Liu, Managing uncertain temporal relations using a probabilistic interval algebra, in *Proceedings of IEEE International Conference on Systems, Man and Cybernetics (SMC'08)* (2008), pp. 3399–3404
19. F. Nakagaito, T. Ozaki, T. Ohkawa, Discovery of quantitative sequential patterns from event sequences, in *Proceedings of IEEE International Conference on Data Mining Workshops (ICDMW'09)*, (2009), pp. 31–36
20. L. Page, S. Brin, R. Motwani, T. Winograd, The pagerank citation ranking: Bringing order to the web. Technical Report, Stanford InfoLab, 1999
21. P. Papapetrou, G. Kollios, S. Sclaroff, D. Gunopulos, Discovering frequent arrangements of temporal intervals, in *Proceedings of Fifth IEEE International Conference on Data Mining* (2005), pp. 354–361
22. Parallel sequential pattern miner homepage (2014), https://github.com/guangchen/parallel-sequential-pattern-miner
23. D. Patel, W. Hsu, M.L. Lee, Mining relationships among interval-based events for classification, in *Proceedings of the 2008 ACM SIGMOD international conference on Management of data (SIGMOD'08)* (Vancouver, 2008), pp. 393–404

24. J. Pei, J. Han, B. Mortazavi-Asl, H. Pinto, Q. Chen, U. Dayal, M.-C. Hsu, PrefixSpan: mining sequential patterns efficiently by prefix-projected pattern growth, in *Proceedings of the 17th international conference on Data Engineering (ICDE'01)* (2001), pp. 215–224
25. H. Pinto, J. Han, J. Pei, K. Wang, Multi-dimensional sequential pattern mining, in *Proceedings of the tenth international conference on Information and knowledge management (CIKM'01)* (Atlanta, 2001)
26. K. Rose, E. Gurewitz, G. Fox, A deterministic annealing approach to clustering. Pattern Recogn. Lett. **11**(9), 589–594 (1990)
27. G. Ruan, H. Zhang, B. Plale, Parallel and quantitative sequential pattern mining for large-scale interval-based temporal data, in *Proceedings of the 2014 IEEE International Conference on Big Data* (Washington, 2014), pp. 32–39
28. P. Shan Kam A.W.-C. Fu, Discovering temporal patterns for interval-based events, in *Proceedings of the Second International Conference on Data Warehousing and Knowledge Discovery (DaWaK'00)* (2000), pp. 317–326
29. A. Shinnar, D. Cunningham, V. Saraswat, B. Herta, M3r: increased performance for in-memory hadoop jobs. Proc. VLDB Endowment **5**(12), 1736–1747 (2012)
30. T. White, *Hadoop: The Definitive Guide*, 3rd edn. (O'Reilly Media/Yahoo Press, Sebastopol, 2012)
31. X. Ye, M.C. Carroll, Exploratory space-time analysis of local economic development. Appl. Geogr. **31**(3), 1049–1058 (2011)
32. C. Yu, Y. Zhong, T.G. Smith, I. Park, W. Huang, Visual mining of multimedia data for social and behavioral studies, in *Proceedings of the IEEE Symposium on Visual Analytics Science and Technology (VAST'08)* (2008), pp. 155–162
33. C. Yu, D. Yurovsky, T. Xu, Visual data mining: An exploratory approach to analyzing temporal patterns of eye movements. Infancy **17**(1), 33–60 (2012)
34. A.B. Zakour, S. Maabout, M. Mosbah, M. Sistiaga, Uncertainty interval temporal sequences extraction, in *Proceedings of 6th ICISTM International Conference (ICISTM'12)* (2012), pp. 259–270
35. H. Zhang, C. Yu, L.B. Smith, An interactive virtual reality platform for studying embodied social interaction, in *Proceedings of the CogSci06 Symposium Toward Social Mechanisms of Android Science* (2006)
36. H. Zhang, D. Fricker, T.G. Smith, C. Yu, Real-time adaptive behaviors in multimodal human-avatar interactions, in *Proceedings of the International Conference on Multimodal Interfaces and the Workshop on Machine Learning for Multimodal Interaction (ICMI-MLMI '10)* (2010)
37. H. Zhang, D. Fricker, C. Yu, A multimodal real-time platform for studying human-avatar interactions, in *Proceedings of the 10th international conference on Intelligent virtual agents (IVA'10)* (2010), pp. 49–56

Chapter 13
Using High Performance Computing for Detecting Duplicate, Similar and Related Images in a Large Data Collection

Ritu Arora, Jessica Trelogan, and Trung Nguyen Ba

Abstract The detection of duplicate and related content is a critical data curation task in the context of digital research collections. This task can be challenging, if not impossible, to do manually in large, unstructured, and noisy collections. While there are many automated solutions for deduplicating data that contain large numbers of identical copies, it can be particularly difficult to find a solution for identifying redundancy within image-heavy collections that have evolved over a long span of time or have been created collaboratively by large groups. These types of collections, especially in academic research settings, in which the datasets are used for a wide range of publication, teaching, and research activities, can be characterized by (1) large numbers of heterogeneous file formats, (2) repetitive photographic documentation of the same subjects in a variety of conditions (3) multiple copies or subsets of images with slight modifications (e.g., cropping or color-balancing) and (4) complex file structures and naming conventions that may not be consistent throughout. In this chapter, we present a scalable and automated approach for detecting duplicate, similar, and related images, along with subimages, in digital data collections. Our approach can assist in efficiently managing redundancy in any large image collection on High Performance Computing (HPC) resources. While we illustrate the approach with a large archaeological collection, it is domain-neutral and is widely applicable to image-heavy collections within any HPC platform that has general-purpose processors.

13.1 Introduction

Digital data collections are increasingly at the center of scholarly research activities. While they can enable and facilitate collaboration and data sharing, there is a large amount of work involved in making them usable, especially if they have

R. Arora (✉)
University of Texas at Austin, Texas Advanced Computing Center, Austin, TX, USA
e-mail: rauta@tacc.utexas.edu

J. Trelogan • T.N. Ba
University of Texas, Austin, TX, USA

© Springer International Publishing Switzerland 2016   269
R. Arora (ed.), *Conquering Big Data with High Performance Computing*,
DOI 10.1007/978-3-319-33742-5_13

270   R. Arora et al.

evolved over a long period of time and have been collected by a large number of people. Organizing, sorting, and documenting the content is a non-trivial challenge. Image-heavy research collections with long histories, in particular, can contain large quantities of both "born-digital" and digitized files, may have been generated by several stakeholders with diverse needs, and may be highly unstructured. In this context duplication and redundancy can quickly proliferate. As research collections continue to grow and as teams and technologies change, it can become increasingly difficult to navigate and make sense of the collections. Routine data curation tasks like file format migration, metadata creation, and archiving can become overwhelming, especially if data management principles have not been prioritized since a project's inception. Without an overarching set of data management strategies applied throughout a collection's history, it can be a challenge to locate specific groups of data and to assess, reorganize, and categorize them.

Common questions that arise during the data curation process include: Can related images be located within an unstructured collection without detailed descriptive metadata (see Fig. 13.1)? Can different versions or copies of the same images be located and connected in the absence of recorded provenance information, even if they have been altered through minor changes like file format migration or editing (see Fig. 13.2)? Can two digital representations of the same photograph be located if they were digitized on two different dates, with different equipment, and have completely different naming conventions?

To address these kinds of challenges within a large and complex collections, automated solutions are needed that can help curators efficiently locate redundant, similar, and related data. Within this chapter we define *duplicate images* as exact copies of a digital file that may have been stored in several different directories with or without the same file names. This type of duplication can be intentional, as with selected sub-collections for publication, or can be the result of data management habits, like multiple backups within the same collection. *Similar images* are near-duplicate but not identical digital copies. These may include (1) copies with slight alteration (e.g., rotation, cropping, or changes to colorspace), (2) photographs of the same subject from different angles, (3) "bracketed" images of the same subject captured with different camera settings, under different lighting condition, or using

Fig. 13.1 Can related images be located within a collection without descriptive metadata? This artifact, for example, was photographed by different people, for different purposes, during many separate photographic campaigns. These photographs contain no object-code either within the photograph or in file names. Finding them and relating them to descriptive records in an associated database required visual inspection

Fig. 13.2 Can different versions or copies of the same photograph be located, even if altered, renamed, and stored in a new location without a record of provenance? The image on the *left* contained descriptive information about the subject and original photographic source in its filename. The version on the *right* was cropped, enhanced, and renamed for inclusion in a specific publication. Provenance information is easily lost if the image is separated from the text that describes how the derivative relates to the original photographic master

different cameras, or (4) multiple scans of the same analog photograph, captured on different dates with different equipment or settings. *Related images* refer to those that can be connected by context or that contain similar, but not necessarily the same subjects. Examples include images from a single photographic campaign, or different groupings or arrangements of the same sets of objects. *Subimages* are extractions from other images via cropping or subsetting and may also contain additional alterations like background removal, color-balancing, sharpening, or rotation.

In the absence of detailed descriptive metadata or clearly structured directories, the analysis of technical metadata can be helpful in detecting duplicates and clusters of related files. Tools like DROID [1] or ExifTool [2] can be run to extract information such as file formats, file dimensions, date stamps, checksums, and capture details. This extracted information can be used as an abstraction of the collection and can thus be helpful to analyze the collections as part of a curation workflow. This type of metadata may be of limited value however in dealing with some of the cases described above, which require deeper inspection of file content. There are several well-known approaches, such as Content-Based Image Retrieval (CBIR) [3, 4] and object-detection [5] that utilize the features extracted from images (*viz.*, color, shape, and texture) and recognize objects in them to find similar, related, and subimages. It can, however, be difficult to find scalable, open-source implementations that use an automated approach for comparing all images in a large collection with each other, such that the images can be classified or filtered according to their content and relationships.

The main goal of our research was to develop a scalable and automated approach for detecting redundant, similar, and related images, along with subimages, in large and complex data collections with speed, accuracy, and precision [6]. In our solution, we classify subimages as a subcategory of related images. Here, speed refers to short time-to-results. Accuracy refers to finding all instances of the desired category of images. Precision refers to having a very low number of false-positives. Another goal was to provide a flexible and user-guided method for iterative assessment and refinement of a data collection, with the active involvement of data curators or other stakeholders. Filters for selectively assessing different subsets of a collection at a given time were needed, as were the options for choosing specific algorithms and thresholds.

13.2 Challenges in Using Existing Solutions

Content-based image assessment may be necessary for detecting related and similar content in image collections where metadata is not available or is of limited value. Manual comparison of image content can be done with a high degree of accuracy and precision within a traditional desktop computing environment. The manual comparison is, however, labor-intensive, and quickly becomes impractical in large image collections (>1000 files). This is especially true if directory structures are deeply nested and complex or if data have been generated over a long span of time, with no consistent organizational principles. For meeting the goals of this project, a number of existing tools were evaluated both within a desktop computing environment and HPC environment. Although several of them performed very well, they mostly proved inadequate for a large (approximately 4 TB) collection. None of the tools were scalable enough to work in batch-processing mode. A brief overview of some of the existing tools that were evaluated in desktop and HPC environments is presented in this section.

There are a variety of CBIR tools that have been shown to be useful in automating the tasks of image comparison [7–9]. Such tools typically segment the images into sets of semantic regions, and compare the image segments (or regions) with a query image (segments) on the basis of features like color, shape, and texture. The tools extract the features from the images (or image segments) and store them in feature vectors. Similarity (or distance) metrics are then used to compare feature vectors associated with different image segments. Large values of similarity mean that the feature vectors are closely related.

Java Content Based Image Retrieval (JCBIR) is a Java-based Graphical User Interface (GUI) tool for CBIR that uses the techniques of K-means clustering and wavelets [10]. When JCBIR was used with a test collection of a small set of images in both desktop and HPC environment, it reported an excessive number of false-positives and missed a large number of possible matches. For our purposes, this tool's accuracy and precision were both considered too low. In terms of usability, the main problem with JCBIR was that it is GUI-based and accepts one query image at a time, thereby, doing one-to-many comparison of images. However, for large datasets, containing thousands of images, this approach is not scalable.

A Matlab-based CBIR tool that was available online was also evaluated. The tool [11] gave errors with the test dataset, and there was no documentation to understand and fix the cause of errors.

Two free off-the-shelf tools were evaluated in a desktop computing environment for benchmarking: dupeGuru [12] and VisiPics [13]. Both of these tools had the advantage of user-friendly interfaces and relatively robust functions to detect matching images and to assess results (e.g., marking result sets or performing actions on them). Neither of them was scalable to deal efficiently with large datasets (>6000 images). Though none of the tools that we tested were perfectly accurate with near-duplicate files that were not exact copies, both VisiPics and dupeGURU performed well at finding similar images, particularly if the color histograms were closely matched. VisiPics by far out-performed dupeGURU in precision (i.e., low numbers of false positives), and was much better at matching images even with very different color histograms. dupeGURU was the only one, however, that was portable to the Linux environment. Tests on Stampede produced results that were very close to expectation. It is very good at finding near-duplicate pairs but missed several rescans of images, and performed poorly if color histograms were not very similar. The processing time was much improved over that of the desktop version, but because this software is used through a GUI, it is not practical to use this tool in a batch-mode in an HPC environment for assessing large data collections. It should be noted here that dupeGURU's GUI includes powerful functionality for viewing and processing result sets, including support for custom scripts. Hence, it could be a useful and convenient tool to use for small data collections.

While none of the content-based image retrieval tools that we explored could find all the similar, non-identical image files in a test collection, they were all helpful in at least guiding the user towards groups of related data, thereby, narrowing the search for related content. Because the process of managing an unstructured collection benefits from an iterative approach, the desired solution was required to work through a command-line interface in batch-mode processing and be amenable to parallelization to reduce the time-to-results.

13.3 New Solution for Large-Scale Image Comparison

Due to the lack of scalable, open-source tools with the desired speed, accuracy, and precision, we developed a new solution, comprising of steps illustrated in Fig. 13.3 and explained further in this section. The steps that are included in the overall workflow can be broken down into three categories: pre-processing, processing, and post-processing.

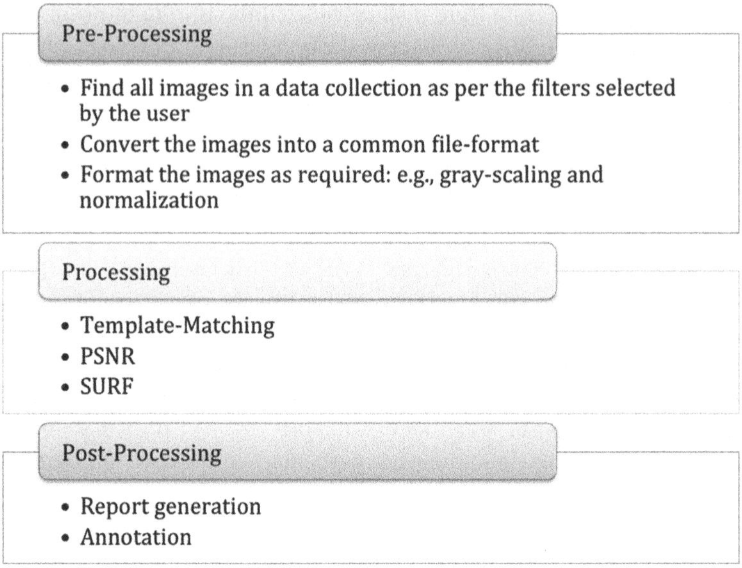

Fig. 13.3 Overview of the key steps in the image-matching workflow

13.3.1 Pre-processing Stage

The pre-processing stage includes finding all image files in a given data collection as per the filters specified by the user. The image files that are discovered are then converted, if necessary, to black-and-white colorspace and to JPG format, and copied to a separate location while maintaining the original directory hierarchy. If required, additional pre-processing can be done during this stage, such as the removal of background noise or histogram normalization. These pre-processing needs of a collection are identified by the user, based on prior knowledge of the collection and requirements for their specific data management challenge.

13.3.2 Processing Stage

After the images are pre-processed, they are compared with one another (a many-to-many comparison) using the algorithms that are implemented for finding duplicate, similar, and related images including subimages. The algorithms include: checking image similarity using Peak Signal-to-Noise Ratio (PSNR) [14], template-matching [15], and SURF [16].

The *PSNR algorithm* calculates the peak signal-to-noise ratio between the images that are being compared. In our implementation, PSNR is used as a similarity metric.

Given an image with dimensions MxN, and another image K of the same dimensions (and possibly containing noise), its PSNR can be calculated as follows:

$$PSNR = 20 \cdot log_{10}(MAX) - 10 \cdot log_{10}(MSE)$$

such that MAX is the maximum possible value of an image pixel, and the Mean Squared Error (MSE) as used in the aforementioned equation is calculated as follows:

$$MSE = \frac{1}{M \cdot N} \cdot \sum_{i=0}^{M-1} \sum_{j=0}^{N-1} \left[I\,(i,j) - K\,(i,j) \right]^2$$

PSNR is measured in decibels (dB). If two images are identical, then their PSNR will be 0 dB. The PSNR of 30–50 dB can imply that the images being compared have a reasonable degree of similarity. However, if PSNR is less than 15 dB, the images being compared are not very similar. The PSNR algorithm requires that the images that are being compared be of the same size. Hence, some pre-processing could be required to adjust the size of images before calculating their PSNR.

Template-Matching is a technique that helps in finding images that match or contain a given image. The given image is known as the template image. The image in which we expect to find areas or patches that match with the template image is called a base image. Hence, the dimensions of a base image cannot be smaller than the given template image. If the base image is smaller in dimension than the template image, then our implementation of the template-matching swaps them. The algorithm works by sliding the template image over base image till a matching area is found. During sliding, the template image is moved left-to-right, and from top-to-bottom one pixel at a time. At each position during sliding, it is determined how well the template matches to the base image using one of the available similarity metrics. There are six similarity metrics that are available to choose from when using the template-matching functionality provided by the [17] OpenCV library: square difference, correlation, correlation coefficient, normalized square difference, normalized correlation, and normalized correlation coefficient. These metrics are explained in detail. The users also provide threshold values for comparing with the values produced by one of the aforementioned metrics. On the basis of this comparison during run-time, it can be determined if an acceptable match has been found or not. Template matching can also be done using PSNR as the similarity metric. It is highly recommended that the users of our solution use PSNR with template-matching for deciding whether a template image is a subimage of the base image. It should be noted that template-matching is a computationally intensive activity and can be time-consuming when done in a serial mode.

Speeded Up Robust Features (*SURF*) is a popular algorithm that is used for image feature detection and image matching. It works by detecting keypoints (or interest points having blob-like structures) at the various points in images, representing the neighborhood of keypoints as descriptors (basically, feature vectors), and

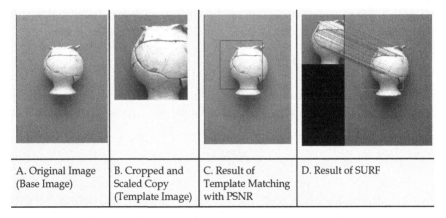

| A. Original Image (Base Image) | B. Cropped and Scaled Copy (Template Image) | C. Result of Template Matching with PSNR | D. Result of SURF |

Fig. 13.4 Results of applying template matching with PSNR, and SURF on images (**a**) and (**b**). Notes on (**c**): PSNR of comparing (**a**) and (**b**) is 36.8111 dB, which means, images are almost the same. The rectangle denotes the patch of the base image that overlaps with the template image. Notes on (**d**): The SURF result shows the matching of interest points in the two images, that is, images (**a**) and (**b**)

doing image matching on the basis of the distance between the image descriptors (or feature vectors) [16]. The version of the SURF algorithm that we used is insensitive to rotation, and scaling but is sensitive to lighting conditions.

The results of comparing two images using Template Matching with PSNR, and the SURF algorithm are shown in Fig. 13.4. As can be noticed from this figure, our solution can detect cropped and scaled versions of images successfully. Through the random sampling of a subset of results, we have found that the accuracy of our solution is 100 % on this front.

In our solution, the user can select any or all of the aforementioned algorithms to find subimages, duplicate images, similar images, and related images in a given data collection. The end-user has the flexibility to experiment with different threshold values and metrics for similarity-checks. Depending upon the quality of the images provided as input, the type of selected algorithms, and the chosen threshold values, the quality of the output can vary. Each of the three algorithms that are used in our solution have limitations and advantages, but when used together, can help in the comprehensive classification of images according to their content. For example, the PSNR algorithm will not find subimages if the template image is significantly smaller than the base image, but the template-matching algorithm can find such matches. If the two images have the same content but have different dimensions, then template matching will not detect them as related in any way but the SURF algorithm will.

The usage of all the algorithms together for image comparison can produce results for different comparison criteria with high accuracy and precision but can be slow as compared to using only one of the algorithms at a time. Therefore, we parallelized our implementation using OpenMP such that we can run the application

Input: list of images (L), selected algorithms (S), threshold values
Distribute **L** into sub-lists of images such that each OpenMP thread gets a distinct sub-list
Read Images in **L** and validate them to eliminate bad images from the comparison process
All threads, do the following:
    outer-loop: for each image, **Img1**, in the sub-list of images, do the following:
        inner-loop: Compare **Img1** with all other images in **L** using **S**, where **S** can be:
            1. PSNR // to find same, similar, or related images
                a. if images being compared are of different dimensions, do image-scaling for making images compatible in size
                b. Compute PSNR
                    I. Make a temporary copy of **Img1** -> **tmpImg1**
                    II. Compute PSNR of **tmpImg1** and the image selected in the inner-loop image, and compare it with the threshold value
                    III. If the images being compared do not match, rotate the copied image 90 degree and execute step 1.a. for the rotated image and inner-loop image
                    IV. repeat II,III until a match is found or the total rotated angle is 360 degree
            2. Template-Matching // to find all subimages of an image
                a. Compare dimensions of **Img1**, and the image selected in the inner-loop, **Img2**. Swap if dimensions of **Img1** are smaller than **Img2**
                b. Slide and compare **Img1** and **Img2**
                    I. Make a temporary copy of **Img1** -> **tmpImg1**
                    II. Find the area in **Img2** that best matches **tmpImg1**
                    III. Crop the best matched patch in **Img2** and compare it with the **tmpImg1** using PSNR as shown in step 1.b.II.
                    IV. If **Img2** and **tmpImg1** do not match, rotate the copied image 90 degree and execute step 2.a.
                    V. Repeat 2.b.II.-IV. until a match is found or **tmpImg1** is rotated to 360 degree
            3. SURF // to check for any near-duplicate, or similar images
                a. Compute keypoint vectors of **Img1**, and the image selected in the inner-loop, **Img2**; the smaller of the two vectors is **base**
                b. Compute keypoint descriptors for each keypoint in the vectors
                c. Use brute force approach to match keypoints of **Img1** to keypoints of **Img2**, this step will give a vector of matches, **matchVec**
                d. Use a well-defined measure to remove false matches from **matchVec**
                e. Compare threshold value to ratio of good-matches and base vectors

Fig. 13.5 Parallel algorithm for image comparison

using multiple threads on a compute-server. The complete algorithm that is used in our solution is outlined in Fig. 13.5.

We tested the OpenMP version of our solution on a compute-server, having two 2.7 GHz processors and 16 cores in total. In order to compare one image with approximately 400,000 images, while using all 16 cores, can take anywhere between 3 and 14 days, depending upon the chosen algorithms, threshold values and the quality of the images. At this rate, an all-to-all comparison of images can take several months if done using only two processors. Hence, either the code needs to be parallelized further or it can be run as is on multiple nodes in the High-Throughput Computing (HTC) mode (see Chap. 1). In the HTC mode, we can run multiple copies of the code independently on different server-nodes such that each copy compares a small subset of images from the dataset with the entire set of images. This HTC mechanism of doing all-to-all image comparison helps in reducing the image processing time, and in improving the process of curating and preserving a data collection. The reduction in time-to-results is commensurate to the number of nodes used and the level of load-balancing between nodes.

13.3.3 Post-processing Stage

During the post-processing stage, the results from different concurrent runs of our solution are combined to form a comprehensive report of the image comparison on the entire dataset. With the involvement of a curator, the results in the report are further verified. The feature of annotating images with metadata will be added in future work.

The flexibility of our software to run in parallel (using HTC and multi-threaded mode), along with the feature to select a combination of image-processing algorithms that can be run with different threshold values, are some of the important features that were missing from the various off-the-shelf tools that we evaluated.

13.4 Test Collection from the Institute of Classical Archaeology (ICA)

The Institute of Classical Archaeology (ICA) at the University of Texas at Austin has been collaborating with the Texas Advanced Computing Center (TACC) for the last several years to assess its digital collection and develop a set of strategies for its curation and long-term preservation. The ICA collection represents over 40 years of archaeological research. Consisting of more than 1,000,000 files scattered throughout a deeply nested structure, it contains a large amount of image data that has been collected, copied, shared, and re-deposited by generations of scholars, students, and specialists, each using an idiosyncratic mix of file formats, data management methods, and naming conventions. Typical of legacy archaeological collections, the photographic documentation is irreplaceable and fragile, in that it represents the only record of sites and artifacts that either no longer exist or are inaccessible to researchers. Likewise, because the dataset has been amassed over generations of research initiatives, there are large sets of related data that have accumulated in disconnected sub-collections that are in need of integration.

In this context, routine data curation tasks are time-consuming, if not impossible, without computational tools to facilitate otherwise manual review. Scalable, automated approaches are needed to improve efficiency in locating related, similar, and redundant content in order to ensure long-term preservation and to facilitate future reuse.

Our initial work in an HPC environment, focused on developing abstract high-level views of the collection, has gone a long way towards that goal. The analysis and visualization of structural and technical metadata have been especially fruitful in helping curators to assess the collection's contents, understand its structure, and begin to reduce some of its inherent complexities. For this work technical metadata, such as date stamps, file size, checksums, and file format identification, was extracted using DROID [18] and various custom scripts to create a series of snapshots of the collection as it evolved over time [19]. OpenRefine [20] was used for exploring, filtering, cleaning, and annotating the collection's structural metadata (file and directory labels). This information was also used as input into a custom-built visual analytics toolkit developed with funding from the National Archives and Records Administration [21]. These tools, as well as Tableau [22], were used to analyze structural patterns, view file formats over time, and to identify duplicate and corrupt data within the collection. To help deal with redundant and related datasets that were not exact duplicates (and as such could not be identified by comparing checksums), descriptive metadata implicit in filenames and directory labels was assessed. In particular, an Entity Resolution-based model was developed to view clusters of related data using Natural Language Processing (NLP) techniques [23]. The methods developed in this prior work were extremely informative and time-saving in initial assessments and in highlighting large areas of files that needed attention. The actual data curation tasks (e.g., deleting, updating, re-organizing, documenting large batches of files) still had to be done manually.

The process of extracting metadata itself proved to be cumbersome and time-consuming. DROID, the tool used for extracting file format identification and other technical metadata, has several limitations and bugs that made it cumbersome to install in an HPC environment and made it challenging to parallelize. We did, however, manage to develop several successful work-arounds for the limitations with DROID and were able to parallelize the process to reduce overall time taken to extract collection-level metadata [19].

Despite the challenges of metadata extraction, it was deemed to be a valuable method for initial assessment and for reducing corruption and irrelevant data within the collection. There is, however, still a great deal of redundancy in the collection that cannot be detected via data abstractions. Technical metadata related to the properties of the files (e.g., checksums and date-stamps) or descriptive metadata (e.g., object codes in file-names) would not help in identifying redundancies where file formats have been modified, scanning efforts have been repeated, or for reconstructing provenance in derivatives without documentation. Because the collection contains a dearth of descriptive metadata, consistent file naming, or control over directory structures, there is no way to discover this type of redundancy, to group related data, or to recreate provenance without looking into the content of the digital objects themselves.

An automated approach was needed to further cull redundancy as well as to identify and integrate related content that would otherwise require visual inspection in a manual review of every file in the collection. Although there is no substitute for the manual, visual inspection of image data in determining its usefulness and in identifying relationships, we needed a way to help guide the process and narrow the problem. While this approach would clearly be useful for ICA's data management needs, it is also widely applicable to other large, unstructured research collections.

13.5 Testing the Solution on Stampede: Early Results and Current Limitations

Using the data collection from ICA, we tested our solution on Stampede, which is a 10 PFLOPS supercomputer at TACC [24]. Stampede has 6400+ Dell PowerEdge server nodes, and each of the server nodes is outfitted with two Intel Xeon E5 processors and Intel® Xeon Phi™ coprocessor. All these processors and coprocessors are multi-core and many-cores. The nodes are connected using high-throughput, low-latency Infiniband™ interconnect.

The ICA data collection that was used for testing our solution is 4.8 TB in size, out of which, 3.3 TB of data are image files. In total, there are 414,193 image files of heterogeneous types, *viz.*, JPG, JPEG, PSD, PNG, and TIF. The main goals of our testing were to estimate the time taken to pre-process and process the ICA data collection on Stampede, and understand any challenges in using an HPC platform for an iterative data curation workflow.

We started by making a copy of the collection on Stampede. It took about 15 h to copy over the collection from one filesystem on Stampede to another using two data transfer processes in parallel. Using more than two data transfer processes in parallel (each working on a different subdirectory of the dataset) would have accelerated the rate of transfer but would have impacted the experience of other users on Stampede—this is because the network and filesystems are shared amongst all users of Stampede. Therefore, the Stampede usage policies restrict the users to only 2–3 data transfer processes at a time.

During the pre-processing step, it took approximately 6 h to convert the images from different formats to the JPG format, and to covert the colored images to grayscale. Twenty-seven processes ran in parallel for doing these conversions on different cores, using the ImageMagick tool [25], such that each process worked on a different subdirectory. Had this task been done using only one process at a time, it would have taken approximately 32 h to complete. It should also be noted here that the load-balancing across the processes was very coarse-grain and hence, a process working on a subdirectory with fewer images than other subdirectories would finish earlier than other processes. There were some corrupt files, on which the aforementioned image formatting steps failed. After the type and color space conversion, the script for creating the list of image files for comparison purposes was run. It took about an hour to prepare the file-list. In total, approximately 7 h of pre-processing was required for a 4.8 TB data collection and utilizing more processes in parallel can reduce the time taken further. Normalization of images was done as a separate step and it took around 2 h to normalize the entire set of images using 27 cores in parallel.

During the processing step, all the three algorithms (PSNR, Template Matching, and SURF) were used together. As noted previously, it can take more than 3 days to compare one image with more than 400,000 images in the dataset while using all the three algorithms in the OpenMP implementation of our solution. The general system policies on Stampede prohibit running a batch job for more than 48 h. Hence, it is not possible to run the serial or OpenMP version of the code with such large number of image files without having to stop and restart the processing several times. It should be noted here that by "restart" we do not imply redoing all the computations that were done before the processing stopped, but what we mean is to resume the computation from a certain point before the processing stopped. Therefore, we are currently extending the OpenMP version of the code to add the checkpointing and restart functionality to it. With the checkpointing feature, the code will periodically write its output to a file, and will also save the values of certain application variables to another file. Using the information about the values of certain application variables, the code can be restarted from the point where it stopped previously such that it does not have to do repeat all the computations that were done before it stopped. Hence, the checkpointing and restart feature will help in overcoming the time-limit restrictions of the various job-queues on Stampede. In addition to checkpointing and restart functionality, the code can be parallelized further so that it can take advantage of distributed-memory parallel programming, and this is part of our future work.

The time taken for post-processing the results is not being accounted for because it involves a data curator to manually verify the results. One of the steps during post-processing involves concatenating the output from different concurrent runs to produce a single report file. The output that is currently produced by our solution is all in textual mode. Reviewing a single very large file of text output for analyzing the results is not convenient to parse through if the number of images is large (over 400,000 in this data collection). As part of our future work, we intend to extend the solution so that it can produce thumbnails of images in the report under different classes—duplicate, similar, related, and subimage (see Fig. 13.8).

To further explain the current functionality of our solution, the quality of the results it can produce, and its performance, we selected a very small subset of the images from the ICA data collection. This subset contained 62 images of artifacts photographed at different angles, with different backgrounds, using different lighting, and having different arrangements. Some images of the artifact/s were colored and some were black-and-white. Figure 13.6 illustrates the known groups or pairs of photographs in this subset. Each group contains 2–4 images of the same artifact/s. Creating such groups of similar, duplicate or related images is a challenging problem to solve manually or in serial mode if the number of images is large, and this challenge gets exacerbated if such grouping is a part of an iterative

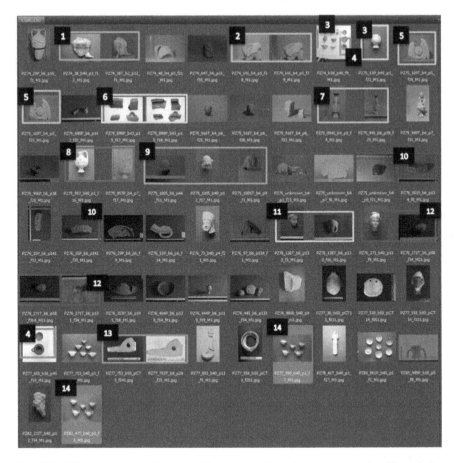

Fig. 13.6 Different images of the same artifact/s grouped together using rectangles. The majority of these groupings were found with the tool

workflow. This challenge can be mitigated, to a large extent, by using the OpenMP version of our solution in HTC mode. Running the OpenMP version of the code on 16 cores of a Stampede compute-node, while selecting all the three algorithms, it took approximately 24 min to compare the 62 images shown in Fig. 13.6. This processing time was brought down to less than a minute by doing such comparisons independently on 31 nodes, using all the 16 cores on each node, and having each node compare only two images with the whole set of images. Therefore, by using the OpenMP version in HTC mode, our time-to-results was shortened by 24 times.

It should be noted here that, depending upon the similarity threshold provided for different algorithms in our solution, the image-comparison results could include a range of very few to many false-positives. Further, depending upon the selection of the algorithm/s for image-comparison, and the quality of the input images, the number of matched images can also vary widely. As can be noticed from Fig. 13.7,

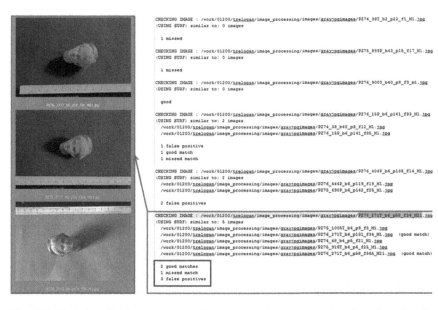

Fig. 13.7 Manual verification of results of image comparison after one iteration of running the code using the test dataset. In this snippet of the report template, two good matches, one missed match, and three false-positives are noted. During the next iteration of application run, when different threshold values were used, the tool matched all the four images accurately (see group 12 in Fig. 13.6), and there were no false-positives. Hence, the user of our solution needs to iteratively experiment with different threshold values to determine the values that would work best for their data collection

our solution can match images of the same artifact that were taken at different angles and using different color-settings. It can find all the duplicates and subimages with 100 % accuracy. Depending upon the threshold values provided by the user, the accuracy of finding similar and related images varied from 0 % (worst-case) to 80 % (best case). Some images in the subset could not be matched by our solution using the threshold values that we provided, and hence, we classified them as missed matches and lowered the accuracy of our solution. However, we found that by iterative testing using different threshold values and enhancement of the images with additional pre-processing steps, like adjusting contrast and normalization of the color histogram, the accuracy of the result improved in some cases.

One surprising outcome was noted in initial tests: photographs that were identified as "false-positives" (i.e., not containing the same objects), are in many cases, useful connections due to photographic backgrounds or other objects, like scale-bars. While those photographs may not constitute redundant subject matter, they are useful for connecting groups of images by context, such as objects photographed by the same photographer on the same date. That connection can provide useful provenance information and help reconstruct resource descriptions. However, such background noise in the images (especially scale-bars) that result in higher than

Base Image	Perfectly Matched Images	Missed Matches	Contextually Related or Similar	False-Positives	Notes
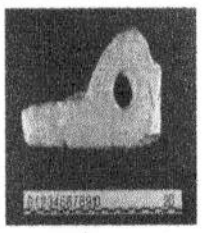		0	0	0	Images in group 13 of Figure 13.6 were matched with 100% accuracy and precision.
		0			Accurately matched the images in group 7 of Figure 13.6. False-positive image matches due to the shape of depression in it.
	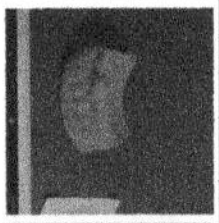 	0	0	0	The images in group 10 of Figure 13.6 are matched with 100% accuracy. The normalization of images helped in finding right matches with no false-positives.
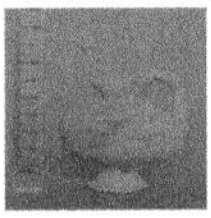		0	0	0	The images in group 8 of Figure 13.6 are matched with 100% accuracy and precision
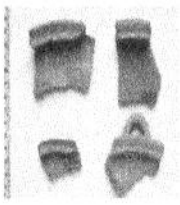	0		0	0	The images in group 6 in Figure 13.6 could not be matched. Images are front- and back-sides of objects.

Fig. 13.8 Classification of images into various categories using the generated report

expected false-positives might be totally undesired during some analysis. In such situations, either the images can be cropped to remove background objects before image comparison, or the objects can be masked with the background color. Efficiently handling the issue of background noise remains part of our future work.

A snippet of the characterization of the images under various categories using the report produced by our solution is shown in Fig. 13.8. While our solution cannot possibly identify all similar photographs without error, it is a useful guide for the data curators to navigate an otherwise totally overwhelming and disordered collection for which none of the other open-source tools have been helpful so far.

13.6 Future Work

Selective masking of the objects in the images to reduce false-positives or to detect images with specific background features is a desideratum for future development. We also intend to provide an annotation mechanism that can facilitate results assessment, annotation, and data management decision-making by the curators— for example, to delete or to keep duplicates. We also intend to extend the solution to produce reports that are easier to parse than a large text file. We have been working on evaluating and integrating the OCR technology in our solution as well. The OCR integration can facilitate in extracting machine-readable text from images and can be used as annotations.

13.7 Conclusion

In this chapter, we have presented a scalable approach for curating a large collection of images using HPC resources. Our approach can help in identifying not only duplicate images and subimages but also nearly identical images including, for example, analog photographs scanned multiple times, derived and/or slightly altered digital images (cropped, color balanced, rotated), and bracketed photos (multiple photographs of the same subject, with slight variations in focus and/or lighting conditions). Our approach also helps in tracking the provenance of the image-data. We have demonstrated our approach by applying it in the curation and preservation process of a large and evolving data collection. There are several applications of this approach beyond the areas of data curation and preservation. Some of the areas in which this approach can be useful are digital piracy, eDiscovery, and cyber-security.

Acknowledgments We are grateful to ICA, XSEDE, TACC, and the STAR Scholar Program for providing us with resources to conduct this research. We are also grateful to our colleague Antonio Gomez for helping during the installation process of dupeGuru on Stampede.

References

1. File profiling tool (DROID): The national archives, http://www.nationalarchives.gov. uk/information-management/manage-information/policy-process/digital-continuity/file-profiling-tool-droid/. Accessed 18 Feb 2016
2. ExifTool by Phil Harvey, http://www.sno.phy.queensu.ca/~phil/exiftool/. Accessed 18 Feb 2016
3. R. Datta, J. Li, J.Z. Wang, Content-based image retrieval: Approaches and trends of the new age, in *Proceedings of the 7th ACM SIGMM International Workshop on Multimedia Information Retrieval* (MIR '05), ACM, New York, 2005, pp. 253–262
4. D.-H. Kim, C.-W. Chung, Qcluster: Relevance feedback using adaptive clustering for content-based image retrieval, in *Proceedings of the 2003 ACM SIGMOD International Conference on Management of Data* (SIGMOD '03), ACM, New York, 2003, pp. 599–610

5. P.A. Viola, M.J. Jones, Rapid object detection using a boosted cascade of simple features, in *Proceedings of the 2001 IEEE Conference on Computer Vision and Pattern Recognition (CVPR 2001)*, 2001, pp. 511–518

6. Y. Ke, R. Sukthankar, L. Huston, An efficient parts-based near-duplicate and subimage retrieval system, in *Proceedings of the 12th Annual ACM International Conference on Multimedia (MULTIMEDIA '04)*, ACM, New York, 2004, pp. 869–876

7. The GNU image finding tool, https://www.gnu.org/software/gift/. Accessed 18 Feb 2016

8. LIRE: Lucene image retrieval, http://www.lire-project.net/. Accessed 18 Feb 2016

9. isk-daemon Github code repository, https://github.com/ricardocabral/iskdaemon. Accessed 18 Feb 2016

10. Java content based image retrieval (JCBIR), https://code.google.com/archive/p/jcbir/. Accessed 18 Feb 2016

11. Content based image retrieval using Matlab, http://www.mathworks.com/matlabcentral/fileexchange/42008-content-based-image-retrieval. Accessed 18 Feb 2016

12. dupeGuru Picture Edition, https://www.hardcoded.net/dupeguru_pe/. Accessed 18 Feb 2016

13. VisiPics, http://www.visipics.info/index.php?title=Main_Page. Accessed 18 Feb 2016

14. Q. Huynh-Thu, M. Ghanbari, The accuracy of PSNR in predicting video quality for different video scenes and frame rates. Telecommun. Syst. **49**(1), 35–48 (2010)

15. R. Brunelli, *Template Matching Techniques in Computer Vision: Theory and Practice* (Wiley, 2009), ISBN: 978-0-470-51706-2

16. H. Bay, A. Ess, T. Tuytelaars, L. Van Gool, Speeded-up robust features (SURF). Comput. Vis. Image Underst. **110**(3), 346–359 (2008)

17. G. Bradski, A. Kaehler, *Learning OpenCV: Computer Vision with the OpenCV Library* (O'Reilly Media, Sebastopol, CA, 2008), pp. 1–580

18. File profiling tool (DROID), http://www.nationalarchives.gov.uk/information-management/manage-information/policy-process/digital-continuity/file-profiling-tool-droid/. Accessed 15 Feb 2016

19. R. Arora, M. Esteva, J. Trelogan, Leveraging high performance computing for managing large and evolving data collections. Int. J. Digit. Curation **9**(2), 17–27 (2014)

20. OpenRefine, http://openrefine.org/. Accessed 18 Feb 2016

21. M. Esteva, J. Trelogan, W. Xu, A. Solis, N. Lauland, Lost in the data, aerial views of an archaeological collection, in *Proceedings of the 2013 Digital Humanities Conference*, 2013, pp. 174–177. ISBN: 978-1-60962-036-3

22. Tableau, http://www.tableau.com/. Accessed 18 Feb 2016

23. W. Xu, M. Esteva, J. Trelogan, T. Swinson, A case study on entity resolution for distant processing of big humanities data, in *Proceedings of the 2013 IEEE International Conference on Big Data*, 2013, pp. 113–120

24. Stampede supercomputer, https://www.tacc.utexas.edu/systems/stampede. Accessed 18 Feb 2016

25. ImageMagick, http://www.imagemagick.org/script/index.php. Accessed 18 Feb 2016

Chapter 14
Big Data Processing in the eDiscovery Domain

Sukrit Sondhi and Ritu Arora

Abstract Legal Electronic Discovery (*eDiscovery*) is a business domain that utilizes large volumes of data, in a variety of structured and unstructured formats to discover evidence that may be pertinent to legal proceedings, compliance needs, litigation or other investigations. The eDiscovery practitioners are typically required to produce results with short turnaround times, utilizing mostly commodity solutions that are available at their disposal, while still conforming to *legally defensible* standards of data management. Therefore, they use optimal strategies for data analysis and management to meet the time and quality requirements of their business. In addition to using such optimal strategies, the time-to-results during eDiscovery can be further reduced by taking advantage of the High-Throughput Computing (HTC) paradigm on High Performance Computing (HPC) platforms.

In this chapter, we discuss the strategies for data management and analysis from the legal eDiscovery domain, and also discuss the advantages of using HTC for eDiscovery. The various techniques that the eDiscovery practitioners have adopted to meet the Big Data challenge are transferrable to other domains as well. Hence, the discussion on these techniques as presented in this chapter could be relevant to a wide range of disciplines that are grappling with the deluge of Big Data.

14.1 Introduction to eDiscovery

Law firms, investigative agencies and legal departments of organizations often engage in discovery of information for use as *admissible evidence* in legal proceedings, or to support civil and criminal investigations. Over time, they have progressed to Electronic Discovery (*eDiscovery*), as a lot of information can now be discovered from digital media. Such information is often referred to as Electronically Stored Information, or *ESI*, and it includes documents, images, accounting databases,

S. Sondhi (✉)
Fulcrum Worldwide, NJ, USA
e-mail: sukrit@fulcrumww.com

R. Arora
Texas Advanced Computing Center, Austin, TX, USA
e-mail: rauta@tacc.utexas.edu

© Springer International Publishing Switzerland 2016   287
R. Arora (ed.), *Conquering Big Data with High Performance Computing*,
DOI 10.1007/978-3-319-33742-5_14

e-mail and even deleted data. eDiscovery is the detection and extraction of evidence from ESI, and its presentation for use in legal proceedings.

The eDiscovery process typically starts with the identification and capture of potentially useful information from various sources such as personal computers, email servers, databases, mobile devices, software applications and social media platforms. The information captured undergoes digital forensic analysis and culling to remove irrelevant parts, reduce the size of the datasets, and organize it better for subsequent processing. This refined information is imported or ingested into eDiscovery solutions that further process the information through operations such as text processing, image processing, indexing, tagging and automated analysis. Further, legal professionals review this processed information to identify *responsive* information and perform redactions. The information is considered as *responsive* if it is relevant to a legal proceeding for which eDiscovery is being done. Finally, the selected information is organized and produced in formats such as paper, PDF and TIFF and presented in the legal proceedings. A strict chain of custody of the data, and a log of the operations performed on it, need to be maintained throughout the eDiscovery process, else, the information may be inadmissible as evidence. Figure 14.1 provides a conceptual view of the eDiscovery process.

Note that the eDiscovery process as depicted in Fig. 14.1 is often iterative, and some of the steps involved may be executed in a different order, or even skipped, depending upon the need of the eDiscovery project. Also, note that the terms "data" and "information" are used almost interchangeably in eDiscovery.

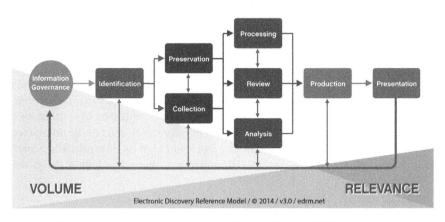

Fig. 14.1 Electronic Discovery Reference Model (*Source*: EDRM.NET [1])

14.2 Big Data Challenges in eDiscovery

Big Data consists of large datasets that are difficult to use and manage through conventional software tools. The difficulties in the management and processing of Big Data are encountered throughout the various stages of its lifecycle. Some of these difficulties include transferring large amounts of data from a storage resource to the computational resource over limited network bandwidth, performing near real-time comparisons across different data collections, and searching for specific subsets of data in a time-bound manner. Despite the aforementioned difficulties, Big Data also offers unprecedented opportunities for developing new insights. Therefore, it is important to develop a holistic understanding of the challenges that impact the timely discovery of new insights from large datasets so that such challenges can be mitigated through scalable tools and strategies.

In order to understand the connection between Big Data and eDiscovery, let us consider the example of the data collected during the accounting scandal of Enron Corporation that was revealed in 2001 [2]. One of the datasets investigated during this scandal consisted of over 1.7 million email messages generated by about 158 Enron executives. These messages are stored in Personal Storage Table (PST) files, contain attachments in diverse formats, and require over 160 GB of storage. There are multiple such datasets from this investigation. In eDiscovery, such heterogeneous datasets generally need to be analyzed for information relevant to the litigation in a timeframe ranging from a few days to a few months.

The analyses can include steps such as extraction of metadata, correlation of information and detailed manual reviews. It may be required to process many such datasets in a single eDiscovery project, and the processing of the datasets often results in an explosion of the data volume, further exacerbating the challenge. Even though the intermediate data can expand in volume during the various stages of processing, the goal of the eDiscovery process, as shown in Fig. 14.2, is to distill the input at each stage such that only relevant evidence is produced as the final outcome.

Like in the eDiscovery process, the Big Data workflows in other domains also need to develop insights and derive actionable information from a large volume and variety of data in a time-bound manner. However, there are some typical challenges and processes that are related to eDiscovery and computer forensics that might not be prevalent in other domains. For example, the ESI captured from various devices for eDiscovery may also include a copy of unused storage-space on the

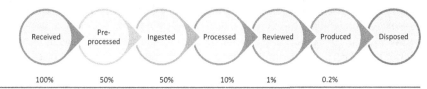

Fig. 14.2 The eDiscovery information lifecycle

device, from which deleted files, if any, can be retrieved. During the processing of heterogeneous data, some of the data may be found to be corrupt, or encrypted, or in formats different from the file-extensions. In addition to these, there could be other exception scenarios as well. Human intervention is required for handling such exceptions and finding workarounds. Another challenge in eDiscovery is that the search and analysis that is performed on a dataset may be based on false assumptions and imprecise search terms because all the facts of the associated legal matter are not known, and there may even have been intentional tampering of the data before it was captured. Therefore, the legal acumen of the professionals reviewing the data is a very important factor in modifying the search criteria during the review and analysis process, so that additional relevant information can be discovered.

14.3   Key Techniques Used to Process Big Data in eDiscovery

eDiscovery practitioners and service providers have developed various strategies in an attempt to overcome the challenges described in the preceding section, while still maintaining the strategic advantages of their proprietary algorithms that are locked within legacy applications. Such strategies are often comprised of unconventional but effective combinations of multiple elements such as data processing techniques, storage and computing platform configurations, application re-engineering, data analysis methodologies and predictive analysis techniques [3].

Some of the key strategies from eDiscovery that can be useful for processing and managing Big Data in other domains as well are: culling, metadata extraction, data-partitioning and archival, sampling and workload profiling, multi-pass inter-active analysis and processing, near-duplicate identification, software refactoring and selective parallelization, fuzzy search, concept search, clustering, predictive analytics and visual analytics. These strategies are further described in this section.

14.3.1   Culling to Reduce Dataset Size

The main goal of processing data in an eDiscovery project is to discover and extract relevant evidence from the large amount of *potentially responsive* information that constitutes the initial dataset. The non-responsive or irrelevant information is eliminated from the dataset being processed through various stages of its lifecycle. However, some of the information captured can be eliminated from the dataset even before any intensive processing is done, through simple actions, such as filtering the dataset by a date range, deduplication, filtering by *custodian* ('keeper' of the data) and filtering by document types (see Fig. 14.3). This narrowing down of the scope of the data to be processed, using readily available characteristics of the data, is known as *culling*. Having an appropriate culling strategy for a dataset is very important in order to reduce the time, effort and cost associated with eDiscovery.

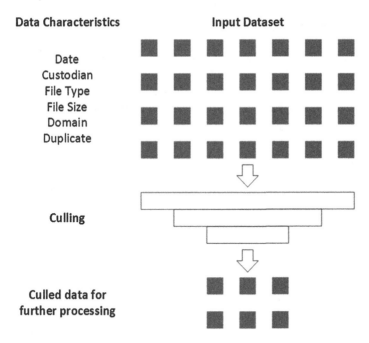

Fig. 14.3 Culling the eDiscovery data

14.3.2   *Metadata Extraction*

In addition to obvious characteristics of eDiscovery data, such as filenames and file sizes, it is also helpful to extract additional metadata from the datasets, such as file formats, authors, versions, tags, comments, creation date, last modification date, image resolutions and access privileges. This is typically done during the early stages of processing the dataset. This metadata extraction may be done using a wide variety of tools, including non-portable desktop applications such as Microsoft Office [4], specialized commercial software such as Oracle Outside In [5], and open-source software such as Apache Tika [6] and DROID [7]. The metadata extracted is used to profile and index the dataset, which helps in taking decisions for further processing for the dataset, and is also instrumental in query and analysis of the dataset during review and production stages of the eDiscovery process.

After metadata extraction, further processing of eDiscovery datasets typically involves extraction of text from various document formats, and also extraction of text from digital images (pictures and photos) using Optical Character Recognition (OCR). This extracted text is indexed, and often correlated with the previously extracted metadata in order to determine whether a document should be considered for inclusion in the evidence produced by the eDiscovery process.

14.3.3   Dataset Partitioning and Archival

The data to be processed and analyzed for a single eDiscovery project may be received as multiple datasets, and in multiple batches. Hence, the datasets may also get processed in separate batches, although they may be interrelated and even overlapping. These datasets and their processed results are typically consolidated in the eDiscovery project, in order to form a complete and holistic view of the information. During processing, intermediate results such as attachments, embedded documents and text are extracted from the files in the datasets, leading to increase in the data and metadata volume. The large volume of data tends to unacceptably slow down many processes in the eDiscovery project, including ingestion, processing, search, analysis and legal review. Essentially, the data to be processed often surpasses the scalability thresholds of the eDiscovery solutions.

To overcome these scalability challenges, the eDiscovery project data is often partitioned (physically separated into groups) in the data stores where it resides. This partitioning is different from traditional database partitioning as it applies to multiple components of the eDiscovery solution, including (1) unstructured source data that may be partitioned by custodian, (2) pre-processed data that may be partitioned by its metadata attributes, (3) indexes and metadata that may be partitioned according to relational database partitioning strategies, and (4) processed data, including extracted text, that may be partitioned by time windows, or other attributes, that provide an equitable distribution of the data across the partitions, to speed up search and analysis operations. The partitioned datasets enable the use of High-Throughput Computing (HTC), with or without using technologies like Hadoop, during the data processing stage. As shown in Fig. 14.4, using HTC, multiple copies of an application can be run concurrently to process the different subsets of data, thereby, reducing the overall time-to-results.

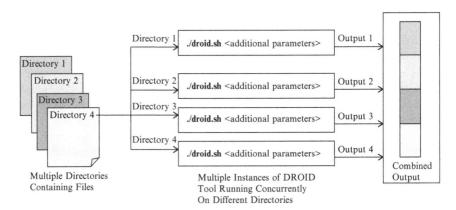

Fig. 14.4 Extracting metadata from a large collection of documents in HTC mode using a software named DROID—each instance of the DROID tool processes files in different directories

Along with partitioning, archival strategies are also important to keep the data volumes at manageable levels. If a significant chunk of data has outlived its usefulness during any stage of processing, it should be considered a candidate for immediate archival, in order to boost the performance and scalability of the solution. The actual decision on "if and when to archive" is taken after factoring in the benefits and the overheads of doing the archival, along with interdependencies of the data.

As an example, in large eDiscovery projects, the review stage may involve multiple teams of legal professionals reviewing the results of the eDiscovery processing by manually inspecting the document sets shortlisted for review. This process may even take many months, and the legal professionals need to search and query the processed data as part of their review process. Some of the search and query operations may be long-running, taking several hours to complete. Partitioning strategies help to some extent, but the queries may need to run across multiple partitions of the data, and may still not be fast enough, as the total data and result-set sizes are still quite large. In such a scenario, it may be possible to divide the review process into several sequential 'investigation areas' that correspond to subsets of data in each partition. As these investigation areas get completed, the related data can be archived from each partition, speeding up the subsequent review process.

14.3.4 Sampling and Workload Profiling

One commonly used strategy in eDiscovery is to use Early Case Assessment (ECA) [8] in an attempt to reduce the size of the dataset to be processed, and to reduce the amount of processing required.

For example, an attorney who is working on a case involving wrongful termination of an employee from an organization may be interested in email communications between key executives of that organization. After processing the documents and email records captured from that organization, it may be discovered that contrary to the expectation, over 90 % of the information processed pertains to irrelevant or *non-responsive* content such as sales interactions, marketing campaigns and pictures of corporate events. Therefore, the processing of the dataset was far more expensive and time-consuming than necessary.

To minimize such scenarios, ECA can be performed on a judiciously selected sample of the input dataset, and better decisions or assumptions can be made about processing the entire dataset. For example, in a case involving possible illegal accounting practices in a business, prosecuting attorneys may first perform ECA on the email messages of a few individuals, covering only one financial quarter. They may proceed to do 'full processing' on a bigger dataset only if they find adequate responsive documents in the ECA phase. Otherwise, they may focus the investigation on other datasets, or on other legal strategies such as summons and subpoenas for witness testimony. The ECA process may also uncover obstacles or exceptions that can occur during processing, such as unexpected formats and password-protected files, thereby, enabling proactive measures to address those challenges.

14.3.5 Multi-Pass (Iterative) Processing and Interactive Analysis

The objective of eDiscovery, as the name suggests, is to discover information pertinent to a legal matter in the ESI available. It is not known beforehand what the relevant information may be, and in what form it may be discovered. Typically, a set of keywords or topics is taken as a starting point to initiate a search, but subsequently, additional topics may be discovered, and the initial set of topics might even diminish in their relative significance. The information discovered may give new direction to the eDiscovery process, requiring a change in strategy.

For example, in a case involving accounting malpractice, the eDiscovery process may reveal a communication pattern that indicates additional complicit individuals, and it may reveal documents that exist only as scanned images of poor quality, including some in an unforeseen language like Spanish, attached to email messages. This discovery would require additional processing, including advanced Optical Character Recognition (OCR) that is configured to recognize Spanish.

In an ideal world, the processing of input datasets in eDiscovery would be so thorough that all relevant information is revealed immediately. However, eDiscovery is generally so costly and time-consuming that the amount of processing to be done needs to be minimized. In such a scenario, it makes sense to conduct eDiscovery as an *iterative* or *multi-pass* process. Each iteration yields information that serves as input to the next iteration, until no further iterations are necessary. The information learned at each stage can be used to process the next stage more intelligently, also incorporating the human knowledge of the legal experts involved to take better processing decisions for subsequent iterations. In the example above, the first iteration might reveal the need for several additional processing tasks, including Spanish-language OCR, which would be performed in the next iteration of the processing. Similarly, there may be other actions taken between processing iterations, such as handling exceptions and narrowing or broadening the search within the dataset. Such feedback and learning mechanisms are critical to having a high-quality, cost-effective and defensible eDiscovery process.

14.3.6 Search and Review Methods

eDiscovery costs for a single case can run into millions of dollars, and are often the largest component of the total litigation costs. The costs involved are high because of the time that legal professionals need to spend in reviewing and analyzing potentially responsive documents. This also leads to delays in the legal process. Therefore, it has become very important to use advanced and automated mechanisms to reduce the overall time and cost involved. The process of using automated mechanisms to support search and review is known as *Technology Assisted Review* (*TAR*) [9] or computer-assisted review.

In order to have an effective TAR process, it is not adequate to extract text from the unstructured input datasets and index the text for convenient querying and search. A simple keyword search may yield a lot of relevant information, but may also miss a lot of information and may include information that is not relevant. For the TAR process to be considered effective and high-quality, the *precision* as well as the *recall* of the eDiscovery results has to be high. Precision is the ratio of responsive results (documents) retrieved to the total number of results retrieved. Recall is the ratio of the responsive results retrieved, to the total number of known responsive documents in the dataset.

Therefore, eDiscovery platforms provide a variety of advanced search and review methods, such as:

- *Stemming*, which broadens the search to include variations and derived terms.
- *Proximity search*, which searches for keywords in close proximity (or *near*) to each other.
- *Concept search*, which uses advanced algorithms to detect matches at the conceptual level, without relying on any specific keywords.
- *Fuzzy search*, which uses common variations of words and provides a tolerance for slight misspellings.
- *Clustering*, which groups related documents together, so that discovering one document from the set may be enough to lead to the others.
- *Near-duplicate identification*, which detects documents that are nearly identical, saving a lot of review and analysis time if the dataset has many such near-duplicates.
- Pattern analysis, such as communication pattern analysis, which may give insights on the flow of information and involvement of individuals in a particular matter.
- *Sentiment analysis*, which detects expression of emotions in textual content, thereby providing a deeper understanding of the matter being investigated.
- *Predictive coding*, wherein software algorithms automatically organize documents in terms of their responsiveness, by first learning the necessary rules and criteria from a human reviewer.

The search and analysis methods used in eDiscovery are generally provided to the eDiscovery practitioners through a variety of command-line and graphical interfaces, with many of the implementations taken from the text mining and Natural Language Processing (NLP) domains. In Sect. 14.5 of this chapter, we provide an example of how clustering and analysis of email messages can be done using the "R" programming language. Details of the search methodologies commonly used in eDiscovery are available at [10]. However, some of the techniques, such as pattern analysis, sentiment analysis and predictive coding, are specialized for eDiscovery, and based on advanced proprietary algorithms of eDiscovery solution providers. The eDiscovery solution providers treat these algorithms as closely guarded trade secrets, as they often give a unique competitive edge to the eDiscovery platforms by helping discover the proverbial needle of evidence in the haystack of data with amazing speed and intelligence.

The aforementioned search and review methods provide a powerful toolbox to the eDiscovery practitioner to cast a wide net that will capture a high percentage of the responsive documents (high-recall), and then narrow down the results quickly to eliminate false positives (high-precision). However, while the burden on the eDiscovery practitioners is reduced, the burden on the eDiscovery technology platforms is increased, which is one of the main reasons for increasing scalability and performance of eDiscovery platforms.

14.3.7 Visual Analytics

In eDiscovery, there are many characteristics of the data and relationships among data elements that need to be discovered or inferred from the data. For example, corporate email and document sets may reveal patterns such as concurrent communication activity on the same topic among separate groups of individuals, suggesting an *offline* communication link, which could be an indicator of collusion or conspiracy. Similarly, there may be other interesting patterns that come to light, such as code words for secret topics and timelines of deleted files and email, resulting from wrongdoers trying to cover their tracks.

Effectively detecting such patterns through manual review and analysis of millions of documents would be exceedingly difficult and not practically achievable within the constraints of typical eDiscovery projects. Even with automated processing of the datasets and traditional reporting mechanisms, it would be very effort-intensive and unreliable to detect such patterns by scanning through numerous reports of multidimensional data. In such a situation, an interactive visualization of the data can help detect broad trends much faster, by focusing the knowledge and intelligence of domain experts on a representation of the "big picture", rather than trying to inspect small parts of the dataset and piece together the big picture.

Visual analytics can be done with the help of a variety of visualization tools that generate intuitive graphical representations of data. Some tools, such as D3.js [11] and dygraphs [12], offer very flexible open-source frameworks for visualization, but are developer-centric and have a learning-curve. There are also some free and user-friendly tools such as Tableau [13], although the free editions of such tools typically have limitations that hinder large-scale or commercial use. Additionally, there are commercial tools like QlikView [14] that offer extensive visualization features with good ease-of-use. Using such tools, it is possible to interactively browse through datasets, discover relationships, drill-down into details, and take decisions about subsequent processing and use of the data.

14.3.8   Software Refactoring and Parallelization

Many legacy software solutions for eDiscovery have advanced algorithms, such as predictive coding and pattern analysis, for detecting potentially responsive information in heterogeneous datasets. However, these solutions do not scale up or perform well in the face of the increasing volumes of data that need to be processed in eDiscovery projects. Consequently, eDiscovery practitioners have evolved the aforementioned techniques to help them process and manage the Big Data in eDiscovery. To take advantage of these techniques, the software architecture of many of the existing eDiscovery solutions needed to be refactored. The refactoring can be classified into two main areas of improvements (1) flexibility and modularity, and (2) scalability and throughput.

The first type of refactoring, done to improve flexibility and modularity of the eDiscovery solutions, includes (1) "externalizing" software configurations and storing them where they can be dynamically updated, (2) automating exception handling, (3) separating concerns like user-interface and data processing, and (4) externalizing workflows so that execution-time decisions can alter subsequent processing steps. These changes enable the legacy software to support techniques like multi-pass processing and interactive analysis as mentioned in Sect. 14.3.5 of this chapter.

The second type of refactoring, done to improve the scalability and throughput of the eDiscovery solutions, includes implementation of workflow management, pipelining of processing tasks, making the processing components *thread-safe*, and selective parallelization of the program logic. Thread-safety is achieved by ensuring that the software programs do not manipulate shared data structures in a way that causes a problem when multiple instances (or threads) of a task are executed concurrently. The refactoring done may also include making the software more platform-independent or portable. Such changes can enhance the data-parallelism and task-parallelism (see Chap. 1) in the solutions so that they can take advantage of HTC or HPC.

14.4   Limitations of Existing eDiscovery Solutions

Traditionally, eDiscovery solutions relied on programmatic execution of native desktop applications (such as Microsoft Office and Adobe components) to extract text and metadata from documents. These solutions offered rich functionality, but suffered from performance, scalability, and manageability problems due to the burden of their legacy, as the desktop applications were not engineered for scalability or performance.

To overcome these problems, many eDiscovery solutions have evolved to leverage modern software architectures, cloud computing and appliance models (a tightly coupled hardware and software solution packaged together as an appliance).

A couple of examples of such solutions are HP eDiscovery [15] and Veritas eDiscovery Platform [16]. Such solutions have replaced the profusion of desktop components with a smaller set of processing utilities that extract text and metadata from many document formats, with much better scalability and performance. However, the rich document manipulation capabilities of the legacy desktop applications had to be sacrificed for this. So while the overall processing is faster and more streamlined, the number of unusual formats and exception scenarios that can be comprehensively handled by such eDiscovery solutions is less than that of legacy eDiscovery solutions.

More recently, several high-end eDiscovery solutions have emerged, that offer high-scalability and significantly faster time-to-results than legacy software by utilizing clusters of commodity (industry-standard) hardware, and software technologies like Hadoop [17]. These high-end solutions struggle to leverage the value locked in legacy software tools and proprietary algorithms, because those legacy components are not designed to take advantage of Big Data technologies like Hadoop.

Hence, the rich legacy solutions for eDiscovery, and the powerful modern software and hardware platforms that are typically used for Big Data processing and management cannot sufficiently take advantage of each other. This gap between the old and new solutions can be bridged to some extent by HPC platforms. The HPC platforms provide a powerful and comprehensive computing environment, where legacy (but portable) eDiscovery software and modern Big Data technologies can coexist synergistically. This landscape of eDiscovery solutions is depicted in Fig. 14.5, wherein, the limitations of existing eDiscovery solutions are highlighted.

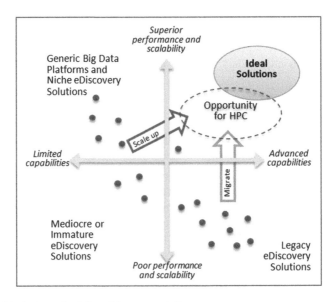

Fig. 14.5 Limitations of existing eDiscovery solutions

Towards the bottom-right of the quadrant depicted in Fig. 14.5, we have the legacy eDiscovery solutions that offer advanced capabilities by virtue of the profusion of legacy components that they utilize, but also suffer from performance and scalability problems due to the same legacy. Many such solutions are developed in portable technologies such as Java and can utilize HPC to scale up, without abandoning their powerful proprietary (and legacy) algorithms. At the diagonally opposite end of the quadrant, we have generic (not specialized for eDiscovery) Big Data platforms from vendors like IBM [18] and Oracle [19], and also niche eDiscovery solutions like Splunk [20], which mines information from IT logs. Such solutions often have Hadoop integrated with them and can run on commodity hardware. Finally, we have the bottom-left quadrant consisting of solutions that have neither advanced capabilities, nor high performance. These solutions may still be considered effective in many cases, because they offer lower costs, or because they are relatively young (in their current form, although they could have legacy components) and 'upwardly mobile', so they may be moving towards a better position on the quadrant. For such upstarts, HPC offers the ability to scale up so that they can improve their standing versus the competition faster. Hence we see that for most segments of the eDiscovery solution landscape depicted, HPC can offer some advantages.

14.5 Using HPC for eDiscovery

HPC platforms (or supercomputers) are an aggregation of high-end computing, storage, and networking resources (as described in Chaps. 1 and 2). Due to their innovative and modern architectural elements, HPC platforms have high theoretical peak performance. These platforms can be used for running both serial (HTC) and concurrent (parallel) applications. A legacy application can be run on HPC platforms without requiring any code reengineering if it is portable (or is platform-independent) and can be used in the batch-processing mode.

Legacy eDiscovery applications could require code reengineering for parallelization so that they can perform efficiently on HPC platforms. However, the performance gains achieved by running such applications "as is" in the HTC mode (see Chaps. 1 and 4) are in many situations sufficient for the needs of the stakeholders. The stakeholders could be more interested in short time-to-results than in developing highly efficient code that optimally utilizes the underlying hardware resources in a platform.

In this section we further describe the various ways in which HPC can be leveraged during the following stages of the eDiscovery lifecycle: Data Collection, Data Ingestion, Pre-processing, Processing, Review and Analysis, and Archival.

14.5.1 Data Collection and Data Ingestion

The key eDiscovery tasks involved during this stage are: data collection and the loading of data into the defined project structure. For this stage, it will be ideal to have HPC platforms with the following characteristic features: (1) very large-scale flash storage tier with high network bandwidth, (2) flash storage racks connected directly to fast processors, (3) storage that is replicated across different geographical locations, and (4) parallel and distributed filesystems. The Wrangler supercomputer [21] at TACC [22] is an example of such a platform.

The high-speed flash storage makes it possible to do millions of I/O operations per second. It enables ultra-fast random access to large numbers of small files. Having data on a parallel filesystem that is shared across different platforms can help in accessing the data from different platforms without involving any data movement. Hence, using a platform with the aforementioned characteristics can significantly accelerate the rate of processing and analytics during eDiscovery. Replicating the storage across geographically distant platforms mitigates the risk of data loss in the event of any catastrophe at a particular site. Hence, high-availability of data can be ensured during the eDiscovery process.

For supporting the activities related to this eDiscovery stage, it is also recommended that the chosen HPC platform supports techniques and tools for data partitioning, efficient and encrypted data transfer protocols like rsync [23], and a data management system like iRODS [24].

14.5.2 Pre-processing

This stage of eDiscovery mainly involves filtering of content, deduplication, metadata extraction, and quality control. Various tools and techniques are used during this stage, like: (1) culling of content is done using customized scripts, (2) data extraction from images is done using tools like Tesseract [25], (3) deduplication of data is done using tools like FSlint [26], and (4) metadata and data extraction is done using tools like DROID, FITS [27], and Apache Tika.

HPC platforms having the following characteristics can impact this stage of eDiscovery: high-end compute servers, high-speed interconnect with low latency, and multiple-levels of memory hierarchy including large amounts of local FLASH memory and DRAM on the compute-servers. These characteristics can help in conducting the various pre-processing steps in a scalable and efficient manner. Portable legacy applications can be run on such high-end hardware in HTC mode, thereby reducing the time-to-results. The applications that require caching of large amounts of data in memory can benefit from the recommended characteristic features of the platform. A parallel filesystem distributes a file across multiple storage servers and provides concurrent access to multiple tasks running in parallel. If large files are involved during eDiscovery such that they cannot be accommodated on a single storage target (hard-disk or other storage media), such files can be distributed across multiple storage targets on a parallel filesystem while still appearing as a unified entity to the end-user.

14.5.3 Processing

During this stage, the data is processed to discover insights through an iterative and interactive process. The various tools and techniques that are involved during this stage include selective parallelization, ECA/sampling and multi-pass processing.

High-end platforms that support iterative and interactive analysis for data-intensive computing, and provide large amounts of memory per compute-server can accelerate the rate of discovery during this stage. Like mentioned before, such platforms provide support for running portable legacy applications on fast hardware in HTC mode, and thereby contribute in reducing the time-to-results. Software packages like Apache Spark [28] can be used during this stage. Such packages can be provisioned on traditional HPC platforms using additional software like myHadoop [29]. The Wrangler supercomputer at TACC and the Gordon supercomputer [30] at the San Diego Supercomputing Center are examples of HPC platforms with the aforementioned characteristics.

14.5.4 Review and Analysis

The processed content is visualized and reviewed during this stage. The tools and techniques used during this stage include interactive analysis, visualization, smart search, visualization tools like Tableau, tools for data mining and statistical analysis (e.g., R [31]).

The HPC platforms that are recommended for this stage of eDiscovery would have compute-servers with the latest Graphical Processing Unit (GPU) accelerators, have large amounts of memory and storage per server, and have fast interconnects between compute-servers to facilitate high-speed internode communication and I/O traffic. An example of such an HPC platform is the Maverick supercomputer [32] at TACC. Such HPC platforms can help in reducing the time taken in data organization, identifying patterns in data at an abstract-level, and performing advanced statistical analysis.

14.5.5 Archival

During this stage of eDiscovery the data is archived as per the standard practices of organizations. Redundant arrays of inexpensive tapes can be used for storing the archival copies of data. Such arrays of tapes ensure high-bandwidth for I/O operations and high reliability of archived data at a low-cost.

The various characteristics of HPC systems that are recommended for the various stages of the eDiscovery process can be made available in a single platform or on separate platforms as well. However, if there are separate platforms used for pre-processing, processing, and analysis of data during the eDiscovery process, then having a shared parallel filesystem is recommended for reducing the data movement, thereby reducing the time-to-results.

14.6   Accelerating the Rate of eDiscovery Using HPC: A Case Study

In order to understand the pros and cons of using HPC platforms for the eDiscovery process, we conducted a few steps in the eDiscovery process on the Stampede supercomputer [33]. We analyzed a mini-corpus of emails of 131 Enron executives on Stampede and on a desktop-class computer. This corpus is available at [34] and is 54 GB in size.

The emails in the Enron mini-corpus were in the PST format and the corpus was directly downloaded to Stampede. Using the readPST [35] tool, the PST files were converted into "mbox" files (that is, the binary to text conversion was done). It took approximately 12 min to convert the PST files into "mbox" format using one process (running on a single core). In total, there were 4055 mbox files generated. We repeated the process of PST to mbox conversion using 26 compute-cores in the HTC mode. Each compute-core had an instance of the readPST tool running and working on PST files starting with a particular alphabet. By using 26 concurrent instances of the tool, the time required for PST to mbox conversion decreased to approximately 2 min.

The large mbox files were parsed using an email parser written in Python. This parser writes each thread of email communication in a separate text file while ignoring certain information in the mail-headers. It took approximately 90 min to run the parser on a compute-core of Stampede to generate the desired text files. We repeated this step by running 18 instances of the parser on 18 compute-cores of Stampede while using the same set of mbox files. By using 18 compute-cores, the processing time during this step came down to approximately 5 min. There were several thousands of small and medium-sized text files that were produced during this step. One of our goals during the analysis of this large collection of email files (in text format) was to categorize them automatically under different classes on the basis of their content and structure. This is known as clustering and we clustered the email corpus using R.

In order to prepare the corpus for clustering, we first pre-process it to transform all the emails to consistent case, remove punctuation and make the text in the emails *sparse* by removing commonly occurring words like, "a", "an", "the" (such words are known as stop-words). Next, we stem the document. During stemming, the words are reduced to their base form. For example, words like "country" and "countries" are stemmed to "countri".

After pre-processing the email corpus, we applied the R function for Latent Dirichlet Allocation (LDA) [36] algorithm in order to do topic modeling. The LDA

Fig. 14.6 Comparison of time taken during certain steps of eDiscovery using a single core and multiple cores on the Stampede supercomputer

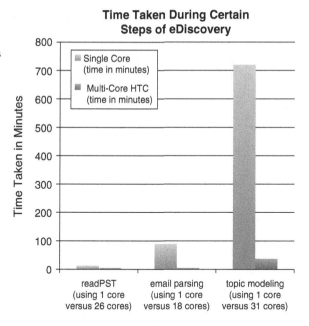

algorithm considers documents (here emails) as mixtures of topics and helps in finding the set of topics that can best describe the documents (here emails). The topic modeling [37] package of R provides the implementation of the LDA algorithm as a function. It takes more than 12 h to do the topic modeling of the entire email corpus, and files need to be incrementally analyzed to avoid failures due to memory issues. However, by running 31 simultaneous copies of the R script independently, such that each copy worked on a different set of emails, the total time taken for topic modeling for the entire corpus was approximately 37 min. Using LDA, we classified emails under ten topics.

The comparison of the time taken for converting the PST files to the mbox format, for parsing emails, and for doing topic modeling using single cores and multiple cores is shown in the graph in Fig. 14.6.

The results of topic modeling were exported to CSV files that were visualized using Tableau on a desktop-class computer. The wordcloud of top 100 words related to couple of topics is shown in Figs. 14.7 and 14.8. As can be noticed from Fig. 14.7, the wordcloud of Topic 9 consisted of the names of different countries, their currency, and financial trading. Therefore, the emails that these words came from are very likely related to financial trading across different countries. Two such emails associated with this wordcloud are shown in Fig. 14.9, and the manual verification confirmed that the wordcloud, and hence the emails under Topic 9 were indeed related to financial trading. On the other hand, the wordcloud shown in Fig. 14.8 indicates that the emails related to Topic 7 are not related to the business of Enron. These words indicated that the emails from which they came could be

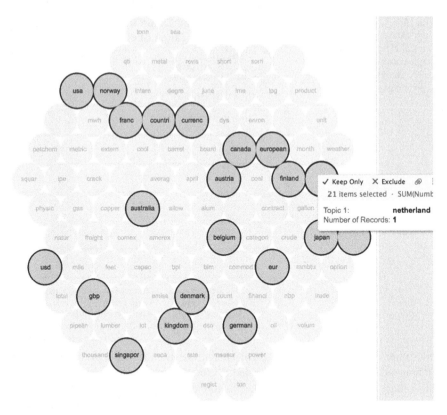

Fig. 14.7 Wordcloud of terms from some of the emails categorized under Topic 9 cluster which is mainly related to countries, regions, currency, and finance

related to informal chitchat. Manual sampling of the emails classified under Topic 7 confirmed that those were indeed related to non-business topics that included jokes, quotes, and informal communication between employees.

14.7   Conclusions and Future Direction

The data processing and management challenges faced by the eDiscovery practitioners are plenty. However, the eDiscovery community has tackled many of those challenges effectively using innovative and well-defined approaches. To further mitigate some of the challenges related to the scalability of their solutions, a lot of eDiscovery solution providers are now looking towards HPC and modernization of legacy applications. The innovative approaches and models for eDiscovery, when implemented on HPC platforms, would yield a powerful solution addressing Big Data challenges.

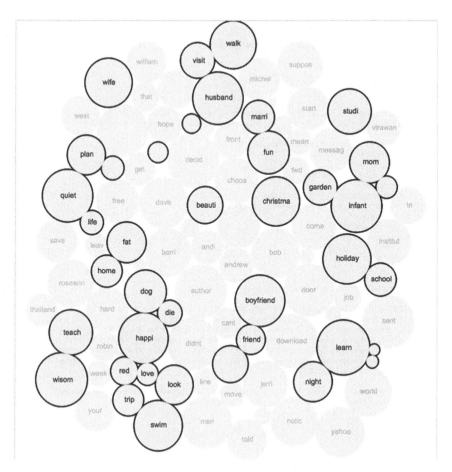

Fig. 14.8 Wordcloud of terms from some of the emails categorized under Topic 7 cluster are mainly related to quotes, jokes, fun, and informal office chitchat

With the continuous growth of data in various disciplines, and the increased adoption of social media, a multitude of mainstream organizations are facing challenges similar to eDiscovery practitioners. For example, like in the eDiscovery domain, several other domains are also having to deal with heterogeneous unstructured content such as business documents, email and personal computer files. The Electronic Discovery Reference Model (EDRM) that we presented in this chapter can be adapted into a general framework for information governance by these other domains as well. Hence, the approaches for processing large datasets in the eDiscovery domain provide many valuable lessons that are transferrable to other domains as well.

```
> sample(which(df.emails.topics$"9" > .95), 10)
[1] 3941 6985 7013 7104 6660 7746 3084 3083 6815 6673
```
R code for sampling emails clustered under topic 9.

```
> as.character(enron[[3941]])
"
```
R code for displaying the content of an email.

Gentlemen
Attached is a fairly comprehensive list of companies in various sectors of the petroleum complex. It is by no means comprehensive and I am sure there are several players that have been left out inadvertently. I broke it down as follows:
Oil & Refined Products
Trading & Marketing Companies (Physical & Financial)
Financial Traders (Generally Financial only)
North American Refiners
Foreign Refiners w/ US Marketing Cos.
Asian Trading Houses
Convenience Store Operators (For rack marketing idea)
Crude Oil Producers (main business, not really into trading)
Oil Products Pipelines
Petchem, Chemical, and NGL
Gas Liquids Companies
Chemical & Petrochemical Companies
Industrial Gas Companies

Product List
List of products with perceived commodity products bolded

It is a bit difficult to put some companies into one bucket or another due to the cross over, but I tried. I also should receive much better information tomorrow on the NGL companies that is more granular. The list is intended to be a beginning and my intent was to begin eliminating companies to focus in on who are the dominant players in the major products in the various parts of the country. Some players such as Global and Northville, for example are dominant in the Northeast, but not as much elsewhere. Methanex, for example is the dominant Methanol producer/trader. Enterprise is a big importer/storage owner in Mt. Belvieu so should be a good company to approach for the NGLs. Once we refine the list a bit more, we will have a basis on who are the most likely candidates.

Let me know what you think, be forgiving of errors, and be mindful that this is a working document. Before we start researching specific companies, let's whittle this list down considerably.

JC
"

```
> as.character(enron[[7746]])
"In today's Daily Update you'll find free reports on Juniper
```
R code for displaying the content of an email.

Networks (JNPR) and the auto industry; an invitation to take advantage of Multex Investor's NEW Personal Finance Channel; Premier Investor Network's Derek Baltimore in the Analyst Corner; reports on Internet infrastructure, telecommunications platforms, and more.
For free research, editor's picks, and more come to the Daily Investor:
http://www.multexinvestor.com/AF004627/magazinecover.asp?promo=unl&d=20001213# investor"

Fig. 14.9 Content of two emails related to Topic 9 confirm that, as predicted by the wordcloud shown in Fig. 14.7, these mails were indeed related to financial trading

References

1. E-Discovery Reference Model (EDRM), http://www.edrm.net. Accessed 9 Mar 2016
2. K. Eichenwald, *Conspiracy of Fools: A True Story* (Broadway Books, New York, 2005)
3. S. Sondhi, R. Arora, Applying lessons from e-discovery to process big data using HPC, in *Proceedings of the 2014 Annual Conference on Extreme Science and Engineering Discovery Environment*, ACM, New York, 2014.
4. Microsoft Office, https://products.office.com/en-US/. Accessed 9 Mar 2016

5. Oracle Outside In technology, http://www.oracle.com/us/technologies/embedded/025613.htm. Accessed 9 Mar 2016
6. Apache Tika, https://tika.apache.org/. Accessed 9 Mar 2016
7. Digital Record Object Identification (DROID) tool, http://www.nationalarchives.gov.uk/information-management/manage-information/preserving-digital-records/droid/. Accessed 9 Mar 2016
8. Early Case Assessment (ECA), http://www.edrm.net/resources/glossaries/grossman-cormack/eca. Accessed 9 Mar 2016
9. Technology Assisted Review (TAR), http://www.edrm.net/resources/glossaries/grossman-cormack. Accessed 9 Mar 2016
10. EDRM search guide, http://www.edrm.net/resources/edrm-stages-explained. Accessed 9 Mar 2016
11. Data-Driven Documents, D3.js, https://d3js.org/. Accessed 9 Mar 2016
12. dygraphs, http://dygraphs.com/. Accessed 9 Mar 2016
13. Tableau, http://www.tableau.com/. Accessed 9 Mar 2016
14. QlikView, http://www.qlik.com/products/qlikview. Accessed 9 Mar 2016
15. HP eDiscovery, http://www8.hp.com/us/en/software-solutions/ediscovery-software/. Accessed 9 Mar 2016
16. Veritas eDiscovery platform, https://www.veritas.com/product/information-governance/ediscovery-platform. Accessed 9 Mar 2016
17. Apache Hadoop, http://hadoop.apache.org/. Accessed 9 Mar 2016
18. IBM eDiscovery solutions, http://www-03.ibm.com/software/products/en/ediscovery. Accessed 9 Mar 2016
19. Oracle Big Data, https://www.oracle.com/big-data/index.html. Accessed 9 Mar 2016
20. Splunk for e-Discovery, http://www.splunk.com/view/SP-CAAACPQ. Accessed 9 Mar 2016
21. Wrangler supercomputer, https://portal.tacc.utexas.edu/user-guides/wrangler. Accessed 9 Mar 2016
22. Texas Advanced Computing Center (TACC), https://www.tacc.utexas.edu/home. Accessed 9 Mar 2016
23. Rsync utility, https://rsync.samba.org/. Accessed 9 Mar 2016
24. Integrated Rule-Oriented Data System (iRODS), http://irods.org/. Accessed 9 Mar 2016
25. Tesseract, https://github.com/tesseract-ocr/tesseract. Accessed 9 Mar 2016
26. FSlint, http://www.pixelbeat.org/fslint/. Accessed 9 Mar 2016
27. File Information Tool Set (FITS), http://projects.iq.harvard.edu/fits/home. Accessed 9 Mar 2016
28. Apache Spark, http://spark.apache.org/. Accessed 9 Mar 2016
29. myHadoop, https://github.com/glennklockwood/myhadoop. Accessed 9 Mar 2016
30. Gordon supercomputer, http://www.sdsc.edu/services/hpc/hpc_systems.html#gordon. Accessed 9 Mar 2016
31. The R project for statistical computing, https://www.r-project.org/about.html. Accessed 9 Mar 2016
32. Maverick supercomputer, https://portal.tacc.utexas.edu/user-guides/maverick. Accessed 9 Mar 2016
33. Stampede supercomputer, https://www.tacc.utexas.edu/stampede/. Accessed 9 Mar 2016
34. The Enron data reconstruction project, http://enrondata.org/content/. Accessed 9 Mar 2016
35. ReadPST tool, http://www.five-ten-sg.com/libpst/rn01re01.html. Accessed 9 Mar 2016
36. D.M. Blei, A.Y. Ng, M.I. Jordan, Latent Dirichlet allocation. J. Mach. Learn. Res. 3(March 2003), 993–1022 (2003)
37. A gentle introduction to topic modeling using R, https://eight2late.wordpress.com/2015/09/29/a-gentle-introduction-to-topic-modeling-using-r/. Accessed 9 Mar 2016

Chapter 15
Databases and High Performance Computing

Ritu Arora and Sukrit Sondhi

Abstract There are many data-intensive applications that require interaction with the database management systems or document management systems for processing, producing, or analyzing Big Data. Therefore, if such data-intensive applications are to be ported to High Performance Computing (HPC) platforms, the database management systems or document management systems that they require should either be directly provisioned on HPC platforms or should be made available on a storage platform that is in close proximity to the HPC platform. Otherwise, the time-to-results or time-to-insights can be significantly high. In this chapter, we present an overview of the various database management systems that can be used for the processing and analyses of Big Data on HPC platforms, and include some of the strategies to optimize the database access. We also present the steps to install and access a relational database management system on an HPC platform.

15.1 Introduction

Several applications such as those for genome sequence-search [1] and for clustering semantic web-data [2] use databases on HPC platforms. Databases are storage spaces in which the data is logically organized for convenient access and management. Most databases have associated logical models that provide structure to the data stored in them. The management of databases (and hence the data stored in them) can be done with the help of Database Management Systems (DBMSs). Depending upon the type of Big Data and the needs of the stakeholders, the DBMSs could be providing capabilities for not only capturing and storing the data, but could also be supporting complex analysis using all the collected data. There are various types of DBMSs that are available for the management and analysis of Big Data.

R. Arora (✉)
Texas Advanced Computing Center, Austin, TX, USA
e-mail: rauta@tacc.utexas.edu

S. Sondhi
Fulcrum Worldwide, NJ, USA
e-mail: sukrit@fulcrumww.com

© Springer International Publishing Switzerland 2016
R. Arora (ed.), *Conquering Big Data with High Performance Computing*,
DOI 10.1007/978-3-319-33742-5_15

309

Both temporary (or transient) and persistent databases can be set up on HPC platforms. A transient database can be used for storing data temporarily in memory and querying it while an application is running. A persistent DBMS can be provisioned at the system-level on the HPC platform such that multiple databases with different access rights can be provided to different users. The administrators of a system control the provisioning of a DBMS at the system-level. If instead of using a system-level installation of a DBMS, a user needs to install a DBMS directly in their account, they should be able to do so without requiring any special privileges (such as "root" access) on the HPC platform. A persistent database is often used for storing large data collections and can be accessed from a computation job. A transient database can be server-less and compact as compared to a persistent database. However, it can be limited in the amount of data it can store or use in memory of a compute-server while a job is running.

Linux is the most commonly used operating system on an HPC platform, especially at open-science supercomputing facilities. Hence, for porting the database-dependent applications to HPC platforms, it is important that the DBMSs that are used by these applications are Linux-compatible. It should also be noted here that, often, there are usage policies associated with the HPC platforms at open-science supercomputing facilities. There could be limits to the amount of storage space that is available to each user on an HPC platform, which in turn can impact the size of the database that can be ported or maintained on an HPC platform.

If a supercomputing facility has a cloud computing resource on which Virtual Machines (VMs) can be provisioned, then a DBMS can be installed in the VM and made web-accessible for storing and sharing results.

In the rest of this chapter, we provide an overview of the various DBMSs that can be used on HPC platforms. We describe the process of installing and using an object-relational database on an HPC platform without requiring any special privileges. We also discuss some strategies for optimizing database access, and present examples of applications running on HPC platforms that require databases.

15.2 Databases on Supercomputing Resources

Supercomputing resources are predominantly Linux-based, and can support the various DBMSs available for Linux. In this section, we discuss such DBMSs that can be used on Supercomputing resources, and their suitability for Big Data. Based on the characteristic of the data and its use, we have classified the DBMSs into four main categories: (1) relational databases, (2) NoSQL or non-relational and Hadoop databases, (3) graph databases, and (4) scientific and specialized databases.

15.2.1 Relational Databases

For structured data that has a well-defined *schema*, relational databases are the obvious choice, as they have evolved over a period of time, and offer a sophisticated framework and features for use as well as management of the database. A relational database is characterized by a tabular structure (database *table*), consisting of rows and columns, for storing information records for each *entity* (or domain concept), such as product or employee. Tables representing entities typically have *key* columns that store identifying information. For example, in a table containing employee records, the employee code might be considered as the primary key, and cannot have any duplicates within that table. Along with tables, which are the central concept of relational databases, the relational databases also provide a variety of supporting constructs and mechanisms. Data in relational databases is typically accessed and managed by a specialized language known as the Structured Query Language (SQL).

Among the relational DBMSs available on Linux, two of the most popular free and open-source options are MySQL [3], and PostgreSQL [4]. However, there could be some scalability challenges in using these DBMSs for managing all types of Big Data. The two popular commercial DBMSs for handling Big Data are Oracle Database Server [5] and IBM DB2 [6].

MySQL is currently the most popular free relational DBMS. It offers comprehensive database management capabilities and enjoys widespread support. While MySQL is scalable and provides good performance for even large relational database implementations, it may not be suitable for all Big Data applications, especially those involving unstructured data, since it is ultimately meant for relational (structured) data. MySQL also does not support the full ANSI SQL standard [7], which might be a disadvantage while migrating to or from another database. Note however, that there are many forks of MySQL available, such as Drizzle [8] and MariaDB [9]. Oracle also offers a commercial edition of MySQL, known as MySQL Enterprise [10], which has additional management and scalability features.

PostgreSQL (also commonly referred to as Postgres) is a powerful object-relational database management system. Its object-relational nature gives it significant advantages in terms of high-level programming constructs and flexibility. It is also highly compliant to the ANSI/ISO SQL standards, so, migrating to or from Postgres would be easier than most other relational databases. However, due to its support for high-level constructs, it may not perform as well for some simple or lower-level operations such as basic read operations. It also has lesser support as compared to MySQL. Postgres may not be the best option for storing and managing Big Data, unless there is an extraordinary amount of code involved that would need to interact on many small subsets of the data in an object-oriented manner.

Two leading commercial relational databases that are Linux-compatible are Oracle Database Server and IBM DB2. Both these databases offer extensive tools and features to support Big Data. This includes highly advanced capabilities such as IBM BLU Acceleration [11] to speed up large-scale analytics and Oracle Exadata Database Machine [12], a pre-packaged, high-end compute and storage system configuration. However, the costs and complexity of Oracle or DB2 as database servers are justified only when the data and its use cases are also very complex and mission-critical, and there is need for advanced database configurations for which the vendor can provide support.

15.2.2 NoSQL or Non-relational and Hadoop Databases

Apache Cassandra™ [13] and Apache HBase™ [14] are wide-column, distributed, shared-nothing databases that do not use SQL for querying and hence are called NoSQL databases. Both these databases are run on clustered nodes and a client can connect to any node in the cluster. Cassandra has a notion of seed nodes, which serve as points for communication with other nodes in the cluster. HBase has the notion of master nodes—some nodes are designated as master nodes and they monitor and coordinate the actions of other servers. The seed nodes in Cassandra and master nodes in HBase ensure high-reliability. These databases have data arranged as rows in a table such that the row key is the primary key of the table, and no two rows can have the same value for a column. Both Cassandra and HBase have scalable architectures, such that, nodes can be added to accommodate the growing data without impacting the existing data storage.

Apache Accumulo [15] is also a distributed key-value storage system but it has cell-level security features allowing only authorized users to view a key-value pair. It is built on top of Apache Hadoop and along with Apache Cassandra and HBase are the most popular NoSQL databases used with Hadoop jobs.

MongoDB [16] is a NoSQL DBMS that is document-oriented. MongoDB supports dynamic schemas and the data can be stored in JSON-like documents (called BSON). It supports indexing, supports querying the documents or data on the basis of regular expressions, field names or range, and provides replication of data. This database can be integrated with Hadoop for offline data processing and can also be used for real-time data processing.

15.2.3 Graph Databases

Based upon graph theory, graph databases use the concepts of a graph—nodes, properties, and edges—for data modeling and storage. They could either use key-value pair style of data storage or could use document-oriented style of storage. They explicitly store connections between different pieces of information that are represented as nodes. The connections between nodes are directed and they can have quantitative properties like weight, cost, and distance.

Neo4j [17] is an open-source NoSQL graph database that seems to support runtime failover, clustering, and reliable processing of database transactions. It stores all information in the form of nodes, edges, or attributes. There can be multiple attributes associated with a node or an edge. As the nodes and edges can be labeled, the labels serve as metadata during querying. Neo4j databases supports visualization of the data stored in them. The visualizations help in showing the relationships between different pieces of information using a query language called Cypher.

Arrangodb [18] is another NoSQL, open-source graph database. It uses a flexible data model for storing documents, graphs, and key-value pairs together and for querying them. It has its own declarative query language called AQL (ArrangoDB Query Language).

15.2.4 Scientific and Specialized Databases

Some scientific applications need to store data in a format that is amenable to complex analytics such that linear algebra operations can be formed on the datasets conveniently. Such data could be generated from scientific instruments or computations and could have some spatial or temporal characteristics due to which querying them in traditional databases can be slow.

SciDB [19] is a scalable computational DBMS that uses a multi-dimensional array data model for storing scientific data and performing analytics on it. With SciDB, the data need not be extracted from a database, reformatted, or exported outside the database for doing analytics on it. Data is never overwritten in SciDB but is only updated. Hence, it helps in recording data provenance as well. It supports automatic indexing and clustering of data. SQL-like data manipulation and analysis is supported on data stored in SciDB.

15.3 Installing a Database on a Supercomputing Resource

At the open-science supercomputing facilities, system administrators provide system-wide installation of DBMSs. However, in some scenarios users might be interested in installing a DBMS locally in their account. In this section, we outline the steps for installing a relational DBMS named PostgreSQL locally in a user's account on a Linux-based HPC or storage platform.

1. As a first step, connect to the HPC or storage platform on which PostgreSQL needs to be installed.
2. Switch to the directory in which the PostgreSQL installation is to be done.
3. Download the compressed source code of PostgreSQL as shown in the following command:
   ```
   wget https://ftp.postgresql.org/pub/source/v9.4.5/
   postgresql-9.4.5.tar.gz
   ```
4. Uncompress the source code of PostgreSQL as shown in the following command:
   ```
   tar -xvzf postgresql-9.4.5.tar.gz
   ```
5. GNU C Compiler (GCC), and Python libraries are required in the standard library path during PostgreSQL installation. If the HPC platform has a module

R. Arora and S. Sondhi

system for the management of the user environment, then check for the "gcc" and "python" modules. If those are available then load them as shown below:

```
module load gcc
module load python
```

Any additional libraries as required by the version of PostgreSQL should be installed during this step.

6. From the directory containing the source code of PostgreSQL, run the configure script and specify the path at which PostgreSQL should be installed with the `-prefix` flag:

```
./configure -prefix=<path-to-the-installation
-directory> --with-python PYTHON=<path-to-the-python
-executable>
```

7. If the configure succeeded, run the `make` and `make install` commands to compile the source code of PostgreSQL and install it.

```
make
make install
```

After step # 7, four directories will be created at the path specified in the source configuration step (which is step # 6): `bin`, `include`, `lib`, and `share`.

15.4 Accessing a Database on Supercomputing Resources

Once a DBMS is installed on an HPC platform it would need to instantiated with a database instance. A database instance would then need to be populated either from previously collected data or from actively running computational job. The steps for instantiating and creating a PostgreSQL database are provided further in this section.

1. While working with databases on an HPC platform, all database queries are run on the compute-server. Either interactive access or batch-mode access is therefore required to a compute-server. For interactively accessing a computer-server, depending upon the job scheduler and job management system available on the HPC platform, there could be different commands available. For example, on an HPC platform that uses the SLURM [20] job scheduler and management system, the following `srun` command can be used to get interactive access to a compute-server from the queue named "development" for one hour:

```
login1$ srun -pty -p development -t 01:00:00 -n 16
/bin/bash -l
```

In the aforementioned command, "`-n 16`" is used to specify that 16 cores are needed. After running the command, the SLURM job scheduler provisions a compute-node with interactive access:

```
c558-204$
```

2. After getting interactive access to a compute-server, switch to the PostgreSQL installation directory.

```
c558-204$ cd <path-to-postgres-installation>
```

3. The `initdb` command of PostgreSQL is used to create a database cluster—a collection of databases in which the data will actually live. The first database that is created is called **postgres**. In the following example, the database cluster is stored in the directory named "`databaseDirectory`" which is inside the current working directory:

```
c558-204$./bin/initdb -D ./databaseDirectory/
```

4. Once the **postgres** database is created, the database server is started using the following command:

   c558-204$./bin/pg_ctl -D ./databaseDirectory/ -l logfile start

5. After the database server has been started, the **postgres** database can be connected to as follows:

   c558-204$./bin/psql -U username postgres

   By running the aforementioned command, the **postgres** prompt as shown below will be displayed for typing SQL queries.

```
psql (9.4.5)
Type "help" for help.
postgres=#
```

6. The following SQL query can be run to see the existing database:

```
postgres=# show data_directory ;
```

   This command will show the path at which the **postgres** database is installed (here it is the path to the directory named "**databaseDirectory**").

7. To quit the PostgreSQL session, "**\q**" can be typed.

```
postgres-# \q
```

8. To create a database, for storing the application data the **createdb** command is used. In the following example, a database named **employee** is being created.

```
c558-204$ ./bin/createdb employee;
```

9. The database named **employee** that is created in step # 9 can then be connected to and tables can be created inside it.

```
c558-204$ ./bin/psql employee;
employee=# CREATE TABLE tempEmployee (name
varchar(80), eid int, date date);
```

10. After creating the database named **employee**, records can be inserted into it and the queries can be run on it as shown in the following SQL commands:

```
employee=# INSERT INTO tempEmployee VALUES ('Donald
Duck', 001, '2015-10-27');
employee=# INSERT INTO tempEmployee VALUES ('Mickey
Mouse', 002, '2015-10-28');
```
    employee=# SELECT * from tempEmployee;
```
name | eid | date
----------+-----+---------
Donald Duck | 1 | 2015-10-27
Mickey Mouse | 2 | 2015-10-28
(2 rows)
```

To quit SQL mode, type the following command:
```
employee=# \q
```
11. The PostgreSQL server can be stopped using the following command:
```
c558-204$./bin/pg_ctl -D ./databaseDirectory/ stop
```
12. To delete the PostgreSQL installation, quit any open PostgreSQL sessions, and delete the installation directory.

If a data management workflow or a data-intensive application on an HPC platform involves steps that might necessitate populating a database with previously collected data, then there could be some bottlenecks during data ingestion related to the available network bandwidth, latency, the size of the database, and some additional factors. In the next section, we discuss how to optimize database access while working at a supercomputing facility.

15.5   Optimizing Database Access on Supercomputing Resources

There are various strategies that can be considered for optimizing database access in general, and especially when handling databases containing very large datasets on supercomputing resources. Some of the strategies are discussed in this section.

A database should be kept close to the compute-server from where it needs to be accessed. As data movement is a costly operation, all the data that an application might need while it is running on an HPC platform, should be staged to the platform before the application starts running.

Indexing of persistent databases (including collection of documents) is often done to improve the speed of data retrieval. Creating an index can be a costly operation, but when the indexing is done, random lookups in databases or searching and sorting often become rapid. However, in the case of indexed relational databases, migration from one platform to another can become a time-consuming operation due to an index created on the source database. Therefore, to reduce the time-taken in database migration, such an index should be dropped on the source platform, and then recreated on the destination platform after completing the migration.

Partitioning is a divide-and-conquer strategy that is applicable to both databases and document collections for speeding up search and retrieval process. In the case of relational databases, by database partitioning, it means that large tables are split into multiple small tables so that queries scan a small amount of data at a time, and hence, speedup the search and retrieval process. Partitioning can be done in relational databases either horizontally or vertically. In horizontal partitioning, a large database table is split into smaller tables on the basis of the number of rows, such that the resulting tables have lesser number of rows than the original table but have the same number of columns. In vertical partitioning, the tables are split on the basis of the columns such that the resulting tables have fewer columns than the original table. The partitioned tables can be stored on different disks, thereby, the problem of overfilling a disk with a single large table can also be mitigated while accelerating the search and retrieval process.

In relational databases, materialized views are pre-computed views (or query-specifications) that are stored like tables for improved performance. Expensive queries, such as those involving joins, that are frequently executed but do not need up-to-the-moment data, can be defined as materialized views. A materialized view can be executed in advance of when an end-user would actually need the results and the result set is stored on disk, much like a table. Because the results of querying a base table are precomputed and stored in the materialized view, the end-user experiences almost instantaneous response-time while querying.

To save disk space and maintain the size of the databases, old data can be periodically compressed and archived for future reference. If the data will not be needed any further, it can also be purged from the database.

In the case of relational databases, normalization is often done to reduce redundancy. With normalization, different but related pieces of information are stored in separate tables. If a join is needed across several normalized tables spread across multiple disks, it can be a very slow process for very large databases. If such data is denormalized, which means grouped together, redundancy will increase but the performance of read operations on databases will increase. Therefore, at times, both normalized and denormalized forms of data can be maintained for performance reasons.

In the case of data-in-motion, event-driven architecture is usually beneficial such that data is processed as soon as it arrives, and in small batches. If any problem arises with the data quality, it is caught in the early stage and the subsequent processing steps can be aborted.

15.6 Examples of Applications Using Databases on Supercomputing Resources

The mpiBLAST [1] application is a parallel computing application that is used for genome sequence-search. It compares a query sequence against a database of sequences, and reports the sequences that most closely match with the query sequence. mpiBLAST involves two interesting divide-and-conquer strategies: query segmentation and database segmentation. Using query segmentation, a set of query sequences is split into multiple fractions such that multiple independent processes running on different cores or compute-servers can independently search for a fraction in a database. Database segmentation is used for searching independent segments or partitions of a database for a query sequence in parallel, and the results of each independent search is combined to produce a single output file. When both query segmentation and database segmentation are used together, they reduce the time-to-results.

Digital Record and Object Identification (DROID) [21] is a file-profiling tool for finding the formats of files to reduce redundancy and to help in the process of management of large data collections in batch mode. DROID collects the file profiling information into a database that can be queried to generate reports about files and their formats. This tool can be used on HPC platforms as well, but it is not inherently designed to work in parallel mode. It creates database profiles while it is actively profiling a data collection and uses the current time-stamp to create database profile names. When multiple instances of the DROID tool are used simultaneously on multiple-cores of a compute-server (in the high-throughput computing mode), there is a high possibility of conflict in the database profile names. This happens because multiple cores can attempt to save a database profile with the same time-stamp. Hence, instead of launching multiple DROID instances at the exact same time to work concurrently with each other, there is a time-gap of few seconds that is introduced between running any two DROID instances.

15.7 Conclusion

A variety of DBMSs can be supported at supercomputing facilities for processing and analyzing Big Data. However, before porting a database application at an open-science supercomputing facility, the users might want to check the information about the usage policies of the desired HPC platforms. For the HPC and storage platforms of their interest, the users might want to check about (1) the availability of the required amount of space for the required amount of time, (2) filesystems, data sharing, data backup, and data replication policies, (3) any data purge policies and compliance needs, (4) availability of infrastructure for transient and persistent storage, (5) options for in-memory databases, (6) network bandwidth and any benchmark information, (7) possibility of shipping data on hard-drives instead of online transfer, and (8) the list of available or supported DBMSs, and their mode of access.

References

1. H. Lin, X. Ma, W. Feng, N.F. Samatova, Coordinating computation and I/O in massively parallel sequence search. IEEE Trans. Parallel Distrib. Syst. **22**(4), 529–543 (2011)
2. E.L. Goodman, E. Jimenez, D. Mizell, S. al-Saffar, B. Adolf, D. Haglin, High-performance computing applied to semantic databases, in *Proceedings of the 8th Extended Semantic Web Conference on the Semantic Web: Research and Applications—Volume Part II (ESWC'11)*, ed. by G. Antoniou, M. Grobelnik, E. Simperl, B. Parsia, D. Plexousakis (Springer, Berlin, Heidelberg, 2011), pp. 31–45
3. MySQL, https://www.mysql.com/. Accessed 12 Mar 2016
4. PostgreSQL, http://www.postgresql.org/. Accessed 12 Mar 2016
5. Oracle Database Server, https://www.oracle.com/database/index.html. Accessed 12 Mar 2016

6. IBM DB2, http://www-01.ibm.com/software/data/db2/. Accessed 12 Mar 2016
7. ANSI SQL Standard, http://www.jtc1sc32.org/doc/N2151-2200/32N2153T-text_for_ballot-FDIS_9075-1.pdf. Accessed 12 Mar 2016
8. Drizzle, http://www.drizzle.org/. Accessed 12 Mar 2016
9. MariaDB, https://mariadb.org/. Accessed 12 Mar 2016
10. MySQL Enterprise Edition, https://www.mysql.com/products/enterprise/. Accessed 12 Mar 2016
11. IBM BLU Acceleration, https://www-01.ibm.com/software/data/db2/linux-unix-windows/db2-blu-acceleration/. Accessed 12 Mar 2016
12. Oracle Exadata Database Machine, https://www.oracle.com/engineered-systems/exadata/index.html. Accessed 12 Mar 2016
13. Apache Cassandra™, http://cassandra.apache.org/. Accessed 12 Mar 2016
14. Apache Hbase™, https://hbase.apache.org/. Accessed 12 Mar 2016
15. Apache Accumulo, https://accumulo.apache.org/. Accessed 12 Mar 2016
16. MongoDB, https://www.mongodb.com/. Accessed 12 Mar 2016
17. Neo4j, http://neo4j.com/developer/graph-database/. Accessed 12 Mar 2016
18. ArrangoDB, https://www.arangodb.com/. Accessed 12 Mar 2016
19. SciDB, http://www.paradigm4.com/try_scidb/compare-to-relational-databases/. Accessed 12 Mar 2016
20. SLURM, http://slurm.schedmd.com/. Accessed 12 Mar 2016
21. DROID, http://www.nationalarchives.gov.uk/information-management/manage-information/policy-process/digital-continuity/file-profiling-tool-droid/. Accessed 12 Mar 2016

Chapter 16
Conquering Big Data Through the Usage of the Wrangler Supercomputer

Jorge Salazar

Abstract Data-intensive computing brings a new set of challenges that do not completely overlap with those met by the more typical and even state-of-the-art High Performance Computing (HPC) systems. Working with 'big data' can involve analyzing thousands of files that need to be rapidly opened, examined and cross-correlated—tasks that classic HPC systems might not be designed to do. Such tasks can be efficiently conducted on a data-intensive supercomputer like the Wrangler supercomputer at the Texas Advanced Computing Center (TACC). Wrangler allows scientists to share and analyze the massive collections of data being produced in nearly every field of research today in a user-friendly manner. It was designed to work closely with the Stampede supercomputer, which is ranked as the number ten most powerful in the world by TOP500, and is the HPC flagship of TACC. Wrangler was designed to keep much of what was successful with systems like Stampede, but also to introduce new features such as a very large flash storage system, a very large distributed spinning disk storage system, and high speed network access. This allows a new way for users to access HPC resources with data analysis needs that weren't being fulfilled by traditional HPC systems like Stampede. In this chapter, we provide an overview of the Wrangler data-intensive HPC system along with some of the big data use-cases that it enables.

16.1 Introduction

An analogy can be made that supercomputers like Stampede [1] are like formula racing cars, with compute engines optimized for fast travel on smooth, well-defined circuits. Wrangler [2], on the other hand, is more akin to a rally car—one built to go fast on rougher roads.

To take the analogy further, a formula race car's suspension will need modification if it races off-road. Even though the car's system has essentially the same components, the entire car will have to be put together differently.

J. Salazar (✉)
Science and Technology Writer, Texas Advanced Computing Center, University of Texas at Austin, USA
e-mail: jorge@tacc.utexas.edu

© Springer International Publishing Switzerland 2016
R. Arora (ed.), *Conquering Big Data with High Performance Computing*,
DOI 10.1007/978-3-319-33742-5_16

For a large number of users who work with big data, their needs and experience are not just about writing and analyzing large amounts of output, which is what is more typically seen in simulation usage. They need to interactively and iteratively develop insights from big data, both during and after the output is produced. Such interactive analysis can necessitate frequent opening and closing of a large number of files. This in turn places extreme stress on the file system associated with an HPC platform, thereby leading to overall degradation of the performance of the system. The Wrangler architecture is designed to meet such needs of manipulating and analyzing large amounts of data that can create bottlenecks in performance for other HPC systems.

Users are now taking advantage of Wrangler's big data processing capabilities. Since its early production period of May–September 2015, Wrangler has completed more than 5000 data-intensive jobs. Wrangler users fell broadly into three categories: first, users who ran the same type of computations they ran on other TACC or Extreme Science and Engineering Discovery Environment (XSEDE) [3] systems, but received a differential performance impact because of Wrangler's unique features (viz., very large flash storage); second, existing users who did entirely different things with the new capabilities due to Wrangler's software stack, particularly in using databases and tools from the Hadoop ecosystem; and third, entirely new users to the TACC or XSEDE ecosystem.

This chapter will describe the capabilities Wrangler offers for data-intensive supercomputing, and a sample of four science use cases that have leveraged Wrangler. These use cases highlight some of the classes of problems that can be effectively solved using Wrangler.

16.1.1 Wrangler System Overview

An overview of the Wrangler system reveals its four main components: (1) A massive 20 PB disk-based storage system split between TACC and Indiana University that provides ultra-high reliability through geographic replication, (2) An analytics system leveraging 600 TB of NAND rack-scale flash memory to allow unprecedented I/O rates, (3) Internet2 connectivity at two sites yielding unsurpassed data ingress and retrieval rates with 100 Gb/s, and (4) the support for the software tools and systems that are driving data research today and are optimized to take advantage of the new capabilities Wrangler provides. A high-level overview of the Wrangler system is shown in Fig. 16.1.

Perhaps Wrangler's most outstanding feature is the 600 TB of flash memory shared via PCI interconnect across Wrangler's over 3000 Haswell compute cores. This allows all parts of the system access to the same storage. The cores can work in parallel together on the data that are stored inside this high-speed storage system to get larger results they couldn't get otherwise. This massive amount of flash storage is directly connected to the CPUs. Hence, the connection from the 'brain' of the computer goes directly to the storage system without any translation

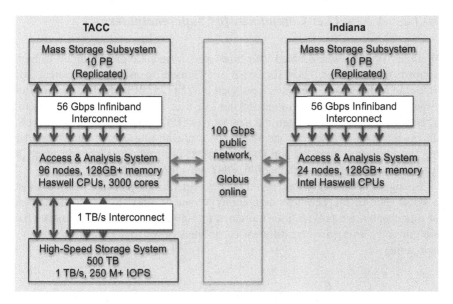

Fig. 16.1 Overview of Wrangler system

in between. This allows users to compute directly with some of the fastest storage available today with no bottlenecks in-between. For writing large blocks of data (approximately 40 MB), the throughput of flash storage can be about 10 times better than disk, and for writing small blocks of data (approximately, 4 KB), the throughput of flash can be about 400 times better than that of the disk.

Users bring data in and out of Wrangler in one of the fastest ways possible today. Wrangler connects to Internet2, an optical network which provides 100 GB per second worth of throughput to most of the other academic institutions around the U.S.

Moreover, Wrangler's shared memory supports the popular data analytics frameworks Hadoop and Apache Spark. Persistent database instances are also supported on Wrangler. The iRods [4] data management system is also provisioned on Wrangler.

What's more, TACC has tools and techniques to transfer their data in parallel. It's like being at the supermarket, to make an analogy. If there's only one lane open, check-out goes only as fast as the speed of one checker. But if you go in and have 15 lanes open, you can spread that traffic across and get more people through in less time.

16.1.2 A New User Community for Supercomputers

Wrangler is more web-enabled than most other systems typically found in high performance computing. A User Portal allows users to manage the system and gives the ability to use web interfaces such as VNC [5], RStudio [6], and Jupyter Notebooks [7] that support more desktop-like user interactions with the system. Therefore, Wrangler is in a sense a new face of HPC systems that are more web-driven, much more graphical, and much less command-line driven. Thus, Wrangler has low barriers to entry for non-traditional HPC users who can take advantage of its data-intensive computing capabilities through a user-friendly interface.

Biologists, astronomers, energy efficiency experts, and paleontologists are just a small slice of the new user community Wrangler aims to attract. In the rest of this chapter, we provide four use cases to highlight the research projects that are currently leveraging the different capabilities of Wrangler for data-intensive computing.

16.2 First Use-Case: Evolution of Monogamy

One of the mysteries of monogamy is whether different species share regulatory genes that can be traced back to a common ancestor.

Scientists at the Hofmann Lab of UT Austin [8] are using the Wrangler data-intensive supercomputer to find orthologs—genes common to different species. They are searching for orthologs in each of the major lineages of vertebrates—mammals, birds, reptiles, amphibians and fishes.

What the scientists are investigating is whether it's possible that some of the same genes—even though they've evolved independently—are important in regulating monogamous behavior, in particular expression of these genes in the brain while monogamous males are reproductively active. One of the difficulties of this research is that resources are limited for genomic analysis beyond the model organisms such as lab rats and fruit flies. For those species, there are online-available databases that group genes together into orthologous groups, groups of gene families that are comparable across species. When scientists study nontraditional species beyond the model organisms, they need to be able to do that on their own with a software package called OrthoMCL. It lets scientists find orthologs, the shared genes that could be candidates for ones that regulate monogamous behavior.

The data that goes into the OrthoMCL [9] code running on Wrangler are protein-coding sequences of RNA from the brain tissue of males of different species of vertebrates. So far the monogamy project has analyzed two species of voles; two species of mice; two species of songbirds; two frogs; and two Cichlid fishes.

During sequencing of the genes that are expressed in a tissue using transcriptomic approaches, the goal is to get gene counts for most of the genes in the genome. This is an astronomically large amount of data to analyze. Across the ten species studied in this research, there were a minimum of 200,000 genes to compare for sequence similarity and to compare in all pairwise fashion. These databases need to be quite large to manage all of this data in a way that is usable by components of the OrthoMCL software.

Supercomputers like Stampede are better suited for arithmetic 'number crunching' instead of handling the massive amount of data transfer between storage and memory that the OrthoMCL code generates. Because Wrangler is designed to have a relational database where individual computational steps can go back and talk to the database and pull out the information it needs, it was used in this research.

Thus far, the results with Wrangler have been encouraging. During one of the prior attempts of gene comparison for this research using online resources, only 350 genes across ten species could be compared. When OrthoMCL was ran on Wrangler, the researchers were able to get almost 2000 genes that are comparable across the species. This is a substantial improvement from what is already available. Researchers want to further use OrthoMCL to make an increasing number of comparisons across extremely divergent and ancient species separated by 450 million years between the different groups.

16.3   Second Use-Case: Save Money, Save Energy with Supercomputers

Saving energy saves money. Scientists at Oak Ridge National Laboratory (ORNL) are using supercomputers to do just that by making virtual versions of millions of buildings in the U.S. The Wrangler data-intensive supercomputer is working jointly with ORNL's Titan [10] in a project called Autotune [11] that trims the energy bills of buildings.

This project takes a simple software model of a building's energy use and optimizes it to match reality. A rudimentary model is created from publicly available data. Then the Autotune project takes utility bill data, whether it's monthly electrical utility bills, or hourly bills from advanced metering infrastructure, and calibrates that software model to match measured data. Once Autotune sufficiently calibrates the model, it can be legally used in multiple ways including for optimal building retrofit packages.

Autotune tunes the simulation engine called EnergyPlus, which essentially describes the salient aspects of a building. But a software description of the building is required for EnergyPlus to run on.

The main hurdle in creating a model of the building is that there are over 3000 parameters to adjust—its "parameter space"—to match 12 data points from monthly utility bills. This is what the supercomputers are being used for. The Autotune research group is sampling the parametric space of inputs to quantitatively determine how sensitive certain parameters are for affecting energy consumption for electricity, for natural gas, and for any other sensor data that they can collect or report from the simulation engine—and then use that to inform the calibration process so that it can create a model that matches the way the building works in the real world.

The second fastest supercomputer in the world, Titan at ORNL, is used in this research to do large-scale parametric studies. Currently, the researcher group is able to run 500,000 simulations and write 45 TB of data to disk in 68 min. The goal though is to scale-out Autotune to run simulations for all 125.1 million commercial and residential buildings in the U.S. It would take about 2 weeks of Titan running nonstop 24/7 to do it. To date eight million simulations have been run for the Autotune project, and the research group has 270 TB of data to analyze.

Wrangler fills a specific niche for this research group in that the analysis can be turned into an end-to-end workflow, where the researcher can define what parameters they want to vary. Wrangler creates the sampling matrix; input files; it does the computationally challenging task of running all the simulations in parallel; it creates the output. Then artificial intelligence and statistical techniques are used to analyze that data on the backend. Doing that from beginning to end as a solid workflow on Wrangler is part of the future work of this research group. Wrangler has enough capability to run some of their very large studies and get meaningful results in a single run.

The main customer segment for Autotune has been energy service companies. EnergyPlus helps in quickly creating software descriptions of buildings. If one has a software description of a building, it would be a very quick analysis to figure, out of the 3000 plus things that you could adjust to your building, which would make it the most energy efficient, save the most money, and give the return on investment. For example, some of those changes could include changing out the HVAC, adding insulation, changing windows, and sealing ducts.

Another usage of Autotune is in national policy-making. Local, state, and federal governments are considering new energy-saving building technology that might not be immediately cost-effective. But incentive structures do exist that can pay for part of it. The ultimate goal of this project is to bring down the energy bill of the U.S.

16.4 Third Use-Case: Human Origins in Fossil Data

The researchers working on the PaleoCore project [12] believe that new discoveries might lie buried deep in the data of human fossils. The PaleoCore project aims to get researchers studying human origins worldwide all on the same page with their fossil data. The project will achieve this by implementing data standards, creating a place to store all data of human fossils, and developing new tools to collect data. Through the integration and sharing between different research projects in paleoanthropology and paleontology, the project will help in developing deeper insights into our origins.

PaleoCore strives to take advantage of some of the geo-processing and database capabilities that are available through Wrangler to create large archives. The big data from this project that will be archived on Wrangler are the entirety of the fossil record on human origins. PaleoCore will also include geospatial data such as satellite imagery. For many of the countries involved, this data is their cultural heritage. Therefore, the researchers need to ensure that not only are the data rapidly available, accessible, and searchable, but that they're safely archived.

PaleoCore also wants to take advantage of the Wrangler data-intensive super-computer's ability to rapidly interlace data and make connections between different databases. Traditionally, relational databases were used to store information in just one way. Now, the databases can be used to store semantic web triples if that's what the request demands. Being able to convert data from one format to another on the fly will meet the different demands of PaleoCore and thereby, the project will take advantage of the linked open datasets.

Linked open datasets are interrelated on the Web, amenable to queries and to showing the relationships among data. What that means for PaleoCore is tying fragments of information collected by individual projects separated by distant points of time and across vast geographical regions. In order to have a comprehensive understanding of human origins and paleontology in general, researchers have to be able to synthesize and pull together all the disparate bits of information in a cohesive and coherent way.

Data collection has come a long way from the days of just cataloging finds with paper and pen. When scientists work in the field in Ethiopia and find a fossil, they now record specific information about it as it's found in real-time on mobile devices. In a typical case they're using IOS devices like iPhones and iPads that automatically record the GPS location of the fossil; as well as who collected it; the date and time; what kind of fossil we think it is; and its stratigraphic position. All of that information is captured at the moment one picks up the fossil.

PaleoCore's future looks to creating Virtual Reality (VR) simulations of human fossil data—enabled in part by Wrangler's ability to manipulate the large data sets in VR and 3D models. Structure From Motion is another technology that's changing the way scientists conduct paleontology and archeology. For example, multiple photographs of a fossil or artifact taken from mobile devices can be combined to construct a VR simulation, an automatically geo-referenced goldmine of information for students. Students can use VR to see for themselves exactly where a fossil came from; what an artifact looks like; be able to manipulate it; and even if they can't do the fieldwork at least in part share in the experience.

16.5 Fourth Use-Case: Dark Energy of a Million Galaxies

A million galaxies billions of light-years away are predicted to be discovered before the year 2020 thanks to a monumental mapping of the night sky in search of a mysterious force. That's according to scientists working on HETDEX, the Hobby-Eberly Telescope Dark Energy Experiment [13]. They're going to transform the big data from galaxy spectra into meaningful discoveries with the help of the Wrangler data-intensive supercomputer. It will require an immense amount of computing storage and processing to achieve the goals of HETDEX.

HETDEX is one of the largest galaxy surveys that has ever been done. Starting in late 2016, thousands of new galaxies will be detected each night by the Hobby-Eberly Telescope at the McDonald Observatory in West Texas. Project scientists will study them using an instrument called VIRUS, the Visible Integral Field Replicable Unit Spectrograph [14]. VIRUS takes starlight from distant galaxies and splits the light into its component colors like a prism does.

With VIRUS, HETDEX can scan a very large region of the sky and perform spectroscopy to discover thousands of galaxies at once. Not only will they be found, but because of the splitting of the light researchers will be able to measure the distance to them instantaneously. That's because light from objects that move away from us appears red-shifted, and the amount of red-shift tells astronomers how fast they're moving away. The faster they move away, the farther away they are. That relationship between speed and distance, called Hubble's Law, will pin down a galaxy's location and let astronomers create a 3D map of a million galaxies with HETDEX.

The main goal with the galaxy map is to study dark energy. Dark energy remains a mystery to science, its presence today undetectable except for its effect on entire galaxies. Basically, galaxies are being pushed apart from each other faster than predicted by science. So astronomers have labeled that mysterious push 'dark energy.' Dark energy's push is so strong that scientists estimate 70% of all the energy in the universe is dark energy.

What HETDEX is attempting to do is measure how strong dark energy is at some point in the distant past. HETDEX scientists will do this by mapping Lyman-Alpha emitting galaxies, which means the galaxies are forming stars in the universe at a time 10 billion years in the past. By making this observation, scientists can rule out many models that say that either the strength of dark energy stays the same or it evolves. They'll do this by measuring the positions of a million galaxies and comparing them to a model for how strong dark energy is.

Data is the biggest challenge with the HETDEX project. Over the course of 3 years, about 200 GB of telescope data will be collected each night, the spectra of 34,000 points of starlight snapped every 6 min. Every time an image is taken, which consists of 34,000 spectra, while the next image is being taken, that previous image is being transferred to Wrangler. By the time the next image is done, it's ready to start transferring that image while it's taking the next one.

Wrangler will also handle the processing of the spectral data from HETDEX to transform the night sky snapshots into galaxy positions and distances. Part of that processing will be calibration of the focal plane of the telescope's camera. A software package will be used to take all the raw telescope data from VIRUS and yield a list of galaxies.

16.6 Conclusion

The use-cases presented in this chapter are from a diverse range of domains but have a common need outside of the realm of traditional HPC for large-scale data computation, storage and analyses. The research work related to these use cases is still in progress but the results accomplished so far clearly underscore the capabilities of Wrangler. With it's capabilities in both HPC and Big Data, Wrangler serves as a bridge between the HPC and the Big Data communities and can facilitate their convergence.

Acknowledgement We are grateful to the Texas Advanced Computing Center, the National Science Foundation, the Extreme Science and Engineering Discovery Environment, Niall Gaffney (Texas Advanced Computing Center), Rebecca Young (University of Texas at Austin), Denne Reed (University of Texas at Austin), Steven Finkelstein (University of Texas at Austin), Joshua New (Oak Ridge National Laboratory).

References

1. Stampede supercomputer, https://www.tacc.utexas.edu/systems/stampede. Accessed 15 Feb 2015
2. Wrangler supercomputer, https://www.tacc.utexas.edu/systems/wrangler. Accessed 15 Feb 2015
3. Extreme Science and Engineering Discovery Environment (XSEDE), https://www.xsede.org/. Accessed 15 Feb 2015
4. iRods, http://irods.org/. Accessed 15 Feb 2015
5. TigerVNC, http://tigervnc.org. Accessed 15 Feb 2015
6. RStudio, https://www.rstudio.com/. Accessed 15 Feb 2015
7. Jupyter Notebook, http://jupyter.org/. Accessed 15 Feb 2015
8. The Hofmann Lab at the University of Texas at Austin, http://cichlid.biosci.utexas.edu/index.html. Accessed 15 Feb 2015
9. OrthoMCL 2.0.9, https://wiki.gacrc.uga.edu/wiki/OrthoMCL. Accessed 15 Feb 2015
10. Titan supercomputer, https://www.olcf.ornl.gov/titan/. Accessed 15 Feb 2015
11. Autotune, http://rsc.ornl.gov/autotune/?q=content/autotune. Accessed 15 Feb 2015
12. PaleoCore, http://paleocore.org/. Accessed 15 Feb 2015
13. Hobby-Eberly Telescope Dark Energy Experiment (HTDEX), http://hetdex.org/. Accessed 15 Feb 2015
14. Visible Integral Field Replicable Unit Spectrograph (VIRUS), http://instrumentation.tamu.edu/virus.html. Accessed 15 Feb 2015

Printed in the United States
By Bookmasters